EMPLOYMENT LAW AND PRACTICE

First Edition

JOHN SPRACK

LONDON
SWEET & MAXWELL
2007

Published in 2007 by
Sweet & Maxwell Limited of
100 Avenue Road,
London NW3 3PF
http://www.sweetandmaxwell.co.uk

Typeset in Great Britain by
LBJ Typesetting Ltd of Kingsclere
Printed in England by
Athenaeum Press Ltd, Tyne & Wear

No natural forests were destroyed to make this product; only farmed
timber was used and re-planted.

A CIP catalogue record for this book is available from the British Library.

ISBN-13 978-1-84703-218-8

PREFACE

This book aims to be an accessible and practical introduction to employment law. The hope is that it will act as a basic text to those who are studying the subject as part of a vocational course, but also that it will be of use to those who represent the parties in employment tribunals, and to employment practitioners generally.

My thanks are due to all at Sweet and Maxwell for their efforts in producing the book, and in particular to Victoria Blanshard for her encouragement. I am grateful also to Jeremy Stein for the work which he put in to planning the project, and wish him all the success which he deserves.

I have endeavoured to state the law as at April 30, 2007.

John Sprack
London
May 2007

CONTENTS

CONTENTS

TABLE OF CASES

(All references are to paragraph number)

TABLE OF STATUTES

(All references are to paragraph number)

TABLE OF STATUTORY INSTRUMENTS

(All references are to paragraph number)

TABLE OF ABBREVIATIONS

ACAS	Advisory, Conciliation and Arbitration Service
AML	Additional maternity leave
CA	Court of Appeal
DDA	Disability Discrimination Act 1995
DDP	Dismissal and Disciplinary Procedure
DTI	Department of Trade and Industry
EA	Employment Act 2002
EAT	Employment Appeal Tribunal
EC	European Community
ECHR	European Convention on Human Rights
ECJ	European Court of Justice
EDT	Effective date of termination (of employment)
EPA	Equal pay Act 1970
ERA	Employment Rights Act 1996
EWC	Expected week of confinement (for childbirth)
EU	European Union
GP	Grievance procedure
HC	High Court
HL	House of Lords
HRA	Human Rights Act 1998
I.C.R.	Industrial Cases Reports
I.R.L.R.	Industrial Relations Law Reports
NIRC	National Industrial Relations Court
PAYE	Pay as you earn
MPLR	Maternity and Paternity Leave Regulations 1999
NMWA	National Minimum Wage Act 1998
NMWR	National Minimum Wage Regulations 1999
NRA	Normal retirement age
OML	Ordinary maternity leave
PALR	Paternity and Adoption Leave Regulations 2002
PCP	Provision, criterion or practice
PILON	Pay in lieu of notice
RRA	Race Relations Act 1976
SDA	Sex Discrimination Act 1975
TULRCA	Trade Union and Labour Relations (Consolidation) Act 1992
TUPE	Transfer of Undertakings (Protection of Employment) Regulations 2006
WFA	Work and Families Act 2006
WTR	Working Time Regulations 1998

CHAPTER ONE

INTRODUCTION

The landscape of employment law is constantly changing. That is **1.01** inevitable, given that it deals with matters which are central to the lives of most people, and which are subject to constant social, economic and political pressures.

Anyone who approaches the subject from the perspective of the traditional notions of freedom of contract will soon end up bewildered by the thicket of statute law which surrounds the subject. Those who, on the other hand, expect that employment law will reflect predominant notions of social justice will find the reality frustrating at times, because the many reforms which have been effected over the past half century have been based upon a foundation of contract law laid down in Victorian times. In addition, the European Union has a powerful influence upon law in this area, perhaps more than in any other. As a result of this eclectic mix, the law can be quite complex at times. Yet the framework which it provides is meant to be understood and applied by those in the workplace with no legal training and little knowledge of the law. And the main legal arena in which disputes are thrashed out is the employment tribunal, which is intended to be accessible to employees and employers who choose to present their own cases, as well as the lawyers and other professionals who frequently do so on their behalf.

The task of this book is to attempt to make sense of the apparent complexity, in a way which will prove useful in practice. Inevitably, that involves a degree of simplification, but the aim is to ensure that there is nothing misleading, and that the reader who has to analyse an employment situation, to advise on a course of action, or to prepare a case, is presented with the basic principles, the relevant statutory provisions, and the leading cases to do so.

The structure of this book

After this brief introduction, Chapter 2 deals with the fundamental **1.02** question of employment status. In order to acquire rights under employment law, an individual has traditionally had to have the status of "employee". The way in which that is defined has shifted in previous years, partly through developments in case law, for example in relation to the position of agency workers. It has also expanded greatly as a result of the wider definition of "employee" applicable to discrimination law. Further,

European law has promoted the less stringent test which defines the "worker", with the result that this area has undergone a radical shift in recent years.

Chapter 3 looks at the individual contract of employment. As has been already mentioned, traditional concepts in this aspect of employment law have been subject to a process of adaptation as the statutory framework has developed. Yet the fundamental principles of the employment relationship continue to be determined by the agreement entered into by employer and employee, and a basic understanding of the topic is crucial to employment law.

Chapter 4 looks at particular aspects of the contract of employment which are not subject to much in the way of statutory intervention—restrictive covenants and confidentiality. Unusually in the field of employment law, the employment tribunals do not have a role in adjudicating upon these matters, which are pursued in the ordinary courts.

1.03   Chapter 5 attempts to describe the main ways in which the wages and hours of workers are governed by statute. This is an area where the contract between the parties is subject to considerable regulation. It is also the subject of substantial intervention on the part of the European Union. The topics in question are important "nitty gritty" ones, affecting such matters as the minimum wage which an employer can pay, and the maximum hours which the employee can be required to work.

The most striking development in the recent history of employment law has been the prohibition of discrimination. This phenomenon is based on the important need to reduce the injustice and detrimental effects for society of discriminatory behaviour and practices. It has rightly come to loom large in the minds of employers and employees. It has given rise to a body of law which is, on occasion, intellectually challenging, and subject to continuing rapid development both internally and from the European Union. Chapter 6 deals with the substantive law relating to discrimination, while Chapter 7 covers the remedies which are available to those who have been discriminated against. Close relatives of the law relating to discrimination are the various "family friendly" rights which are described in Chapter 8 ("family friendly" is not a very satisfactory label, but the one which seems to be most frequently adopted). This group of statutory rights derived its impetus from the wish to mitigate the detrimental effects which maternity and childcare have upon the employment position of women, but it has expanded way beyond that goal, so that it encompasses paternity and adoption rights, in addition to flexible working for those who care for adults as well as children.

Unfair dismissal is the area of law which retains its primacy as far as the operations of the tribunals are concerned, and (one would suspect) is the area which provides most food for thought among employers and aggrieved employees. This topic forms the focus for Chapter 9 (which deals with the law relating to liability for unfair dismissal), and Chapter 10, which outlines the remedies available once liability has been determined. Unfair dismissal overlaps with redundancy, which forms the subject of Chapter 11, dealing with the individual and the collective aspects of redundancy.

Few topics provide the practitioner with more headaches than the **1.04** transfer of undertakings (referred to without much affection as "TUPE"). Chapter 12 attempts to provide a summary of this important, but sometimes perplexing area, which is again dominated by European Directives and jurisprudence.

The final three chapters deal with various aspects of practice and procedure. Chapter 13 looks at the matter from the point of view of the procedure adopted in the tribunal. Chapter 14 describes the provisions (important in practice, and sometimes counter-intuitive in their operation) relating to the time limits applicable to tribunal claims. Chapter 15 looks at the topic of settlement or compromise, relevant to those who wish to avoid the formal trial process, for whatever reason.

The Appendices provide material which is of particular relevance to the pursuit and defence of tribunal claims. The tribunal claim and response forms are reproduced, so that those unfamiliar with their format can see what information the parties are required to provide. The Employment Tribunal Rules, together with the Regulations of which they form a part, are also reproduced.

The Code of Practice produced by the Arbitration and Conciliation Service (ACAS) plays a central role in providing the yardstick for "best practice" in respect of disciplinary and grievance procedures. In consequence, it figures prominently in the deliberations of many employers and trade unions, and in the way in which employment tribunals approach their task of deciding whether a dismissal is fair. It is reproduced in full as an Appendix.

The last of the Appendices contains a statement of terms such as is **1.05** required by s.1 of the Employment Rights Act 1996.

Publications and research

As is all too apparent, employment law is a rapidly developing subject, and **1.06** it is even more important than usual to keep up to date. Fortunately, there are a number of websites which assist in this process. In particular:

- *www.emplaw.co.uk* provides a useful portal for a number of other sites, free newsletters and free trials of other relevant services;

- *www.dti.gov.uk* gives details of current and forthcoming legislation, as well as employment law topics of general interest;

- *www.acas.org.uk* sets out the guidance provided by the Arbitration, Conciliation and Advisory Service, constituting suggestions as to "best practice" on various matters;

- *www.employmentappeals.gov.uk* is the site to access for the judgments of the Employment Appeals Tribunal. It contains a useful search facility and is right up to date.

As far as hard copy reference works are concerned, the standard work in the area is *Harvey on Industrial Relations and Employment Law* (looseleaf,

London: Butterworths). Its size and expense are somewhat daunting, but it should be found in any decent law library. The law reports most often used in practice are now the Industrial Relations Law Reports, which appear monthly, and contain an excellent introductory summary of each month's cases written by Michael Rubinstein. The IDS Employment Law Brief (published twice monthly by Thomson—access via *www.IDSBrief.co.uk*) is a first-rate method of keeping up to date. It contains case reports and features on employment law summarising topics of current interest.

Chapter Two

EMPLOYEES AND WORKERS

The acquisition of rights under employment law is dependent upon the status of the individual concerned. As a result, it becomes important to determine, whenever someone might lay claim to a particular right, whether they have acquired the necessary status. This chapter begins by setting out the main categories of employment rights, in accordance with the status necessary to claim entitlement. It then goes on to deal with the tests which are used to draw the main distinctions—between those who are "employees", "workers" or "in employment". Finally, it discusses some of the categories which have caused the most controversy in practice, and have generated the most case law.

2.01

Rights and status

Each of the major sets of employment rights applies to a differently defined group of individuals. These are set out in the Table entitled "Statutory Rights and Status", which is below.

2.02

Status of those Entitled to statutory rights

Statutory right	Employees	Workers	Those "In Employment"
Redundancy payment	Yes	No	No
Unfair dismissal	Yes	No	No
Written reasons for dismissal	Yes	No	No
Right to be accompanied at disciplinary and grievance meetings	Yes	Yes	No
Maternity leave	Yes	No	No
National minimum wage	Yes	Yes	No
Holiday pay under WTR	Yes	Yes	No

Statutory right	Employees	Workers	Those "In Employment"
Right not to have deductions from wages	Yes	Yes	No
Right not to be discriminated against on grounds of race, sex, disability, sexual orientation, religion or belief, age	Yes	Yes	Yes
Right to equal pay	Yes	Yes	Yes

The categories set out at the top of each of the above columns are described in the paragraphs which follow.

Employees

2.03   Most of the rights which are now contained in the Employment Rights Act 1996 ("ERA") are restricted to employees. The right not to be unfairly dismissed, the right to a redundancy payment, the right to maternity leave and the right to written reasons for dismissal, for example, are all dependent upon the individual in question establishing "employee" status. Section 230 of the ERA defines an employee as "an individual who has entered into or works under . . . a contract of employment", and goes on to state that "contract of employment" means a "contract of service or apprenticeship, whether express or implied, and (if it is express) whether oral or in writing. The use of the phrase "contract of service" introduces the basic common law distinction between those under a contract of service (who are employed) and those under a contract for services (who are self-employed). What the statute does not do is to give any guidance as to how the distinction is to be drawn between contracts of service and contracts for services. That is done by the case law, and the relevant tests are set out in paras 2.07 to 2.12.

Workers

2.04   There are a number of statutory rights which are available to those who are classified as workers. "Worker" is a category which is more widely defined than "employee", with the result that some people who might be classed as "workers" are self-employed. Generally, the definition is similar whichever statute or statutory instrument it appears in. For example, the definition in the Working Time Regulations covers those who work under:

(a) a contract of employment; or

(b) any other contract

"whereby the individual undertakes to do or perform personally any work or services for another party to the contract whose status is not by virtue of the contract that of a client or customer of any profession or business undertaking carried on by the individual".

The statutory definition has been subject to interpretation in case law, and this is dealt with in paras 2.13 to 2.16.

As far as the rights to which "workers" are entitled, they include the right to protection of wages (ss.13–17 of the ERA), rights under the minimum wage legislation, the right to holiday pay under the Working Time Regulations, and the right to be accompanied at disciplinary and grievance hearings.

Rights for those "in employment"

The various statutes and statutory instruments which outlaw discrimina-   **2.05**
tion have broader coverage than those who fall within the categories of "employee" and "worker". Each of them covers discrimination "in employment" but this does not reflect the definition of "employee" which is set out in the ERA, or in the common law. Race discrimination, for example, is prohibited for those "in employment", which is defined (s.78(1) of the Race Relations Act 1976) as "employment under a contract of service or of apprenticeship or a contract personally to execute any work or labour".

It follows that the definition is broader than that for a "worker", because it does not exclude those who provide work for customers or clients in the course of a profession or business (see para.2.17). The definition set out in the RRA is identical to that in the legislation dealing with discrimination on grounds of sex, disability, religion or belief, sexual orientation and age.

The tests

Different tests apply to each of the three main categories of rights which   **2.06**
have been summarised.

What is an "employee"?

The statutory definition, as set out in s.230 of the ERA, has been   **2.07**
mentioned in para.2.03. That definition relies heavily upon the concept of a "contract of service" as the hallmark of the employee. Developing case law has set out the following conditions which must be present before a contract of employment can exist:

(a) a contract between the "employee" and the "employer";

(b) an obligation on the "employee" to provide work personally;

(c) mutuality of obligation between the parties; and

(d) control of the "employee" by the "employer".

Each of these conditions must be present before a contract of employment can exist. If they are present, that does not conclude the matter. One must then look at all the terms of the contract in order to ascertain whether it does constitute a contract of employment. The following paragraphs consider each of these elements in turn.

2.08   Contract. There must be a contract in existence between the individual who is providing the work or services, and the person for whom it is provided. Such a contract may be express or implied and, if it is express, the terms may be oral or written.

   The question of whether there is any contract at all is, of course, fundamental to whether there is any employment relationship. It has arisen particularly in recent times in relation to agency work, and this category of workers is the focus of paras 2.26 to 2.31 below.

2.09   Work provided personally. For a contract of service to come into existence, the "employee" must agree to carry out the work personally. In *Express and Echo Publications v Tanton* [1999] I.R.L.R. 367, CA, the contract contained a clause which provided that if the claimant was unable to carry out his work personally, he was to arrange a substitute at his own expense. It was held that this precluded the agreement from being a contract of service. In *Byrne Bros (Formwork) Ltd v Baird* [2002] I.R.L.R. 96, EAT, the contract stated that the services could be provided by someone else only where the "employee" was "unable" to provide the work himself. In addition, "the express approval of the contractor" was required for such a substitution. It was held that this did not prevent the agreement being a contract of service because "a limited power to appoint substitutes is not inconsistent with an obligation of personal service".

2.10   Mutuality of obligation. For a contract of employment to exist, there should be an obligation on each side: an obligation on the employer to provide work and on the employee to carry out that work: *Nethermere (St Neots) Ltd v Gardiner* [1984] I.R.L.R. 240. This requirement was somewhat relaxed by the Court of Appeal decision in *Clark v Oxfordshire Health Authority* [1998] I.R.L.R. 125. That case considered what was necessary where a "global" or "umbrella" contract was being argued—a contract which covered periods of work interspersed with periods of inactivity. In such a case, the Court of Appeal decided, it may be enough if there is an obligation on the part of the "employee" to do work if it is offered, coupled with an obligation on the part of the "employer" to pay a retainer during the periods of inactivity when no work was being offered.

   The issue as to whether there is mutuality of obligation arises with greatest frequency where the individuals claiming employment status work on a casual, irregular, seasonal or temporary basis. Their situation is looked at in more detail in paras 2.21 to 2.23. The argument is often around whether there is an exchange of promises (usually implied rather than express) about what will happen in the future. Will work be provided? Will it be performed? In answering these questions, an employment tribunal will usually have no documents, nor even an express oral agreement to rely upon. As a result, it will often look for any inferences which can be drawn from the conduct of the parties, e.g. from the pattern of work done. From this, it may be possible to conclude that there is an umbrella contract. If there is not, then each of the short periods worked may constitute a period of employment. In this latter situation, however, the "employee" will usually not acquire sufficient continuity of employment to become entitled to rights such as those not to be unfairly dismissed, or to receive a redundancy payment.

Control. Traditionally, control was the factor which the common law used   **2.11** to distinguish the contract of service from the contract for services. The question frequently asked was: did the "employer" have control over what the "employee" did and the manner in which it was done? The greater the degree of control, the more likely it was that the relationship was one of employment. In determining whether the requisite degree of control existed, the courts would look at matters such as:

- the extent to which the "employer" controlled the work which was done;

- the control which he had over the hours which the "employee" worked;

- the extent to which he determined where the work was done;

- whether he could control the manner in which the work was done.

Obviously, as the worker becomes more skilled, one would expect him to exercise independent judgment, and it is difficult to see how, for example, an NHS Trust can be said to control the manner in which a surgeon does his work. As a result, this part of the control test has tended to undergo a change, so that the question is usually posed as: does the "employer" have the right to tell the "employee" how to do the job? (Rather than: does it actually tell him how to do it?)

In any event, control is no longer seen as the primary condition for the existence of an employment relationship. It is clear, however, that it is still a necessary condition, in the sense that, without the right to control, there can be no contract of service: *Montgomery v Johnson Underwood Ltd* [2001] I.R.L.R. 269, CA.

Other factors. The above elements are all essential for the existence of a   **2.12** contract of employment. Even if they are all present, however, that does not conclude the matter. The context of the relationship has to be considered in order to determine whether it really does constitute a contract of employment. Some of the relevant factors are:

(a) whether the person doing the work provides their own equipment;

(b) whether they take any financial risk;

(c) whether they hire staff;

(d) any restrictions upon working for someone else;

(e) payment for periods of sickness, and for holidays;

(f) membership of a pension scheme;

(g) whether there is a disciplinary code administered by the "employer";

(h) the intentions of the parties.

These are merely factors in the equation. The absence or presence of one or more of them will not be conclusive one way or the other. Nor is it a case of looking at the number of factors present by comparison with those which are absent and comparing the totals. It is rather a case of looking at the various aspect of the relationship, and determining whether they amount to a contract of service or not. In any event, it is worth repeating that the four elements dealt with in paras 2.07 to 2.11 must all be present before the factors outlined as (a) to (h), together with any others which are relevant, can enter into the picture.

What is a "worker"?

2.13   The definition of "worker" , and the rights to which workers are entitled are set out in para.2.04. The definition includes all those who are subject to a contract of employment, but its scope is broader than that, so as to encompass some independent contractors. It does not, however, extend to those who might be thought of as totally self-employed.

It includes anyone who provides personal services under a contract, subject to an exception. The exception is that the other party to the contract may not be a client or customer of the individual in question. It follows that:

(a) there must be a contract;

(b) it must be to carry out personal services for another party to the contract; and

(c) that other party must not be a client or customer of the "worker's" profession or business undertaking.

2.14   **Contract.** The work must be carried out in accordance with an agreement—express or implied and if express, oral or written.

2.15   **Personal Service.** The worker must perform the services personally. Just as the unrestricted ability to delegate will be fatal to the formation of a contract of employment (see para.2.09), it will also prevent an individual from acquiring the status of "worker": *Byrne Bros (Formwork) Ltd v Baird* [2002] I.R.L.R. 96.

2.16   **The Client or Customer Exception.**   In *Byrne Bros (Formwork) Ltd v Baird* [2002] I.R.L.R. 96, the EAT said that the Working Time Regulations had created an intermediate group of protected workers. On the one hand they were not necessarily employees, but on the other hand they were not involved in carrying on a business. Deciding whether an individual fell into this intermediate category would mean considering the same factors as were relevant in deciding whether someone was an employer e.g. degree of control, who provides the equipment, who takes the financial risk. However, the hurdle was lower for the achievement of the status of "worker" than it was for the status of "employee". Nevertheless, it is clear from the wording of the various pieces of legislation which define "worker" that those who are carrying on a business undertaking do not qualify. Hence in *Commissioners of Inland Revenue v Post Office Ltd* [2003] I.R.L.R. 199, it was held that sub-postmasters fell outside the ambit of the definition of worker for this reason (as well as the fact that they were able to choose whether to do the work themselves).

What constitutes "in employment"?

An individual will qualify for protection under the various strands of anti- **2.17** discrimination legislation if he is "in employment". The definition, as set out in para.2.05 covers not only contracts of service or apprenticeship but also "a contract personally to do any work or labour". It will be seen that this covers the same territory as the definition of worker, but it is wider, because it is not subject to the exception for clients or customers of a business or profession. There are therefore two requirements:

(a) a contract; and

(b) personal work or labour.

Contract. In order to be in employment for the purposes of the anti- **2.18** discrimination legislation, the individual doing the work must have a contract with the person for whom the work is done. The contract need not necessarily involve payment. Hence in *Murray v Newham Citizens Advice Bureau* EAT 1096/99, the absence of pay was held not to be fatal to the claim of a trainee voluntary adviser that he was discriminated against contrary to the Disability Discrimination Act 1995. It was still possible for him to be "in employment", given the wide meaning attributed to that term by the DDA (and other anti-discrimination legislation).

Personal work or labour. The contract must have as its dominant purpose **2.19** the execution of work or labour. Hence, in *Tanna v Post Office* [1981] I.C.R. 374, a postmaster was held not to be covered by the definition, since he was responsible merely for seeing that the work of the Post Office was effected, and did not have to perform any of the duties himself. An independent wholesale newspaper distributor who held an agency for the Mirror Group was excluded for similar reasons in *Mirror Group Newspaper Ltd v Gunning* [1986] I.R.L.R. 27.

Types of employee and worker

There has been a shift in recent years away from the traditional pattern **2.20** of employees in regular, full-time employment. Some employers have seen an advantage in hiring workers who fall outside the traditional model, for example in casual work, often performed on a part-time basis and sometimes at home. Often, a core of regular full-time employees is supplemented by such workers, who are regarded as expendable when demand is reduced. One of the reasons for the evolution of these new patterns is an attempt to skirt around employment protection legislation. Sometimes the attempt is successful, and sometimes it is not. Each case must be looked at on its facts, and the label attributed by the parties to the relationship is not conclusive—the mere fact that the worker is, for example, described as "self-employed" does not mean that he is not, in reality, an employee. In addition, as has been seen in paras 2.13 to 2.16 the status of "worker" (introduced primarily in response to the European framework) means that many who formerly had no employment rights at all are now entitled to certain of the rights historically attributed to employment status, e.g. to holiday pay and protection of wages.

The sections which follow examine the position with regard to certain groups of people whose work falls outside the traditional pattern, and who have been the focus of a disproportionate amount of case law as a result.

Casual workers

2.21   In certain industries (for example catering, tourism, agriculture), it is common for people to work irregularly, often on a seasonal basis. They are often referred to as "casual workers", although there is no defined legal category with that label. The patterns in question can vary widely. A part-time teacher may work a number of hours during term time for several years. A student may take on a job as a fruit-picker for a few months one summer holiday. A waiter may take a job with the same employer in a tourist resort over the summer for a number of successive years. Does the individual in question qualify as an "employee", and even if he does not, is he a "worker"?

There are really two distinct questions where the individual has a working relationship which is irregular or seasonal. First, is he employed during the time when he is actually working? To take the example of the waiter in the preceding paragraph, is there a contract of employment during the summer? This might be established with relative ease, but will be of limited value if the waiter is looking for protection against unfair dismissal which would require (in normal circumstances) employment for at least a year (see paras 9.07 to 9.12). Second, is there a global or umbrella contract which covers the periods when the waiter is not actually working, with the result that he can acquire those rights which need a longer period of continuous employment?

As to the first question, it is possible for each period to give rise to a contract of employment, depending on whether it satisfies the tests for such a contract set out in paras 2.07 to 2.12 (*McMeechan v Secretary of State for Employment* [1997] I.C.R. 549).

2.22   The second question raises a more difficult hurdle for the prospective employee to clear. The central problem is that there may well be no mutuality of obligation between the parties during the non-working period (the winter in the case of the waiter). In *Carmichael v National Power plc* [2000] I.R.L.R. 43, HL tour guides were held to have no contractual relationship with the tour guide operator. There were no mutual obligations to offer and perform work. Although there were documents dealing with the relationship between the parties, they merely provided a framework for a series of successive ad hoc contracts which they might make from time to time.

In *Clark v Oxfordshire Health Authority* [1998] I.R.L.R. 125, CA, lack of mutuality was held to be fatal to the claim for unfair dismissal of a "bank nurse", who was offered work whenever an appropriate temporary vacancy occurred. She was not regarded as employed under a global contract of employment during the periods between engagements because the employer was under no obligation, during those periods, to offer work, and she was under none to accept it. She was not entitled to pay when not working, and had no entitlement to holiday or sick pay within the terms of her contract.

By contrast, a global contract was held to exist in the "homeworkers" case of *Nethermere (St Neots) Ltd v Gardiner* [1984] I.R.L.R. 240, the facts of which are dealt with in para.2.24.

In *Stevedoring and Haulage Services Ltd v Fuller* [2001] I.R.L.R. 627, CA, **2.23** it was stressed that where a contract contained clear express terms excluding mutual obligations, it was not possible to imply a term conferring such obligations. A docker, employed on a casual basis, with a contract stating that no mutual obligations as to the provision and acceptance of work existed, could not be an "employee".

There are several factors, however, which mitigate the position of casual employees. First, it is perfectly possible that an employment contract exists in relation to the period during which the individual is actually working, with the result that they acquire certain rights which do not require a longer period of continuous employment. Second, there are various provisions which allow periods where an individual is not actually working to be taken into account as part of a period of continuous employment (see paras 9.10 to 9.11). Finally, even where employment status cannot be established, casual staff may well provide personal services under a contract which is not with a client of customer, and hence be classified as workers. In any event, they will generally be "in employment" within the meaning of the discrimi-nation legislation, with the result that they will be able to claim its protection.

Homeworkers

Again, there is no statutory definition for the term, but a home worker is **2.24** one who does all or much of their work at home, rather than at a workplace under the control of the person who hires them, A variety of work can be done in this way—for example the sewing of garments as in *Nethermere (St Neots) Ltd v Gardiner* [1984] I.R.L.R. 240. More recently, the growth in home working has been led by technology-based services, and call-centres in particular.

In principle, the difference between working from home and working from the normal workplace is that the home worker gains a measure of independence from control, and can exercise discretion as to how the workload is timed and managed. In addition, cases have frequently highlighted the absence of mutuality of obligation between the parties.

In *Nethermere*, the company manufactured boys' trousers. The claimants had worked for the company for a number of years from home, sewing flaps and pockets on to the garments, using machines provided by the company. There were no fixed hours of work, but they normally worked for four or five hours a day, and were paid weekly by piece-rate, filling out time sheets and receiving deliveries on a regular basis. They were not obliged to accept any particular work. The arrangement came to an end, and the workers claimed that they were unfairly dismissed. The employer argued that they were self-employed. The Court of Appeal decided that the relationship between the parties had developed into an "umbrella" contract, which obliged the company to continue to provide and pay for work, and the workers to continue to accept and perform the work provided. There was no reason why home workers should be excluded from an enforceable contract of service (ie employment) where there was a regular course of dealing which involved mutuality of obligation. However, where work is sporadic and the putative employer is under no obligation to provide work, the relationship will not amount to an "umbrella" contract: *Market Investigations Ltd v Minister of Social Security* [1969] 2 W.L.R. 1.

2.25   Even if a home worker does not qualify for employment status, he may well be providing personal services under a contract, and the other party to the contract may not be a client or customer of his business of profession. If so, he will classified as a "worker" and will be entitled to some of the rights to employment protection. In any event, he may fall within the definition of "in employment" contained in the anti-discrimination legislation, and be able to rely upon its protection.

The National Minimum Wage Act 1998, s.35 contains a special provision in relation to home workers. Even if a home worker is not a "worker" because he does not provide services "personally", he will be entitled to the national minimum wage (see paras 5.05 and 5.06 for details of the national minimum wage). As a result, the home worker is entitled to delegate work, and still paid the national minimum wage for the hours worked by those who actually carry the work out. It is worth noting that, in order to qualify as a "homeworker" under s.35, the worker need not actually work at home: *James v Redcats (Brands) Ltd*, EAT 0475/06.

Agency workers

2.26   There has been a considerable volume of recent case law about the status of those who are "on the books" of an employment bureau. (Employment bureaux are frequently referred to as "employment agencies" although that term is reserved in law for recruitment consultants or "headhunters".) Such agency workers (sometimes called "temps") are then found work with a third party—the "hirer". The engagement may be for a fixed-term, or it may be open-ended. The relationship is a tri-partite one, and is depicted in the diagram below.

Agency workers

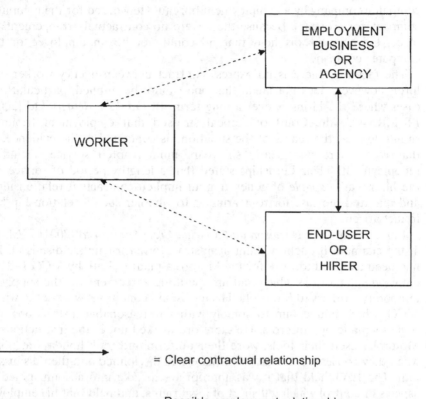

←———————→	= Clear contractual relationship
◄----------------►	= Possible employment relationship

When dealing with the employment status of an agency worker, two questions arise:

(a) Is he an employee of the hirer (or end-user)?

(b) Is he an employee of the agency?

It is of course possible that both of these questions must be answered in the negative, because the agency worker is self-employed, for example.

Employee of the hirer?

There are two contracts which are fundamental to the tri-partite arrange-   **2.27** ment depicted in the diagram. First, there is a contract between the worker and the employment business, which will govern their relationship. Second, there is a contract between the employment business and the hirer, which governs the relationship of the businesses in question.

The question which needs to be answered, however, is whether there is a contract in existence between hirer and agency worker. It is of course necessary that there should be one for the worker to be employed by the hirer, in line with the general principles set out in paras 2.07 to 2.08. This was the basis of the decision in *Hewlett Packard Ltd v O'Murphy* [2002] I.R.L.R. 4, EAT. In that case, the claimant was found work with a computer company by an employment bureau. He worked for the computer company for six years. Because there were no contractual arrangements in place, however, it was held that he could not be an employee of the computer company.

The fact that there is no express contract between agency worker and hirer, however, does not mean that one cannot be implied, particularly in cases where the hiring is over a long term. In *Franks v Reuters Ltd* [2003] I.R.L.R. 423, the Court of Appeal stressed that employment tribunals should look at the reality of the situation, as contained in the evidence. In that case, there was nearly six years uninterrupted service, including redeployment. Their Lordships stated that a lengthy period of service for the hirer was "*capable* of generating an implied contractual relationship", and remitted the case for re-hearing as to whether such a relationship had in fact arisen.

2.28   In *Motorola Ltd v Davidson and Melville Craig Group Ltd* [2001] I.R.L.R. 4, the claimant brought a claim against Motorola for unfair dismissal. He had been assigned to work for the Motorola plant in Bath by MCG Ltd, an employment business which had an operating agreement for the supply of temporary workers to Motorola. His terms and conditions were set down by MCG, which bound him to comply with any reasonable instructions and requests made by Motorola. He therefore worked under the instructions of Motorola, used their tools, wore their uniform and took holidays at times when they consented. It was Motorola which disciplined and then dismissed him. The EAT held that it was appropriate to take into account practical aspects of control which fell short of legal rights, and held that his employer was Motorola.

In cases where the agency worker has no contract with the hirer, he will not be either an employee or a worker. However, under the anti-discrimination legislation, discrimination against "contract workers" by "principals" is unlawful in respect of their work. A "principal" is defined as one who makes work available for doing by individuals who are employed by another person who supplies them under a contract. A "contract worker" is an individual supplied to a principal under such a contract. It follows that the designation "principal" is equivalent to the term "hirer" which has been used in this section. The term "end-user" is also sometimes found.

Employee of the employment bureau?

2.29   The Conduct of Employment Agencies and Employment Businesses Regulations 2003 (SI 2003/3319) state that an employment bureau must have a contract with each member of staff whom it supplies to a hirer, and must make that fact clear. The crucial question, however, is whether that contract is a contract of employment or not.

In *Montgomery v Johnson Underwood Ltd* [2001] I.R.L.R. 269, the Court of Appeal stressed the need for mutuality of obligation and control, in accordance with general principles. However, their Lordships stated that:

"an offer of work by an employment agency, even at another's workplace, accepted by the individual for remuneration to be paid by the agency, could satisfy the requirement of mutuality of obligation."

It is submitted that it will more usually prove to be a lack of control by the employment bureau which will exclude a finding that there is an employment relationship between it and the worker. Usually, control will be exercised at the workplace by the hirer, rather than the bureau, although there may be a degree of indirect control exercised by the bureau.

The individual may be a worker as far as the employment bureau is concerned, even if he is not an employee. The bureau is legally obliged to provide him with a contract. It will generally be founded upon an obligation to supply work personally to the hirer (who will be a client of the employment business, and not of the worker. The worker will also usually be "in employment" as far as the employment bureau is concerned, for the purposes of the anti-discrimination legislation.

Not employed at all? The *Dacas* case

In *Dacas v Brook Street Bureau (UK) Ltd* [2004] I.R.L.R. 358, the   **2.30**
claimant was a cleaner who was sent by the bureau to work as a cleaner at a hostel run by Wandsworth Council for some four years until her assignment was terminated. She then claimed unfair dismissal against either the agency or the council. The employment tribunal held that she was not employed by either. The EAT held that she was employed by Brook Street, on the basis that it exercised considerable control over her, and that there was mutuality of obligation as between Mrs Dacas and the bureau. It was therefore not open to the parties to exclude the employer-employee relationship by agreement, as they had originally attempted to do. The label put on the contract by the parties was only decisive where, after balancing the pointers for against employment, there is still some doubt or ambiguity as to the true nature of the contract.

The decision of the EAT was appealed to the Court of Appeal, which held that Mrs Dacas was not employed by the bureau. There was no obligation on her to accept any work which it offered, and it did not exercise any relevant control over her. The employment tribunal had failed to address the possibility that Mrs Dacas was in fact employed by Wandsworth Council—the "hirer", on the basis of an implied contract of service. However, as Mrs Dacas had not appealed against the finding that she was not employed by the council, the employment tribunal's decision must stand, and Mrs Dacas was left without a remedy. In the course of its judgment, the Court of Appeal indicated its dissatisfaction with the suggestion that Mrs Dacas might have been employed by no-one, with the result that she was left without employment rights. Sedley L.J. stated that:

"The conclusion that Mrs Dacas was employed by nobody is simply not credible. There has to be something wrong with it."

He went on to say that there was:

"an inexorable inference . . . that by the date of her dismissal she was an employee of the borough with the statutory right not to be unfairly dismissed".

He suggested that this inexorable inference would have arisen after a year. Mummery L.J. said that a finding that the council was the legal employer of the agency worker would "accord with practical reality and common sense". Both Sedley L.J. and Mummery L.J. made the point that, if temporary workers are not employees, there can be no vicarious liability if they carelessly injure someone in the course of their work. Munby J. delivered a dissenting judgment, which stated that the views of the majority would "put in question the most basic assumptions upon which the whole of [the employment bureau] industry has hitherto conducted its business". Whilst there is some truth in that statement, it does beg the question of whether the basic assumptions are in accordance with the way in which the law has developed, and the purpose of the employment protection legislation.

In *Cable and Wireless plc v Muscat* [2006] I.R.L.R. 354, the CA approved and applied the approach in *Dacas*. However, in *James v Greenwich Council* [2007] I.R.L.R. 168, the EAT suggested that the circumstances in which an employment tribunal should imply that there was a contract of employment with the end-user should be tightly defined. Elias P. stated that when agency arrangements genuinely represented the actual relationship between the parties, it would be rare that there would be evidence entitling the tribunal to imply a contract between worker and end-user. In particular, it would be necessary to show that there were mutual obligations between worker and end-user.

CHAPTER THREE

THE INDIVIDUAL CONTRACT OF EMPLOYMENT

Traditionally, the dealings between employer and employee are founded **3.01** upon the individual contract of employment. With the growth of statutory controls over the contents of the contract, however, it is no longer possible to say with any degree of certainty that its terms form the bedrock of the employment relationship. Nevertheless, before one can answer many of the important questions about how employer and employee ought to behave towards each other, it is necessary to determine what is in the individual contract of employment.

In doing so, one needs to remember that it will be most unusual for that contract to be contained within a single document. Usually there will be a number of documents which contain various terms of the contract. Often important terms in the contract will not have been reduced to writing at all, but will have been the subject of oral agreement or be assumed by the parties to take a particular form. Sometimes, there will be no document which can in any meaningful sense be called a contract.

This chapter looks at the following aspects of the individual employment contract:

(a) the formation of the contract;

(b) the various sources from which the terms of the contract are derived;

(c) the statutory statement of terms and conditions (which represents an effort by legislators to simplify the confusing position outlined in the previous paragraph);

(d) the typical major terms contained within a contract of employment;

(e) variation of contract;

(f) termination;

(g) remedies for breach.

Formation of the contract

The general principles applicable to the law of contract are equally **3.02** relevant to employment, and reference should be made to the standard works on the law of contract for details. Offer and acceptance are required, together with consideration. In practice, the offer is usually from the employer, and acceptance is by the employee. Consideration takes the form of paying wages and doing the work respectively. The parties must intend the agreement, and the terms which it contains, to create legal relations.

The formation of the contract may well take place as a result of an interview. The employer then sends an offer of appointment, which the prospective employee is asked to sign and return. But sometimes the offer may be oral, and acceptance may even be by conduct, in that the employee turns up at the appointed time and place and begins work. There is no need for the contract to be in writing to be binding. However, s.1 of the Employment Rights Act 1996 ("the ERA 1996") requires the employer to provide a written statement of certain specified important terms to the employee (see paras 3.13 and 3.14).

Source of terms

3.03   The main sources of terms in the contract of employment are:

(a) written express terms;

(b) works' rules and staff handbooks;

(c) collectively agreed terms;

(d) orally agreed terms;

(e) custom and practice;

(f) implied terms;

(g) statute.

Each of them will be dealt with briefly, in turn.

Written express terms

3.04   Generally, the employee should be given, at the start of employment, a document which contains his contractual terms. Ideally, this document will be comprehensive, and he will have signified his agreement that it is accurate by signing a copy of it. In other words, his contract will consist of a series of written express terms. Unfortunately, all too often this is not done, and any subsequent enquiry as to what the terms of the contract are will sometimes involve a complex investigation ranging over a variety of pieces of paper and accounts of what was or was not agreed in various conversations.

Sometimes the question arises whether a tribunal or court is entitled to look outside the terms of written documentation to determine the terms of the contract of employment. The principles would appear to be as follows (*Carmichael v National Power plc* [2000] I.R.L.R. 43, HL, as summarised in *Ministry of Defence Dental Services v Kettle* EAT 0308/06):

(1) A tribunal faced with a document(s) said to be contractual should decide whether the parties intended it to be the exclusive record of the terms of their agreement.

(2) That question is a question of fact for the tribunal.

(3) If it was the intention of the parties that the document(s) should be the exclusive record of the terms of their agreement, the tribunal is generally restricted to consideration of the document(s). The meaning of the documents is a question of law.

(4) If it was not the parties' intention that the document(s) should be the exclusive record of their terms of agreement, the tribunal will look at other relevant materials to determine the terms of the contract.

In order to ensure that question (1) is answered in the affirmative, some employers now rely upon "entire agreement" clauses, which specify that nothing other than what is contained in the contract may amount to a contractual term. In *White v Bristol Rugby Club* [2002] I.R.L.R. 204, HC, for example, a clause in the written contract stated:

> "this agreement and its schedules together with the documents referred to in this agreement contain the whole agreement between the parties and. . . they have not relied upon oral or written representations made to them by other persons, its employees or agents".

H.H. Judge Havelock-Allan Q.C. stated that such "entire agreement" **3.05** clauses, if clearly worded as this one was, were effective to exclude claims based on collateral warranties or oral terms outside the four corners of the written document.

Policies, works' rules and staff handbooks

A frequent practice, particularly in larger companies, is to set out policies **3.06** which relate to employment in a Staff Handbook, or Works' Rule Book. This may then be pinned to the notice board, or kept in the manager's office, or posted on the intranet for employees to access from their computers. The aim is to flesh out the skeleton contained in the letter of appointment or other main contractual document issued to the employee when he started working. A frequent formula is for the employee to sign a declaration (sometimes appended to his letter of appointment) that he accepts the conditions set out in (for example) the staff handbook (using that phrase to cover works' rulebooks, policies etc). To have effect, however, it is not necessary for the employee to acknowledge acceptance of the term specifically. It may be prominently displayed, for example, or handed out.

The legal question is: are the contents of the staff handbook incorporated as terms of the individual's contract? There are some aspects of the typical staff handbook which are not susceptible to becoming terms in a contract. They may be matters which fall within the prerogative of the employer, or they may by their nature be variable. For example, in *Secretary of State for Employment v ASLEF (No.2)* [1972] 2 Q.B. 455, the rail driver's union embarked upon a "work to rule" as a form of industrial action, i.e. they instructed their members to follow the detailed instructions laid down in the employers' rule book, comprising some 239 rules in an attempt to clog up the working of the railways. The Court of Appeal held that the "work to rule" was a breach of contract. The rules in question were not part of the contract. They were instructions to each worker as to how to do his work, and they could be altered at will by the employer.

In *Grant v South West Trains Ltd* [1998] I.R.L.R. 188, it was held that an equal opportunities policy was not incorporated into the individual's contract of employment. Similarly, in *Dryden v Greater Glasgow Health Board* [1992] I.R.L.R. 469, the EAT determined that a ban on smoking was not a breach of the employee's contract of employment, since it was a work rule which came within the employer's prerogative.

3.07   The crucial test is: do the parties intend the policy or rule in question to be a contractual term? In determining what that intention is, the nature of the term will be important. Is it the sort of term which typically forms part of a contract of employment? Clearly, if it is one of those terms which are required by the statutory statement (see paras 3.13 and 3.14), then it is more likely to be deemed to have been intended by the parties to be contractual.

Collectively agreed terms

3.08   For large sectors of the working population, terms and conditions of employment are negotiated and agreed collectively between employers and trade unions. For the workers in question, the position will be that their main contractual document will refer them to the collective agreement which deals with the topic in question, e.g. pay, hours, holidays.

Where there is a collective agreement between employers and unions, the question posed is: are its terms incorporated in the contract of the individual? Some parts of a collective agreement will clearly not be susceptible to such incorporation, e.g. those which govern relations between union and employer, procedural agreements as to negotiation, what should happen in the event of dispute, and the like. Assuming that the term in question is susceptible of incorporation in this sense, however, the question still remains: is it in fact incorporated? For that to be the case, there must be a "bridge" between the collective agreement and the individual contract. The simplest way in which this is achieved is by means of an express statement in the individual contract, e.g.

> "rates of pay are to be determined by the national agreement between the recognised unions and the employers which is in force for the time being".

This will mean that the contract need not be amended after each round of negotiation, when a new national agreement is in place. It is worth emphasising that the individual does not need to be a member of the union in question in order for the term in the collective agreement to be incorporated in his contract. Indeed, he need not know of the terms of the agreement, or the fact that it has been changed.

Orally agreed terms

There is no difference in theoretical status between written and oral **3.09** terms. An oral term concluded after a written agreement is signed, for example, can override the relevant term in the written agreement. In practice, the problem is one of proof—the document is relatively easy to establish in evidence in any subsequent proceedings, whereas the existence of the oral term may be hotly disputed. Subject to proof, however, the oral term will become part of the contract.

In cases where there is a dispute as to whether an oral term is to be taken as altering contractual documents, the principles set out in *Carmichael v National Power* are likely to be relevant, as is the presence of any "entire agreement" clause (see para.3.04 above).

Custom and practice

The way in which things are done, and have been done in the past, in the **3.10** workplace and elsewhere, will sometimes give rise to a contractual term based upon "custom and practice". For such a term to be recognised, it must be "reasonable, certain and notorious" and there must be nothing in the express or necessarily implied terms of the contract to exclude it. As to certainty, what is necessary is that the term must be capable of being stated precisely. It will be notorious if it is generally known by the workforce— which does not mean that the particular worker whose contract is being scrutinised must have known of it. In the leading case of *Sagar v Ridehalgh and Son Ltd* [1931] 1 Ch. 310, the Court of Appeal was called upon to decide whether deductions which had been made from the wages of weavers in the same way for 30 years had been incorporated in their contracts. As it was put by Romer L.J., an employee entering the company's service:

> "upon the same terms as the other weavers employed by them . . . must be deemed to have subjected himself to those terms whatever those terms might turn out to be".

Implied terms

Custom and practice may be viewed as one way in which a term is **3.11** implied into a contract. There are various others, and some terms, such as the implied mutual duty of trust and confidence, are implied into contracts of employment as a matter of course.

Leaving aside those terms implied into a contract as a matter of law, there is also the possibility of a term being implied into a contract from the conduct of the parties. Such implication must be based upon the presumed intention of the parties. The test for the inclusion of such an implied term is that it must be necessary to give business efficacy to the contract: *Reigate v Union Manufacturing Co Ltd* [1918] 1 K.B. 592. It is not enough that it should be reasonable to imply a term: *Liverpool CC v Irwin* [1977] A.C. 239. An alternative and striking test was articulated by McKinnon L.J. in *Shirlaw and Southern Foundries (1926) Ltd* [1939] 2 K.B. 206 when he said that, for a term to be implied, it must be:

"something so obvious that it goes without saying; so that, if, while the parties were making their bargain, an officious bystander were to suggest some express provision for it in their agreement, they would testily suppress him with a common 'Oh, of course!'"

In addition to being obvious in this sense, it must also be precise, so that the courts are aware of exactly what it is that they are supposed to enforce.

Statute

3.12   There are certain terms which are implied into the employment contract as a result of the operation of statute. Examples include the right to statutory notice, to the minimum wage, to maternity leave and to equal pay. All of these are dealt with in other chapters, and Chapter 5, in particular, is devoted to the statutory regulation of wages and hours.

Statement of Terms

3.13   A statutory duty is laid down for employers by s.1 of the ERA 1996: to supply an employee employed for one month or more with a statement of terms and conditions. This document must contain, in accordance with ss.1 to 7 of the ERA, the following:

    (a) the names of employer and employee;

    (b) the date when employment began;

    (c) the date on which the employee's period of continuous employment began (this may be the same as (b), or it may be an earlier date so as to take into account employment with a TUPE transferor, for example—the operation of TUPE is dealt with in Chapter 12);

    (d) the rate of remuneration, or method of calculating it;

    (e) the intervals at which it is paid;

    (f) hours of work;

    (g) holidays;

    (h) sick pay;

    (i) pensions;

    (j) notice required;

    (k) the job title or brief description;

    (l) if the employment is not permanent, the period for which it is meant to last and, if for a fixed term, the end date;

    (m) the place of work or an indication that the employee is required or permitted to work at various places, together with the employer's address;

(n) any collective agreements affecting terms and conditions;

(o) any details as to work outside the United Kingdom;

(p) any disciplinary rules (or a reference to the document which specifies them;

(q) any procedure applicable to the taking of disciplinary decisions or decisions to dismiss, or a reference to the relevant document;

(r) the person with whom grievances can be raised, and the manner in which that should be done;

(s) a note about whether there is a certificate relating to the employment being contracted out under the Pensions Schemes Act 1993.

The employee acquires the right to receive such a statement after a month in employment. The statement need not actually be issued until after two months (so that an employee dismissed after between one and two months' employment will become entitled to have a document as a record of his former job, which may be useful in the event that he wishes to make a claim based on his rights at that time). If there is a change in any of the matters of which particulars are required, then the employer is obliged to issue a statement containing the particulars of change as the earliest opportunity and in any event within a month.

Generally, the required details must be contained within the statement itself. However, in respect of certain matters (disciplinary procedures, grievance procedures) the statement may refer to other documents reasonably accessible to the employee.

As to the status of the written statement, there has been a certain **3.14** amount of case law. What is clear is that it does not of itself constitute the contract. Nor is it conclusive evidence of the terms of the contract. However, according to *System Floors (UK) Ltd v Daniel* [1982] I.C.R. 54, it "provides very strong prima facie evidence of what were the terms of the contract". In practice, given the frequent dearth of documentation relating to contractual terms in many disputed cases, the court or tribunal will often turn to the statutory statement with something approaching relief.

If the employer fails to provide a statement in accordance with the statute, there are two main consequences in law. First, the employee can refer the matter to a tribunal, which has the power to determine what the statement should have contained (ERA 1996, s.11). Second, the Employment Act 2002, s.38 sets out a financial penalty for the employer who is in default. Where one of the tribunal claims listed in Sch.5 of that Act succeeds, the tribunal must make an award of two weeks pay to the employee, unless there are exceptional circumstances which make it unjust or inequitable to do so. Further, if it considers it just and equitable to increase the award to four weeks' pay, it may do so. A week's pay is capped at the statutory amount (£310 per week with effect from February 1, 2007). The claimant has no need to make a specific claim for this amount. The tribunal should raise the matter on its own initiative.

Typical major terms in the contract

3.15   There are a number of terms which are typically contained in a contract of employment, and which impose duties and rights on each of the parties. It is convenient to consider first the duties imposed on the employer, and then those to which the employee is subject.

Employer's Duties

3.16   The duties of the employer include the following:

(a) To pay wages. This is an area which is heavily regulated by statute, and is dealt with in Chapter 5. Nevertheless, perhaps the most obvious contractual duty to which the employer is subject is that of remunerating the employee. In the absence of agreement on the amount which he is to be paid, there is still a right to reasonable remuneration (which, according to statute, must be at least at the level of the national minimum wage for those who qualify). One area of potential controversy is whether the employer is bound to pay sick pay. In *Mears v Safecar Security Ltd* [1982] I.C.R. 626, there was no express term in the employee's contract. The Court of Appeal held that there was no presumption that an employer was obliged to pay sick pay (as the tribunal had suggested), and that it was necessary to look at the surrounding circumstances to determine whether there was any such duty. It is worth noting that there is a scheme of statutory sick pay under the Statutory Sick Pay Act 1994, although the details of the scheme are beyond the scope of this book.

(b) To take reasonable care for the safety of the employee. The employer has a duty to provide a safe system of work, adequate material and premises, and competent fellow employees: *Wilsons & Clyde Coal Co v English* [1938] A.C. 57. This duty extends not only to physical safety, but to the avoidance of actions which will cause psychiatric damage, e.g. caused by stress as a result of the amount of work which they are required to do. In *Sutherland v Hatton* [2002] I.R.L.R. 263, the Court of Appeal set out the boundaries to this aspect of the employer's duty. The central test laid down was: is a harmful reaction to the pressures of the work reasonably foreseeable, with regard to the individual in question?

(c) Mutual trust and confidence. This is actually, as the label makes clear, a two-way obligation, but it arises more frequently in the context of an allegation by the employee that the employer has failed to comply with the duty, often as the foundation for a claim of constructive dismissal (see paras 9.21 to 9.29 for details on constructive dismissal). It is applicable in a variety of contexts, e.g. where there is harassment or victimisation by the employer, or a middle manager is undermined in front of his subordinates by a senior manager, or a refusal to afford a reasonable opportunity to obtain redress for a legitimate grievance. As it was put by the Court of Appeal in *Woods v WM Car Services (Peterborough) Ltd* [1982] I.R.L.R. 413, the employers must not:

"without reasonable and proper cause conduct themselves in a manner calculated or likely to destroy or seriously damage the relationship of mutual confidence and trust between employer and employee."

(d) Grievances. There is an implied term that the employer should provide the employee with a reasonable opportunity to resolve a legitimate grievance: *WA Goold (Pearmak) Ltd v McConnell* [1995] I.R.L.R. 516, EAT. It should be noted in this context that there is a statutory grievance procedure which is applicable to all employees, and which has important consequences both in terms of procedure, and with respect to compensation, in the event of a subsequent tribunal claim (see paras 3.33, 10.18 and 14.08).

(e) References. There is a duty on the employer to take reasonable care in giving a reference. If the employer acts negligently, he will be liable to the current or former employee for economic loss, based on an action for negligent misstatement: *Spring v Guardian Assurance plc* [1994] I.R.L.R. 460. This does not mean, however, that there is any general duty to provide a reference—merely that when one is provided, it should be "true, accurate and fair": *Bartholomew v Hackney LBC* [1999] I.R.L.R. 246, CA.

Employee's duties

The following is a short selection from the duties of the employee: **3.17**

(a) Obeying lawful orders. The employee must not wilfully disobey a lawful order. In this context, "lawful" means within the scope of the contract. It does not mean that the order must be reasonable, although the contractual term upon which the employer bases himself to render the instruction lawful must be reasonably interpreted. To take an extreme example, in *Ottoman Bank v Chakarian* [1930] A.C. 277, an Armenian employee was ordered to work in Turkey, where he was under sentence of death. It was held that he was within his rights in refusing.

(b) Exercising reasonable care and skill. The employee is under a duty to exercise reasonable care and skill in the performance of his duty, and will be in breach of that duty in the event that he acts negligently or with a degree of competence below his capabilities: *Janata Bank v Ahmed* [1981] I.R.L.R. 457. This contractual duty is now tempered by the right of the employee to claim unfair dismissal if dismissed for incompetence where the employer has failed to follow a reasonable procedure (see Chapter 9).

(c) Acting in good faith. There is a general duty upon the employee to act loyally and honestly towards his employer. Clearly, any theft from, or fraud committed against the employer would be in breach of contract. Also under this heading come the duty not to disclose confidential information (see Chapter 4) and the duty not to compete with the employer: *Hivac Ltd v Park Royal Scientific Instruments Ltd* [1946] Ch. 169.

(d) Duty of co-operation. The employee has a duty not to disrupt the employer's business interests. Hence a "work to rule" can in certain circumstances amount to a breach of contract where its aim is to cause disruption: *Secretary of State for Employment v ASLEF (No.2)* [1972] 2 Q.B. 455.

Variation of contract

3.18   Either party to the contract may wish to vary its terms, as a result of changing circumstances. Crucially, any variation in contractual terms will require the consent of both parties, and should be supported by consideration. It is necessary to distinguish, however, between:

(a) a variation in contractual terms; and

(b) a variation in the conditions of employment which is provided for within the original contract. This may be done by means of a "flexibility clause", e.g. that the employee "will carry out such duties as are from time to time notified to him by the Managing Director." This will not of itself constitute a variation in contractual terms.

Consent may be either express or tacit and the employee may, for example, signify his consent by continuing to work under the varied terms. However, where the employee makes his opposition sufficiently clear to the change in terms, a court or tribunal may not be willing to accept that the employee has consented by his conduct (see, for example, *Marriott v Oxford and District Cooperative Society (No.2)* [1970] 1 Q.B. 186).

The question of whether there is agreement to the variation of the contract arises most frequently in connection with business reorganisation. On occasion, the employer may be able to argue that the variation is within the four corners of the contract (e.g. there is a flexibility clause, or that there is an implied term which covers the proposed change). More difficult is the situation where the proposed changes in working practice fall outside the scope of the contractual terms. Various factual situations may ensue:

(a) The employee may agree to the change, and stay in employment. There will then be a change in the terms of the contract which is supported by the consent of both parties, and will be effective. Often the agreement in question is achieved through collective bargaining with the trade unions, where unions are recognised.

(b) The employee may stay in the job, without agreeing to the change. In such a case, the conduct of the employee may amount to assent, but his protests may mean that there is an ineffective unilateral variation (see *Marriott* above). Further, if the employee concludes that the change has little practical effect, his consent will not necessarily be implied by the courts or tribunals: *Jones v Associated Tunnelling Ltd* [1981] I.R.L.R. 477, EAT.

(c) The employee refuses to accept the new terms and resigns. If the employer's actions constitute a fundamental breach of contract, the employee can claim that he was constructively dismissed, and bring an action for unfair dismissal (see Chapter 9).

(d) The employer dismisses the employee, on the basis that he has failed to accept the changes necessary to the business. The employee may be able to bring an action for wrongful dismissal, if there is, for example, a failure to give contractual notice or to go through the procedure for dismissal laid down in the contract. In addition, the employee may bring a claim for unfair dismissal, although it may be open to the employer to argue that he dismissed for "some other substantial reason" and acted reasonably rather than unreasonably (see Chapter 9).

(e) The employer dismisses the employee, and re-engages him under the new contract, with the terms as varied. The advantage to the employer is that his obligations under the old contract are extinguished, subject to any claims on the part of the dismissed employee for wrongful or unfair dismissal. In order to take this course of action, the employer must make it clear that he is terminating one contract and offering another. It is not sufficient to announce the change without terminating, as that will mean that the contract continues in existence, and the employee's rights under it are preserved. In *Rigby v Ferodo* [1987] I.R.L.R. 516, the employer reduced wages unilaterally, which was a repudiation of the contract. However, that repudiation was not accepted by the employees. As a result, they were entitled to recover lost wages right up to the date of trial, rather than just for the period of notice, as the employer argued. In any event, there are major disadvantages to a strategy of termination and re-engagement, even if it is clearly flagged. Quite apart from the prospect of claims for unfair dismissal, an employee working out a period of notice is likely to be resentful and uncooperative, and the industrial relations consequences are likely to be extremely negative. It is also worth noting that the strategy may trigger off a duty on the part of the employer to consult both individually and collectively where dismissals arise out of restructuring (*GMB v Man Truck and Bus Ltd* [2000] I.R.L.R. 636, and see Chapter 11).

Termination of contract

The following are the main ways in which the contract of employment **3.19** comes to an end:

(a) Dismissal by the employer. This may well give rise to a claim for wrongful dismissal (see paras 3.27 to 3.30), or unfair dismissal (see Chapter 9). Dismissal may be with or without notice, and this aspect is dealt with in paras 3.20 and 3.21.

(b) Resignation by the employee. Where the employee alleges that the resignation flowed from a fundamental breach of contract, there may again be a claim for unfair dismissal.

(c) Agreement. The parties can agree that the contract should be terminated. In such a case, there is no breach of contract, and no claim for wrongful or unfair dismissal should arise.

(d) Frustration. Where the contract of employment is frustrated, it terminates automatically, by operation of law. There will be no breach of contract arising from the termination itself. Events which would result in frustration of the contract include:

- The death of either party.
- Long-term illness or injury on the part of the employee. In practice, the courts and tribunals will usually require a very long term before they will hold that the contract has been frustrated. The employer may well be entitled to dismiss long before that point is reached on grounds of incapability (see Chapter 9).
- Imprisonment of the employee for a term of any substantial length.

(e) The winding up of a company, i.e. a compulsory winding up. The appointment of a receiver, or the making of an administration order would not of itself constitute termination of the contracts of the company's employees.

(f) The dissolution of a partnership (not a mere change of partners, unless the identity of the partners is, unusually, material to the contract).

(g) Expiry of a fixed-term contract. This terminates the contract but does not, at common law, constitute a dismissal. However, it does constitute a dismissal for the purposes of the statutory provisions relating to unfair dismissal (see Chapter 9).

Notice and summary dismissal

3.20   A contract of employment which is of indefinite duration can be terminated by notice on either side. Where the employer dismisses with the requisite notice and according to the procedure required by the contract, the dismissal will not be wrongful, the employee will have received his rights in accordance with his contract, and no contractual claim ought to be forthcoming. That does not mean that there will not be a claim for unfair dismissal, because the statute lays down various rules outside the traditional domain of contract law to determine whether a dismissal is unfair (see Chapter 9).

Summary dismissal

If an employee is dismissed without notice, that is termed a summary **3.21** dismissal, and it is in breach of contract unless the employee is in repudiatory (or fundamental) breach of contract. Gross misconduct is a repudiatory breach of contract, and it entitles the employer to dismiss without notice.

Fixed-term contracts

If a contract is for a fixed term, then there will be no breach of contract if **3.22** the employee is not taken on for a further period, whatever the position may be with regard to unfair dismissal. What is the position, assuming that there is no repudiatory breach on the part of the employee, if the employer wishes to end the contract before its expiry? The answer will depend on whether there is a "break" clause within the contract, entitling the parties (or the employer, in any event) to give notice if they do not wish the contract to continue to full term. If there is such a clause, then the employer could lawfully terminate the contract before the fixed term comes to an end. If there is no "break" clause, then the employer can only end the contract early if he is willing to pay the employee to the end of the contract (unless there has been repudiatory conduct on the part of the employee).

Length of contractual notice

The contract will usually contain a term which sets out the amount of **3.23** notice to which the parties are entitled. If there is no express term, then there is an implied term that the contract can be terminated by either party on the giving of reasonable notice to the other. As to what constitutes reasonable notice, that will depend upon all the circumstances—in particular the sphere of employment concerned, and the position of the employee. As a rule of thumb, the more senior the employee in terms of position, the longer the period of notice to which he is entitled. A professional employee or a manager might well attract a period of reasonable notice of three months or more. As much as a year might be reasonable notice in the case of a company chief executive officer. The reasonable period of notice for an employee in a more junior or less skilled position might be a week or a fortnight.

Statutory notice

In any event, whether the contractual notice term is express or implied, it **3.24** will be subject to the statutory provisions. The rule is that the employee is entitled to the contractual period, or the statutory period, whichever is the longer. The statutory periods of notice which an employer must give are laid down in s.86 of the ERA 1996, as follows:

Period of continuous employment	Length of notice
One month to two years	One week
Two years to 12 years	One week per year
Over 12 years	12 weeks (the maximum statutory notice

Pay in lieu of notice

3.25 Sometimes the employer will dismiss the employee without notice, or with less than the requisite period of notice, and make a "payment in lieu of notice" (PILON). This could be done, for example, if the employer wanted a potentially disaffected employee to leave, rather than spreading ill-feeling among the workforce. Or it could be done as part of a compromise agreement, to enable an employee to look for other employment. In any event, the question arises; what is the legal effect of the PILON?

The first point is that the date on which the employee is dismissed with payment in lieu of notice will normally be the effective date of termination (s.97(1) of the ERA 1996, and see Chapter 9). There will be an exception where the employer requires the employee to adhere to obligations under the contract during the period of notice. In that case, the effective date of termination will be on the expiry of the notice.

Second, if there is no provision in the contract that the employer is entitled to pay in lieu of notice, the employer is technically in breach of contract. Normally, it will not be worth the employee's while to pursue a claim for wrongful dismissal, since he will have received notice pay which will be the equivalent of the damages which he will receive for a successful wrongful dismissal claim. If he accepts the PILON without demur then he will have, in effect, waived the breach of contract for the consideration which he has received.

3.26 However, if there is a provision in the contract entitling the employer to pay in lieu of notice, the dismissal will not be wrongful, even if the employer fails to make the PILON. In that situation, the employee's claim is for a debt owed, rather than for damages for breach of contract: *Abrahams v Performing Rights Society Ltd* [1995] I.R.L.R. 486, CA. An important consequence of this distinction is that the employee is not, in these particular circumstances, subject to a duty to mitigate his loss, e.g. by getting alternative employment. Where he succeeds in a claim for wrongful dismissal, by contrast, he is under a duty to mitigate.

In *Cerberus Software v Rowley* [2001] I.R.L.R. 160, the relevant provision in the claimant's contract stated: "It is agreed that the employer may make a payment in lieu [of notice] to the employee". The claimant was entitled to six months' notice, and obtained new better-paid employment after five weeks. The employer argued that he should be restricted to damages for wrongful dismissal, namely five weeks' pay. The employee argued that a debt had been created, and mitigation was irrelevant. By a majority, the Court of Appeal held that the employer was entitled to choose whether or not to make a PILON. As a result, their non-payment was a breach of contract, and the duty to mitigate applied, with the result that the employee could only claim five weeks' pay. It would appear, therefore, that an employer who reserves the right to decide whether to make a PILON or not will restrict any claim against him to one for damages rather than debt, and will benefit from the employee's duty to mitigate.

Remedies for breach of contract

In accordance with the general rule in contract, the basis for the award of damages is to put the injured party in the position which he would have been if the contract had been fulfilled: *Hadley v Baxendale* (1854) 9 Ex. 341. The damages must not be too remote—they must arise naturally from the breach, or be such as may reasonably be supposed to be within the contemplation of the parties. In an action for wrongful dismissal, the usual measure of damages relates to the period of notice. Where there are mandatory contractual procedures which the employer has failed to carry out, however, the period upon which damages are based will be the period which it would have taken for the employer to dismiss in accordance with the contract. **3.27**

Damages for the employee

The employee will be entitled to the wages which he would have earned during the notice period (if there is one). If the contract is for a fixed term, without a "break" clause, then the wages in question are those to the end of the fixed term. **3.28**

In addition to wages proper, the employee may also suffer loss through a failure to receive other benefits during the period in question, e.g. loss of commission, use of a company car, pension benefits. Many of the relevant considerations arise also in the compensation of unfair dismissal, and are dealt with in Chapter 10.

One controversial area has been whether the employee is entitled to damages for the loss of a discretionary benefit which he expected to receive under the contract—for example, a discretionary bonus. In *Clark v BET plc* [1997] I.R.L.R. 348, it was held that a term which stated that the employee should receive a salary increased "by such amount as the board shall in its absolute discretion decide" fixed the employer with an obligation to increase his salary each year. He was also given an award in respect of a discretionary bonus scheme under his contract.

There has also been a series of cases dealing with the situation where an employee claims that his wrongful dismissal has deprived him of the chance of bringing a claim for unfair dismissal. Assume, for example, that an employee is dismissed without notice after 11 months continuous employment, and that his contract states that he is entitled to a month's notice (or, alternatively, that a month is a reasonable period of notice in all the circumstances). If dismissed in accordance with his contract, he would have **3.29** a year's continuous employment and be able to claim unfair dismissal. Can he claim, under damages for wrongful dismissal, that the employer's breach of contract has deprived him of the prospect of claiming unfair dismissal, with the result that he can add the amount which he would have received for unfair dismissal to the wrongful dismissal damages? In *Harper v Virgin Net Ltd* [2004] I.R.L.R. 390, the Court of Appeal held that the employee was not entitled to compensation for the loss of the opportunity to bring an unfair dismissal claim.

An employee is not entitled to recover contractual damages for psychiatric illness which arises from a wrongful dismissal: *Johnson v Unisys Ltd* [2001] I.R.L.R. 279, HL.

There are certain deductions which have to be made from an award to the employee for breach of contract:

(a) Mitigation. There is a common law duty to mitigate any loss from a breach of contract. This matter is dealt with in more detail in discussing the equivalent duty in unfair dismissal cases (see Chapter 9 and also paras 3.25 and 3.26 dealing with the position in relation to payment in lieu of notice). Briefly, the general rule is that there must be deducted from the damages any amount which the employee has actually received as a result of his mitigation, or what he ought to have received if he had mitigated reasonably.

(b) Taxation. The damages are based upon the wages which the employee has lost, and are therefore paid net of tax. However, payments over £30,000 are taxable in the hands of the employee. As a result, the assessment of the claimant's loss should be increased by such amount as is necessary to leave him, after tax, with the net compensation due to him. This will then put him in the same position as he would be if the contract had been properly performed: *Shove v Downs Surgical plc* [1984] I.R.L.R. 17.

(c) Benefits such as jobseekers' allowance and income support are deducted from the award. The position is different from that which pertains to unfair dismissal, where the amounts paid in respect of these benefits are subject to the Recoupment Regulations. Other benefits received as a result of a period of unemployment should also be deducted, to avoid double compensation. A redundancy payment is not deducted, however, as it is a recognition for past service; nor is any pension benefit.

A claim for damages for breach of contract in the employment tribunal is limited to £25,000. If the claim is for more than that amount, it should be brought in the ordinary courts (see Chapter 13).

Damages for the employer

3.30   The contract usually provides that the employee should give notice to the employer in the event of resignation. The period designated is often the same as that which has to be given by the employer. As far as the statutory position is concerned, the employer is only ever entitled to a week's notice (s.86, ERA 1996). The employer is entitled to whichever is the longer of the contractual and statutory periods.

What is the situation if the employee fails to give the requisite notice, whether statutory or contractual? In theory, the employer is entitled to bring an action for breach of contract. In practice, it is often difficult for the employer to produce evidence of quantifiable damage caused by the lack of notice, and any action under this head is a rarity. In the event that a claim is brought, the usual measure of damages is the additional cost of providing a substitute to do the work.

An employer can claim damages for breach of contract in the employment tribunal only by means of a counterclaim (see para.13.12).

Injunctions

An injunction has to be sought in the courts, and cannot be obtained from a tribunal. The usual obstacle to an injunction sought by an employer is that the court will not order specific performance of the contract. Injunctions are more commonly sought and granted to maintain confidentiality or uphold a non-competition clause (see Chapter 4). **3.31**

As far as the employee is concerned, it is possible to seek an injunction, for example, preventing the employer from dismissing unless and until he has complied with a mandatory contractual procedure relating to, say, redundancy or discipline: *Jones v Lee* [1980] I.C.R. 310, CA.

Statutory Grievance Procedure

The Employment Act 2002 laid down statutory procedures in relation to dismissal and dismissal (the statutory DDP) and for grievances (the statutory GP). Both are set out in Appendix Two. Commentary on the statutory DDP is set out in paras 9.30 to 9.39. **3.32**

As far as the statutory GP is concerned, it takes either the standard or the modified form. A grievance is defined in the Employment Act 2002 (Dispute Regulations 2004, reg.2 as "a complaint by an employee about action which his employer has taken or is contemplating taking in relation to him."

In the standard grievance procedure, there are three steps:

Step 1: the employee makes a complaint in writing against the employer.

Step 2: the employer must have at least one meeting to discuss the grievance with the employee. Thereafter, he must tell the employee of his decision in relation to the grievance, and inform him of his right of appeal.

Step 3: if the employee wishes to appeal, the employer must hold a meeting to consider it.

The modified grievance procedure applies only:

- Where employment has ended without the grievance being raised, or the procedure being completed; and

- Both parties agree in writing to use the modified procedure.

It consists of two steps only:

Step 1: the employee sets out the nature and the basis for the grievance, in writing. This involves more detail than Step 1 in the standard procedure. In *City of Bradford Metropolitan District Council v Pratt* [2007] I.R.L.R 192, the EAT held that the employee must set out not only the grievance, but the essential reasons why he holds the grievance, in sufficient detail to enable the employer to respond.

Step 2: the employer sends a written response to the employee.

The consequences of the statutory GP as far as tribunal procedure is concerned is dealt with in paras 13.06 and 14.08. Its impact upon compensation is dealt with in para 10.18.

CHAPTER FOUR

RESTRICTIVE COVENANTS AND CONFIDENTIALITY CLAUSES

This chapter deals with two topics which are related to the employee's **4.01** duty of fidelity or good faith to his employer (see para.3.17). The employee owes a duty not to compete with his employer, and not to reveal or make use of certain types of confidential information. The two duties—not to compete, and not to reveal confidential information—are often inter—related. For example, the employer may fear that confidential information learnt in the course of working for him will be used by the employee to compete. From the employer's point of view, it is often important to ensure that these duties are complied with, both during the subsistence of the employment relationship, and after it is over. There are other issues at stake, however, and the law places strict limits on the extent to which the employer's interests can be protected.

This chapter will deal with the following topics:

  (a) confidentiality during the course of employment;

  (b) competition while employed;

  (c) confidentiality and the ex-employee;

  (d) restraint of trade and restrictive covenants for the ex-employee.

Confidentiality during employment

An employee will be in breach of the duty of good faith if, during his **4.02** employment, he makes use of trade secrets or other confidential information: *Faccenda Chicken v Fowler* [1986] I.R.L.R. 69, CA. For example, it is a breach of duty to:

  • agree to work personally for existing customers of the employer: *Sanders v Parry* [1967] 2 All E.R. 803;

  • make a list of the employer's customers, intending to use it once he has left the job: *Roger Bullivant v Ellis*: [1987] I.R.L.R. 491, CA;

  • reveal company accounts: *Camelot v Centaur Communications Ltd* [1998] I.R.L.R. 80, CA;

  • reveal a secret formula for the manufacture of gold ink for use in the printing process: *Johnson & Bloy (Holdings) Ltd v Wolstenholme Rink plc and Fallon* [1987] I.R.L.R. 499, CA.

In certain circumstances, this duty will persist after the employment relationship has ended, but its operation will not be as wide, even if it is the subject of an express clause—see para.4.04. Where the information is protected as confidential, both the employee and those who receive it may be liable.

In considering whether information is sufficiently confidential to be protected, the courts have found the following factors to be particularly relevant:

(a) Whether disclosure of the information to a competitor would be likely to cause significant damage to the employer.

(b) Current practice in the industry in question.

(See *Thomas Marshall v Guinle* [1979] Ch. 227.)

Competition during employment

4.03 The courts will generally avoid any interference with an employee's legitimate activities, carried on outside working hours. However, they will protect an employer against an employee who acts directly against him, thereby causing harm to that employer's interests. In *Hivac Ltd v Park Royal Scientific Instruments Ltd* [1946] Ch. 169, skilled manual workers who assembled hearing aids worked for their employer's sole competitor on Sundays. The Court of Appeal held that their actions breached the duty of fidelity, emphasising the secret nature of their work and the considerable degree of potential harm which might be inflicted upon their employers.

It will be different if the employee is not in a position to acquire confidential information or put the employer's business at risk in some other way. In *Nova Plastics Ltd v Frogatt* [1982] I.R.L.R. 146, for example, it was held that an odd-job man who worked for his employer's competitor in his spare time was not in breach of the implied contractual duty not to compete.

After his employment is over, an ex-employee may compete with his former employer without restriction, subject to any valid restrictive covenant (see paras 4.05 to 4.16) and provided that he has not deliberately used his employer's time and facilities to prepare for the competitive business whilst still employed (see para.4.02). Thus, in *Wessex Dairies v Smith* [1935] 2 K.B. 80, an employee milkman was held to be in breach of contract where he informed customers, on his last day of employment, of his plans to set up in business himself. However, an employee will not be a breach of contract if his actions are merely preparatory to setting up in competition on his own account: *Laughton v Bapp Industrial Supplies* [1986] I.R.L.R. 245.

Confidentiality and the ex-employee

4.04 Once the employment relationship has ended, the protection given to confidential information is reduced. In essence, the implied term of confidentiality will then only cover trade secrets and information which is of such a confidential nature as to require the same protection as a trade secret. In *Faccenda Chicken v Fowler* [1996] I.R.L.R. 69, the defendant had been Faccenda's sales manager. He and several other employees then resigned and set up a business which competed with Faccenda. None of the ex-employees had express restrictive clauses in their contracts, but the employer claimed that they had used confidential sales information in a way which damaged its business. The Court of Appeal set out a series of questions to assist in determining whether information is sufficiently confidential to be protected by the implied term after employment has ended:

(a) What was the nature of the employment?

(b) What was the nature of the information?

(c) Did the employer make it clear to the employee that the information was confidential?

(d) Could the information easily be isolated other information which the employee was entitled to use or disclose?

On the facts, it was held that, although the information held by Mr Fowler as to customers, sales and prices was confidential, it was not equivalent to a trade secret. It would have been in breach of contract for him to use it (or even gather it) during the period of his employment. However, because it did not constitute a trade secret, the employer was not entitled to an injunction to prevent an ex-employee from using it.

Restrictive covenants

The purpose of a restrictive covenant is to ensure that an ex-employee **4.05** cannot compete with the employer after the employment ends. Such a restriction is, on the face of it, void as being in restraint of trade, and the employer has to establish that it is valid. The general rule is that the employer must have a legitimate business interest to protect, the restraint must be reasonable in time and area, and it must be in the public interest. Further, if the employer dismisses the employee wrongfully (repudiating the contract) then he will be unable to rely on any restrictive covenant. There are particular rules where the employee is put on "garden leave" and paid notice without being required to work.

This section deals with various aspects of restrictive covenants as follows:

(a) What constitutes a restraint of trade?

(b) The different types of restraint.

(c) The effect of wrongful dismissal.

(d) What amounts to a legitimate interest on the part of the employer?

(e) What is reasonable?

(f) What is in the public interest?

(g) The role of drafting, severance and the blue pencil test.

(h) Garden leave.

(i) Enforcement.

What constitutes a restraint of trade?

4.06   The employer may well wish to protect himself against competition by an ex-employee by the insertion in the contract of employment of a restrictive covenant. This would typically state that, after the contract is terminated by either party the employee will not work for another employer or set up a competing business, within a certain geographical area for a defined period of time. As an express term in the contract, it will purport to bind the employee even after he has left the job. However, the common law rule against restraint of trade operates in this area. As it was put by Lord Atkinson in *Herbert Morris v Saxelby* [1916] 1 A.C. 688:

> "It is in the public interest that a man should be free to exercise his skill and experience to the best advantage for the benefit of himself and of all others who desire to employ him."

As a result, a restrictive covenant taking any of the forms (a) to (d) described in para.4.07 will be prima facie void as being in restraint of trade, and the onus will be on the ex-employer to show that the circumstances are such that it should be held to be valid, so that he can claim its protection.

The different types of restraint

4.07   There are four main types of restraint (although there are many variations and combinations, depending on circumstances):

(a) Non-competition restraints. These prohibit the employee from carrying on or being associated with the same type of business as that run by the employer. It will typically set out a geographical area from which such activity is prohibited, and specify the number of months or years for which the prohibition is to last.

(b) Non-solicitation restraints. The terms of such a covenant will prohibit the ex-employee from seeking business from former customers of the employer. By contrast with (c), however, it will not prevent the employee from accepting as customers those who transfer their business to him without being solicited for that purpose. Often such a clause is limited to customers with whom the ex-employee has had personal contact over a limited period prior to the termination of the contract e.g. 12 months.

(c) Non-dealing restraints. A clause of this nature will prohibit the ex-employee from dealing with customers even if they approach him. It is consequently more drastic in its effect than a non-solicitation clause.

(d) Non-poaching restraints. This will prohibit the ex-employee from encouraging his former colleagues to join him in the new enterprise. Frequently such clauses are limited to prohibit the poaching of "senior employees", sometimes defined by status or salary.

Effect of wrongful dismissal

An employer who repudiates the contract by dismissing the employee **4.08** wrongfully will be unable to rely upon the contract thereafter. It follows that any post-termination restrictive covenant which it contains will be unenforceable, even if it is otherwise valid: *General Billposting Co Ltd v Atkinson* [1909] A.C. 118, HL. This will be the effect if the employer fails to give proper notice of termination, or is in breach of a procedural provision for the termination of the contract. The employer will also be precluded from relying upon the clause where an employee is given pay in lieu of notice, and is not allowed to work out his notice, unless there is a provision in his contract which states that he must accept the pay in lieu. If there is such a provision, the employer is entitled to insist that he accepts the pay in lieu rather than working out his notice, and can still rely upon any otherwise valid restrictive covenant: *Rex Stewart Jeffries Parker Ginsberg Ltd v Parker* [1988] I.R.L.R. 483, CA.

In the situation where the contract is terminated without breach by the employer, or where the employee is rightfully dismissed for his own breach, the restrictive covenant will be enforceable by the employer, subject to its validity in accordance with the tests set out in the paragraphs which follow. This will still be the case even if the employee is *unfairly* dismissed, provided that there is no repudiatory breach of contract by the employer.

Some employers draft the restrictive clause in such a way that it purports to be effective even if the employee is wrongfully dismissed, e.g. "after termination of employment howsoever that happens, whether lawfully or not". Such a clause will be invalid in the event of a wrongful dismissal, as it will still be caught by the rule in *General Billposting* (see *Living Design (Home Improvements) Ltd v Davidson* [1994] I.R.L.R. 69). The mere fact that the clause is phrased in such a way, however, will not mean that it is invalid, provided that there is no repudiation of contract by the employer: *Rock Refrigeration Ltd v Jones* [1996] I.R.L.R. 675.

What constitutes a legitimate interest?

For a restrictive covenant to be enforceable, the employer must be **4.09** protecting a legitimate business interest by its inclusion in the contract. This is because the court is striking a balance between the interest of the employee in acquiring further employment (or starting up a business), and the interest of the employer in preserving his business from harmful action by the ex-employee.

The classic categories of legitimate business interest are:

(a) preventing the disclosure of confidential information; and

(b) preventing the employee from incursions upon the employer's trade connections.

As to (a), confidential information must be such that "if disclosed to a competitor, [it] would be liable to cause real or significant damage to the owner of the secret": *Lansing Linde Ltd v Kerr* [1991] 1 All E.R. 418, CA. Examples might include technical information, scientific formulae, or the terms upon which customers are supplied. With respect to (b) trade connections might include the employer's customers, suppliers and employees.

It should be emphasised that the mere fact that the interest which the employer seeks to defend is a legitimate one does not mean that the means adopted (the clause included in the contract of employment) is a reasonable one. This latter aspect of the test for validity is dealt with in the next section.

What is reasonable?

4.10   The restraint must be no wider than is necessary to protect the employer's legitimate interest. In considering whether a particular clause meets this test, the geographical area which it covers and its duration in time need to be considered. In considering the cases, it should be stressed that this is an area which is particularly fact-sensitive, with the result that, even within one industry, it is impossible to lay down general rules based on precedent, e.g. that duration of over a year is unreasonable. It will depend upon the circumstances as a whole.

4.11   Area.   As to the area covered, the larger the area covered, the less likely it is that the clause will be reasonable, although the density of the population in the area comes into the equation, as does the likelihood that communication with customers and the like may be by telephone, mail, or by electronic means. In *Littlewoods Organisation Ltd v Harris* [1977] 1 W.L.R. 1472, a restrictive covenant was upheld. The ex-employee was a director who left the plaintiff's mail order business to work for their rivals, Great Universal Stores Ltd. The covenant was upheld because it was the only way to protect Littlewoods' trade secrets (fashion designs which were due to appear in next year's catalogue and to which the defendant had access). The clause purported to impose a one-year worldwide ban, but the Court of Appeal interpreted it to apply only to the United Kingdom, which was the only country where the two companies competed for business. It was also construed to apply only to the type of business where the companies were rivals.

In *Greer v Sketchley* Ltd [1979] I.R.L.R. 445, by contrast, the Court of Appeal held that a ban was too wide in its geographical scope. Mr Greer had been employed by Sketchley Ltd for some 20 years in London and the Midlands, finishing as a director with special responsibility for the Midlands. The restrictive clause provided that he was not to engage directly or indirectly in any similar business anywhere in the United Kingdom for a period of 12 months after termination. The Court of Appeal held that the ambit of the clause was too wide, because Mr Greer had only had responsibility for part of the country.

Duration. Time is likely to be a critical factor in considering whether **4.12** knowledge of confidential information is likely to cause damage to the ex-employer's business. To take the example in *Littlewoods* (see para.4.11), the fashion designs in question would have a limited shelf-life, with the result that a ban which lasted more than 12 months would not be a reasonable means of protecting the company's legitimate business interest. In the field of technology, also, it is likely that advances will quickly reduce the value of any confidential information with the result, once again, that a lengthy restrictive covenant will be likely to be held invalid.

What is in the public interest?

To be valid, a restrictive covenant must be in the public interest. In other **4.13** words, there is a judicial discretion in every case. Where a clause is based upon a legitimate business interest, however, and constitutes a reasonable way of protecting that interest, it is rare for it to be struck down on this ground. One case where this did happen was *Bull v Pitney-Bowes* [1967] W.L.R. 273. A clause which adversely affected the pension rights of a retired employee if he competed with the employer was held to be contrary to the public interest, and hence invalid.

Drafting, severance and the blue pencil test

Where the court has decided that a clause is unreasonable in the form **4.14** which it appears in the contract, the question arises whether it can be rewritten in a form which is reasonable. This is obviously of great practical importance, both in terms of deciding the position as far as the parties in a particular case are concerned, and for the drafter, in attempting to arrive at a suitable form of words. To put it crudely, can the drafter rest safe in the knowledge that, even if he has got it wrong, the court will do his job for him?

The short answer to the question is: No. The court will usually resist any role which involves the rewriting of a clause so that it is reasonable. In some circumstances, however, it will construe a restraint in a reasonable way rather than hold it invalid.

Among the tools potentially available to the court in limiting the ambit of a restrictive clause so that it is reasonable are those of severance and editing. The court may, provided that certain conditions are fulfilled, sever, or "blue pencil", by removing words or phrases which make the clause unreasonable. In *Sadler v Imperial Life Assurance of Canada Ltd* [1988] I.R.L.R. 388, it was stated that the following conditions were necessary for the editing process to take place:

(a) the unenforceable provision must be removable without the need to add or modify the remaining part;

(b) those terms which remained must be supported by adequate consideration; and

(c) the removal of the objectionable part must not so change the nature of the clause that the contract became substantially different from that which the parties entered into.

Garden leave

4.15   The term "garden leave" has been given to a period when an employee is paid for his notice period, but does not have to work, and can stay at home—in the garden, if he chooses! The concept has relevance to the restrictive clause, in the sense that the employee is bound by any clauses in his contract relating for example to confidentiality or non-competition for the duration of the "garden leave". He will not generally be in a position to take up employment with a competitor for that period. By the time that the notice period comes to an end, any confidential information or trade connections will have lost their usefulness. Further, since the contract remains in existence, and the employee is not suffering financially, the court is more likely to look sympathetically on the employer's efforts to restrict his activities.

In *Evening Standard Co v Henderson* [1987] I.R.L.R. 64, the production manager of a newspaper attempted to resign from his post, in order to take up a position with a rival. He gave two months notice, although the contractual period was 12 months. His employers sought to hold him to the notice period, and put him on a period of garden leave. They were granted an injunction to prevent him from working for any other employer during the notice period, on giving the court an undertaking that they would pay his full salary and contractual benefits. In *Provident Financial Group plc v Hayward* [1989] I.R.L.R. 84, however, an injunction to prevent an employee going to work for another employer during a period of garden leave was refused. The facts were distinguished from the *Evening Standard* case because the company which Mr Hayward was going to work for was not in direct competition with his ex-employer.

Enforcement

4.16   The standard remedy for breach of a restrictive covenant is an injunction (although damages may be claimed, the employer's usual aim is to prevent the ex-employee from acting in the way which is prohibited). In deciding whether to grant an injunction, the court will usually apply the test in *American Cyanimid v Ethicon Ltd* [1975] A.C. 396. In summary, the test is:

(a) is there a serious issue to be tried at the full hearing? and

(b) if so, does the balance of convenience favour the granting of the injunction?

In so far as this is the test which is applied, it is sufficiently relaxed to favour the employer who is claiming the injunction. However, if a speedy trial is not possible, so that the case may not be determined before the restrictive clause expires, then the judge should consider examine the substantive merits of the case, and consider the likelihood of success at trial: *Lansing Linde v Kerr* [1991] I.R.L.R. 80. In such a case, the employer has a more difficult task.

CHAPTER FIVE

WAGES AND HOURS: THE STATUTORY FRAMEWORK

Traditionally, the contract of employment has been a matter for the **5.01** parties to agree. They have been free to negotiate their own terms, although it has always been clear that the inequality of bargaining power between employee and employer means that the phrase "freedom of contract" has a somewhat hollow ring. In the past few decades, "freedom of contract" has been increasingly circumscribed by legislation whose purpose is to protect employees—and the vulnerable employee in particular. The various strands of discrimination law form part of that protection, as does the law on unfair dismissal.

This chapter concentrates on the role which statute plays in regulating wages and hours. The areas dealt with are:

(a) the itemised pay statement;

(b) deductions from wages;

(c) the national minimum wage; and

(d) the Working Time Regulations.

The first three of those areas relate to the pay which the worker receives. The fourth deals mainly with the hours that he works (although it also covers the subject of holiday pay). The list is inevitably selective, and does not deal, for example, with the limited protection which shop workers receive under the Sunday Trading Act 1994. Other topics, such as the range of family friendly rights (Chapter 8), are dealt with elsewhere.

Itemised pay statement

Section 8 of the Employment Rights Act 1996 ("ERA 1996") grants an **5.02** employee the right to be given a written itemised pay statement. It must be given to him no later than the time at which his wages are paid and must set out:

(a) his gross wages;

(b) any deduction from the gross wages, with the reason why they are made (e.g. income tax or national insurance)

(c) his net wages;

(d) where different parts are paid in different ways, the amount and method adopted for each part.

While the "right" in question may seem to be rather formalistic, it is important to the employee in enabling him to check whether he is receiving the wages to which he is entitled, and provides useful evidence in the event of a later dispute. If the employer fails to comply with his obligations, the employee may refer the matter to an employment tribunal. There is no compensation for failure to provide a pay statement, but the tribunal will make a declaration as to the terms which the pay statements ought to have included and (more crucially) will order the employer to pay any wages which ought to have been paid in accordance with those terms (ERA 1996, ss.11 and 12).

Deductions from wages

5.03   The employer may not make a deduction from wages in respect of any worker unless the deduction is authorised by statute (e.g. income tax payable on a PAYE basis), by contract, or by previous consent in writing on the part of the worker: ERA 1996, s.13. There is also a right for employers in retail employment to make deductions for cash shortages and stock deficiencies, subject to various limits, including an overall maximum of 10 per cent of gross pay: ERA 1996, ss.17 to 22.

The right to receive wages without unauthorised deductions was formerly contained in the Wages Act 1986, and such claims are still sometimes referred to as "Wages Act claims". The right not to have deductions made from wages is one which all "workers" have, and is not confined to "employees" (see Chapter 2 for the respective definitions and criteria).

"Wages" are defined in s.27 of the ERA 1996, so as to include: "any fee, bonus, commission, holiday pay or other emolument referable to his employment, whether payable under his contract or otherwise". It also includes statutory sick pay as well as statutory maternity, paternity and adoption pay. It does not, however, include pay in lieu of notice (*Delaney v Staples* [1992] I.C.R. 483, HL) which is viewed as liquidated damages, referable to the termination of employment, rather than to employment itself. The failure to pay notice pay to which an employee is entitled is a breach of contract, and it can be claimed as such in the ordinary courts, or in the employment tribunal.

5.04   Other exceptions from the ambit of the provisions relating to deduction from wages include:

(a) a deduction made by the employer to recover an overpayment of wages or expenses (ERA 1996, s.14(1));

(b) a deduction made because the worker took part in a strike or other industrial action.

Although the statute is framed in terms of "deduction from wages", a total failure to pay wages in respect of a particular period is classed as a deduction and can be claimed under these provisions. The claim under s.23 of the ERA 1996 is to an employment tribunal. It must be made within three months of the deduction complained of. However, where a complaint is brought in respect of a series of deductions, it must be made within three months of the "last deduction. . . in the series" (i.e. the most recent deduction made). This means that the claim can potentially extend over a considerable period where there have been a number of deductions made: s.23(3) of the ERA 1996.

The right to bring a claim in the employment tribunal for deduction from wages is one which can be exercised by current employees. In this, it differs from the tribunal's jurisdiction in relation to breach of contract, which is limited to claims which arise or are "outstanding on the termination of the employee's employment" (Employment Tribunals Extension of Jurisdiction (England and Wales) Order (SI 1994/1623), Art.3(c)). It is also worth noting that a claim for deductions from wages will not trigger off a right on the part of the employer to bring a counter-claim for breach of contract, whereas an action by the employee for breach of contract will. These distinctions mean that care must be exercised by representatives in deciding whether to frame their claim as one for deduction from wages or one for breach of contract, because of the procedural consequences which will flow from the choice which they make.

National Minimum Wage

Workers have the right to be paid the national minimum wage provided **5.05** that they ordinarily work in Great Britain, and are above the compulsory school leaving age. The right is set out in the National Minimum Wage Act ("NMWA") 1998, as fleshed out by the National Minimum Wage Regulations 1999 ("NMWR"). Those who are given the right are "workers" rather than "employees" (see Chapter 2 for the distinction). In addition, agency workers are given the right to the minimum wage, even if there is no contract between the worker, the agent and the principal (end-user or hirer). In effect, whoever is responsible for the payment of the agency worker is also responsible for ensuring that they receive the national minimum wage (s.34 of the NMWA). The rates for the national minimum wage are set by regs 11 and 13 of the NMWR, which are amended annually on October 1. The current rates, with effect from October 1, 2007 are:

- Those aged 22 and over: £5.52;

- Those aged 18 to 21: £4.60;

- Those aged 16 and 17: £3.40.

Determining the rate is relatively simple. The difficulty lies in determining whether the payment made by the employer meets the minimum wage. The formula is set out in reg.14 of the NMWR which requires that the hourly rate is determined by dividing the amount paid over the pay reference period (e.g. a month) by the total number of hours which the worker is deemed to have worked over the pay reference period.

As to the amount paid, that excludes benefits in kind, but it does include a certain amount in respect of accommodation, which is limited to £3.90 per day. In performing the calculation, any shift or overtime premium paid must be excluded, as must any service charge, tip or gratuity paid by customers (unless it is paid through the payroll): NMWR, reg.31.

5.06   The calculation of the number of hours worked is more complex. This will form the figure by which the remuneration is divided, so it will be critical to the calculation. In brief, the hours to be taken into account are:

> (a) Salaried hours work (NMWR, reg.4). This is work for which the worker is paid for a basic number of hours, excluding overtime. It covers the usual arrangement by which a worker is paid weekly or monthly, irrespective of the number of hours which he works (leaving aside considerations of overtime).
>
> (b) Time work (reg.3). This is work paid according to set or varying hours, which is not salaried hours work. It would cover, for example, a worker who clocks in and out and is paid only in accordance with the number of hours actually worked.
>
> (c) Output work (reg.5) is work which is paid for by measure of output, e.g. the number of articles produced, or items sold.
>
> (d) Unmeasured work (reg.6) is a catch-all provision. It is defined so as to include any work which does not fall under (a), (b) or (c) above.

The category within which the work in question falls is important because different provisions apply to determine what counts towards the number of hours which the worker has worked. This is a case where the devil is very definitely in the detail, and reference should be made to the regulations in question in order to see, in a particular case, which hours have to be counted in the calculation referred to above.

Section 17 of the NMWA makes receipt of the minimum national wage a contractual right for the worker concerned. If the employer fails to pay it, it can be enforced as a breach of contract. Where an employment tribunal adjudicates on another statutory right (e.g. unfair dismissal or redundancy payment), the national minimum wage becomes the minimum payable to the employee in respect of a week's wages (say, for the calculation of the basic award). An employee who is dismissed for claiming the national minimum wage will have been automatically unfairly dismissed for assertion of a statutory right (ERA 1996, s.104A—no period of qualifying employment is required). He is also protected against suffering any detriment other than dismissal for asserting his right to the national minimum wage (NMWA, s.23). In addition, Her Majesty's Revenue and Customs is charged with enforcement of the national minimum wage, and may prosecute employers who fail to pay it, or fail to keep adequate records to show that they are paying it.

The Working Time Regulations

The Working Time Regulations 1998 ("the WTR") were passed to **5.07** implement the European Working Time Directive 93/104. They set out a series of minimum rights, which can be improved by agreement between employer and employee. The rationale for the Directive, and hence for the Regulations, was to safeguard the health and safety of workers. Like most of the rights discussed in this chapter, they cover "workers" rather than "employees" (see Chapter 2 for the distinction between the two). Agency workers are brought within the ambit of the WTR by reg.36, and the paying party is given the responsibility of ensuring that the regulations are complied with.

There are exemptions from the coverage of the WTR generally (e.g. seafarers) and from specific provisions (e.g. the armed services, the police, doctors in training). Details are to be found in regs 18–22 of the WTR.

Working time

The definition of "working time" is critical to the interpretation of the **5.08** various rights contained within the WTR. It is defined in reg.2(1) to mean:

(a) any period during which a worker is working, at his employer's disposal and carrying out his activity or duties;

(b) any period during which he is receiving relevant training; and

(c) any additional period which is to be treated as working time for the purpose of these Regulations under a relevant agreement.

In *SIMAP v Conseilleria de Sanidad y Consumo de la Generalidad Valenciana* [2000] I.R.L.R. 845, ECJ, the position of doctors on call was considered. It was held that the time spent on call at the health centre was "working time" within the Directive. Where they were not at the health centre, however, only time spent in the actual provision of care was to be counted as working time.

Maximum weekly hours

A limit is placed upon the maximum number of hours in a worker's **5.09** working week. The maximum is 48 per week averaged over a "reference period" of 17 weeks (which may be extended by mutual agreement to 26 weeks (reg.4)). A worker who is prepared to work for more than the maximum may sign an opt-out, and will then have to give seven days' notice if he wishes to opt back in and insist on the maximum 48 hour week to which he is entitled. The employer for his part can extend the notice up to three months if there is a specific agreement to that effect.

Certain categories of people are excluded from the provisions relating to maximum weekly hours, over and above those subject to a general exemption such as members of the armed services and the like. The additional exemption applies to "managing executives or other persons with autonomous decision making powers" as well as the clergy and family workers. As they can fix their own working time, so the argument goes, the limit is not appropriate.

Rest breaks

5.10   A worker must be given a daily rest break of 11 hours in a period of 24 hours (reg.10). He must also be given a weekly rest break of a day per week (or two days in a fortnight) (reg.11). If he works more than six hours work at a stretch, he must be given a rest break of 20 minutes (reg.12). In addition, if the pattern of his work puts his health and safety at risk, in particular because of its monotony, or because the work rate is pre-determined, he must be given rest breaks which are adequate.

Young workers (defined as those over compulsory school age but under 18) must be given more generous rest breaks, as follows:

- two days per working week;

- 12 hours rest in every 24;

- a rest break of at least 30 minutes after working for four and a half hours.

Annual leave

5.11   Workers are entitled to four weeks paid annual leave in accordance with reg.13 of the WTR. This entitlement includes any paid bank holidays, e.g. Christmas, Easter. The Work and Families Act 2006, s.13, gave the government power to make regulations to change this. Its intention is to increase the minimum amount of paid leave to 5.6 weeks per year. This would mean that the worker was entitled to paid bank holidays in addition to the four weeks which already constitute the minimum. At the time of writing, the government has stated that it intends to increase the statutory minimum to 4.8 weeks in October 2007, with the remaining .8 weeks to follow no later than October 2009.

Some employers make "rolled up" payments to their workers which expressly include an element of holiday pay, and then make no further payment when the worker actually takes his holiday. There has been a cluster of case law around whether this method of paying holiday pay is in accordance with the WTR and with the Directive. The matter was referred to the ECJ in *Robinson-Steele v R D Retail Services Ltd* [2006] I.R.L.R. 386. The ECJ concluded that the payment of such "rolled-up" holiday pay was contrary to the Directive. It indicated, however, that its ruling was not intended to be retrospective, provided that the holiday element had been clearly paid by the employer as an additional sum. The position now, therefore, is that payment for statutory annual leave should be made at the time when the leave is taken.

Enforcement

The provisions relating to the working week are enforced by the Health 5.12
and Safety Executive, which can prosecute employers who fail to observe
the limits. Those flowing from the right to a weekly or daily rest period or
break are enforceable by a claim to the employment tribunal, as is the right
to paid annual leave.

CHAPTER SIX

DISCRIMINATION

The general principle in our law is that discrimination is legal unless it is **6.01**
specifically forbidden. Further, the common law does not prescribe any
particular form of discrimination as illegal—that is left to a series of
statutes, which were enacted from the 1960s onwards, and have been
affected by the framework laid down by the European Union.

Over the years which have followed, the law relating to discrimination
has achieved increasing importance in the field of employment. During the
year 2005–6, about 21 per cent of the claims accepted by the Employment
Tribunals Service, according to its Annual Report, related to discrimination
(including equal pay). The cases concerned are very often complex and
disproportionately time-consuming. Whereas a typical unfair dismissal case
is heard by the tribunal in the course of a day, three days is perhaps the
typical length of a discrimination case (obviously, both types of case can be
very much longer, or shorter). In addition, the average level of compensation for a discrimination case is substantially higher than that for an unfair
dismissal case. The average compensation for different categories of case in
2005–2006 is set out in the table in para.7.05.

The focus of this chapter is upon the law as it relates to discrimination in
employment. It deals with:

    (a) The grounds upon which discrimination is unlawful.

    (b) The forms which discrimination can take.

    (c) The scope of the prohibition.

    (d) The exceptions.

    (e) Who can claim?

    (f) Against whom?

    (g) The employer's defence.

    (h) Disability discrimination.

    (i) Age discrimination.

    (j) Part-time workers.

    (k) Fixed-term workers.

    (l) Trade union membership and activities (and non-membership).

(m) Equal pay.

(n) Procedure in so far as it is peculiar to discrimination cases.

6.02   The matters dealt with in the sections labelled (b) to (g) above relate to discrimination on grounds of sex, race, sexual orientation and religion or belief. The other forms of unlawful discrimination are sufficiently different to merit separate treatment, and this is done in sections (h) to (m). Parts (n) and (o) deal with matters of more general relevance.

Prohibited grounds

6.03   As stated in the introduction to this chapter, there is no general prohibition against discrimination, In fact, it is not merely lawful but rational for employers to be involved in a constant process of discrimination—as to which employee to hire, promote or make redundant for example. For discrimination between employees to be rational, the reasons for selection have to be sensible ones. Again, there is nothing in the law to make irrational decisions unlawful. It is only upon certain grounds, specifically prohibited by statute, that it is forbidden to discriminate. The forbidden grounds can be summarised as follows.

Gender

6.04   This is covered by the Sex Discrimination Act ("SDA") 1975, which outlaws discrimination based upon sex or marital status. It is complementary to the Equal Pay Act ("EPA") 1970. The EPA deals with pay, and the SDA deals with other areas, particularly non-contractual matters. The precise scope is dealt with in the later section on Equal Pay. Legislation against sex discrimination and equal pay, in particular, has been shaped by the European Union: see for example:

- Article 141 of the Treaty of Rome,
- The Equal Treatment Directive (76/207)

and the numerous cases from the ECJ dealing with the provisions of domestic law in the light of the Treaty and the Directive.

Clearly, the SDA is primarily meant to alleviate the discrimination faced by women in the workplace. However, there are two fundamental points about its ambit which are worth noting. First, its provisions can equally be utilised by a man who claims to have been discriminated against on grounds of his sex. Second, the SDA also protects those who are married from discrimination (but not those who are single).

Race

6.05   The Race Relations Act 1965 was the first statute to be passed in this country which outlawed discrimination. Its provisions have now been subsumed within the Race Relations Act ("RRA") 1976. It prohibits discrimination on racial grounds, which is defined so as to mean "any of the following grounds, namely colour, race, nationality or ethnic or national origins". The main definitions of what constitutes a discriminatory act are similar to those in the SDA, as are the principles which are contained within the two acts. Again, the European Union has influenced the shape of legislation in this area, as can be seen from the Race Discrimination Directive 2000/43.

Sexual orientation

Discrimination on grounds of sexual orientation in the employment field is prohibited by the Employment Equality (Sexual Orientation) Regulations 2003.
    6.06

"Sexual orientation" is defined to mean:

"a sexual orientation towards—

  (a) persons of the same sex;
  (b) persons of the opposite sex; or
  (c) persons of the same sex and of the opposite sex."

As a result, homosexuals, heterosexuals and bisexuals are protected against discrimination, but that protection is not extended to other forms of sexual orientation: sado-masochism or paedophilia, for example. The regulations are based upon the Equal Treatment Framework Directive of the European Union (2000/78)

Religion or belief

The Employment Equality (Religion or Belief) Regulations 2003 forbade discrimination in the field of employment on grounds of religion, religious belief or similar philosophical belief. The Equality Act 2006 broadened the definition so that:
    6.07

(a) religion means any religion,

(b) belief means any religious or philosophical belief,

(c) a reference to religion includes a reference to a lack of religion, and

(d) a reference to belief includes a reference to a lack of belief.

As a result, the atheist or agnostic is entitled to protection in the same way as the Hindu, Jew, Muslim or Christian.

Like the law on discrimination on grounds of sexual orientation, this area has been shaped by the Equal Treatment Framework Directive of the European Union (2000/78).

Disability

The law relating to discrimination on grounds of disability is contained in the Disability Discrimination Act 1995. The concepts involved are rather different from those which are common to the four types of discrimination
    6.08

outlined above. As a result, this area is dealt with in the separate section entitled "Disability Discrimination" below.

Age

6.09   The Employment Equality (Age) Regulations 2006 outlaw discrimination in the employment field on grounds of age. Once again, there are significant differences between this area of the law and those relating to sex, race, sexual orientation and religion or belief. As a result, the subject is dealt with in the section entitled "Age Discrimination" below.

Part-time status

6.10   Part-time workers receive protection from the Part-time Workers (Prevention of Less Favourable Treatment) Regulations 2000. The part-time worker must not be treated less favourably than a comparable full-time worker (on a pro rata basis in so far as that is appropriate). The relevant European Directives are 97/81 and 98/23. Again, the subject is treated in a separate section below.

Fixed-term status

6.11   Those employed on a fixed-term basis are covered by the Fixed-Term Employees (Prevention of Less Favourable Treatment) Regulations 2002. The impetus for the regulations came from the EU Fixed-Term Work Directive (99/70). They are dealt with in a separate section below.

Trade union membership

6.12   It is unlawful, in a general way, for an employer to treat a trade union member less favourably than a non-member, or vice versa. The subject is dealt with in a separate section below.

The forms which discrimination can take

6.13   This section deals with discrimination on grounds of sex, race, sexual orientation, and religion or belief. These areas have sufficient in common to make it possible to deal jointly with them as far as the forms which discrimination can take are concerned. Disability, age and the other forms of unlawful discrimination are then dealt with separately.

In summary, the legal forms which a discriminatory act can take are:

(a) direct discrimination;

(b) indirect discrimination;

(c) victimisation;

(d) harassment; and

(e) instructions to discriminate.

Direct discrimination

This occurs where one person treats another less favourably than another **6.14** on grounds of her sex (or race, or sexual orientation or religion or belief— in the subsequent discussion, only one alternative will be mentioned, but it will be of general applicability to all four of the grounds of discrimination which are currently being dealt with).

Assume that the act of discrimination complained of arises from an unsuccessful application for employment. The claimant, who alleges she is the victim of the discrimination, must be compared with someone in order to determine whether she has been less favourably treated. That person is known as the "comparator". Sometimes the comparator is an actual person—in the example given, it might be the person who was appointed to the job in question. But the comparator may be a hypothetical person. For example, a woman who is not given promotion after a number of years may allege she has been discriminated against even if there is no actual comparator. Her case may be: "If I were a man with the same attributes, competence and qualifications, I would have been promoted". Clearly she would have more difficulty mustering the evidence for such an assertion, but if she can do so there is no reason why her case, based upon comparison with a hypothetical person, should not succeed. However, the comparison, whether it is with a real or a hypothetical person, must be such that "the relevant circumstances in the one case are the same, or not materially different in the other" (s.3(4) of the RRA—and there are similar provisions in each of the other sets of statutory provisions).

For an act to constitute direct discrimination, there must not only be less favourable treatment—it must be "on grounds of" sex (or race, or whatever the type of discrimination that is alleged). But the motive of the alleged discriminator is not material. For example, someone may fail to appoint a black person to a job because of a wish to protect them from the racially prejudiced customers with whom he will have to deal. There is less favourable treatment on grounds of race, and it is no defence for the discriminator to argue that he was only trying to avoid injury to the victim or his feelings.

As far as direct discrimination is concerned, it is also important to bear **6.15** in mind that there is no defence of justification (age discrimination is an exception to this principle, which will be dealt with in the section on that topic below). For example, an employer who refused to appoint a woman to a sales position could not argue that his target customers were males who were unlikely to buy from a woman, even if he could put forward evidence to that effect. He would be treating her less favourably on grounds of her sex, it would be direct discrimination, and a defence of justification is not available. Justification is, however, a valid defence to a claim of indirect discrimination.

Indirect discrimination

6.16   The wording of the various statutory provisions on indirect discrimination is slightly different, as a result of the impact of two European Directives—the Burden of Proof Directive (97/80) and the Race Directive (2000/43). However, the differences in the concepts involved are not all that great, and the differences in practice are likely to be minimal.

The definition which is set out in the SDA, s.1(2)(b) relates to the employment field and states that indirect discrimination is:

   (a) the application of a provision, criterion or practice to a woman which he would apply equally to a man, but which

   (b) puts women at a particular disadvantage compared with men, and

   (c) which puts her at that disadvantage, and

   (d) which the employer cannot show to be a proportionate means of achieving a legitimate aim.

There are a couple of preliminary points to note about this definition. First, the provision, criterion or practice ("PCP") is applied equally to men and women. If it were not, then it might well constitute <u>direct</u> discrimination. Second, while the definition is framed in terms of a woman being disadvantaged, a man could equally claim indirect discrimination—to see whether he satisfied the test, one would need to substitute "man" for "woman" in the definition, and vice versa.

6.17   *Example.   To take a practical example, assume that an employer operates a "flexitime" system but requires all employees to carry on working until 5.30pm, as a condition of continued employment. Evidence can be produced which shows that female employees in the company find it more difficult to comply with this finishing time than male employees, because more of them have unavoidable child care duties, and have to pick their children up from school between 3.30pm and 4pm. One of the employees, Emily, is a single mother who has two children of five and eight.*

If one looks at this factual situation in the light of the definition of indirect discrimination, it is clear that there is a PCP (obligation to work until 5.30pm). It puts women at a particular disadvantage (not being able to continue working for the company because they have to meet their child care obligations). It puts Emily at that disadvantage because she has children to collect. As a result, there is a prima facie case of indirect discrimination. There is a defence open to the company. Can it produce evidence to show that its rule about working until 5.30pm is a proportionate means of achieving a legitimate aim?

"Proportionate means of achieving a legitimate aim" is sometimes referred to in shorthand as "objective justification" or just "justification". In determining whether an indirectly discriminatory PCP can be justified, it is necessary to ask:

(a) whether it has been adopted to further a legitimate aim; and

(b) whether proportionate means have been used to further that aim.

In the example which we are examining, the employer may have in mind the need to deal with a rush of customers at the end of the working day, so as to meet the business need of coping with demand for the services which the company offers. That would seem to constitute a legitimate aim— business need, in shorthand. One then needs to consider whether the company is adopting proportionate means to achieve that aim. In considering that part of the test for justification, there are, it is submitted, three questions which need to be asked:

(a) Does the PCP actually contribute to the achievement of the legitimate aim? Is there actually increased customer demand at the end of the day? Is it necessary to have additional staff there to deal with it? If not, it is not a proportionate means of achieving the legitimate aim of meeting a business need.

(b) The importance of the legitimate aim should be weighed against the discriminatory effects which it produces. Here the discriminatory effect will depend on the number of women who are disadvantaged, and the extent to which they are disadvantaged, e.g. does it mean that they will lose their jobs. The importance of the legitimate aim will depend to a large extent upon the answers to the questions posed in (a) above.

(c) If the legitimate aim can be achieved just as well by a measure which has less discriminatory effects, then the less discriminatory measure should be used. The employer ought to choose the least discriminatory means, or the means will not be proportionate. For example, would it be possible to cope with any increased customer demand at the end of the working day by drafting in additional part-time workers, whose pay might come from the reduced hours worked by those who decided not to work until 5.30? The reasoning process in relation to indirect sex discrimination is illustrated in the flowchart below.

Indirect sex discrimination

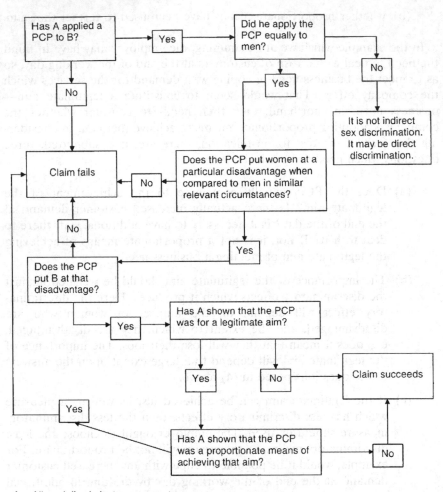

A = Alleged discriminator. e.g. employer

B = Alleged victim, e.g. employee

PCP = provision, criterion or practice

In the chart, it is assumed the B is a woman, but the alleged victim may be a main, in which case the wording needs to be changed accordingly.

6.18   The RRA sets out the position in regard to indirect discrimination on racial grounds in s.1(1)(b) and 1(1A). The RRA as a whole covers discrimination on grounds of colour, race, nationality or ethnic or national origin. An amendment was introduced to the statute as a result of the Race Directive, which relates only to racial or ethnic origin.

The definition in s.1(1A) is very similar in structure to the equivalent definition in relation to sex, although it deals with indirect discrimination in relation to race, ethnic or national origins (rather than in relation to sex). The explanation set out above with regard to indirect sex discrimination has relevance to this definition.

The definition in s.1(1)(b) is narrower in scope, and will have effect where the case is brought on the basis of discrimination on racial grounds which are not in relation to race, ethnic or national origins (i.e. they are in relation to colour or nationality). The main differences are these:

(a) It refers to a "requirement or condition" rather than a "provision, criterion or practice".

(b) The claimant has to show that the proportion of persons of the same racial group who can comply with the requirement or condition is considerably smaller than the proportion of persons not of that racial group who can comply with it.

(c) The employer has to show justification, rather than a proportionate means of achieving a legitimate aim.

(d) The claimant must show a "detriment", rather than a "disadvantage."

Overall, it may be more difficult to establish a claim under the definition in s.1(1)(b) of the RRA than under s.1(1A). However, most factual situations which fit one definition will fit the other one as well. **6.19**

The definition of indirect discrimination in the regulations relating to sexual orientation and religion or belief is in line with that in the SDA and the RRA, s.1(1A), i.e. it is the easier test to satisfy.

Victimisation

The word "victimisation" is frequently used in ordinary conversation in the sense that someone is being "picked on". In the context of the anti-discrimination legislation, however, it has a much more specific and specialised meaning. It is defined as less favourable treatment of an employee by reason that the person victimised has done one of a series of acts, which are known as protected acts. The acts in question are: **6.20**

(a) bringing proceedings against the discriminator or anyone else under the legislation in question;

(b) giving evidence or information in connection with any proceedings under the legislation;

(c) otherwise doing anything under or by reference to the legislation;

(d) alleging that the discriminator or any other person has committed an act which would amount to a contravention of the legislation.

Any knowledge or suspicion on the part of the discriminator that the claimant has done or intends to do any of these protected acts is also covered. However, there is no protection in so far as any allegation made was false and not made in good faith.

To take an example, suppose that an employee genuinely believes that he has been failed to achieve promotion because he is gay. He invokes the grievance procedure against the managers who took the decision not to promote him, stating that he believes he was discriminated against because of his sexual orientation. It is in fact, an unfounded suspicion, and he was not promoted because his record did not warrant it. If the management decided that, because of the trouble he had caused, they would dismiss him, that would be an act of victimisation. The fact that his claim of discrimination was not well-founded does not deprive him of protection, provided that it was made in good faith. The same protection would be available if he pursued the matter to an employment tribunal. It would also cover witnesses who gave evidence on his behalf, provided that they, too, acted in good faith.

Harassment

6.21   Each of the four sets of statutory provisions which we are considering (sex, race, sexual orientation, religion or belief) makes it unlawful to harass another person upon the forbidden ground. The definitions of harassment are broadly similar in relation to race, sexual orientation and religion or belief, but are rather different in relation to sex. For example, the Employment Equality (Religion or Belief) Regulations 2003 state that:

> "5.(1). . . a person ("A'") subjects another person ("B") to harassment. . . where on grounds of religion or belief, A engages in unwanted conduct which has the purpose or effect of—
>
> (a) violating B's dignity, or
> (b) creating an intimidating, hostile, degrading, humiliating or offensive environment for B.
>
> (2) Conduct shall be regarded as having the effect specified in paragraph (a) or (b) of subsection (1) only if, having regard to all the circumstances, including in particular the perception of B, it should reasonably be considered as having that effect."

The definition therefore covers unwanted conduct which intentionally violates the dignity of another ("purpose"). It also covers intentional conduct which creates an environment which is intimidating etc for the other person. In addition, it will cover unwanted conduct which has either of these effects, provided that it can reasonably be considered as having the effect in question. In determining what is reasonable, all the circumstances have to be considered, including the perception of the alleged victim.

In practice, the majority of claims of harassment are for sexual harassment. Until the SDA was amended in 2005, there was no separate basis for a claim of harassment—the claim had to be brought as an act of discrimination. However, as sexual harassment is gender-specific, it was held that there was no need for a male comparator: *British Telecommunications plc v Williams* [1997] I.R.L.R. 668.

The statutory definition is somewhat expanded when compared with that for race, sexual orientation and religion or belief, in order to cope with the particular characteristics of sexual harassment. It is set out in the SDA, s.4A:

"4A.(1). . . a person subjects a woman to sexual harassment if—

    (a) on the ground of her sex, he engages in unwanted conduct that has the purpose or effect—

        (i) of violating her dignity, or

        (ii) of creating an intimidating, hostile, degrading, humiliating or offensive environment for her,

    (b) he engages in any form of unwanted verbal, non-verbal or physical conduct of a sexual nature that has the purpose or effect—

        (iii) of violating her dignity, or

        (iv) of creating an intimidating, hostile, degrading, humiliating or offensive environment for her, or

    (c) on the ground of her rejection of or submission to unwanted conduct of a kind mentioned in paragraph (a) or (b), he treats her less favourably than he would treat her had she not rejected, or submitted to, the conduct.

(2) Conduct shall be regarded as having the effect mentioned in sub-paragraph (1) (a) or (b) only if, having regard to all the circumstances, including in particular the perception of the woman, it should reasonably be considered as having that effect."

There are two significant differences between this definition and that **6.22** which pertains to harassment in the other strands of discrimination law. First, there is a specific prohibition against unwanted conduct "of a sexual nature". Second, less favourable treatment of the object of such conduct on the grounds that she has rejected it (or submitted to it) is specifically prohibited.

The definition of harassment in the SDA was inserted by the Employment Equality (Sex Discrimination) Regulations 2005 (SI 2005/2467). This was done in order to implement the EC Equal Treatment Amendment Directive (2002/73), which made certain changes to the original Equal Treatment Directive. However, the Equal Opportunities Commission challenged the government's amendments by way of judicial review, claiming that the scope for bringing a successful harassment claim was narrower than the Directive required, so that the protection from harassment was inadequate according to the requirements of European law. In *Equal Opportunities Commission v Secretary of State for Trade and Industry* [2007] EWHC 483, Burton J. agreed, and held that the s.4A (above) would have to be recast so that:

    (a) the requirement that the unwanted conduct should be "on ground of her sex" should be replaced by "related to the sex of a person", so that the claimant would no longer have to show that the conduct was directed towards her because she was a woman;

    (b) the employer could in certain circumstances be held liable for harassment carried out by a third person—for example where he knowingly fails to protect an employee from repetitive harassment by a customer.

The requirement that the conduct in question should be "unwanted" has given rise to some important case law. In *Insitu Cleaning Co Ltd v Heads* [1995] I.R.L.R. 4, the EAT considered whether a single act of verbal sexual harassment was sufficient, and concluded that "unwanted" was essentially the same as "unwelcome" or "uninvited". As a result, a single act might be sufficient to constitute harassment in certain circumstances.

6.23   The issue was further explored in *Reed and Bull Information Systems Ltd v Stedman* [1999] I.R.L.R. 299. The EAT stated that some conduct could properly be described as unwelcome. A woman did not have to make it clear in advance that she does not want to be touched sexually. At the other end of the scale, a woman may appear, objectively, to be unduly sensitive to what might otherwise be regarded as unexceptional behaviour. But it was for each person to define their own levels of acceptance. The question would then be whether by words or conduct the woman had made it clear that she found such conduct unwelcome. Provided that any reasonable person would understand her to be rejecting the conduct of which she was complaining, continuation of the conduct would generally be regarded as harassment. Morison P. also pointed out that a tribunal should not dissect a course of conduct into individual incidents and measure the effect of each separately. Once an unwelcome sexual interest has been displayed, the victim may be bothered by further incidents which might have been unobjectionable in a different context.

Scope of prohibited discrimination

6.24   Although the ambit of the legislation relating to sex and race is wider than the field of employment, so that it covers goods and services, the focus in this text is upon employment. It is worth setting out, however, the different aspects of employment which come within the scope of the prohibition against discrimination.

6.25 **Recruitment.** First, it covers "arrangements for recruitment". As a result, any discrimination in the process of short-listing or interviewing for a job is prohibited, as would be a discriminatory decision to appoint one person rather than another. In each case, the person who was not short-listed, suffered from less favourable treatment in the interview, or was not appointed, would be able to claim discrimination on one of the prohibited grounds (race, sex, sexual orientation, religion or belief). However, the publication of an advertisement which was, for example, gender-specific, (e.g. "man required to fill vacancy") would not necessarily constitute in itself discrimination such as to enable a woman to bring a claim for sex discrimination: *Cardiff Women's Aid v Hartup* [1994] I.R.L.R. 357 EAT. The reason is that the placing of the advertisement does not in itself discriminate against an individual, in that no detriment results to the individual—it is a "victimless act". The detriment will take place at a later stage when a woman applies and is not short-listed, for example. Although the placing of such an advertisement is unlawful (because of the public interest in prohibiting sex discrimination), the law in such a case has to be enforced by the Commission for Equality and Human Rights (RRA, s.29, SDA, s.38). It is worth pointing out, however, that in the event of a later potentially discriminatory act (e.g. the appointment of a man to the position, and the rejection of an application from a woman), the tribunal may well draw an inference that the less favourable treatment was "on grounds of her sex".

Terms and conditions of employment. It is generally unlawful to discriminate on the grounds currently under discussion in relation to the terms and conditions which the employer affords to an employee.   **6.26**

Where the prohibited ground of discrimination is sex, however, the remedy will have to be pursued under the Equal Pay Act 1970, rather than the SDA if the claimant has been offered and accepted the job. If the prospective employee does not accept the job because of the discriminatory terms which she is offered, however, then the SDA is the applicable statute (see s.6(6) of the SDA and the section on the Equal Pay Act below).

Transfer, training or promotion. The relevant statutes prohibit discrimination in the fields of transfer, promotion or training. Assume that Husssain, who is a Muslim, is denied promotion from assistant manager to manager for that reason. He would be able to claim discrimination on grounds of his religion or belief. He would similarly have a claim if he was, for the same reason, denied managerial training or transfer to a department which he sought.   **6.27**

Access to benefits. Discrimination in relation to the provision of "other benefits, facilities or services" is prohibited by the legislation. For example, if male employees are provided with free travel passes by the bus company which employs them, but female employees are not, then that would constitute sex discrimination.   **6.28**

In *Eke v Commissioners of Customs and Excise* [1981] I.R.L.R. 334, EAT, it was held that a refusal to investigate complaints of unfair treatment, whether based on grounds of race or otherwise, could amount to a refusal of access to "any other benefits, facilities or services" within the meaning of the RRA.

Dismissal. Dismissal of an employee upon one of the prohibited grounds is a particularly blatant act of discrimination, and is expressly prohibited by each of the statutes in question. Assume that two employees are caught fighting. The white one is given a final warning, and the black one is sacked. In the absence of any material lawful distinction between the two, this would be a clear case of racial discrimination, and the black employee could claim on that basis. In many cases, he could also succeed in an action for unfair dismissal, but there are distinct advantages to a claim under the RRA: **6.29**

- he does not need a year's continuous employment in order to claim;

- if he succeeds, he can claim for injury to feelings, over and above his financial loss; and

- there is no limit on the compensation which he can be awarded for discrimination, whereas there is a limit upon the compensatory award for unfair dismissal.

6.30   Any other detriment.   Although the relevant statutes set out certain areas of employment in which discrimination is prohibited, as described in the preceding paragraphs, there is a catch-all category as well: "subjecting. . . to any other detriment". The wording is comprehensive in its coverage, but a few examples help to give an idea of its scope:

- the removal of counselling responsibilities for members of staff: *Shamoon v Chief Constable of the RUC* [2003] I.R.L.R. 285, HL;

- transfer to employment which was less interesting: *Kirby v Manpower Services Commission* [1980] I.R.L.R. 229, EAT;

- continuation of an investigation by employers into the actions of an employee for a longer period than usual because of her ethnic origins: *Garry v London Borough of Ealing* [2001] I.R.L.R. 681. This was held to be a detriment even though the employee was not award that the investigation was continuing.

6.31   Post termination.   The relevant statutes cover discrimination which occurs after the employment relationship has ended. It continues to be unlawful to discriminate on one of the prohibited grounds after the termination of employment, if the act in question "arises out of and is closely connected with" employment. Assume, for example, that an employee leaves his employment on bad terms because he has (in good faith) pursued a grievance about discrimination which he genuinely believes was related to his sexual orientation. He seeks new employment, and a reference is requested from his old employers. They provide one which brands him as a trouble-maker and warns against offering him employment. The protection against victimisation which he will have had as a result of committing a protected act (see the section on "Victimisation" in para.6.20 above) will continue despite the fact that he has ceased to be employed by the company, and he would appear to have a claim against them.

Genuine occupational requirements (or qualifications)

6.32   Some occupations are regarded as being outside the scope of the statute in question, because of their particular characteristics. The result is that a restriction on the person to be employed which would otherwise be unlawful is not prohibited.

The jobs in question vary according to the type of discrimination. In the RRA, s.5(2) the following are defined as being cases where membership of a particular racial group may be a genuine occupational qualification:

(a) actors and other entertainers;

(b) artists and photographic models;

(c) waiters in a place where food or drink is consumed by members of the public;

(d) those providing personal welfare services for members of a particular racial group.

The SDA, s.7 permits genuine occupational qualifications as follows:

(a) where for reasons of physiology (excluding stamina or strength) a man is required;

(b) where for reasons of authenticity, e.g. in a dramatic performance, a man is required;

(c) to preserve decency or privacy;

(d) in a private home where close personal contact is involved;

(e) in single-sex hospitals and prisons;

(f) the provision of personal services promoting welfare or education;

(g) the job entails work in a country such as Saudi Arabia whose laws or customs require that it should not be held by a woman;

(h) where the job is one of two to be held by a married couple or two civil partners.

Some of the qualifications in question involve additional conditions, and examination of the statutory provisions is necessary in order to see their precise scope.

The Employment Equality (Religion or Belief) Regulations 2003 set out **6.33** genuine occupational requirements more broadly. Regulation 7 makes it lawful to discriminate on grounds of religion or belief where being of a particular religion or belief is a genuine and determining occupational requirement, it is proportionate to apply the requirement in the particular case, the employer is not satisfied that the person concerned meets the requirement, and it is reasonable for him not to be satisfied. This exception applies whether the employer has an ethos based on religion or belief or not. Examples would be an army chaplain and an imam attached to a school. A similar but differently worded exception applies where the employer does have an ethos based on religion or belief.

The Employment Equality (Sexual Orientation) Regulations 2003 provide in reg.7 for genuine occupational requirements as follows:

(1) Employment is excepted from the operation of the Regulations if being of a particular sexual orientation is a genuine and determining occupational requirement, it is proportionate to apply the

requirement in the case in question, and the person concerned does not meet it, or the employer is not satisfied that he does so (and it is reasonable for him not to be satisfied).

(2) Employment is excepted where it is for the purposes of an organised religion, the employer applies a requirement related to sexual orientation to comply with its doctrines or to avoid conflict with the strongly held religious convictions of a significant numbers of the religion's followers. For this requirement to apply, it is also necessary that the person to whom it is applied should not meet the requirement, or that the employer is not satisfied that he does so (and it is reasonable for him not to be satisfied).

Positive action

6.34   Positive discrimination is unlawful. This follows from the general principle that a man can complain of sex discrimination, a white person can bring a claim for racial discrimination, a heterosexual for less favourable treatment on grounds of sexual orientation, etc. Any attempt to implement a policy of positive discrimination, such as by the imposition of a quota system, would be subject to claims made by those who fell outside the quota.

Whilst positive discrimination is unlawful, positive action within the specific confines of the legislation is allowed. Employers may provide specialist training where the purpose is to compensate for under-representation of a particular group. In addition, members of an under-represented group may be encouraged to apply for particular jobs (see ss.35–38 of the RRA, ss.47–48 of the SDA, reg.25 of the Employment Equality (Religion or Belief) Regulations 2003 and reg.26 of the Employment Equality (Sexual Orientation) Regulations 2003).

Who can claim?

6.35   The group of people who can claim for discrimination at work is generally wider than those who are employed under conventional contracts of employment. For example, s.82 of the SDA defines "employment" to mean "employment under a contract of service or of apprenticeship or a contract personally to execute any work or labour". There are similar provisions in relation to race, sexual orientation, and religion or belief. There are various other groups which are protected by the legislation (e.g. police, partners, office-holders), although coverage varies from one set of provisions to another, and the precise position needs to be checked in relation to any particular group of workers.

As far as contract workers (e.g. cleaners, temporary secretaries) are concerned, they are generally afforded protection within the various strands of discrimination law. It is unlawful for the "principal" to discriminate against a "contract worker". The principal is the person for whom the work is done, not the person who actually employs the contract worker and supplies the contract worker under a contract made with the principal (see, for example, s.7 of the RRA). Such provisions are necessary because it will be the client company, rather than the employer which will generally have scope for discrimination—it will control the contract worker's environment.

Against whom can a claim be brought?

An employer is liable for an act of discrimination carried out by his **6.36** employee, provided it is carried out in the course of employment. The phrase "in the course of employment" should be determined in accordance with everyday speech, rather than the case law relating to vicarious liability for torts committed by an employee: *Jones v Tower Boot Co Ltd* [1997] I.R.L.R. 168, CA.

In *Chief Constable of Lincolnshire Police v Stubbs* [1999] I.R.L.R. 81, the EAT considered whether a police officer was acting in the course of his employment when he subjected a female colleague to inappropriate sexual behaviour at social events away from the police station. It was held that, where there was a social gathering of work colleagues, the tribunal should consider whether what was occurring was an extension of their employment. In this case, the incidents had been at social gatherings involving officers from work, and what happened was in the course of employment of the officer who committed the discriminatory act.

There is, however, a defence available to the employer. He will escape liability if he can show that he:

> "took such steps as were reasonably practicable to prevent the employee from doing that act, or from doing in the course of his employment acts of that description"

(RRA s.32, with equivalent provisions in the other strands of discrimination law currently under consideration). In determining whether such steps have been taken, a tribunal will be likely to scrutinise, for example:

- Any relevant policies relating to equal opportunities in the field in question.

- Whether members of staff had the policy brought to their attention.

- Any relevant training in equal opportunities.

- Any relevant monitoring exercise.

- The existence and effectiveness of grievance procedures relating to discrimination.

- Whether complaints of discrimination were investigated properly.

The tribunal should concentrate on whether the employer took the **6.37** reasonably practicable steps to prevent the discriminatory act, rather than whether any such steps would have been effective. In *Canniffe v East Riding of Yorkshire Council* [2000] I.R.L.R. 555, a tribunal had decided that there was nothing the employers could have done to prevent their employee from assaulting the claimant. The EAT held that this was not the right approach. The tribunal should first have identified whether the employer took any steps at all to prevent the employee doing the act complained of. Then they should consider whether there were any further steps which they could have taken which were reasonably practicable. Whether such further steps would have been successful in preventing the discriminatory act is not determinative, although it may, of course, be relevant in deciding what is reasonable.

In addition to employer's liability, anyone who aids a discriminatory act is himself liable for that act. Aiding includes helping, co-operating or collaborating, whether the help is substantial or not, provided that it is not so insignificant as to be negligible: *Anyanwu v South Bank Students' Union* [2001] I.R.L.R. 305, HL.

In *Gilbank v Miles* [2006] I.R.L.R. 538, a manager was held personally liable for bullying carried out by her colleagues. G was employed in a hairdressing salon as a trainee manager. There was a friendly atmosphere in the salon until she told M, the salon manager, that she was pregnant. Thereafter, there was, in the words of the tribunal's judgment, an "inhumane and sustained campaign of bullying and discrimination" against G by M and her other managers. The company was held liable under s.41(1) of the SDA for the actions of M and its other managers. Moreover, M was held liable for her own discriminatory acts by virtue of s.42(2), and also for the discriminatory acts of other managers, because she had aided them to commit an unlawful act, contrary to s.42(1). The tribunal awarded £25,000 for injury to feelings, in addition to its award for unpaid maternity pay. The award was made jointly and severally (see the Remedies section below). M appealed to the EAT and in due course to the CA, both of which upheld the tribunal's judgment. The CA held that M had consciously fostered and encouraged a discriminatory culture that targeted G. She had knowingly aided the unlawful acts of the other managers. In addition, she had aided the acts of the company in unlawfully discriminating against G. The unsuccessful appeal against the amount of the award is dealt with in the "Remedies" section.

Disability discrimination

6.38   The Disability Discrimination Act 1995 made it unlawful to discriminate against people who are disabled. The fundamental thinking behind the Act is different from that which underpins the SDA and RRA, and the Regulations which prohibit discrimination on grounds of sexual orientation and religion or belief. These latter strands of discrimination law are concerned to ensure a level playing field—between men and women, people of different races, those of different religious beliefs or sexual orientation. Thus, it is possible for a man to complain of sexual discrimination—and this is not just a theoretical possibility but one that happens in a significant minority of cases. Similarly, a white person can complain that he was subjected to racial harassment, and a heterosexual can claim that he was discriminated against on grounds of his sexual orientation. All this is so, although the policy in each case is to reduce discrimination against women, ethnic minorities and gays respectively.

In the case of disability discrimination, however, it is not possible for someone to base his claim on discrimination because he was not disabled. This is because the statute aims to compensate disabled people for the disadvantages which they face owing to their disabilities. It does not have a level playing field as its objective—it aims to tilt the ground in favour of those whom it seeks to protect.

This underlying aim is reflected in the pattern which the statute adopts in its definition of discrimination. It is particularly marked when it comes to the duty on the employer to make reasonable adjustments. The purpose of such adjustments, after all, is to offer positive assistance to disabled people. It follows also that there is no prohibition on "positive discrimination" as there is in the case of the other strands of discrimination law, since positive discrimination in favour of disabled people is (within the limits of what is reasonable) part of the policy of the DDA. Since positive discrimination is not forbidden, it follows also that there is no need for the statute to incorporate permission for "positive action" as is seen in the other anti-discrimination legislation.

Materials. Although the field is governed by the DDA, there are other   **6.39** important materials which play a part in its interpretation and implementation. In particular, the following are the subject of frequent references by tribunals and the appellate courts:

- The Disability Rights Commission Code of practice: Employment and Occupation (2004).
- Guidance on matters to be taken into account in determining questions relating to the definition of disability (2006).
- Various statutory regulations dealing with the statutory duties of public authorities and trade organisations, and people with particular disabilities, e.g. those who are blind.

Scope. The DDA prohibits discrimination in the provision of goods and   **6.40** services. However, in accordance with the general focus of this book, our coverage will concentrate upon the employment field. The DDA, like the other strands of discrimination law, adopts the wide definition of "employee" to cover anyone who is subject to a contract personally to do any work, and gives protection to job applicants as well as employees. It also extends that protection to discriminatory acts which are closely related to employment which has come to an end, e.g. provision of a reference.

One area of controversy is whether the DDA protects someone who is associated with a disabled person—for example as a carer. For some other strands of discrimination law (e.g. race), the protection extends to someone who associates with a member of the protected group. But the DDA protects only "disabled persons". However, the European Framework Employment Directive (2000/78) requires member states to prohibit discrimination "on grounds of disability". In *Attridge Law v Coleman* [2007]

I.R.L.R. 88, the claimant was a legal secretary with a young disabled son requiring care. She claimed that she had been subjected to unfair treatment and harassment as a result. The chairman of the employment tribunal referred the matter to the ECJ to determine whether the DDA should be read in such a way as to put such "associative discrimination" within its scope. The EAT held that the reference was correct in principle. As a result, the decision of the ECJ is awaited on this important point.

Whilst there are exceptions for "genuine occupational qualifications" in the case of other strands of discrimination law, there is no such exception in the DDA. Employers who had fewer than 15 employees were initially exempt from some of the duties imposed by the Act, but this was removed with effect from October 1, 2004. The only general exception from the duties imposed is that relating to the armed forces.

6.41   **Meaning of disability.** Before a claimant can establish rights under the statute, he must show that he is disabled. In view of the wide ambit of the protection given by the DDA, the definition of "disabled" assumes considerable importance. Section 1 states that:

> ". . . a person has a disability for the purposes of this Act if he has a physical or mental impairment which has a substantial and long-term adverse effect on his ability to carry out normal day-to-day activities."

There is, then, a series of issues which have to be determined in order to judge whether a claimant is disabled. It is worth stressing from the outset that it is not a matter of defining certain conditions as "disabilities" and others as falling outside the definition. To ask, for example, "Is depression a disability?" is to pose the wrong question. Whether the depression suffered by a particular person is a disability or not will depend upon whether its effects on that person fit within the definition. In the case of some people at particular times, it will, and in the case of other people (or even the same people at different times) it will not. Each of the constituent parts of the definition needs to be examined in turn.

6.42   **Physical or mental impairment.** The stereotypical view of disability focuses upon a physical impairment. However, the legislation makes it quite clear that mental, as well as physical impairments are covered—so that depression, dyslexia, schizophrenia and learning difficulties are all potentially within the scope of the protection. It all depends upon whether, in the particular factual situation, the claimant fulfils the various components of the definition.

6.43   **Long-term effects.** This phrase within the definition is interpreted in Sch.1 of the DDA which states that an effect is long-term if it

(a) has lasted for at least 12 months;

(b) is likely to last for at least 12 months; or

(c) is likely to last for the rest of the life of the person concerned.

If it ceases to have a substantial adverse effect on a person's ability to carry out normal day-to-day activities, it is treated as continuing to have that effect if it is likely to recur.

Substantial. The Guidance on the Definition of Disability (2006) issued **6.44** by the government under s.3 of the DDA states that a substantial effect is one which is greater than "minor" or "trivial" (B1). In *Goodwin v The Patent Office* [1999] I.R.L.R. 4, the EAT stated that it meant "more than minor or trivial" rather than "very large". In *Abadeh v British Telecommunications plc* [2001] I.R.L.R. 23, the EAT considered the role of medical evidence, and stressed that it was not the role of the medical expert to tell the tribunal whether an impairment was or was not substantial. That was a question for the tribunal to answer. Whilst this is, with respect, undoubtedly correct, in practice a tribunal will frequently rely upon medical evidence in approaching its task and in *Kapadia v London Borough of Lambeth* [2000] I.R.L.R. 699, the CA held that uncontested medical evidence on the degree of effect is generally conclusive. Further, where the tribunal rejects medical evidence, it is under a duty to explain its reasons: *Edwards v Mid Suffolk DC* [2001] I.R.L.R. 190.

As a matter of practice, where the parties wish to rely on medical evidence. the tribunal will take into account the procedural guidance given in *De Keyser Ltd v Wilson* [2001] I.R.L.R. 324, EAT:

- the preferred course of action is to ensure that the parties instruct a joint expert;
- any letter of instruction should specify in detail the particular questions which the expert is asked to answer;
- instructions should avoid partisanship.

Normal day-to-day activities. The impairment must have a substantial **6.45** effect upon the claimant's ability to carry out "normal day-to-day activities". This latter phrase is defined in Sch.1, para.4 of the DDA so that it includes the following (and no other activities):

(a) mobility;

(b) manual dexterity;

(c) physical co-ordination;

(d) continence;

(e) ability to lift, carry or otherwise move everyday objects;

(f) speech, hearing or eyesight;

(g) memory or ability to concentrate, learn or understand; or

(h) perception of the risk of physical danger.

The list is exhaustive, so that the claimant has to demonstrate that at least one of the areas in question is affected substantially and adversely. The focus is upon "day-to-day activities" rather than the performance of work duties. This has the result that the claimant may not be able to perform his duties at work on a long-term basis, but does not come within the definition of "disabled". Of course, evidence of the claimant's work duties and the way in which they are performed, particularly if they include "normal day-to-day activities" will very often be relevant to the tribunal's assessment of the claimant's case: *Law Hospital NHS Trust v Rush* [2001] I.R.L.R. 611, CS.

As was pointed out in *Goodwin* the fact that a person can carry out such activities does not mean that his ability to carry them out has not been impaired. The focus of the DDA is on the things that the claimant <u>cannot</u> do, or can only do with difficulty, rather than on the things which he <u>can</u> do.

Forms of Disability Discrimination

6.46   The DDA gives a disabled person the right to claim in respect of each of the following categories of unlawful act:

    (a) direct discrimination;

    (b) disability-related discrimination;

    (c) failure to make reasonable adjustments;

    (d) harassment;

    (e) victimisation.

As far as (d) and (e) are concerned, the definitions are similar to the other strands of discrimination law. Consequently what has been said above is equally applicable to harassment and victimisation under the DDA. There are particular features about (a), (b) and (c), however, which make it necessary to treat them separately here.

6.47   **Direct discrimination.**   The definition of direct disability discrimination is set out in s.3A(5) of the DDA:

> "3A(5) A person directly discriminates against a disabled person if, on the ground of the disabled person's disability, he treats the disabled person less favourably than he treats or would treat a person not having that particular disability whose relevant circumstances, including his disability, are the same as, or not materially different from, those of the disabled person."

The definition is similar to that in the other strands of discrimination law, but it is worth reiterating that there is no reciprocal right for the non-disabled person to claim discrimination on the basis that his treatment is less favourable than that afforded to a disabled person. In addition, some attention needs to be given to the selection of the comparator. The comparator could also be a person who has a disability, provided that it is not the "particular disability" which the claimant has. Consequently, a claimant with schizophrenia, for example, could use as a comparator a person who is blind. As in other areas of discrimination, the comparator can be a hypothetical person, but the choice of an appropriate comparator may be fraught with difficulty.

In *High Quality Lifestyles v Watts* [2006] I.R.L.R. 850, the EAT considered the case of an HIV positive care-worker who helped provide services for people with learning disabilities and autistic disorders. After he disclosed his HIV positive status to his employers, they carried out a risk assessment and concluded that, because HQ Ltd's employees frequently sustained bites and injuries from its service-users which resulted in broken skin, there was a high risk that this could lead to the transmission of HIV and other infectious diseases. This ran counter to guidance from the Department of Health which stated that the risk of transmission in such circumstances was "theoretical". The employers dismissed him and W brought claims of direct discrimination, disability-related discrimination, and failure to make reasonable adjustments (as to the latter two matters, see the next sections). The tribunal found that he had been directly discriminated against, comparing his treatment with that which would have been received by someone who was in the same position but without HIV. HQ Ltd appealed and the EAT held that, in coming to a decision on direct discrimination, the tribunal should have selected a comparator with an attribute (whether caused by a medical condition or otherwise) which carried the same risk of causing illness or injury to others as W's condition.

Disability-related discrimination. There is no concept of "indirect discrimination" within the DDA. Instead, there is a prohibition against what is generally termed "disability-related discrimination". The relevant definition is contained within s.3A(1): **6.48**

> "**3A.**(1) . . . a person discriminates against a disabled person if—
>
> (a) for a reason which relates to the disabled person's disability, he treats him less favourably than he treats of would treat others to whom that reason does not or would not apply, and
> (b) he cannot show that the treatment in question is justified."

The difficult question of interpretation here has been in respect of the phrase "others to whom that reason does not. . . apply". In *Clark v TDG Ltd t/a Novacold* [1999] I.R.L.R. 318, the CA considered a case where C had been dismissed for long-term absence, which resulted from a disability. Should he be compared with

(a) a non-disabled person who had an equivalent pattern of absence? or

(b) someone who had not been absent at all?

The CA reasoned that the language of the DDA was different from that of the RRA and the SDA. In the latter statutes, the comparison had to be with the cases of persons in the same, or not materially different circumstances. That was not required for the DDA, whose statutory focus was narrower. The CA concluded that others without C's disability would not have been absent to the same extent. They would therefore not have been dismissed. C's treatment was, therefore, less favourable. That left open the question of justification. Was the employer justified in dismissing C, given the level of absence and the other relevant circumstances? The case was remitted to the tribunal to decide whether the employer had been justified.

As far as justification is concerned, the definition is set out in s.3A(3) which states:

> "**3A.**(3) Treatment is justified for the purposes of subsection (1)(b) if, but only if, the reason for it is both material to the circumstances of the particular case and substantial."

6.49   As can be seen, the test is a relatively undemanding one. It must merely relate to the individual circumstances in question (rather than consisting of a generalised, stereotypical assumption, for example) and it must not be merely trivial or minor: *HJ Heinz Co Ltd v Kenrick* [2000] I.R.L.R. 144, EAT.

Further, when considering justification, a tribunal should not substitute its own judgment for that of the employer. It has to adopt the "range of reasonable responses" test in the same way as it does with regard to the question of whether the employer acted reasonably or unreasonably in a claim for unfair dismissal. It should decide whether the employer acted inside or outside the range of what a reasonable employer would have done: *Jones v Post Office* [2001] I.R.L.R. 384, CA.

There is an important link between justification for disability-related discrimination and the duty to make reasonable adjustments (which is looked at in more detail in the following section). Section 3A(6) of the DDA states that, in a claim for disability-related discrimination, where the employer is under a duty to make a reasonable adjustment but fails to do so, his treatment of the disabled person cannot be justified unless it would have been justified even if he had made the reasonable adjustment.

6.50   Another issue of some importance is whether the employer needs to know of the disability for disability-related discrimination to occur. As will be seen from the next section, actual or constructive knowledge is required for the duty to make a reasonable adjustment to arise. However, as far as disability-related discrimination is concerned, the employer does not need to have knowledge of the disability, nor as to whether it falls within the statutory definition of a disability: *H J Heinz*.

6.51   **Duty to make reasonable adjustment.** The central plank of the law relating to disability discrimination is the duty imposed on the employer to make reasonable adjustments to alleviate any disadvantage suffered by the disabled person in relation to his employment. Whilst the other forms of discrimination set out in the DDA have their rough equivalents in other strands of discrimination law, the duty to make reasonable adjustments is unique. It is the clear expression of the statute's policy—not to create a level playing field, but to tilt it in favour of the disabled person.

Section 3A(2) makes it clear that the failure to make reasonable adjustments is unlawful:

> "**3A.**(2) . . . a person also discriminates against a disabled person if he fails to comply with a duty to make reasonable adjustments imposed on him in relation to the disabled person."

The duty is set out in s4A(1):

> "**4A.**(1) Where—
>
> (a) a provision, criterion or practice applied by or on behalf of an employer, or
> (b) any physical feature of premises occupied by the employer,
>
> places the disabled person concerned at a substantial disadvantage in comparison with persons who are not disabled, it is the duty of the employer to take such steps as it is reasonable, in all the circumstances of the case, for him to have to take in order to prevent the provision, criterion or practice, or feature, having that effect."

There is an exception set out in s.4A(3), which states that there is no duty imposed if an employer does not know, and could not reasonably be expected to know that the person has a disability and is likely to be affected in the way set out in 4A(1). Ignorance is not sufficient to avail the employer of this defence. It must be reasonable ignorance!

So, what might constitute a reasonable adjustment? Some examples are given in s.18B(2)

   (a) making adjustments to premises;

   (b) allocating some of the disabled person's duties to another person;

   (c) transferring him to fill an existing vacancy;

   (d) altering his working hours;

   (e) assigning him to a different place of work;

   (f) allowing him to be absent during working hours for rehabilitation, assessment or treatment;

   (g) giving him, or arranging for him to be given, training or mentoring (whether for the disabled person or any other person);

   (h) acquiring or modifying equipment;

   (i) modifying instructions or reference manuals;

   (j) modifying procedures for testing or assessment;

   (k) providing a reader or interpreter;

   (l) providing supervision or other support.

The list is not exhaustive. For example, in *Nottinghamshire CC v Meikle* [2004] I.R.L.R. 703, the CA held that the payment of full sick pay by an employer can be an adjustment falling within the scope of what is now s.4A. The context was important, however, as the reason why the employee was unable to return to work was partly because the employers had failed to make reasonable adjustments by providing her with appropriate work equipment. That undermined the justification which the employers put forward for reducing her sick pay. In *O'Hanlon v Commissioners for HM Revenue and Customs* [2006] I.R.L.R. 840 the employee was in a sick pay scheme which provided for a reduction to half pay after six months' absence, and an overall maximum period of 12 months' sick pay in any four-year period. After that, the rate of pay was reduced. O was absent for 365 working days during a four year period, 320 of which related to her disability. She claimed that she should have received full pay, rather than sick pay for all disability-related absences. The EAT concluded that there was a duty of reasonable adjustment on the employers. However, it was not a reasonable adjustment to require them to pay her full pay in respect of absences which were related to her disability. Further, her claim for disability-related discrimination failed on the basis that the employers were justified in not paying her full salary, even though she was absent from work as a result of disability-related sickness. The decision of the EAT was upheld by the CA: [2007] EWCA Civ 283.

6.52   In *Archibald v Fife Council* [2004] I.R.L.R. 651, the HL held that the duty to take reasonable steps could include transferring without competitive interview a disabled employee for a post she can no longer do to a post which she can do. The employer's duty might require moving the disabled person to a slightly higher grade.

Certain factors are set out in s.18B(1) to which regard must be had in deciding whether a particular step is reasonable:

- the extent to which taking the step would prevent the effect in question;
- the extent to which it is practicable for the employer to take the step;
- the financial and other costs which would be incurred by the employer in taking the step and the extent to which taking it would disrupt any of his activities;
- the availability to the employer of financial or other assistance with respect to taking the step;
- the nature of his activities and the size of his undertaking;
- where the step would be taken in relation to a private household, the extent to which taking it would
  - disrupt that household; or
  - disturb any person residing there.

In *Morse v Wiltshire County Council* [1999] I.R.L.R. 352, the EAT set out guidance for a tribunal hearing an allegation of failure to make a reasonable adjustment. It should go through the following steps:

- it must decide on whether the provisions of s.4A impose a duty on the employer in the circumstances of the case;

- if such a duty is imposed, it must determine whether the employer has taken such steps as are reasonable to prevent the arrangements or feature placing the disabled person at a substantial disadvantage when compared with people who are not disabled;

- this involves the tribunal in inquiring whether the employer could reasonably have taken any of the steps set out in s.18B(1);

- at the same time, the tribunal must have regard to the factors set out in s.18B(2) which gives a series of examples of steps which might constitute a reasonable adjustment (it is not meant to be an exhaustive list).

It was made clear in *Morse* that the tribunal must scrutinise the **6.53** employer's explanation and reach its own decision on what steps were reasonable. In other words, this is not one of those areas where it must look at whether the employer has acted within the "reasonable band of responses" (contrast disability-related discrimination—see above). It has to come to its own judgment as to what is reasonable.

In *Mid-Staffordshire General Hospitals NHS Trust v Cambridge* [2003] I.R.L.R. 566, the EAT held that a proper assessment of what is required to eliminate a disabled person's disadvantage is a necessary part of the duty imposed by s.4A(1). The reason is that the employer cannot comply with its duty unless it makes a proper assessment of what is to be done. The duty to make a reasonable adjustment does not, however, extend to consulting a disabled employee about what adjustment might be made. The wise employer will nevertheless consult with the employee in question, to determine what adjustments might reasonably be made: *Tarbuck v Sainsbury's Supermarkets Ltd* [2006] I.R.L.R. 644.

Age discrimination

The Employment Equality (Age) Regulations 2006 came into force on **6.54** October 1, 2006. Like the regulations on sexual orientation, and those on religion or belief, they aim to implement the EC's Council Directive 2000/78 on Equal Treatment. Many of the provisions of the regulations also reflect those of the legislation prohibiting discrimination on grounds of sex, race and disability. However, there are sufficient distinctive features to the new strand of age discrimination law to merit its separate treatment in this section.

Scope. The Regulations do not deal with discrimination on the grounds of **6.55** age in relation to the supply of goods and services. Their ambit is confined to employment (broadly defined: see below) and vocational training. They do, however, cover institutions of further and higher education, whether the courses concerned are vocational or not (reg.23).

As far as employment is concerned, protection is given to those who fall within a definition of "employee" which is similar to that found in the other areas of discrimination law. In addition, office-holders, contract workers, police officers, partners and barristers come within the scope of the regulations, as do those in Crown and Parliamentary employment. The way in which the Regulations are framed means that people who are applying to be an employee (or to be recruited as a member of one of the other groups listed above) are protected. However, some of the individual regulations only operate in respect of some of the groups in question.

6.56   **The Forms of Discrimination.** The regulations make the following activities unlawful:

(a) direct discrimination

(b) indirect discrimination

(c) victimisation

(d) harassment; and

(e) instructions to discriminate.

The definitions of the various categories of unlawful activity generally follow those which are familiar from other strands of discrimination law, although there are some distinctive points which are worth noting.

Direct discrimination is defined as less favourable treatment by A of B "on grounds of B's age". This is defined to include "B's apparent age." Assume, for example, that an employer is set on appointing someone who is over 50 to a particular position, because of a wish for "maturity". If Dominic, who is over 50 but of exceptionally youthful appearance, fails to get the job, he can still claim age discrimination, because he has been less favourably treated on the grounds of his apparent age.

Justification. The major difference from the other strands of discrimination law is that direct discrimination on grounds of age is capable of being justified. In the case of the various other forms of discrimination (e.g. on grounds of sex or race), direct discrimination cannot be made lawful by a process of justification. However, in the case of age discrimination, the Regulations make it clear that the employer is entitled to show that its discriminatory treatment of an employee is justified. If it succeeds in doing so, then it will have a valid defence, and its actions will not be unlawful.

6.57   This sharp difference from discrimination law generally poses the question: is this major exemption allowed by the EC's Equal Treatment Directive which the Regulations aim to implement? The Directive (Art.6) allows member states to permit justification of differences of treatment on grounds of age, without distinction between direct and indirect discrimination, if:

> "they are objectively and reasonably justified by a legitimate aim, including legitimate employment policy, labour market and vocational training objectives, and if the means of achieving that aim are appropriate and necessary."

Indirect discrimination is the application of a provision, criterion or practice "which puts or would put persons of the same age group as B at a particular disadvantage when compared with other persons". "Age group" means "a group of persons defined by reference to age, whether by reference to a particular age or a range of ages". If indirect discrimination can be justified by the employer, then it will not be unlawful. In this case, the situation mirrors that for other forms of indirect discrimination (e.g. on grounds of sex, race, etc.), which are also capable of being lawful if justified.

As is the case with discrimination law generally, the Employment Equality (Age) Regulations do not in fact use the term "justification". Instead they refer to: "a proportionate means of achieving a legitimate aim".

However, it is clear from the case law, both European and domestic, that **6.58** justification involves establishing that the employer had a legitimate aim which it sought to achieve by proportionate means.

The provisions in relation to victimisation and harassment are similar to those for other types of discrimination law. In addition, reg.5 makes unlawful less favourable treatment on the grounds that an employee has failed to carry out instructions to commit an act which is unlawful by virtue of the Regulations, or has complained about such instructions.

General exceptions. There are general exceptions to the operation of the **6.59** Regulations in respect of:

- statutory authority (reg.27);

- national security (reg.28);

- positive action (reg.29);

- genuine occupational requirements (paragraphs of particular regulations).

Recruitment. The prohibited areas of discrimination for applicants and **6.60** employees are set out in reg.7. It makes unlawful any discrimination in relation to the process of recruitment for the categories of person protected by the Regulations. There is, however, an exception to the prohibition on discrimination in the recruitment process set out in reg.7(4). This lays down that it is not unlawful to discriminate in the recruitment process against those who are:

(a) over 65 if the employer does not have a normal retirement age (NRA);

(b) over the employer's NRA if that is over 65;

(c) within six months of the NRA or (if there is none) the age of 65 on the date of the application for employment.

This important exclusion from the right for job applicants not to be discriminated against flows from the power which employers are given to retire employees compulsorily at the age of 65 (see the section on Retirement in paras 6.62 to 6.69 below). It would not make much sense to force employers to consider job applicants close to or over the age of 65 if they were able to retire them compulsorily once they achieved that age.

This recruitment exception applies only to those who, if they were appointed, would be subject to a contract of employment (including those in Crown or Parliamentary employment). As a result, it would still unlawful to discriminate in the recruitment process against those aged 65, etc. who are seeking other positions (such as an applicant for office or a partnership).

6.61   **Terms of Service.** Discrimination is prohibited in relation to terms of employment, opportunities for promotion, transfer, training and other benefits. However, there is an exception in relation to benefits based on length of service, which is set out in reg.32 (reproduced below). In summary, this states:

    (a) discrimination on the basis of length of service is permitted; but

    (b) if the person alleging discrimination has five years service or more, it must "reasonably appear" to the employer that his use of the criterion of length of service "fulfils a business need of his undertaking" (e.g. by encouraging loyalty or motivation or rewarding experience).

The exception contained in reg.32 applies to those who are employees, office-holders, police officers, partners, and those in Crown or Parliamentary employment.

There are also exceptions to the prohibition on discrimination in relation to benefits in respect of:

    (a) the national minimum wage—employers can pay workers aged 16/17 less than those aged 18/21 and both age bands less than those aged 22 and over;

    (b) enhanced redundancy pay—this can be based upon the present formula for statutory redundancy pay; which gives increased benefits to older workers; and

    (c) life assurance cover for workers who have retired early on grounds of ill health.

6.62   **Retirement.** The most controversial provisions in the Regulations deal with retirement. In particular, the issue which took up most of the government's extensive process of consultation was whether employers should be able to retire employees compulsorily at a certain age, without putting forward any justification (in the sense of a legitimate aim achieved by a proportionate means). Broadly, during the process of consultation, the trade unions and groups representing the interests of older workers, such as

Age Concern, argued that there should be no general compulsory retirement age, and that each compulsory retirement should have to be
individually justified. The employers' organisations were in favour of a
"default retirement age" over which any employer could retire an employee
compulsorily, without the need for individual justification. At the end of the
day, the government came down in favour of the arguments of the
employers—at least for the time being. As a result, the Regulations specify
that it is not unlawful to dismiss someone who is over the age of 65 where
the reason for the dismissal is retirement (reg.30). The impact is that any
such dismissal is excluded from the ambit of the prohibition against age
discrimination. It may, however, constitute unfair dismissal, as the age limit
for unfair dismissal claims has now been removed (Sch.8, para.25).
However, the government has promised to review the issue of the
retirement age in 2011.

Regulation 30 applies only to employees within the meaning of s.230(1)
of the Employment Rights Act ("ERA") 1996 (those under a contract of
employment but including Crown employees and members of Parliamentary staff). Its ambit is much narrower than that of the Regulations
generally. With regard to office holders, for example, any retirement age
would have to be justified (in the sense that the retirement was based upon
a legitimate aim achieved by proportionate means).

Unfair Dismissal. The Regulations brought about major changes in the   **6.63**
law of unfair dismissal. In summary:

- Employees over the age of 65 were given the right to bring a claim
  for unfair dismissal (prior to the commencement of the Regulations, they were barred from claiming unfair dismissal);

- "Retirement of the employee" was added to the fair reasons for
  dismissal set out in s.98 of the ERA 1996 (see the chapter on
  Unfair Dismissal);

- There is a duty placed upon the employer to consider whether the
  employee should continue after the retirement date;

- A procedure is laid down for such consideration (the "duty to
  consider" procedure—see paras 6.64 and 6.65 for the details);

- This procedure replaces the statutory dismissal and disciplinary
  procedure (DDP) in respect of retirement dismissals;

- There are various presumptions as to whether retirement has been
  established as the reason for the dismissal (see paras 6.66 and
  6.67);

- There is a special test for fairness in respect of retirement
  dismissals (see para.6.68).

The "duty to consider" procedure. An important part of the Regulations   **6.64**
was the introduction of a duty on employers to consider requests from
employees who are coming up for retirement to continue working for a

longer period. The stated purpose of the government is to bring about a culture change, so that employers consider the positive benefits of extending the working life of their employees, rather than enforcing a strict retirement age. Whether it will achieve this purpose remains to be seen. The model which the government has in mind is the duty under "family friendly legislation" (see Chapter 8) to consider a request for flexible working by a worker with childcare commitments.

The "duty to consider" procedure in the Employment Equality (Age) Regulations (for further details see paras 9.73 to 9.80) may be summarised as follows:

- The employer who intends to retire an employee must notify the employee of the date upon which he intends him to retire, and of his right to make a request to continue working after that date;

- The notification must be given between six months and one year before the intended date of retirement (Sch.6 para.2). Failure to notify within these limits constitutes a separate right of action for which a tribunal shall award compensation up to eight weeks' pay;

- Thereafter, the employer remains under a continuing duty to notify, until the 14th day before the intended date of retirement (Sch.6 para.4);

- The employee may make a request to the employee not to retire on the intended date;

- The employer has a duty to consider the request;

- The employer must hold a meeting to consider the request within a reasonable period after receiving it;

- If the request is refused, the employee must be told of his right to appeal. No reasons for the refusal need be given;

- Notice of appeal must be given as soon as is reasonably practicable after notice of the refusal, setting out grounds of appeal;

- The employee is entitled to be accompanied by a worker employed by the same employer at both the initial and the appeal meeting;

- The deadlines are set out in tabular form below.

The "duty to consider" procedure: deadlines

DATE (and authority)	EVENT
12 months before intended date of retirement (Sch.6 para.2)	Earliest date for employer to issue notice of intended retirement
Six months before intended date of retirement (Sch.6 para.2)	Latest date for employer to issue notice of intended retirement without incurring penalty of up to eight weeks' wages* AND Earliest date for employee to make request to continue working
Three months before intended date of retirement (Sch.6 para.5(5))	Latest date for employee to make request to continue working if employer gave notice between six and 12 months before intended date of retirement
14 days before date of dismissal (Sch.6 para.4 and s.98ZG of ERA 1996)	If employer has not issued date of intended retirement, any dismissal for retirement will be automatically unfair
Intended date of retirement/ dismissal	Employee will be dismissed OR Date of retirement altered
Three months after * above or the date on which the employee knew (or should have known) that date (Sch.6 para.11)	Deadline for claim in respect of failure to issue notice under Sch.6, para.2 (subject to any extension because it was "not reasonably practicable" to present claim, etc.)

The table above summarises the provisions in Sch.6 of the Regulations relating to the "duty to consider" procedure.

Compulsory retirement can be for a "fair reason". As mentioned above, 6.66 employees over the age of 65 can now be able to bring claims for unfair dismissal. However, where the dismissal is by reason of retirement, that will be a fair reason for dismissal (although, as described below, failure to adopt the correct procedure may still mean that the dismissal is unfair).

The employer must show that the reason is retirement, but certain presumptions are set out in ss.98ZA to 98ZH, which are inserted in the ERA 1996 (see paras 9.53 and 9.54 for details).

In summary, the reason for dismissal will be deemed to be retirement if:

- The dismissed employee is at or over the age of 65;

- He is at or over the normal retirement age (which is itself 65 or over);

- The employer complies with the notification duty in para.2 of sch 6 to the Regulations (notification between 6 and 12 months before the intended date of retirement); and

- The dismissal is carried out on the intended retirement date.

6.67   In addition, there are a few cases where it is left to the tribunal to decide whether retirement is the reason for dismissal:

- where the employer has not notified the employee in accordance with para.2 of Sch.6—perhaps he notified late or not at all (whether or not the employee has a normal retirement age); or

- where the employer notified the employee in accordance with para.2 of Sch.6, but the dismissal takes effect after the intended date of retirement.

In other situations, the dismissal will not be retirement.

Where the tribunal concludes that retirement is the reason for dismissal, whether or not the dismissal is fair is assessed in accordance with the new s.98ZG of the ERA 1996. This test is to be applied by the tribunal once it is established that the dismissal in question is a retirement dismissal. The test amounts to a procedural fairness test. The tribunal must ask whether the employer has complied with the following obligations under the duty to consider procedure:

- service of notice of date of intended retirement, etc. (must be by the 14th day before the date);

- consideration of any request to continue in employment;

- holding a meeting to consider the request;

- holding any appeal if notice of appeal served.

If there has been a failure on the part of the employer to comply with any of the above, the employee is to be regarded as unfairly dismissed. If there has not, then the dismissal is fair (for details, see paras 9.73 to 9.80).

The test is a rather mechanical one, depending as it does on whether certain formalities have been complied with. It should be contrasted with the usual test in unfair dismissal cases. As will be seen from the discussion in the chapter on Unfair Dismissal, the tribunal must ask (in relation to all potentially fair reasons other than retirement) whether in the circumstances (including the size and administrative resources of the employer's undertaking) the employer acted reasonably or unreasonably in treating it as a sufficient reason for dismissing the employee.

As can be seen, the test for whether a <u>retirement</u> is fair is much simpler   **6.68**
and, arguably, less consistent with common notions of what is fair or unfair.
The question whether a retirement dismissal is fair is dealt with in the
flowchart below.

Retirement dismissal

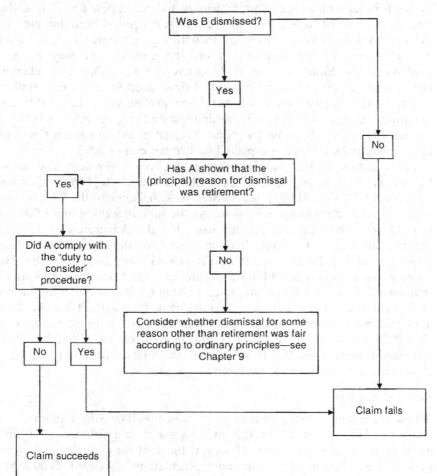

A = Employer

The chart assumes that B (the claimant) has the right to claim unfair dismissal e.g. one year's
continuous employment

Challenges.   Although the law on age discrimination reflects other strands   **6.69**
of discrimination law, it has features which are unique. The scope of the

legislation, excluding as it does the supply of goods and services, is markedly different. In addition, there are a number of exceptions, exemptions and defences, some of the most important of which are not to be found in the equivalent legislation prohibiting other forms of discrimination.

These distinctive features have already created controversy, and are likely to result in legal challenges both by way of judicial review and also in the European Court of Justice. The first major challenge has been mounted by the organisation Heyday (closely allied with Age Concern). It has sought judicial review of the Regulations on the ground that they do not implement the Equal Treatment Directive, because they give blanket justification for compulsory retirement of those aged 65 and over. Another aspect of the Regulations which has been challenged is the ability for employers to justify direct age discrimination on the same basis as indirect age discrimination. The case has been referred to the European Court of Justice, and judgment is not expected before the end of 2007.

The question of the lawfulness of compulsory retirement also arose before the ECJ in the Spanish case of *Palacios de la Villa v Cortefiel Servicios SA* (Case C-411/05). It consisted of a challenge to the Spanish law which permits compulsory retirement. At the time of writing, the ECJ had not yet delivered judgment on that case, but the Advocate-General had recommended that the Court find no breach of the age discrimination provisions in the Equal Treatment Framework Directive (2000/78). He based his view upon recital 14 in the preamble to the Directive, which states that the Directive is without prejudice to national provisions laying down retirement ages. He further recommended that, even if the Directive does apply, setting a national retirement age is justified direct age discrimination. The Advocate-General's opinion is not binding on the ECJ, but it is followed in most cases. If it is followed in the Spanish case, that will have clear relevance to the Heyday reference.

Part-time workers

6.70   Discrimination against part-time workers may well constitute indirect sex discrimination, in view of the fact that a greater proportion of part-time workers are women than men. However, the Part-time Workers (Prevention of Less Favourable Treatment) Regulations 2000 (SI 2000/1551) introduced a more direct form of protection for this group of people. As is clear from their title, the Regulations cover "workers" rather than "employees" in the sense of those subject to a contract of employment. The part-time worker has to show that less favourable treatment was given to him than to a comparable full-time worker. The protection is subject to the "pro rata principle". In respect of pay or other benefits, a part-time worker is to receive not less than the proportion that the number of his weekly hours bears to the number of weekly hours of the comparable full-time worker. The sex of the claimant, and of the comparator, are irrelevant. The Regulations deal with less favourable treatment, and are thus concerned, in effect with direct discrimination. There is no prohibition of indirect discrimination, and such a claim would have to be framed within the SDA.

The comparable full-time worker and the claimant must both be:

(a) employed by the same employer under the same type of contract; and

(b) engaged in the same or broadly similar work having regard, where relevant, to whether they have a similar level of qualification, skills and experience.

The leading case in this area is *Matthews v Kent & Medway Fire Authority* [2006] I.R.L.R. 367, in which the House of Lords held that 12,000 part-time retained fire-fighters could claim equality with full-time firefighters (principally in relation to access to the pension fund) because they were doing the same or broadly similar work.

The employer is entitled to put forward a defence of justification on objective grounds to the allegation of direct discrimination. In this respect, there is a similarity to the law relating to age discrimination which, unlike discrimination law generally, allows a defence of justification to direct discrimination. **6.71**

The employer is prohibited from dismissing a part-time worker, or subjecting him to a detriment, for a reason relating to the exercise of his rights under the Regulations. This is broadly equivalent to the prohibition against victimisation found in other discrimination law.

Where a successful claim is brought under the Regulations, the tribunal can award compensation, but there is no award for injury to feelings (in contrast with most other strands of discrimination law).

Fixed-term workers

The Fixed-term Employees (Prevention of Less Favourable Treatment) Regulations 2002 (SI 2002/2034) follow the pattern of the Part-time Workers Regulations, as described in the preceding section. Unlike the latter set of provisions, however, it is fixed-term employees rather than workers, who are protected. The claimant must select a comparable permanent employee who is engaged in "the same or broadly similar work". The employer is prohibited from "less favourable treatment" of the fixed-term employee, but this is subject to a defence of justification. The employee has the right not to be dismissed or subjected to a detriment for asserting his rights. In the event of a successful claim, the tribunal can award compensation, but not for injury to feelings. **6.72**

Peculiar to the Fixed-term Employees Regulations is a right which applies where an employee has been continuously employed under a fixed-term contract for a period of four years or more. If the fixed-term nature of the contract cannot be objectively justified, then the provision which restricts the duration of the contract is of no effect. In other words, the contract becomes a permanent one.

Trade union membership and activities

An employer is generally prohibited from discriminating against trade union members on the grounds of their membership by the Trades Union and Labour Relations (Consolidation) Act 1992. There is a similar prohibition with regard to discrimination against non-members of trade unions. By **6.73** virtue of s.144, it is unlawful to take any action short of dismissal against an employee for the purpose of:

(a) stopping the employee from being a member of a trade union;

(b) stopping an employee from taking part in trade union activities; or

(c) forcing an employee to join a trade union (whether one particular union, or any trade union).

The prohibition is more narrowly cast than that in discrimination law generally. There must be an intention on the part of the employer to discriminate—it is for the purpose of deterring or forcing.

Section 137 makes unlawful the practice of making offers of employment on the basis of trade union membership or non-membership, or willingness to become a trade union member.

As to dismissal, that is automatically unfair where the reason (or principal reason) is actual or proposed membership of, or participation in the activities of a trade union (s.152). An employee who is so dismissed is entitled to claim unfair dismissal even though he does not have the period of continuous employment (one year) normally required to qualify for such a right. Further, he is entitled to interim relief (s.161) in the form of reinstatement or suspension on full pay until the case has been fully heard.

6.74   Various other rights attached to trade union membership are contained within the TULRCA 1992, but are beyond the scope of this work, which concentrates upon individual employment rights.

Equal pay

6.75   The Equal Pay Act 1970 (EPA) aims to remedy a particular form of discrimination—the fact that women overall receive pay which is appreciably lower than men. The law in this area is complex, and because of the procedural and legal difficulties which surround it, few practitioners have experience of handling equal pay cases to trial. What follows is a short summary of the main rules.

The EPA deals with discrimination not only in relation to "pay" in the generally accepted meaning of the word, but also with regard to all other contractual terms, e.g. bonuses, overtime, shift payments, length of service increments, holiday pay and sick pay. Its provisions cover employees, and the term is widely defined to include those under contracts personally to execute any work (in this respect it is similar to the SDA). Whilst the EPA covers contractual terms, non-contractual terms must be dealt with under the provisions of the SDA. It is also open to a man to claim under the EPA, using a woman as a comparator. However, a comparator of the same sex is not permitted, as the purpose of the EPA is to promote equality of contractual terms as between men and women.

It is also worth pointing out that the EPA does not cover discrimination on other unlawful grounds, e.g. race, disability. Any discrepancy in pay which is alleged to be discriminatory on such grounds must be dealt with under the statute in question, e.g. the RRA, DDA.

The fundamental mechanism of the EPA is that every woman's contract **6.76** of employment is deemed to include an equality clause wherever she and a man in the same employment are employed on:

(a) like work;

(b) work rated as equivalent under a job evaluation scheme; or

(c) work of equal value.

The effect is that, if any term in the claimant's contract is less favourable than a term of a similar kind in the contract of her comparator, her term is changed so that it is no less favourable than his. If there is a term in the comparator's contract which is of benefit to him, and which does not appear in the claimant's contract, her contract is taken to include such a term. The equality clause does not operate, however, if the employer can justify the difference between the claimant and her comparator on the basis of a genuine material factor other than the difference of sex. If the equality clause is established by any of these three methods, it can be enforced like any other term of the contract, e.g. by an action for breach of contract, or for unlawful deduction of wages. It should be stressed that the equality clause operates in relation to each individual term in the claimant's contract. The employer cannot defeat the claim by arguing that, taken overall, she is treated as favourably as her comparator. There is no offset of one term against another: *Hayward v Cammell Laird Shipbuilders Ltd* [1988] I.R.L.R. 257, HL.

Same employment. The comparison must be with a man "in the same **6.77** employment". The comparator must be an actual person of the opposite sex, and not a hypothetical comparator (such as would be permissible in a claim under the SDA). In addition, the comparator must be working for the same employer as the claimant, or an associated employer. In addition, they must either

(a) work at the same establishment, or

(b) at an establishment in Great Britain to which terms and conditions apply which are "common" to those at which the claimant works.

Employers are associated if one is a company of which the other has direct or indirect control, or both are companies of which a third person (e.g. a holding company) has control.

For example, assume that Kwiki-Mart stores have a number of branches. At the branch in the north of town, all the counter assistants are women. At the branch in the south of the town, some are men and some are women. A claimant from the northern branch is entitled to select her comparator (who must be male) from the northern branch if the same general terms apply to both branches.

A claimant can select as a comparator someone who was employed in the past, but was no longer employed at the time of the presentation of the claim to the tribunal: *McCarthys Ltd v Smith* [1980] I.R.L.R. 210. In this case, the claimant, who was a stockroom manageress, sought to compare her job with that of her predecessor, who had received higher wages. The CA interpreted the use of the present tense in the statute so as to hold her comparator invalid. The ECJ, however, held that she was entitled, in accordance with Art.141 of the EC Treaty, to compare herself with her predecessor. In *Diocese of Hallam Trustee v Connaughton* [1996] I.R.L.R. 505 the EAT held that the scope of Art.141 also included equal pay claims based upon the use of an immediate successor as a comparator.

6.78 **Like work and work rated as equivalent.** As far as ground (a) in the list in para.6.76 is concerned, jobs will be regarded as "like work" if they are the same or broadly similar in practice. It is the practical, rather than the contractual difference which is relevant. Trivial differences should be ignored, and the time at which the work is done is generally not important.

As to ground (b), jobs will be regarded as "rated as equivalent" if they have been given comparable value by a job evaluation scheme which is analytical and non-discriminatory. On the other hand, if such a scheme has found that the comparator's job is rated as of higher value than that of the claimant, that will block the equal pay claim.

If either ground (a) or ground (b) is established, then the claim should succeed, unless the employer can establish that there is a genuine material factor in which results in the difference between the jobs of claimant and comparator (see below).

6.79 **Work of equal value.** With regard to ground (c) in the above list, the relative value of the jobs done by the claimant and her comparator is usually evaluated by an independent expert appointed by the tribunal. There is provision, however, for the parties to adduce their own expert reports. The evaluation aims to determine the relative values of their jobs by evaluating the demands which each job makes upon the person who does it. The method chosen must be analytical and non-discriminatory. Again, there is a defence open to the employer if the jobs of claimant and comparator are shown to be of equal value—if there is a genuine material factor which results in the difference between the two jobs.

6.80 **Genuine material difference.** There is substantial case law on the question of what constitutes a genuine material factor such as to provide the employer with a defence where the claimant has established one of the grounds (a) to (c) in paras 6.78 and 6.79 above. The following points emerge from consideration of the statute and the leading cases:

- the claim will fail if the employer shows that the difference in pay is genuinely due to a material factor which is not the difference of sex. In the case of grounds (a) and (b) the factor must be a material difference between the claimant's and the comparator's case. In respect of ground (c), it may be such a material difference;

- if the factor relied on by the employer is tainted by sex discrimination, the defence will not succeed;

- if the difference in pay arises from indirect discrimination, the employer must objectively justify it for the defence to succeed: *Enderby v Frenchay Health Authority* [1993] I.R.L.R. 591, ECJ, applying Art.141 of the EC Treaty;

- among the reasons which may be successfully argued as the basis for the defence are skills, experience, length of service, qualifications, market forces and red-circling (e.g. where an employee is downgraded and permitted to retain his previous rate of pay—but the process must not be a means of continuing past discrimination or the defence will fail: *Snoxell v Vauxhall Motors Ltd* [1977] I.R.L.R. 123, EAT).

Procedure in discrimination cases

The procedure in relation to tribunal cases generally (including discrimination cases) is covered in Chapter 13. Similarly, the position with regard to time limits is dealt with in Chapter 14 on that subject. However, there are certain procedural features which are unique to discrimination cases. **6.81**

The first such feature is that there is a questionnaire procedure applicable to discrimination cases. A claimant has the right to serve upon the employer a questionnaire, setting out his version of events, asking the employer to comment on it, and asking specific questions. The employer cannot be compelled to reply, but failure to reply, or a reply which is late or evasive, will be admissible in evidence, and may prove the basis for an inference to be drawn by the tribunal. In addition, the answers to the question may well assist the claimant in assembling his case, e.g. by revealing the position as far as relevant policies and procedures are concerned, or helping to muster statistical evidence.

There are time limits attached to the service of questionnaires. As far as tribunal cases are concerned, the questionnaire must be served within three months of the act complained of (i.e. the alleged act of discrimination) if it is served before the claim has been presented to the tribunal. If the questionnaire is to be served after proceedings have been commenced, then it must be served within 21 days of commencement. Otherwise, the leave of the tribunal is required. The questionnaire in relation to each form of discrimination is contained within the relevant statutory instrument.

Burden of proof. An important procedural issue in discrimination claims is the burden of proof. Claimants are in a difficult position, in that the employer is the one who is in possession of information, and is also best able to provide an explanation in regard to the alleged act of discrimination. The burden of proof is on the claimant, but he is assisted by a provision which has been inserted in each of the pieces of legislation as a result of the Burden of Proof Directive (98/52) and related Directives from the EU. This provision lays down that, where the claimant proves facts **6.82**

from which the tribunal could conclude, in the absence of an adequate explanation, that the employer has committed an unlawful act of discrimination or harassment, then it is for the employer to prove otherwise. It does not appear in the Equal Pay Act 1970.

Important guidance as to the application of the burden of proof provision in cases of sex discrimination was provided by the Court of Appeal in *Igen Ltd v Wong* [2005] I.R.L.R. 258. Although the references in the extract which follows are to sex discrimination, the provisions in the various other strands of discrimination law are identical in all material respects to those in the SDA, and the guidance is equally applicable:

(1) Pursuant to s.63A of the SDA, it is for the claimant who complains of discrimination to prove on the balance of probabilities facts from which the tribunal could conclude, in the absence of an adequate explanation, that the respondent has committed an act of discrimination against the claimant which is unlawful by virtue of s.41 or 42 of Pt II or which by virtue of s.41 or 42 of the SDA to be treated as having been committed against the claimant. These are referred to below as "such facts".

(2) If the claimant does not prove such facts he or she will fail.

(3) It is important to bear in mind in deciding whether the claimant has proved such facts that it is unusual to find direct evidence of sex discrimination. Few employers would be prepared to admit such discrimination, even to themselves. In some cases the discrimination will not be an intention but merely based on the assumption that "he or she would not have fitted in".

(4) In deciding whether the claimant has proved such facts, it is important to remember that the outcome at this stage of the analysis by the tribunal will therefore usually depend on what inferences it is proper to draw from the primary facts found by the tribunal.

(5) It is important to note the word "could" in [the burden of proof provision]. At this stage the tribunal does not have to reach a definitive determination that such facts would lead it to the conclusion that there was an act of unlawful discrimination. At this stage a tribunal is looking at the primary facts before it to sees what inferences of secondary fact could be drawn from them.

(6) In considering what inferences or conclusions can be drawn from the primary facts, the tribunal must assume that there is no adequate explanation for those facts.

(7) These inferences can include, in appropriate cases, any inferences that it is just and equitable to draw in accordance with section 74(2)(b) of the SDA from an evasive or equivocal reply to a questionnaire or any other questions that fall within s.74(2) of the SDA.

(8) Likewise, the tribunal must decide whether any provision of any relevant code of practice is relevant and if so, take it into account in determining, such facts pursuant to s.56A(10) of the SDA. This means that inferences may also be drawn from any failure to comply with any relevant code of practice.

(9) Where the claimant has proved facts from which conclusions could be drawn that the respondent has treated the claimant less favourably on the ground of sex, then the burden of proof moves to the respondent.

(10) It is then for the respondent to prove that he did not commit, or as the case may be, is not to be treated as having committed, that act.

(11) To discharge that burden it is necessary for the respondent to prove, on the balance of probabilities, that the treatment was in no sense whatsoever on the grounds of sex, since "no discrimination whatsoever" is compatible with the Burden of Proof Directive.

(12) That requires a tribunal to assess not merely whether the respondent has proved an explanation for the facts from which such inferences can be drawn, but further that it is adequate to discharge the burden of proof on the balance of probabilities that sex was not a ground for the treatment in question.

(13) Since the facts necessary to prove an explanation would normally be in the possession of the respondent, a tribunal would normally expect cogent evidence to discharge that burden of proof. In particular, the tribunal will need to examine carefully explanations for failure to deal with the questionnaire procedure and/or code of practice.

In *Madarassy v Nomura International plc* [2007] I.R.L.R. 246, the CA reaffirmed the guidance in *Igen v Wong*. Mummery L.J. emphasised that the burden of proof does not shift to the employer simply on the claimant establishing a difference in status (e.g. sex) and a difference in treatment. The words "could conclude" in the relevant statutory provisions must mean that "a reasonable tribunal could properly conclude from the evidence". It is not enough, in other words, that there should just be a possibility of discrimination. Mummery L.J. also looked at the question of what evidence from the employer is relevant at this stage. He concludes that, although the discrimination provisions involve a two-stage analysis of the evidence, they do not exclude the tribunal from considering at the first stage evidence adduced by the respondent employer which disputes or rebuts the claimant's evidence of discrimination e.g. where the respondent produces evidence to show that the allegedly discriminatory acts never happened, or that they did not constitute less favourable treatment. Similarly, in *Appiah v Governing Body of Bishop Douglass Roman Catholic High School* [2007] I.R.L.R. 264, CA, Maurice Kay L.J. stated that a court or tribunal is not required to "assess the evidence of the complainant in isolation, in the way that, for example, a court deals with a submission of no case to answer. That would be absurd in the present context where the consideration is taking place after all the evidence from both sides has been heard."

6.83 **Interim relief.** A claimant for discrimination on the basis of trade union membership or activities may claim interim relief. This is a special procedure which provides for reinstatement pending hearing of the full claim. It is also available to an employee who is dismissed for refusing to join a trade union, and to those dismissed for certain other specified reasons—making a protected disclosure (whistle-blowing), health and safety activities and trustees of occupational pension schemes. Application for interim relief must be made to the tribunal within seven days of dismissal, supported by a certificate signed by an official of the employee's union (where applicable) who has been authorised for the purpose, and stating the reasons why interim relief is available. The tribunal is charged with hearing the application as soon as possible, and must decide whether it is "likely" that the tribunal will, at the full merits hearing, find that the claimant has been unfairly dismissed for an inadmissible reason. If so, it should order reinstatement or re-engagement pending the final decision. In order to secure interim relief, the claimant's prospects of success in the eventual hearing should be "pretty good": *Taplin v C Shippam Ltd* [1978] I.R.L.R. 450.

CHAPTER SEVEN

REMEDIES FOR DISCRIMINATION

The remedies for discrimination are calculated on a different basis from   **7.01**
those for unfair dismissal. Broadly speaking, the principles are similar for
each of the statutory regimes dealing with discrimination, so that the
statutory formula in respect of sex discrimination is similar to that which
appears throughout the various strands of discrimination law. Section 65 of
the Sex Discrimination Act ("SDA") 1975 states:

> "65(1) Where an employment tribunal finds that a complaint presented to it. . .
> is well-founded the tribunal shall make such of the following as it considers just
> and equitable—
>
> (a) an order declaring the rights of the complainant and the respondent in
>   relation to the act to which the complain relates;
> (b) an order requiring the respondent to pay to the complainant compensa-
>   tion of an amount corresponding to any damages he could have been
>   ordered by a county court or by a sheriff court [in Scotland] to pay to the
>   complainant if the complaint had fallen to be dealt with under section 66;
> (c) a recommendation that the respondent take within a specified period
>   action appearing to the tribunal to be practicable for the purpose of
>   obviating or reducing the adverse effect on the complainant of any act of
>   discrimination to which the complaint relates."

Section 66(4) of the SDA states that:

> "For the avoidance of doubt it is hereby declared that damages in respect of an
> unlawful act of discrimination or harassment may include compensation for
> injury to feelings, whether or not they include compensation under any other
> head."

Equivalent provisions are to be found in the Race Relations Act
("RRA") 1976, s.56; the Disability Discrimination Act ("DDA") 1995, s.8;
the Employment Equality (Religion or Belief) Regulations 2003, reg.30; the
Employment Equality (Sexual Orientation) Regulations 2003, reg.30; and
the Employment Equality (Age) Regulations 2003, reg.38.

The "declaration" referred to in s.65(1)(a) of the SDA is as to the rights   **7.02**
of the parties. It usually consists of the tribunal's judgement that an
unlawful act of discrimination or harassment has been committed by the
respondent against the claimant.

Recommendation

7.03   The terms of SDA, s.65(1)(c) (and similar provisions in all the other anti-discrimination legislation) give the tribunal the power to make a recommendation that the respondent take action within a specified period. This power is not much used in practice. Any recommendation must be "practicable for the purpose of obviating or reducing the adverse effect on the complainant of any act of discrimination to which the complaint relates". Its effect is therefore focussed upon cases where employment continues. There are several cases which have indicated that the power is restricted by the statutory terms in which it is set out. For example, it was held in *Bayoomi v British Railways Board* [1981] I.R.L.R. 431 that no general recommendation could be made affecting the employer's recruitment policies, since the recommendation had to be restricted to matters which could obviate or reduce the adverse effect on the claimant.

Compensation

7.04   This is the central core of the remedies which are awarded to the claimant. Originally, there was a limit to the amount which could be awarded as compensation for discrimination, in line with that for unfair dismissal claims. That limit was removed in 1993 for sex discrimination, and in 1994 for race discrimination. When the remaining anti-discrimination legislation was introduced, no limits were laid down. As can be seen from the table in para.7.05, the awards for compensation for discrimination are substantially higher than those for unfair dismissal.

7.05 **Average levels of compensations awarded 2005–6**
(source: Employment Tribunals Service—Annual Report)

Type of case	Average award
Unfair dismissal	£8,679
Race discrimination	£30,361
Sex discrimination	£10,807
Disability Discrimination	£19,360

7.06   The measure of compensation is that which could be ordered in the ordinary courts. It is compensation for the statutory tort of discrimination, and it is important that tortious principles should be applied in determining compensation, rather than those applicable to, for example, unfair dismissal.
Hence:

- Reinstatement or re-engagement are not within the remit of the tribunal in a discrimination case (although, if a dismissal is unfair as well as discriminatory, reinstatement or re-engagement would be among the remedies which the tribunal must consider).

- There is no reduction for contributory fault.

- There is no *Polkey* reduction as such (see para.10.17 for the operation of such a reduction in the unfair dismissal context). The tribunal must consider, however, the chances of the claimant's loss continuing, just as it would have to do in respect of any other tort.

Financial loss

The principle behind compensation is to ask what would have happened **7.07** if it had not been for the discriminatory act(s). The claimant should then be put in the same position as they would have been, but for the unlawful act(s). Hence in a case where servicewomen were dismissed on grounds of pregnancy, the tribunal had to calculate the sum they would have earned had they remained in employment. Then it had to deduct the amount they earned (or should have earned) elsewhere. Finally, it had to discount the net loss by a percentage to reflect the chance that they might have left the job in any event: *Ministry of Defence v Wheeler* [1998] I.R.L.R. 23, CA.

The claimant is entitled to be compensated for the loss which arises naturally and directly from the wrong. Unlike the position in the tort of negligence, it is not necessary for the claimant to show that the particular type of loss was reasonably foreseeable: *Essa v Laing* [2004] I.R.L.R. 313, CA.

The employee is obliged to mitigate his loss. The burden of proving any failure to mitigate is on the party asserting it. Earnings which should have been earned had it not been for a failure to mitigate should be deducted before, rather than after, the deduction for a percentage chance that the employee might have left the job. In other words, one should calculate the loss first, and then go on to make deductions for contingent events: *Ministry of Defence v Hunt* [1996] I.R.L.R. 139, EAT. The undertaking of a period of training need not indicate a failure to mitigate. It depends upon what is reasonable in the circumstances: *ITCS (UK) Ltd v Tchoula* [2000] I.R.L.R. 643. In *Tchoula*, the claimant had been dismissed from his job as a security officer. He retrained in computers because he could not pursue work in security. To have done so, he would need a clean record, and his dismissal meant that his record was marred. It was not, therefore, appropriate to find that he had failed to mitigate his loss.

State benefits should be deducted from the amount awarded for loss. The **7.08** position is different from unfair dismissal, where the Recoupment Regulations apply (see paras 10.27 to 10.29 for an account of the recoupment process): *Constable of West Yorkshire Police v Vento (No.2)* [2002] I.R.L.R. 177.

Where an employee receives compensation for future loss, he has the benefit of receiving it immediately, rather than waiting to receive it in instalments. Consequently (where the compensation is for loss over a substantial period e.g. several years) it is right to make a deduction for "accelerated receipt": *Brentwood Bros (Manchester) Ltd v Shepherd* [2003] I.C.R. 1000.

Psychiatric injury

7.09   This is a different concept from injury to feelings. The Tribunal has
power to award both. As already indicated, since the award is based on the
statutory tort of discrimination, rather than common law tort of negligence,
the injury does not need to have been reasonably foreseeable. What is
necessary is causation. Provided that causation is established, a tribunal
may award compensation for personal injuries suffered, including psychiatric injury: *Sheriff v Klyne Tugs (Lowestoft) Ltd* [1999] I.R.L.R. 481.

However, it is not always easy to separate psychiatric injury from injury
to feelings, and care must be taken to avoid the risk of double compensation. The existence and extent of psychiatric injury are matters of fact to be
determined by the Tribunal, which may (not must) be assisted by psychiatric evidence: *HM Prison Service v Salmon* [2001] I.R.L.R. 425, EAT. In
practice, the Tribunal will usually welcome medical evidence where the
alleged psychiatric injury is disputed and substantial, especially where issues
of causation are at stake.

Injury to feelings

7.10   The principles are set out in *Armitage v Johnson* [1997] I.R.L.R. 162,
EAT, as follows:

- the award is to be compensatory, not punitive. It should not be
  inflated by feelings of indignation at the wrongdoer's conduct;

- awards should not be so low as to diminish respect for the anti-
  discrimination legislation. Nor should they be so excessive as to be
  seen as a way to untaxed riches;

- awards should bear some broad general similarity to the whole
  range of awards in personal injury cases (rather than any particular type of such award);

- tribunals should remind themselves of the value in everyday life of
  the sum which they have in mind e.g. by reference to purchasing
  power, or earnings.

The leading case on the levels which should be awarded under this head
is *Vento v Chief Constable of West Yorkshire Police (No.2)* [2003] I.R.L.R.
102, CA, which set out three bands for compensation for injury to feelings
(distinct from psychiatric injury), as follows:

(a) The top band between £15,000 and £25,000 to be awarded in the
    most serious cases e.g. where there has been a lengthy campaign
    of sexual, etc. harassment. It was stated that only in the most
    exceptional case should an award of compensation for injury to
    feelings exceed £25,000;

(b) The middle band of £5,000–£15,000 should be used for serious
    cases other than those in the top band;

(c) Awards of between £500 and £5,000 are appropriate for less serious cases, such as where the act of discrimination is an isolated or one off occurrence. Awards lower than this should generally be avoided.

It is submitted that the figures set out in *Vento* should be revised in order to take account of inflation since the case was decided in 2003.

In *Voith Turbo Ltd v Stowe* [2005] I.R.L.R. 228, the EAT upheld a **7.11** tribunal which had assessed compensation for injury to feelings in the middle band of *Vento* where the act of racial discrimination was dismissal. H.H. Judge McMullen Q.C. stated that dismissal on grounds of race discrimination is a very serious incident, and cannot be described as one-off or isolated.

In assessing injury to feelings, the willingness of the employer to admit that it has acted in breach of the law may help to reduce the hurt felt by sparing the claimant from the indignity and further hurt of rehearsing the nature of her treatment: *Orlando v Didcot Power Station Sports and Social Club* [1996] I.R.L.R. 262, EAT.

Aggravated damages

These are awarded where the respondent behaved in a high-handed, **7.12** malicious, insulting or oppressive manner in committing the act of discrimination: *Alexander v Home Office* [1988] I.C.R. 685. It may also cover cases where an employer has failed to investigate a complaint of discrimination, or used his power to inflict further distress, or acted insensitively and treated a serious matter as trivial. Conduct in the course of litigation (including unsatisfactory answers to a statutory questionnaire under SDA, s.74 or RRA, s.65) may be taken into account in deciding whether to make an award of aggravated damages: *City of Bradford Metropolitan Council v Arora* [1989] I.R.L.R. 442, EAT.

After several cases which gave conflicting guidance on the matter, it would seem that aggravated damages should not be aggregated with, or treated as part of the damages for injury to feelings: *Scott v Commissioners of Inland Revenue* [2004] I.R.L.R. 713, CA.

Aggravated damages should be distinguished from exemplary damages which are punitive in nature and cannot be awarded for discrimination, in view of the rule that exemplary damages are limited to those torts for which they had been awarded prior to the decision of the House of Lords in *Rookes v Barnard* [1964] A.C. 1129: *Deane v London Borough of Ealing* [1993] I.R.L.R. 209, EAT.

Interest

The rules are different from those which generally apply in the employ- **7.13** ment tribunals. With respect to a tribunal award for unfair dismissal or breach of contract, for example, interest only begins to accumulate six weeks after the judgment is sent to the parties. In discrimination cases, by contrast, the award itself normally includes an element of interest relating to the period between the unlawful act and the judgment.

The parties may agree the amount. Any calculation by the Tribunal is governed by the Employment Tribunals (Interest on Awards in Discrimination Cases) Regulations 1996. These state that, for injury to feelings, interest should be awarded for the period starting with the date of the act of discrimination, and ending on the day on which the amount of interest is calculated. For the other elements of the award (e.g. present financial loss), interest is calculated from the date at the mid-point between the act of discrimination and the date of calculation. Clearly, no interest can be awarded on future loss. The rate of interest is the rate for the Special Investment Account (currently 6 per cent).

7.14   Compensation for indirect discrimination. No compensation can be awarded for indirect discrimination (other than in cases of sex discrimination in employment) unless the employer intended the discrimination to occur. The relevant point at which the intention is to be gauged is when the provision, criterion, practice, etc. is applied, rather than the time at which it was introduced. The intention to apply the provision, etc. together with knowledge of its impact upon the claimant as a member of the disadvantaged group, is sufficient to establish intention: *London Underground v Edwards* [1995] I.R.L.R. 355, EAT. Intention can be inferred from the knowledge of the consequences: *JH Walker Ltd v Hussain* [1996] I.R.L.R. 1. The position is different for indirect sex discrimination in employment, as a result of the Sex Discrimination and Equal Pay (Miscellaneous Amendments) Regulations 1996. In those circumstances, the Tribunal can award compensation if it is just and equitable to do so after it has made any recommendations.

7.15   Joint and several awards. In discrimination cases, the claimant may bring a claim not only against the employer, but also against an individual employee who is alleged to have been responsible for the act of discrimination or harassment in question. Where the claimant is successful against both the employer and the individual, the question arises: against whom should compensation be awarded? From the claimant's point of view, it will usually be the employer who is best able to satisfy judgment and ensure that the compensation is paid. It would therefore not be in the claimant's interest for the tribunal to make the major part of the award payable by the individual. The usual practice, therefore, is to make the bulk of the award payable by the employer, with a relatively small additional amount to be paid by the individual respondent.

7.16   *Example.   C has won her claim for sexual harassment against R Ltd (her employer) and H (the person who harassed her). The tribunal assesses the compensation to be paid as £50,000 in total, and decides that R Ltd must pay £47,500 and H must pay £2,500.*

There is an alternative way of proceeding, which is that the tribunal can decide that the respondents are to be jointly and severally liable for the payment of the award. In effect, this means that the claimant can decide which of the respondents to proceed against, and in what sum (up to a limit of the total award) in respect of each respondent.

Example.   In the case described above, the tribunal awards £50,000 and   **7.17**
states that the respondents are jointly and severally liable to pay it. C can then
decide, for example, whether to pursue H for the whole amount, or R Ltd for
the whole amount, or to seek proportions making up the total of £50,000 from
each.

It was held in *Way v Crouch* [2005] I.R.L.R. 603 that it is not generally appropriate for a tribunal to make a joint and several award (i.e. 100 per cent against each respondent). It should apportion liability between employer and the individual employee who has discriminated. Apportionment should be based upon the responsibility of each tortfeasor—taking into account their relative culpability and the extent to which they caused the damage. If the tribunal does make a joint and several award, it should make clear its reasons for doing so.

Chapter Eight

FAMILY FRIENDLY RIGHTS

This chapter deals with a number of different rights which relate to **8.01** maternity, paternity, or the family generally. Although the term is not an ideal one, they are frequently referred to as "family friendly rights", and as that seems to be the only umbrella description which is appropriate, it has been adopted as the title for this chapter.

One general point needs to be made. The rights which are described are statutory—sometimes owing their shape to the European Union, sometimes being of domestic origin. Frequently, employers and employees have contractual arrangements which are more favourable to their employees in respect of, for example, maternity leave. If that is the case, the general position is that the statute creates a floor, not a ceiling. In other words, the employee is entitled to whichever is the better of the statutory and contractual rights.

Maternity rights

The main benefits in employment law which attach to pregnancy are: **8.02**

(a) ordinary maternity leave (ERA 1996, s.71);

(b) compulsory maternity leave (ERA, s.72);

(c) additional maternity leave (ERA, s.73);

(d) statutory maternity pay (Social Security Contributions and Benefits Act 1992, ss.164–166);

(e) ante-natal care (ERA, s.55); and

(f) suspension on full-pay because of maternity (ERA, s.66).

Ordinary maternity leave

All pregnant employees are entitled to 26 weeks of ordinary maternity **8.03** leave, no matter how short their length of service. In order to take up her entitlement, the employee must notify her employer no later than the fifteenth week before the expected week of confinement ("EWC") or as soon as is reasonably practicable. The notification must cover the fact that she is pregnant, identify the EWC (providing a medical certificate if the employer requests one), and state when she wishes to start her maternity leave. The employer is then obliged to respond within 28 days, and inform her of when the leave will end. As to when the employee can start her ordinary maternity leave, she has some discretion, but it cannot start before the eleventh week preceding the EWC, unless the baby is born before that, in which case the leave starts immediately.

During the period of ordinary maternity leave, her contract of employment continues in existence. She is entitled to all the benefits which she would have received if she had not been absent, including non-contractual benefits, with the exception of remuneration (which is defined as "sums payable to the employee by way of wages or salary"). So, if she is entitled to private use of a company car when working, and private medical insurance, she must remain in receipt of those benefits when on leave, even if they are stated to be discretionary and not part of her contract. As far as remuneration is concerned, the position is covered by statutory maternity pay (see para.8.08). For her part, she continues to be bound by the obligations arising from her contract, e g those arising from the mutual duty of trust and confidence, and any duty to keep information confidential. She will not, of course, be bound by the normal contractual obligation to work, since that would be inconsistent with the right to maternity leave.

As a result of amendments introduced by the Work and Families Act 2006, an employee can do up to 10 days work during the maternity leave period without losing statutory pay for the week in question, or bringing the leave to an end. These are termed "keeping in touch" days. They do not have the effect of extending the maternity leave period.

8.04   If the employee wishes to return to work at the end of her period of ordinary maternity leave, she can do so without serving notice upon the employer. However, if she wishes to return before that date, she must give at least eight weeks notice—increased by the Work and Families Act 2006 ("WFA 2006") from 28 days. Any failure to do so entitles the employer to postpone her leave so that he, in effect, acquires the requisite notice, but he cannot postpone to a date beyond the end of the period of ordinary maternity leave.

On her return to work the employee returns to the same job. Her seniority, pension rights and other terms and conditions are to be the same as they would have been if she had not been on leave. The period of ordinary maternity leave will count towards continuity of employment.

Compulsory maternity leave

8.05   During the two week period after the date when the child is born, the mother is not allowed to work for reasons of health and safety, and the employer must not allow her to do so (ERA 1996, s.72).

Additional maternity leave

8.06   After the expiry of ordinary maternity leave, the employee is entitled to additional maternity leave. Prior to the WFA 2006, this right was restricted to those who had 26 weeks or more of service with the employer. The position now is that all women whose EWC begins on or after April 1, 2007 are entitled to 26 weeks additional maternity leave as well as their ordinary maternity leave.

On expiry of the period of additional maternity leave, the employee is entitled to return to her old job, or, if it is not reasonably practicable for the employer to permit her to do so, to "another job which is suitable for her and appropriate for her to do in the circumstances" (MPLR, reg.18). In any event, on return to work, she is to have the same seniority, pension and other similar rights as she had on commencing the period of additional maternity leave. This period, unlike the ordinary maternity leave period, does not count towards continuity of service in relation to contractual rights (MPLR, reg.18A). It does, however, count as continuous employment for statutory purposes e.g. in acquiring the right not to be unfairly dismissed (ERA, s.212).

If the employee returns at the end of the period of additional maternity **8.07** leave, there is no legal obligation to give the employer notice of her intention. However, if she returns early, she must give eight weeks notice, under similar conditions to that required for ordinary maternity leave (see para.8.04).

Maternity pay

An employee who is on ordinary maternity leave is entitled to maternity **8.08** pay. This is paid by the employer, who is able to reclaim from the government (Social Security Contributions and Benefits Act 1992, s.167). The rate at which it is to be paid is:

(a) an earnings-related rate of 90 per cent of normal weekly earnings for six weeks; and

(b) thereafter, at whichever is the less of the earnings-related rate and the statutory maximum of £108.85 (amended in April each year).

The WFA 2006 has extended the period of maternity pay from the period of 26 weeks set out above. Initially, this will be to 39 weeks for women whose EWC is after April 1, 2007. At a date yet to be announced, the government will extend the period further, up to a maximum of 52 weeks. When that happens, the employee will be paid for both the ordinary and additional maternity leave periods.

Ante-natal care

A pregnant employee is entitled to paid time off for any ante-natal **8.09** appointments which she is medically advised to attend, and may not be unreasonably refused leave to attend them. There is no qualifying period for this right.

Suspension on maternity grounds

Where a woman is suspended from work on maternity grounds, she is **8.10** entitled to certain rights. These rights come into play if she is suspended from work:

(a) because she is pregnant, has recently given birth, or is breastfeeding a child; and

(b) the suspension results from a requirement imposed by or under any statutory requirement, or Code of Practice issued under the Health and Safety at Work Act 1974.

She then has a right to be offered any suitable alternative employment which is available, on terms and conditions not less favourable than those applicable to her usual job (ERA, s.67). If there is no such work available, then she is entitled to be paid remuneration by her employer while she is suspended (ERA, s.68).

Paternity leave

8.11   This area is governed by ss.80A to D of the ERA 1996, and the Paternity and Adoption Leave Regulations 2002 ("PALR"). An employee is eligible for paternity leave if he:

(a) was continuously employed for 26 weeks ending with the 15th week before the EWC;

(b) has, or expects to have, responsibility for the upbringing of the child; and

(c) is the father of the child or the partner (of either sex) of the child's mother or adopter (on this basis, a woman may claim an entitlement to paternity leave).

The right is to either one or two weeks of paid paternity leave (and not occasional days). The employee must give notice of his intention to take paternity leave at least 14 weeks before the EWC or as soon as is reasonably practicable. There are limits on when the leave can be taken e.g. it must be completed within eight weeks of the actual date of birth of the child or the EWC. The employee has the same terms and conditions of employment as those applicable to a woman on ordinary maternity leave, and is entitled to return on terms and conditions no less favourable than they would have been if he had not been absent. The rate of statutory paternity pay is the same as that for the latter period of ordinary maternity pay (see para.8.08).

The WFA 2006 has laid down a new right for those eligible for paternity leave to be absent from work for a maximum of 26 weeks to care for a child. This will be known as additional paternity leave, and it will have to be taken before the child's first birthday. At the time of writing, details had not been announced, although the right in question is contained within the WFA.

Adoption leave

8.12   This is dealt with in ss.75A–D of the ERA, and the PALR 2002. It is paid leave for a period of 26 weeks on conditions which reflect closely those for maternity leave. There are certain conditions to establish eligibility:

(a) the employee must have been employed for at least 26 weeks at the end of the week in which she is notified of being matched for adoption;

(b) the employee must be the child's adopter, i.e. the person who has been matched with the child for adoption. Where two people have been jointly matched, they must decide who is the adopter for the purposes of adoption leave. The other person may then be eligible for paternity leave;

(c) the employee must have notified the adoption agency that he agrees to adopt the child, and the date of placement;

(d) the employee must notify the employer of the date when the child is expected to be placed, and the date when he will start his adoption leave.

Any employee who is entitled, as a result of fulfilling these conditions, to ordinary adoption leave, will qualify also for additional adoption leave of a further 26 weeks.

During the period of adoption leave, the rules relating to terms and conditions of employment and the right to return to work are similar to those which apply to ordinary or additional maternity leave. Statutory adoption pay is payable at the same rate as that applicable to the latter portion of statutory maternity pay (see para.8.08). Where the placement takes place on or after April 1, 2007, statutory adoption pay will be paid for a total of 39 weeks, and the government has announced its intention to extend that to 52 weeks.

Parental leave

This is a right which originates in the European Parental Leave Directive **8.13** (96/34). The details are to be found in the Maternity and Parental Leave, etc. Regulations 1999 ("MPLR"). It is a right to unpaid time off for both parents. An employee is eligible to take the leave if he is the parent of a child under five years old, for whom he has responsibility, provided that he has one year's continuous employment with the employer. In the case of a disabled child, the child must be under 18, rather than under five.

Each parent may take up to 13 weeks unpaid leave in respect of each child. In the case of a disabled child, the allowance is increased to 18 weeks. The leave cannot be taken in odd days (except in the case of a disabled child—see Sch.2, para.7 for the details), but must be in blocks of one week: *South Central Trains Ltd v Rodway* [2004] I.R.L.R. 777, EAT. An employer who refuses to allow an employee to take one day's leave is therefore entitled to do so. Since the leave is unpaid, the necessity to take it in chunks of a week at a time may mean that it is not always be an attractive option. There is a maximum of four weeks leave per child in any one year.

Notice of the start of leave must be given at least 21 days in advance, and it should specify when the leave is to end. There are provisions for the employer to postpone the leave because of disruption to the business in certain circumstances (see Sch.2 of the MPLR for details). Refusal or unreasonable postponement of parental leave can be grounds for a claim to the employment tribunal (s.80(1) ERA).

8.14   When the employee returns to work after a period of four weeks or less parental leave, he is entitled to return to the same job. If leave is for a period of more than four weeks, or it is added on to the end of a period of additional maternity leave, the right to return is the same as it is after additional maternity leave (see para.8.06). The right to return is generally to return terms and conditions not less favourable than those which would have been applicable if the employee had not been absent on parental leave. However, where an employee returns from a period of parental leave taken immediately after additional maternity leave, the right is to return to the terms and conditions which preceded her period of additional maternity leave.

8.15   On return from parental leave, an employee must be treated as though she had never been absent for the purpose of calculating seniority, pension and similar rights. This mirrors the position on return from ordinary maternity leave, but is different from that after return from additional maternity leave.

Leave to care for dependants

8.16   There is a right to a reasonable amount of unpaid leave to make arrangements for the care of dependants. The right (like that to parental leave) originates from the European Parental Leave Directive 96/34. It has been implemented in ss.57A and 57B of the ERA.

Section 57A(3) defines an employee's dependants as:

(a) a spouse or civil partner;

(b) a child;

(c) a parent;

(d) a person who lives in the same household as him, provided that that person is not his employee, tenant, lodger or boarder.

Section 57A(1) sets out the circumstances in which the employee is entitled to take a reasonable amount of time off during working hours. It includes those cases where it is necessary to take action which is necessary:

(a) to provide assistance where a dependant falls ill, gives birth or is injured or assaulted;

(b) to make arrangements for the provision of care for a dependant who is ill or injured;

(c) in consequence of the death of the dependant;

(d) because of the unexpected disruption or termination of arrangements for the care of a dependant; or

(e) to deal with an incident which involves a child of the employee
and which occurs unexpectedly at school.

With regard to (a) or (b), "dependant" is to include anyone who reasonably
relies on the employee for assistance when they fall ill or are injured or
assaulted, or to make arrangements for care when ill or injured. With
regard to (d), "dependant" is to be interpreted to include anyone who
reasonably relies on the employee to arrange care if ill or injured. (see
s.57A(4) and (5) of the ERA). It might therefore cover an elderly
neighbour who falls and breaks a leg, or an uncle who falls ill, and whose
nearest relative is the employee.

The employee must tell the employer as soon as reasonably practicable,   **8.17**
and (save where he is unable to do so before he returns to work) how long
he expects to be absent. If the employer unreasonably refuses to permit him
to take unpaid leave, then the employee is entitled to present a claim to the
employment tribunal (ERA, s.57B). There is no limit to the amount of time
off, provided that it is reasonable. If the employee is dismissed for taking
time off within the ambit of these provisions, the dismissal will be
automatically unfair (s.99, ERA—see Chapter 9 for unfair dismissal).

In *Qua v John Ford Morrison Solicitors* [2003] I.R.L.R. 184, EAT, Ms
Qua was a single mother whose son had medical problems. She was absent
from work for 17 days during the ten months that she worked as a legal
secretary for the respondent solicitors before she was dismissed. She
claimed that her dismissal was automatically unfair under s.99 of the ERA,
because she had been dismissed for taking time off for a dependant under
s.57A. The tribunal found that she had failed to tell her employer for how
long she had expected to be absent, and hence that she did not have the
protection of s.57A and s.99, so that she was not automatically unfairly
dismissed. The EAT found that the tribunal had erred in finding that she
had not complied with the requirements of s.57A. In particular, it was
wrong to suggest that there was a duty to report to the employer "on a daily
basis". The duty was to tell the employer about the reason for her absence
and, save where she us unable to do so before she returns to work, how
long she expects to be absent. There was no continuing duty on an
employee to update the employer on her situation. Further, the tribunal
had wrongly directed themselves that the disruption to the employer's
business by the employee's time off was relevant to the question of whether
the amount of time off was reasonable. The EAT stressed that the right was
essentially a right to take time off to deal with the unexpected. The
operational needs of the employer could not be relevant to the amount of
time an employee needed to deal with the kind of emergency specified in
the legislation.

Example.   C's child falls ill with chickenpox. It is an emergency, and she   **8.18**
needs to take steps to arrange for his care. She should inform her employer as
soon as possible of the reason for her absence and (if she is able to do so) how
long it is likely to be. However, the period of absence would not normally be

such as to enable C herself to take care of the child. It is rather to give her a chance to deal with the immediate care of the child, to visit the doctor and to make longer-term care arrangements.

Flexible working

8.19   From April 2003, ss.80F to 80I of the ERA have given employees the right to ask the employer for a different work pattern in order to care for a young or disabled child. The change in terms and conditions may relate to:

(a) hours of work;

(b) times of work;

(c) place of work, as between the employee's home and the employer's place of business.

There are criteria for eligibility:

(a) the employee must have 26 weeks continuous service;

(b) the child must be aged under 6 (18 if disabled);

(c) the employee must be the mother, father, adoptive parent, guardian of foster parent of the child, or be the spouse or partner of such a person;

(d) the employee must have, or expect to have, responsibility for the child's upbringing;

(e) the purpose of the application must be to look after the child; and

(f) the employee must not have another application in the preceding 12 months.

With effect from April 6, 2007, the right to request flexible working was extended by the WFA 2006 to employees with caring responsibilities for adults. The Flexible Working (Eligibility, Complaints and Remedies) (Amendment) Regulations 2006 (SI 2006/3314) cover any employee who is, or expects to be, caring for an adult who:

• is married to, or is the partner or civil partner of the employee; or

• is a near relative of the employee (parent, parent-in-law, son or daughter-in-law adult child, adopted adult child, sibling (including in-laws), uncles, aunts, grandparents and step-relatives); or

• does not fall into either of the above categories, but lives at the same address as the employee.

The request must be in writing and dated, state whether a previous application has been made and when, and specify what change in working pattern is requested. It should also state when the change should come into effect, explain what effect the employee thinks it will have on the employer (if any) and how that effect might be dealt with. It should explain how the employee meets the conditions with regard to relationship to the child (s.80F(2) of the ERA, and the Flexible Working (Eligibility, Complaints and Remedies) Regulations 2002, reg.4).

Once the application is received, there is a statutory procedure set out in **8.20** the Flexible Working (Procedural Requirements) Regulations 2002. In summary:

(a) within 28 days of receipt of the application, the employer must arrange a meeting with the employee to discuss it;

(b) a meeting must be held, and the employee has a right to be accompanied by a colleague;

(c) within 14 days of the meeting, the employer must give the employee written notice of his decision;

(d) if the request is accepted, the written notice should be dated and state the variation agreed and the date it is to take effect;

(e) if the request is rejected, the employer must specify which of the permitted grounds for refusal apply (see below) and inform the employee of the right to appeal;

(f) within 14 days, the employee can appeal against the decision setting out the grounds in writing and dated;

(g) within 14 days, the employer must either uphold the appeal or meet the employee to discuss it (again, the employee has the right to be accompanied by a colleague); and

(h) within 14 days of the appeal meeting, the employer must notify the employee of the result of the appeal. If it is upheld, the notice must state the contractual variation agreed to, and the effective date. If it is rejected, the grounds for rejection and the reasons why they apply must be stated.

There are certain grounds set out in s.80G(1)(b) as being the only ones on which the employer can refuse the application for flexible working:

(i) the burden of additional costs;

(ii) detrimental effect on ability to meet customer demand;

(iii) inability to re-organise work among existing staff;

(iv) inability to recruit additional staff;

(v) detrimental impact on quality;

(vi) detrimental impact on performance;

(vii) insufficiency of work during the periods the employee proposes to work; and

(viii) planned structural changes.

The employee is entitled, in the event of a refusal by the employer to grant his application, to bring a claim to the employment tribunal under s.80H on the grounds that the employer:

(a) has failed to carry out the correct procedure;

(b) did not reject the application on one of the grounds (i) to (viii) above; or

(c) made his decision based upon incorrect facts.

If the employer is successful, the tribunal can award up to eight weeks pay, capped at the statutory maximum (£310 with effect from February 1, 2007).

Protection against dismissal

8.21   The exercise of the rights detailed in this chapter is subject to protection, and generally speaking, an employer who dismisses an employee for their exercise will be held to have dismissed her unfairly.

Thus, dismissal for reasons connected with any of the following will be automatically unfair:

- pregnancy;
- giving birth to a child;
- the fact that the employee is under maternity suspension;
- the fact that she took or sought to take ordinary or additional maternity leave;
- a failure to return after ordinary or additional maternity leave where the employer failed to give her notice of the date on which it ended and she reasonably believed that it had not ended;
- a failure to return after maternity leave when the employer gave notice of less than 28 days notice of the leave ending, and it was not reasonably practicable for her to return on that date;
- selection for redundancy for any of the above reasons.

If the tribunal finds that the reason for the dismissal is one of those in the list above, then it will be automatically unfair, and there is no need to consider whether the employer acted reasonably or unreasonably in all the circumstances. Further, the employee does not need to have the usual qualifying period of one year for unfair dismissal (see s.99 of the ERA and MPLR 1999, reg.20).

Where an employee is subjected to a detriment for one of these prohibited reasons, she will be entitled to claim compensation for the detriment from an employment tribunal (ERA, s.47C).

Similar protection is extended to those who take or seek: **8.22**

- paternity leave

- parental leave

- adoption leave

- dependant care leave

- flexible working

in accordance with the rights and procedures detailed above. If dismissed for a connected reason, they will be regarded as automatically unfairly dismissed.

If subjected to a detriment for a connected reason, they will be entitled to claim for compensation (see ss.47E, 99 and 104C of the ERA; PALR 2002, regs 28 and 29; MPLR 1999, regs 19 and 20).

CHAPTER NINE

UNFAIR DISMISSAL

The concept of unfair dismissal is central to employment law in Great **9.01**
Britain, and arguably constitutes the most important of the employment
protection rights conferred by statute. It is a creature of statute, and was
unknown to our law before its introduction in the Industrial Relations Act
1971.

Wrongful dismissal and unfair dismissal

It is commonly confused with wrongful dismissal, yet the two are quite **9.02**
different—sharing only the necessary foundation that the employee must
have been dismissed, and the prospect of a claim in the employment
tribunal by the aggrieved employee. Wrongful dismissal is discussed in
more detail in Chapter 3, but it is essentially a dismissal which is contrary to
contract, and its legal roots lie in the common law. The remedy is usually
limited to payment for the notice period. It can be pursued either in the
employment tribunal or in the courts. Unfair dismissal is dismissal contrary
to statute—the primary legislative source being the Employment Rights Act
("ERA") 1996. A claim for unfair dismissal must be taken to an employment tribunal. The remedy is, potentially, the reinstatement of the
employee or compensation for the financial loss which flows from the
dismissal. Unfair dismissal is, therefore, usually a much more substantial
right for the employee, and the consequences for the employer of dismissing unfairly are usually much more serious than those which attend a
wrongful dismissal.

It follows from the distinction between unfair and wrongful dismissal that
a dismissal may be:

  (a) wrongful but not unfair;

  (b) unfair but not wrongful;

  (c) unfair *and* wrongful;

  (d) lawful, in the sense that it is neither unfair nor wrongful.

The issues in an unfair dismissal claim

The right not to be unfairly dismissed is set out in general terms in the **9.03**
ERA 1996, s.94: "(1) An employee has the right not to be unfairly
dismissed by his employer."

This general right is, however, subject to various qualifications and exclusions. Further, the question whether the employee has in fact been unfairly dismissed is one which has to be determined according to the statutory tests, as opposed to a commonsense notion of "fairness" (which would in any event be suspect because of the subjective nature of "fairness").

When a tribunal deals with a claim for unfair dismissal, it will have to deal with the following issues:

(1) Does the claimant qualify for the right not to be unfairly dismissed? (see paras 9.4–9.16)

(2) Was the claimant dismissed? (see paras 9.17–9.29)

(3) Did the employer comply with the statutory Dismissal and Disciplinary Procedure (DDP)? (see paras 9.30–9.39)

(4) What was the reason for dismissal, and was it one of the potentially fair reasons laid down by statute? (see paras 9.40–9.55)

(5) Did the employer act reasonably or unreasonably in deciding to dismiss? (see paras 9.55–9.81)

(6) If the answers to the above questions lead to the conclusion that the claim succeeds, what remedy is the claimant entitled to (see Chapter 10)?

Questions (3) to (6) are set out in flowchart form below.

Unfair dismissal

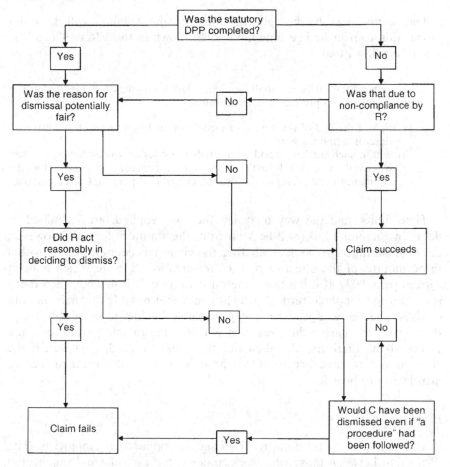

DDP = Dismissal and Disciplinary Procedure

C = Claimant

R = Respondent

The chart assumes that C is able to make a valid claim, e.g. it is presented in time, he has a year's continuous employment, etc. It focuses upon the unfair dismissal decision-making process itself.

Eligibility

There are certain exclusions and qualifications which must be examined **9.04** in order to determine whether the person making a claim for unfair dismissal is entitled to have it heard by the employment tribunal.

Time limits

9.05   The claim must be brought in time, or the tribunal will have no jurisdiction to hear it. The time limit is laid down in the ERA 1996, s.111, which lays down that

> "an employment tribunal shall not consider a complaint made under this section unless it is presented to the tribunal—
>
> (a) before the end of the period of three months beginning with the effective date of termination, or
> (b) within such further period as the tribunal considers reasonable in a case where it is satisfied that it was not reasonably practicable for the complaint to be presented before the end of that period of three months."

Time limits, and the way in which they are applied, are examined in detail in Chapter 14. As will be seen from the statutory formula, however, the tribunal must first look at whether the claim has been presented within three months of the effective date of termination (a term which is dealt with in para.9.07). If it has been, then it is in time. If it has not, then there is a (narrow) loophole through which it may still pass. If the claimant can establish that it was not reasonably practicable for him to present it within that time, and that he did present it within a reasonable period after the expiry of the three months, then the claim can proceed. However, if the claim is out of time according to these tests, then the tribunal has no jurisdiction to hear it.

Employees only

9.06   The right not to be unfairly dismissed is confined to employees. The distinction between those who work under a contract of employment and those who do not is dealt with in Chapter 2.

One year's continuous employment

9.07   Generally, an employee must have been continuously employed for at least a year before he acquires the right not to be unfairly dismissed. As a result, he must establish that he was continuously employed for at least a year before the effective date of termination.

The effective date of termination is defined in s.97 of the ERA 1996 as:

(a) where notice is given, the date upon which it expires;

(b) where no notice is given, the date upon which the termination takes effect;

(c) the date upon which a limited term contract expires without being renewed.

It follows that the date of dismissal is not the date upon which the employee is <u>notified</u> that he is dismissed. It is the date upon which any notice which he is given expires. The notice begins to run on the day after notification.

Example. An employee is given a week's notice on Thursday, with the result   **9.08**
that the notice period expires on the following Thursday, and that is the effective date of termination.

What happens in a case where an employer dismisses the employee without notice, but with payment in lieu of notice? The position was summarised in *Adams v GKN Sankey Ltd* [1980] I.R.L.R. 416, EAT as follows:

(1) Where notice of termination is given, the effective date of termination is the date when the notice expires. The fact that a person is not required to work during the period of notice does not mean that the employment ends earlier than the specified date.

(2) If the date of termination of employment is immediate but money is paid in respect of a subsequent period (in lieu of notice), it is to be taken as compensation for immediate dismissal and not by way of continuation of employment.

What is the position where the employee is dismissed, but is entitled to pursue an internal appeal, either in terms of his contract or by virtue of the statutory DDP? Assuming that the decision to dismiss is confirmed on appeal, is the effective date of termination the date of the original decision to dismiss, or the date upon which the unsuccessful appeal is notified? The general rule is that it is the date of the initial decision to dismiss which constitutes the effective date of termination, subject to any contractual provision to the contrary: *West Midlands Co-operative Society Ltd v Tipton* [1986] I.R.L.R. 112, HL.

A limited extension to the effective date of termination results from the operation of s.97(2) of the ERA 1996. This states that, where an employee is dismissed with less than the statutory period of notice, the effective date of termination is postponed to the date of the expiry of the statutory notice. The minimum statutory notice is in turn laid down in s.86 as follows:

- one week where the employee has been continuously employed for at least one month, but less than two years;

- one week's notice for each year of continuous employment if the employee has been employed for two years or more but less than 12 years;

- 12 weeks' notice if the period of continuous employment is 12 years or more.

Example. C starts to work for R Ltd on September 1, 2005. She is dismissed   **9.09**
without notice on August 28, 2006. The stated reason for her dismissal is that her performance is well below the standard which the company requires. She is

entitled to a week's statutory notice (which she did not receive). This must be added to her period of employment to determine whether she has worked for long enough to acquire the right not to be unfairly dismissed. The notice begins to run on August 29, 2006, and will end on September 4, 2006. As a result, she has a year's continuous employment and is entitled to have her case heard by the tribunal. (Note that she must present her claim to the tribunal on or before November 27, 2006. The extension by adding the statutory notice does not apply to time limits—see Chapter 14.)

The one year's employment required to qualify for the right to claim unfair dismissal must be continuous, and the continuity must be with the dismissing employer. The exceptions to this rule are when a business or undertaking is transferred (see Chapter 12 for the circumstances in which this might occur), or when an employee is taken into employment by an associated employer. Section 231 of the ERA 1996 states that two employers are associated if:

- one is a company of which the other has direct or indirect control; or
- both are companies of which a third person has direct or indirect control.

Apart from these exceptions, continuous employment must be with one employer, or continuity will be broken: *Secretary of State for Employment v Globe Elastic Thread Co Ltd* [1979] I.R.L.R. 327 HL.

9.10 **Calculating continuous employment.** The rather complex and occasionally counter-intuitive rules for computing a period of continuous employment are set out in s.210–218 of the ERA 1996. It should be stressed that these rules are applicable to other employment rights as well as unfair dismissal, e.g. redundancy payments and the acquisition of the right to notice. The main rules are as follows:

- There is a presumption that employment is continuous (s.210(5)).
- Any week during the whole or part of which an employee's relations with his employer are governed by a contract of employment counts in computing the employee's period of employment (s.212(1)).
- If there is no contract of employment governing relations between the parties in a particular week, then the general rule is that continuity is broken.
- However, in certain circumstances, continuity will not be broken, and the week in question will count towards the period of continuous employment (s.212(3)). Those weeks are those in which:
  (1) The employee is incapable of work in consequence of sickness or injury (up to a maximum of 26 weeks).

(2) The employee is absent from work on account of a temporary cessation of work. The work which must cease is that of the employee, rather than the employer: *Fitzgerald v Hall, Russell & Co Ltd* [1970] A.C. 984, HL.

(3) The employee is absent from work in circumstances such that, by arrangement or custom, he is regarded as continuing in the employer's employment for any purpose. In *Curr v Marks & Spencer plc* [2003] I.R.L.R. 74, CA, the Court of Appeal examined this provision in the light of an agreed career break to care for children. It was held that there must be a meeting of minds about the fact that the employee continued in employment for some purpose. Although there had been an agreement as to the break, there was not sufficient evidence to support continuity.

- In other circumstances, the week in question will not count, but continuity will not be broken e.g. in an industrial dispute (s.216).

Example. B starts to work for Q Ltd on January 1, 2006. During May 2006, he takes part in a strike which lasts for three days. In August 2006, he is ill for three weeks. During that time, he is unable to work, and the company does not pay his wages or any sick pay. He resumes work for the company at the end of August. In October 2006, the company ceases operations for a fortnight due to problems with its main supplier. B is not paid by them during that time, but is told there will be a job for him when the factory opens again. In late October, the factory resumes operation, and B starts to work there again. On December 26, 2006, he is dismissed for redundancy, being given one week's notice to expire on January 2, 2007. Despite the interruptions to his employment, he has acquired the necessary one year's continuous employment to bring an unfair dismissal claim: **9.11**

- *As the industrial action only lasts three days, he will have been subject to a contract of employment in each week during that time.*

- *The period during which he is incapable of working is deemed not to interrupt his employment, even if there was no contract with the employer during that period.*

- *The period during which the factory is closed is a temporary cessation of work, and once again is deemed to count towards his period of continuous employment.*

- *The effective date of termination is not the date on which he is told that he is dismissed, but the date upon which his notice expires.*

Exceptions to the one year qualification rule. There are some categories **9.12** of unfair dismissal which do not require a year's continuous employment to enable a claim to be brought. They are set out in s.108 of the ERA 1996, and include dismissal on the following grounds:

- Dismissal for reasons relating to jury service;

- Dismissal for taking time off for dependants;
- Dismissal for a reason relating to pregnancy, childbirth or family leave;
- Dismissal for a health and safety reason;
- Dismissal of certain shop and betting workers in connection with Sunday working;
- Dismissal in relation to the entitlement to paid annual leave and other rights under the Working Time Regulations;
- Dismissal of a trustee of an occupational pension scheme in connection with his duties under the scheme;
- Dismissal of an employee representative serving in that capacity in connection with redundancies or the transfer of an undertaking;
- Dismissal for the assertion of a statutory right;
- Dismissal for making a protected disclosure ("whistle—blowing");
- Dismissal in connection with the entitlement to the national minimum wage;
- Dismissal in connection with working tax credit to which the employee might be entitled;
- Dismissal in connection with the right to request flexible working;
- Dismissal in connection with trade union membership, activities or use of union services;
- Dismissal in connection with activities relating to trade union recognition or bargaining rights;
- Dismissal for taking official industrial action in certain circumstances;
- Dismissal relating to the activity of a European Works Council;
- Dismissal in connection with the exercise of a statutory right to be accompanied;
- Dismissal in connection with the exercise of rights of part-time workers or limited-term employees;
- Dismissal in connection with the establishment of a European public liability company;
- Dismissal in connection with certain information and consultation rights;
- Dismissal in connection with certain duties relating to occupational and pension schemes;
- Selection for redundancy in connection with any of the above reasons (other than that dealing with the statutory right to be accompanied).

In addition, a claim for unfair dismissal arising out of suspension on medical grounds requires one month, rather than one year, continuous employment.

Although the list is a long one, some of the exceptions to the one year rule are quite restrictively drafted, and others are very rarely encountered in practice. The great majority of claims for unfair dismissal do in fact require a minimum of one year's continuous employment.

Employment outside Great Britain

Until 1999, s.196 of the ERA 1996 provided that the right not to be unfairly dismissed did not apply "to employment where under the employee's contract of employment he ordinarily works outside Great Britain". That provision was repealed in 1999. The question of the territorial scope of the right not to be unfairly dismissed fell to be considered in *Lawson v Serco* [2006] I.R.L.R. 289, HL. The House of Lords held that the question should still ordinarily be: was he working in Great Britain at the time he was dismissed? Where an employee was peripatetic (e.g. an airline pilot, or an international management consultant), his base could be treated as his place of employment for the purposes of the statute.   **9.13**

Expatriate employees who work and are based abroad, were very unlikely to qualify in terms of the unfair dismissal provisions, unless they were working for a employer based in Great Britain. Even that would not be enough. Something more was necessary, e.g. that the employee was posted abroad for the purposes of a business carried on in Great Britain.

Normal retirement age

Up until 1 October 2006, employees who had reached "normal retire-   **9.14** ment age" or the age of 65 lost the right to bring a claim for unfair dismissal. Clearly, this provision was discriminatory on grounds of age, and it was abolished by the Employment Equality (Age) Regulations 2006 (see Chapter 6). Those dismissed *before* the commencement of the Regulations on October 1, 2006, however, will still be unable to bring a claim for unfair dismissal if they were above the normal retirement age for the position which they held (if there was one) or 65 (if there was no normal retirement age).

Excluded categories

Although members of the armed forces are given the right not to be   **9.15** unfairly dismissed by s.192 of the ERA 1996, that section has not yet been brought into force.

Those employed in the police service are excluded from unfair dismissal rights (s.200(1)). This includes service in any capacity by virtue of which the person has the powers and privileges of a constable. The exclusion was originally thought to apply to prison officers, but that is no longer the case (s.126 of the Criminal Justice and Public Order Act 1994). In any event, where the dismissal is on the health and safety grounds set out in s.100, or for making a protected disclosure under s.103A, the person holding the office of constable or police cadet will be treated as employed under a contract of employment.

Illegal contracts

9.16   An employee cannot rely upon a contract which is tainted by illegality to found a claim for unfair dismissal. The legal principle is sometimes set out in the Latin tag: *ex turpe causa non oritur action*. The humorous legal writer, A.P. Herbert translated it rather loosely as "The dirty dog gets no dinner here".

In practice, the illegality which is most commonly raised in the tribunals is tax evasion. An employee may consequently find that his contract of employment is tainted with illegality where the failure to pay tax is really the fault of the employer. The appellate courts have sought to soften what is potentially a harsh doctrine by stating that:

- The employee must know of the illegality: *Newland v Simons & Willer (Hairdressers) Ltd* [1981] I.C.R. 521. It is worth stressing that the knowledge required is of the facts. It does not matter that the employee did not know that what was being done was illegal: ignorance of the law is no excuse.

- If the employee is less blameworthy, then he may be permitted to enforce the contract where he has been subject to fraud or duress by the employer.

- Where it is possible, illegal terms may be severed, leaving the remainder of the contract enforceable, so that a claim for unfair dismissal can be brought.

Dismissal

9.17   In order for a claim for unfair dismissal to succeed, the employee must have been dismissed. The statutory definition is wider than that which is used in everyday discussion, and is contained in s.95 of the ERA 1996. It includes:

(a) termination of the contract by the employer (with or without notice);

(b) expiry of a limited-term contract without renewal; and

(c) termination by the employee of the contract, with or without notice, "in circumstances in which he is entitled to terminate it without notice by reason of the employer's conduct.

So dismissal for the purposes of the statute encompasses express dismissal, expiry of a limited-term contract, and resignation which results from repudiatory conduct by the employer (constructive dismissal). Each of these will be discussed in turn.

Express dismissal

This is by far the most common of the three statutory forms of dismissal. **9.18**
If the employer disputes that there was an express dismissal, then the
burden of proof is upon the employee. The tribunal may have to consider
whether the employee was dismissed, or resigned, or whether he and the
employer agreed that the contract was ended.

There are occasional problems over whether the words used by an
employer constitute a dismissal. Sometimes it will be clear that the
employee has been sacked:

> "You are dismissed"

> "You can collect your P45 on the way out".

Equally, it may be clear that he has resigned. On other occasions, the words
used may be ambiguous, perhaps being intended as a rebuke but being
taken by the employee as meaning dismissal or being meant as a protest or
a "cry for help" by the employee and taken by the employer as a
resignation.

Where the words used are unambiguous words of dismissal or resignation, the other party to the contract is entitled to treat them as such:
Sothern v Frank Charlesly & Co [1981] I.R.L.R. 278, CA. Where there is
ambiguity, the question is: How would a reasonable person have understood the words (or, possibly, the actions) in question? If he would regard
them as amounting to a dismissal, then that is what they are. If he would
not, and the employee walked out, then it will amount to a resignation. A
resignation may be a breach of contract on the part of the employee. On
the other hand, it may be that the words in question constitute a breach of
the mutual duty of trust and confidence, such that the employee is entitled
to accept the repudiatory conduct, resign and claim constructive dismissal.
Logically, however, the first question is whether there was an express
dismissal by the employer.

Sometimes, a surprising result comes about when ambiguous words are **9.19**
put in their context. In *Futty v D and D Brekkes Ltd* [1974] I.R.L.R. 130,
ET, the claimant was a fish-filleter working on the docks in Hull. The
foreman became tired of his complaining, and said "If you do not like the
job, fuck off". Mr Futty thought that he had been sacked, and found
another job. The foreman had expected him to get over his bad temper and
return to work, so they denied dismissing him. Evidence was called from
other fish-filleters, and the tribunal found that the words were not a
dismissal but a "general exhortation to get on with the job". To use a
phrase much employed in the tribunals, the foreman had made use of
"industrial language".

In addition, words (even unambiguous ones) may be uttered in the heat
of the moment. In some exceptional circumstances, it has been held that
there may not be a resignation or a dismissal despite appearances to the
contrary. In *Kwik-Fit (GB) Ltd v Lineham* [1992] I.R.L.R. 156, EAT, the
claimant received a humiliating warning from the employer, threw down his

keys and drove away. His employer treated his actions as constituting a resignation. Wood J. stated that where special circumstances exist, before accepting a resignation at its face value, an employer should allow a reasonable period of time to elapse, such as a day or two, during which facts may arise that cast doubt upon whether the employee did resign.

Looking at the other side of the coin, what appears to be a dismissal may not actually be a dismissal if the employer acted in the heat of the moment and immediately withdrew the words of dismissal: *Martin v Yeomen Aggregates Ltd* [1983] I.R.L.R. 49, EAT.

Termination of a limited-term contract

9.20   A contract may be for the completion of a specific task, or for a fixed period of time. In either case, it can be described as a "limited-term" contract. If it expires without being renewed, then the employee is dismissed. This is the case even if the employee knew from the outset that it would not be renewed: *Nottinghamshire County Council v Lee* [1980] I.C.R. 635, CA. Of course, the mere fact that the employee is dismissed does not mean that there will be a successful claim for unfair dismissal. The fact that the contract is for a limited term may well assist the employer to show that the dismissal is fair. However, that is a matter which needs to be tested against the statutory questions: Can the employer show that the dismissal was for a potentially fair reason? Did the employer act reasonably or unreasonably in deciding to dismiss?

Constructive dismissal

9.21   Section 95(1)(c) of the ERA 1996 makes it clear that, when an employee resigns in circumstances where he is entitled to terminate the contract as at an end by reason of the employer's conduct, that will be treated as a dismissal. The term "constructive dismissal" is usually used to describe this situation, although that phrase does not appear in the ERA 1996.

To establish that he has been constructively dismissed, the employee must show that:

   (a) the employer has committed a fundamental breach of contract;

   (b) that fundamental breach has caused his resignation; and

   (c) he has not delayed to such an extent that he has, in effect, accepted the breach.

9.22   **(a) Fundamental breach of contract.** Most of the case law surrounds this first requirement. The employee must be entitled to resign. What gives rise to that entitlement? Until the case of *Western Excavating (ECC) Ltd v Sharp* [1978] I.R.L.R. 27, CA, there was a conflict in the case law; some decisions tended towards the view that unreasonable conduct on the part of the employer was sufficient to trigger off an entitlement to resign, while others held that a fundamental breach of contract on the part of the employer was necessary. *Western Excavating* resolved the controversy definitively in favour of the latter view. In that case, S was suspended from work without pay for taking time off to play cards. As a result, he was in need of cash, and asked his employer for a loan, or alternatively for his accrued holiday pay. When this was refused, he resigned, and claimed that he had been constructively (and unfairly) dismissed. Perhaps somewhat surprisingly, the tribunal and the EAT found in his favour on the preliminary issue of whether he had been dismissed. When the case reached the Court of Appeal, however, this decision was held to be perverse. Lord Denning M.R. held that the employee was entitled to resign and claim that he had been constructively dismissed only if conditions (a) to (c) set out above were satisfied. A test of "unreasonable conduct" was not correct: The test had to be determined in accordance with the law of contract. He stated:

> "An employee is entitled to treat himself as constructively dismissed if the employer is guilty of conduct which is a significant breach going to the root of the contract of employment; or which shows that the employer no longer intends to be bound by one or more of the essential terms of the contract. The employee in those circumstances is entitled to leave without notice or to give notice, but the conduct in either case must be sufficiently serious to entitle him to leave at once".

What type of conduct will constitute a fundamental breach of contract? Clearly, that will be determined by the facts, and in many cases it will be the degree to which the relevant term of the contract has been breached which will be decisive, rather than the category within which the conduct falls. However, a few examples from the scores of reported cases will give the flavour of the conduct involved:

- a reduction in pay which is significant and deliberate: *Industrial Rubber Products v Gillon* [1977] I.R.L.R. 389;
- a unilateral variation of the employee's job content or status: *Coleman v Baldwin* [1977] I.R.L.R. 342;
- failure to provide a safe system of work: *Keys v Shoefayre Ltd* [1978] I.R.L.R. 476;
- failure to ensure a smoke-free environment so that employees could safely perform their duties: *Waltons and Morse v Dorrington* [1997] I.R.L.R. 488;
- a significant change to the place of work: *McAndrew v Prestwick Circuits Ltd* [1988 I.R.L.R. 514.

A number of the reported cases concerning constructive dismissal deal with alleged breaches of the implied term of mutual trust and confidence. In *Courtaulds Northern Textiles Ltd v Andrew* [1979] I.R.L.R. 84, Phillips J. stated that there was an implied term in every contract of employment that employers would not

> "without reasonable and proper cause conduct themselves in a manner calculated or likely to destroy or seriously damage the relationship of confidence and trust between the parties".

Some examples of conduct found to be a breach of the implied duty of trust and confidence are:

- the use of foul and insulting language, particularly where there is a close working relationship between employer and employee. For example, in *Isle of Wight Tourist Board v Coombes* [1976] I.R.L.R. 413, EAT the company's director said to another employee about his secretary: "She's an intolerable bitch on a Monday morning". This shattered the relationship, and entitled the secretary to resign and claim constructive dismissal;
- undermining the authority of a manager over the staff for whom he was responsible;
- falsely accusing an employee of criminal conduct: *Robinson v Crompton Parkinson Ltd* [1978] I.R.L.R. 61;
- unwanted and bullying behaviour by a manager, amounting to sexual harassment: *(1) Reed and (2) Bull Information Systems v Stedman* [1999] I.R.L.R. 299, EAT.

9.23   Not every breach of contract will be fundamental. If it is not fundamental, then the employee is not entitled to resign and, if he does, he will not be able to establish that he was constructively dismissed. Some examples of factual situations where the breach was not fundamental:

- A failure to pay the employee in full, due to a mistake: *Cantor Fitzgerald International v Callaghan* [1999] I.R.L.R. 234.
- A requirement for the employee to transfer his place of work to another depot one mile down the road: *Courtaulds Northern Spinning Ltd v Sibson and TGWU* [1988] I.R.L.R. 305, CA. However, reasonable notice of a transfer should be given: *Prestwick Circuits Ltd v McAndrew* [1990] I.R.L.R. 507.
- Failure to consult a manager over the appointment of a subordinate: *Walker v Josiah Wedgwood & Sons Ltd* [1978] I.R.L.R. 105, EAT.
- Instigating disciplinary action against an employee where there are good grounds to do so.

However, where there is conduct which amounts to a breach of the implied term of mutual trust and confidence, such a breach must inevitably be held to be fundamental, with the result that the breach constitutes a repudiation of the contract: *Morrow v Safeway Stores* [2002] I.R.L.R. 9. This is because this particular implied term is so fundamental to the operation of the contract.

9.24   (b) The breach must have caused the resignation. There must be a causative link between breach and resignation.

9.25   *Example. A has decided to seek new employment, and makes a number of job applications. His employer then makes an unwarranted accusation against his honesty. Following on from that, A finds the job he has been looking for,* *and resigns, citing the employer's unacceptable behaviour towards him. There might well be a fundamental breach of contract, but it will not have caused the resignation.*

Example.   B has decided to look around for another job, but finds nothing he   **9.26**
particularly wants. The employer then commits fundamental breach, and as a result B decides to resign and take one of the jobs which he formerly found unattractive. The breach will have caused the resignation, and B will have been constructively dismissed.

In practice, a tribunal will look with some care at what was said or written by the employee at the time. If there is a resignation letter, does it cite the fundamental breach as the cause? If it does, that will be powerful evidence of causation although it will not be conclusive because the employee may be deliberately setting up a claim for constructive dismissal. If the breach was not mentioned at the time of resignation, that will be a strong argument against causation. Again, however, it will not be conclusive. For example, the employee may be too embarrassed to deal with the matter expressly. In any event, there is no requirement in law that the employee should state that he is leaving because of the employer's repudiatory conduct: *Weathersfield Ltd v Sargent* [1999] I.R.L.R. 94, CA.

(c)   Without such delay as to constitute acceptance. This is the third   **9.27**
condition for constructive dismissal set out in *Western Excavating (ECC) Ltd v Sharp.* As Lord Denning put it:

> "The employee must make up his mind soon after the conduct of which he complains; for if he continues for any length of time without leaving, he will lose his right to treat himself as discharged."

To look at it another way, if the employee delays for too long before resigning, then he will be treated as having accepted the employer's repudiation of the contract. How long a delay will constitute acceptance? There is no simple answer, as it will inevitably depend upon the facts. Turning up to work and, in due course, accepting pay for having done so, are acts which in theory put the employee at risk of having affirmed the contract. However, if an employee makes clear his objection to what is being done, he will not be taken to have affirmed the contract by continuing to work and draw pay for a limited period of time. In *Cantor Fitzgerald International v Bird* [2002] I.R.L.R. 267, HC, for example, the employees were held not to have affirmed their contracts by waiting for over two months before resigning. They had made clear their dissatisfaction with their jobs, and the fact that they intended to leave.

An employee may continue to work after a breach of contract, and then add it to other later breaches, so that they cumulatively amount to a breach of the implied duty of trust and confidence: *Lewis v Motorworld Garages Ltd* [1985] I.R.L.R. 465. This is sometimes referred to as the "last straw" doctrine. The initial breach did not precipitate the resignation but, taken together with the later breach(es) it constituted the fundamental breach which provides the foundation for constructive dismissal. This doctrine is particularly important in relation to the question of delay. The primary focus is likely to be on whether the employee delayed unduly after the "last straw" rather than after the initial breach.

9.28 *Example. D is entitled, in accordance with his contract, to payment at a premium rate for overtime. He does overtime for two months, but in successive pay slips, no mention is made of the money which he ought to have got for overtime. He protests, but then despairs of getting any money for the extra work which he has done, and leaves the matter rest for another month. He requests leave but this is refused arbitrarily by his line manager, whom he suspects of having blocked his overtime payments. D resigns and brings an action for unfair dismissal claiming that he was constructively dismissed, and that the refusal of leave for no good reason constituted the "last straw" which caused him to resign.*

In assessing whether the employee has delayed unduly before resigning, the tribunal will now need to bear in mind the impact of the statutory Grievance Procedure (see para.3.32 for details of its operation). This aims to ensure that employers and employees should attempt to resolve any dispute in the workplace before going to a tribunal. Failure to utilise the statutory procedures may mean that the tribunal will refuse to admit the claim. In addition, there are consequences in terms of a reduction or increase in compensation for failure to make use of the procedures.

9.29 Is a constructive dismissal unfair? The fact that an employee has been constructively dismissed does not mean that he has been unfairly dismissed. By satisfying conditions (a),(b) and (c) above, the employee merely proves that he has been dismissed. The tribunal must then go on to consider whether that dismissal was for a fair reason, and whether the employer acted reasonably or unreasonably in deciding to dismiss, as it does in respect of other types of dismissal. However, the fact that the tribunal will already have found that the employer has acted in such a way as to repudiate the contract does mean that it will face an uphill struggle.

Statutory dismissal and disciplinary procedures

9.30 The Employment Act ("EA") 2002 introduced two sets of statutory procedures which form a framework for resolving disputes in the workplace:

(a) statutory dismissal and disciplinary procedures ("DDP"); and

(b) statutory grievance procedures ("GP").

The stated aim of the new scheme is to promote the resolution of employment disputes in the workplace. The desired result is that fewer cases will find their way to the tribunals.

The new procedures are reproduced in Appendix 3. Their role within the contract of employment is dealt with in Chapter 3. The focus in this section is upon the way in which the statutory DDP, in particular, affects the law relating to unfair dismissal. In brief, the statutory DDP lays down a minimum procedure which the must be followed in dismissing an employee. If it is not, and the failure to do so is the fault of the employer, then any dismissal will be automatically unfair, regardless of the cogency of the reason for the dismissal. In addition, compensation awarded to the employee may be enhanced (see para.10.18). This bald statement of the result needs some elaboration, however.

Applicability of the statutory DDP

The DDP applies whenever the employer "contemplates dismissing or taking relevant disciplinary action against an employee" (reg.3 of the Employment Act 2002 (Dispute Resolution) Regulations 2004—"the Dispute Resolution Regulations". It has general application to dismissals, whatever the reason may be, except that it does not apply to dismissals for retirement. Hence the statutory DDP applies to dismissal for redundancy, as well as for misconduct or capability (although there are certain exceptions dealt with in the next paragraph). As far as retirement is concerned, that is subject not to the DDP but to the "duty to consider" procedure (see paras 9.73 to 9.80). The statutory DDP also applies to disciplinary action short of dismissal (other than warnings) but that is outside the scope of this chapter. **9.31**

The general applicability of the DDP to all dismissals is excluded by reg.4 of the Dispute Resolution Regulations where the employee in question:

- belongs to a category of employees, all of whom are dismissed and then offered re-engagement on new terms;

- is one of 20 or more employees who are collectively declared redundant within a period of 90 days or less;

- is taking part in certain forms of industrial action at the time of dismissal;

- is employed in a business which suddenly ceases to function because of an event not foreseen by the employer, so that it is impractical for him to employ anyone;

- cannot continue in the job because to do so would contravene a statutory duty or restriction;

- is subject to a dismissal procedures agreement designated by an order under s.110 of the EA 2002.

The categories set out above are relatively limited, however. A more important limitation in practice is that the statutory DDP does not cover constructive dismissals. In fact in the case of a constructive dismissal the employee is generally obliged to lodge a grievance under the statutory GP. Even with these exclusions, the great majority of dismissals are subject to the statutory DDP.

9.32   There are certain situations in which the parties are deemed to have complied with the DDP. These include situations where:

- the behaviour of one party or the other makes it impossible or impracticable to continue e.g. because of harassment or a threat to a person or property (reg.11 of the Dispute Resolution Regulations);

- other specialist procedures interrupt the DDP (reg.5).

Standard or modified DDP?

9.33   The EA 2002 lays down two forms of statutory DDP. The standard DDP applies to all dismissals other than those to which the modified DDP applies. The modified DDP is limited to cases where the employer:

- dismissed the employee by reason of his conduct without notice;

- immediately he became aware of the conduct;

- was entitled to dismiss the employee without notice or pay in lieu; and

- it was reasonable to dismiss the employee before enquiring into the circumstances in which the conduct took place.

The modified DDP is therefore in effect confined to those few cases of gross misconduct where investigation would be futile. The great majority of cases will have to be dealt with under the statutory DDP.

General requirements

9.34   The EA 2002, Sch.2, Pt 3 sets out certain general requirements which apply to both forms of DDP (and also to the GP):

(a) each step must be taken without unreasonable delay;

(b) the timing and location of meetings must be reasonable;

(c) meetings must be conducted in a manner that enables both employer and employee to explain their cases; and

(d) in the case of appeal meetings which are not the first meeting, the employer should as far as is reasonably practicable, be represented by a more senior manager than attended the first meeting.

The first three points are self-explanatory. As far as (d) is concerned, the reason behind this requirement is that a more senior manager is needed to ensure that the initial decision can be overruled. It will be difficult, if not impossible, for a more junior manager to overturn a decision already made by a superior.

The meetings described in the statutory DDP fall within the ambit of s.13 of the Employment Relations Act 1999. This gives employees the right to be accompanied at disciplinary hearings and grievance hearings by a work colleague or a trade union official.

Standard DDP: the steps

The standard DDP consists of three steps, which are set out in the Table **9.35** below.

Step 1: statement of grounds for action and invitation to meeting	(1) The employer must set out in writing the employee's alleged conduct or characteristics, or other circumstances, which lead him to contemplate dismissing or taking disciplinary action against the employee.
	(2) The employer must send the statement or a copy of it to the employee and invite the employee to attend a meeting to discuss the matter.
Step 2: meeting	(1) The meeting must take place before action is taken, except in the case where the disciplinary action consists of suspension.
	(2) The meeting must not take place unless,—
	(a) the employer has informed the employee what the basis was for including in the statement under para.1(1) the ground or grounds given in it, and
	(b) the employee has had a reasonable opportunity to consider his response to that information.
	(3) The employee must take all reasonable steps to attend the meeting.
	(4) After the meeting, the employer must inform the employee of his decision and notify him of the right to appeal against the decision if he is not satisfied with it.
Step 3: appeal	(1) If the employee does wish to appeal, he must inform the employer.
	(2) If the employee informs the employer of his wish to appeal, the employer must invite him to attend a further meeting.

Step 3: appeal—cont.	(3) The employee must take all reasonable steps to attend the meeting.
	(4) The appeal meeting need not take place before the dismissal or disciplinary action takes effect.
	(5) After the appeal meeting, the employer must inform the employee of his final decision.

9.36   In *Alexander v Bridgen Enterprises Ltd* [2006] I.R.L.R. 423, EAT, guidance was given as to what was required for compliance with these steps. Elias P. emphasised that the purpose of the statutory procedures is to prevent a dispute from going to a tribunal if possible by providing an opportunity for differences to be resolved internally at an earlier stage. He went on to say that:

> "to achieve that purpose, the information provided must be at least sufficient to enable the employee to give a considered and informed response to the proposed decision to dismiss. . .At the first step the employer merely has to set out in writing the grounds which lead him to contemplate dismissing the employee, together with an invitation to attend a meeting. At that stage, in our view, the statement need do no more than state the issue in broad terms. . .at step one the employee simply needs to be told that he is at risk of dismissal and why. In a conduct case this will be identifying the nature of the misconduct in issue, such as fighting, insubordination or dishonesty. In other cases it may require no more than specifying, for example, that it is lack of capability or redundancy. . .Of course, most employers will say more than this brief statement of grounds, but compliance with the minimum procedure is in our view met by a limited written statement of that nature. It is at the second step that the employer must inform the employee of the basis for the ground or grounds given in the statement. This information need not be reduced into writing; it can be given orally. The basis for the grounds are simply the matters which have led the employer to contemplate dismissing for the stated ground or grounds . . .the employee must be given sufficient detail of the case against him to enable him properly to put his side of the story. The fundamental elements of fairness must be met."

Modified DDP

9.37   The steps in the modified DDP are set out in the table below.

Step 1: statement of grounds for action	The employer must—
	(a) set out in writing—
	(i) the employee's alleged misconduct which has led to the dismissal,

	(ii) what the basis was for thinking at the time of the dismissal that the employee was guilty of the alleged misconduct, and
	(b) send the statement or a copy of it to the employee.
Step 2: appeal	(1) If the employee does wish to appeal, he must inform the employer.
	(2) If the employee informs the employer of his wish to appeal, the employer must invite him to attend a meeting.
	(3) The employee must take all reasonable steps to attend the meeting.
	(4) After the appeal meeting, the employer must inform the employee of his final decision.

As can be seen, the modified DDP is a pared-down version of the standard DDP. At the time of writing, it had not been the subject of interpretation in the appellate courts.

Consequences of failing to complete the relevant statutory DDP

9.38 Where the statutory DDP applies, the parties must follow it. In the event that it is not completed, s.98A of the ERA 1996 comes into play. It states that:

> "A(1) An employee who is dismissed shall be regarded for the purposes of this Part as unfairly dismissed if—
>
> (a) on of the [statutory DDP] procedures . . . applies in relation to the dismissal,
> (b) the procedure has not been completed, and
> (c) the non-completion of the procedure is wholly or mainly attributable to failure by the employer to comply with its requirements."

In other words, if the relevant statutory DDP has not been completed because of a failure by the employer, any dismissal is automatically unfair.

Consequences of completing the relevant statutory DDP

9.39 Where the statutory DDP has been completed, or its non-completion is not attributable to the fault of the employer, the dismissal will not be *automatically* unfair. However, it may still be unfair. This is because the DDP merely lays down a minimum standard of procedural fairness, applicable to all cases. As Elias P. put it in *Alexander*:

"It must be emphasised that the statutory dismissal procedures are not concerned with the reasonableness of the employer's grounds, nor the basis of those grounds, in themselves. It may be that the basis for a dismissal is quite misconceived or unjustified, or that the employer has adopted inappropriate or vague criteria, or acted unreasonably in insisting on dismissing in the light of the employee's response. These are of course highly relevant to whether the dismissal is unfair, but it is irrelevant to the issue whether the statutory procedures have been complied with."

Once the issue relating to the statutory DDP has been resolved, therefore, there are still two questions to be resolved:

(1) what was the reason for the dismissal?

(2) Was it a potentially fair reason in terms of the statute?

(3) Did the employer act reasonably or unreasonably in deciding to dismiss?

The steps of the enquiry are set out in the flowchart on page 119.

The reason for the dismissal

9.40   If the employee is eligible to claim unfair dismissal, and has established that he was dismissed, the next stage of the enquiry is: What was the reason for the dismissal? The onus is on the employer to show the reason. Closely bound up with this question is: Was the reason a potentially fair one in terms of the statute (the ERA 1996)?

The reason for the dismissal is a set of facts known to the employer, or beliefs held by him which cause him to dismiss the employee: *Abernethy v Mott, Hay and Anderson* [1974] I.R.L.R. 213, CA. This must be distinguished from the label which the employer attaches to the facts or beliefs in question. The reason for dismissal does not have to be correctly labelled at the time of dismissal.

In *Abernethy*, the claimant was a civil servant who refused to work away from head office, and was dismissed for "redundancy". At the tribunal, the employer stated that the reason for dismissal was redundancy and/or incapability. The tribunal held that the reason for dismissal was not redundancy, but incapability, and that he had been fairly dismissed for that reason. On appeal, it was argued that the employer should not have been allowed to rely on a different reason before tribunal from that stated at the time of dismissal. The Court of Appeal held that the "reason" for the dismissal was a set of facts which led to his dismissal. As these had been made clear to him at the time of dismissal, the employer's failure to attach the correct label to the facts did not matter.

9.41   It is different if the employee is not made aware of the true nature of the allegations at the time of dismissal. He will not then have had a proper opportunity to consider the allegations, and answer them. In *Hotson v Wisbech Conservative Club* [1984] I.R.L.R. 422, EAT, for example, the original reason given for sacking a barmaid was lack of capability in handling the bar takings. During the course of the tribunal hearing, it transpired that the real reason was dishonesty. The EAT held that the difference between inefficiency and dishonesty was more than a mere change of label. The charge of dishonesty should have been stated at the outset, or not pursued at all. The employee had not had a proper opportunity to consider the implications of the allegation, or to answer it.

Subsequent events

In deciding what the reason was for the dismissal, the focus is upon the   **9.42** employer's state of mind at the time of the dismissal. In *W. Devis & Sons v Atkins* [1977] I.R.L.R. 314, HL, the employee managed the company's abattoir. He was dismissed for failing to carry out the company's purchasing policy. After dismissal, the company found various evidence of dishonest conduct on his part during the course of his employment. They sought to rely on it as the reason for dismissal, although they had not known about it at the time. The House of Lords held that, in determining whether a dismissal is fair, an employment tribunal cannot have regard to matters of which the employer was unaware at the time. It is worth pointing out, however, that although the subsequently discovered matters cannot affect the reason for, or the fairness of, the dismissal, they will be relevant to compensation. In *Devis*, in fact, the claimant received no compensation because he had suffered no injustice and hence it would not be just and equitable to make a compensatory award (see the "Remedies" section of this chapter).

Although the focus is upon the situation at the time of dismissal, an event which occurs during the notice period may have to be taken into account by the employer. For example:

- In *Williamson v Alcan (UK) Ltd* [1977] I.R.L.R. 303, EAT, the employee was dismissed because of chronic ill health. During the notice period he made a spontaneous recovery. It was held that the employer should have reconsidered the position in the light of new evidence.

- In *Stacey v Babcock Power Ltd* [1986] I.R.L.R. 3, EAT, an employee was dismissed for redundancy and given three months notice. During the notice period the employer obtained a new contract, which required a number of workers. They recruited new workers, and did not offer one to the dismissed employee. The EAT held that what was initially a fair dismissal became an unfair one as a result.

It follows from the case law that the employer should be careful to specify accurately the reason why the employee is being dismissed. This care should be exercised at the time when the internal hearing and appeal take place, and also at the time of the tribunal hearing. It is always risky for an employer to change horses in mid-stream, because it is potentially prejudicial to the employee when that is done. Where an employer is in doubt, it is better that the reasons should be set out in the alternative, e.g. "dismissal was because of lack of capability or, in the alternative, for a reason related to conduct".

More than one reason

9.43   Sometimes the employer will have more than one reason for dismissal. What the statute lays down (s.98(1) (a)) is that: "it is for the employer to show (a) the reason (or, if more than one, the principal reason) for the dismissal."

That does not mean that there must be a single reason for dismissal. However, where there is more than one, the employer must identify the principal one. This means that the employer is prevented from using a "scattergun" approach. In *Smith v City of Glasgow D C* [1987] I.R.L.R. 326, HL, the Council set out four reasons for dismissal in a letter to the employee, all of which related to conduct or capability. The tribunal held that the Council had not established, in relation to one of the four charges, that it had believed it to be true on reasonable grounds. Nevertheless the tribunal decided that the dismissal was fair. When the case eventually came to the House of Lords, it was held that the Council had failed to show what the principal reason for dismissal was. It might have been that the charge which was not established was the principal reason or part of it. An important part of the reason for dismissal had not been made out. As a result, the dismissal was unfair.

Written reasons

9.44   The employee who has been dismissed has a right to receive written reasons for the dismissal from his employer (s.92 of the ERA 1996). This applies to a dismissal by the employer, with or without notice, or the failure to renew a limited-term contract but it does not (for obvious reasons) apply to constructive dismissal. In order to acquire the right, the employee must have continuous service of at least a year with that employer. However, an employee dismissed while pregnant or during maternity or adoption leave does not require any length of service to acquire the right.

The right is exercised once the employee makes a specific request for written reasons. Again, this is subject to an exception in the case of an employee who is pregnant or on maternity or adoption leave. Such an employee is entitled to receive written reasons without having to make a request.

The request, if one is needed as is usually the case, need not itself be in writing. The employer is then obliged to provide written reasons within 14 days. An unreasonable failure to do so, or the provision of reasons which are untrue or inadequate, will result in an award of two weeks' pay. The award is not subject to the statutory cap for a week's pay which applies to the calculation of the basic award or a redundancy payment. Some of the issues dealt with by the case law are:

- A failure to provide reasons may be justified if the employer has a genuine and reasonable belief that there was no dismissal:

Broomsgrove v Eagle Alexander Ltd [1981] I.R.L.R. 127, EAT. There is, however, some authority for suggesting that the belief in question must merely be "conscientious":*Brown v Stuart Scott & Co* [1981] I.C.R. 166. This latter suggestion, however, does not flow so easily from the statutory condition that the employer "unreasonably failed to provide".

- The fact that an employee is well aware of the reasons for dismissal is of itself no excuse for a failure to provide written reasons. One of the aims of s.92 is to provide documentation as to the basis for the employer's decision, which may be shown to third parties, or produced in subsequent proceedings, e.g. in a tribunal: *McBrearty v Thomson t/a Highfield Mini-Market* EAT 653/90.

- The employer's response to the request should "at least contain a simple statement of the essential reasons for the dismissal" but no particular formalities are required: *Horsley Smith and Sherry Ltd v Dutton* [1977] I.R.L.R. 172, EAT.

- An employer may answer the request by referring to existing documents which are available to the employer: *Kent CC v Gilham* [1985] I.R.L.R. 16, CA, which also held that sending the letter to the employee's representative could constitute compliance.

- As to the degree of detail required, it is submitted that the bare description of the statutory label e.g. misconduct, capability (see the next section) is not sufficient. In accordance with *Abernethy v Mott, Hay and Anderson* [1974] I.R.L.R. 213, CA, the reason is a set of facts known to the employer, or beliefs held by him, which have caused him to dismiss the employee. Those facts can be briefly summarised, and need not be set out in detail.

The statutory reasons

Section 98 of the ERA 1996 sets out the potentially fair reasons for dismissal. In sum they are: **9.45**

(a) a reason relating to the capability or qualifications of the employee for the work which he was employed to do;

(b) a reason relating to the conduct of the employee;

(c) that the employee was redundant;

(d) that continuation in the position held by the employee would contravene a statutory duty or restriction;

(e) retirement of the employee;

(f) some other substantial reason.

There are, by contrast, certain cases where the dismissal can be described as automatically fair:

(a) where dismissal is to safeguard national security (s.10(4) of the ERA 1996);

(b) where the employee was taking part in unofficial industrial action (unless the reason for dismissal is for one of certain automatically unfair reasons—see s.237 of the Trades Union and Labour Relations (Consolidation) Act (TULRA) 1992);

(c) where the employee was taking part in official industrial action or the employer was conducting a lock-out, provided that the employer dismisses all relevant employees and does not re-employ any of them within three months. This is subject to certain exceptions (ss. 238 and 238A of the TULRA 1992).

Finally, there are various reasons which are <u>automatically unfair</u>. By and large, these do not require a year's service before a claim for unfair dismissal can be pursued. Reference can be made to the list in para.9.12 entitled "Exceptions to the one year qualification rule". To that list should be added dismissals for the following reasons (which are automatically unfair, but <u>do</u> require a year's service to qualify):

- dismissal where there has been a failure to complete an applicable statutory DDP, and that failure is attributable to the employer (s.98A of the ERA 1996);

- dismissal where there is a transfer of an undertaking and the transfer, or a reason connected with it, is the reason or the principal reason for the dismissal (reg.7 of the Transfer of Undertakings (Protection of Employment) Regulations 2006) ("the TUPE Regulations");

- dismissal because of a "spent" conviction within the meaning of the Rehabilitation of Offenders Act 1974, unless the employee falls within a category excluded by statutory instrument (s.4(3)(b) of that Act).

Potentially fair reasons

9.46   The great majority of unfair dismissal claims in the tribunals concern dismissals where the employer claims that it had a potentially fair reason for dismissal. What follows is a brief description of what each of the reasons in question entails. In paras 9.65 to 9.81, there is a more detailed discussion of what will constitute a fair dismissal in relation to each of the potentially fair reasons.

9.47   Capability or qualifications.   The first of the potentially fair reasons is:

"a reason [which] relates to the capability or qualification of the employee for performing work of the kind which he was employed by the employer to do".

There are in fact several totally different factual situations to which this reason can be applied as a label.

First, it can apply to a lack of qualifications. Some guidance is provided by s.98((3)(b) of the ERA 1996, which states that this means "any degree, diploma or other academic, technical or professional qualification relevant to the position". Cases where employers rely upon this particular limb are uncommon. One example is a requirement for a clean driving licence: *Tayside Regional Council v McIntosh* [1982] I.R.L.R. 272, which made it clear that this could be a qualification even though it had not been included in a written contract of employment.

Second, it can apply to ill-health. Section 98(3)(a) of the ERA 1996 states that capability is "assessed by reference to skill, aptitude, health or any other physical or mental quality". If an employee is absent from work to an extent which means that he is incapable of performing the job, with the result that the employer decides to dismiss him, it would fall within this category. Such absence might consist of a number of short absences over a period of time, or a prolonged absence. It is worth reiterating that at this stage, the focus is upon the reason for the employer's decision to dismiss. Whether such a decision would be reasonable or not is a separate issue, which is dealt with in paras 9.65 to 9.68.

Third, s.98(3)(a) defines "capability" so that it covers competence. In **9.48** other words, an employer may decide to dismiss an employee for incompetence, e.g. a poor production rate, failure to deal properly with customers, low sales figures. Again, the question of the reasonableness of such a decision is postponed for a later discussion (see paras 9.64 to 9.68).

There is the possibility of overlap between the categories described above and the other potentially fair reasons. For example, if the employee is dismissed for persistent absence where the employer has concluded that he has dishonestly been claiming to be sick when he is in fact moonlighting as a minicab driver, the set of facts constituting the reason may be more accurately labelled as "misconduct". The dismissal would then be on the (potentially fair) ground that it was "related to conduct".

Conduct. A reason is potentially fair if it "relates to the conduct of the **9.49** employee". It is worth emphasising that the reason need merely "relate" to the employee's conduct. It can include (to take a few examples from a virtually unlimited list) the following examples of misconduct:

- fighting;
- dishonesty;
- setting up in competition to the employer;
- abusive language;
- failure to obey a lawful order;
- drunkenness;
- lateness;

- breaches of health and safety procedures;

- computer misuse.

9.50   **Redundancy.**   Unlike the previous two potentially fair reasons, what is required here is actual redundancy, and not merely a "reason related to redundancy". The employer must first show that there was what may be referred to in shorthand as a "redundancy situation", and then that redundancy was the reason, or the principal reason, for the dismissal.

"Redundancy" is defined in s.139 of the ERA 1996. In summary, it occurs where:

(1) there is a cessation of business;

(2) the business is no longer carried on in the place where the employee is employed; or

(3) the requirement for employees to carry out work of a particular kind has ceased or diminished, or is expected to do so;

(4) the requirement for employees to do work of a particular kind at the employee's workplace has ceased or diminished, or is expected to do so.

If the employer can show that any of these conditions is satisfied, it will constitute a redundancy situation. The tribunals will not challenge the commercial decision of the employer to require redundancies, as long as the decision is a genuine one, and not a sham. In *Moon v Homeworthy Engineering (Northern) Ltd* [1977] I.R.L.R. 298, EAT, employees claimed that, because the factory where they were working was still economically viable, there was no redundancy. It was held that "there cannot be any investigation into the reasons for creating redundancies or into the rights and wrongs of the declared redundancy". In practice, if it is alleged that the redundancy is a sham, and that the employer wished to get rid of the employee for some other reason, the tribunal will be obliged to carry out at least some investigation into the reasons why redundancy was declared, in order to ascertain whether it was genuine or not.

9.51   Once the employer has shown that a redundancy situation existed, it must go on to show that the employee who alleges unfair dismissal was in fact dismissed by reason of redundancy. That still leaves open the question of whether the employer acted reasonably e.g. by consulting properly—and, again, discussion of that aspect is postponed until later (see para.9.71).

9.52   **Statutory illegality.**   Where it would contravene a statute or statutory instrument for an employee to continue to work in the position which he holds, that will be a fair reason to dismiss him. The commonest example is a driving disqualification for someone whose job depends on being able to drive. This provision would also apply where the Secretary of State for Education determines that someone is no longer fit to teach: *Sandhu v Department of Education and Science* [1978] I.R.L.R. 208. Another area where it is relevant is where it is discovered that someone does not have permission to work in this country (s.8 of the Asylum and Immigration Act 1996).

Retirement. The Employment Equality (Age) Regulations 2006 ("the Age Regulations") outlawed discrimination on grounds of age (see paras 6.54 to 6.69 for a summary of their effect as far as unlawful discrimination is concerned). The Age Regulations repealed the bar on those over normal retirement age (or 65 where there was none) from bringing a claim for unfair dismissal. However, it remains lawful for an employer compulsorily to retire someone who is aged 65 or over. It is also lawful compulsorily to retire an employee at an earlier age if the employer can show that his actions are objectively justified. As a result, a new potentially fair reason was inserted into s.98(2) of the ERA 1996, namely "retirement of the employee", with effect from October 1, 2006.

9.53

The Age Regulations introduced into the ERA 1996 a set of irrebuttable presumptions which determine in a number of instances whether a dismissal is by reason of retirement. These presumptions are to be found in ss.98ZA to 98ZH, which were inserted in the ERA 1996 by the regulations. The presumptions make a number of references to the "normal retirement age" (NRA). This is defined in s.98ZH as:

> "the age at which employees in the employer's undertaking who hold, or have held, the same kind of position as the employee are normally required to retire".

This places the emphasis upon the contractual position, by the use of the phrase "required to retire".

As far as the presumptions are concerned, retirement is deemed to be the only reason for dismissal where:

(a) the employee has no normal retirement age (NRA), the employer gives notice of between six to twelve months in accordance with the "duty to consider" procedure and the dismissal takes effect on or after the employee's 65th birthday and on the intended date of retirement;

(b) the employee has an NRA which is over 65, the employer gives notice of six to twelve months in accordance with the "duty to consider" procedure and the dismissal takes effect on or after the employee has reached the NRA and on the intended date of retirement;

(c) the employee has an NRA which is below 65 but which does not amount to unlawful age discrimination, the employer has given the required notice of six to twelve months under the "duty to consider" procedure and the dismissal takes effect on or after the employee has reached the NRA and on the intended date of retirement.

9.54   There are various sets of circumstances where retirement is deemed not
to be the reason for dismissal:

(a) where the employee has no normal retirement age, but the
dismissal takes effect before the employee reaches the age of 65;

(b) where the employee has no normal retirement age, the employer
gives notice under the "duty to consider" procedure, but the
dismissal takes effect before the intended date of retirement
notified to the employee;

(c) where the employee has a normal retirement age (whether above
or below 65), but the dismissal takes effect before the employee
reaches that age;

(d) where the employee has a normal retirement age over the age of
65, the employer gives notice, but the dismissal takes effect before
the intended date of retirement date so notified;

(e) where the employer does not notify the employee in accordance
with the "duty to consider" procedure, but he does notify the
employee of an intended date of retirement, and the dismissal
takes effect before that intended date of retirement;

(f) where the employer has a normal retirement age which is below
the age of 65, the dismissal takes effect after that age, but it is
unlawful age discrimination for the employee to have that retirement age (i.e. the retirement age is not objectively justified);

(g) where the employer has a normal retirement age which is below
the age of 65, that retirement age is objectively justified, the
employer has notified the employee in accordance with the "duty
to consider" procedure, but the dismissal takes effect before the
intended retirement date.

These two sets of presumptions will govern the great majority of factual
situations. As a result, the question of whether the reason for dismissal is
retirement is in most cases actually determined by a series of technical
rules, rather than by an examination of what went on in the employer's
mind (as would be the case with other reasons for dismissal).

There are a few cases which are not governed by the presumptions, so
that it is left to the tribunal to decide whether retirement is the reason for
dismissal:

(a) where the employer has not notified the employee six to twelve
months in advance of retirement in accordance with the duty to
consider procedure; or

(b) where the employer did give the employee such notice, but the
dismissal takes effect after the intended date of retirement.

Where (a) above applies, the tribunal *must* take the matters listed in s.98ZF
of the ERA into account. Where (b) applies, it may take them into account.
The matters in question are.

(a) whether or not the employer has notified the employee by the fourteenth day before termination;

(b) if notice was given, how long before the intended retirement date it was given; and

(c) whether or not the employer followed, or sought to follow, the procedure laid down for a meeting to consider the request not to retire.

Some other substantial reason. The ERA 1996, s.98(1)(b) sets out as **9.55** potentially fair.

"some other substantial reason of a kind such as to justify the dismissal of an employee holding the position which the employee held".

The phrase has an all-embracing ring about it, and is frequently used as a safety net where a cogent reason for dismissal is not one of those specified in s.98(2). It is submitted that full weight should be given to the word "substantial", which is clearly meant to be an important part of the statutory formula.

The classic case where "some other substantial reason" is pleaded by the employer is a business reorganisation which, while not fulfilling the strict criteria for redundancy, means that some employees are "surplus to requirements". This is not the only situation caught by the safety net, however, and other examples include:

- An employee's plan to marry someone who worked for a rival business: *Skyrail Oceanic Ltd t/a Goodmos Tours v Coleman* [1980] I.R.L.R. 226, EAT.

- Third party pressure to dismiss an employee: *Dobie v Burns International Security Services (UK) Ltd* [1984] I.C.R. 812, CA.

- A personality clash with other employees: *Terganowan v Robert Knee & Co Ltd* [1975] I.R.L.R. 247, HC.

- Expiry of a limited-term contract: *Terry v East Sussex County Council* [1976] I.R.L.R. 332, EAT.

Reasonableness

Leave aside dismissals by way of retirement (which have their own **9.56** procedure and presumptions). Further, assume that it has been established that the statutory DDP was followed. In addition, let us assume that the employer has shown that the reason for dismissal was a potentially fair one in terms of s.98 of the ERA 1996 (other than retirement). The next stage of the enquiry for the tribunal is laid down in s.98(4):

"(4) Where the employer has fulfilled the requirements of subsection (1), the determination of the question whether the dismissal is fair or unfair (having regard to the reason shown by the employer)—

(a) depends on whether in the circumstances (including the size and administrative resources of the employer's undertaking) the employer acted reasonably or unreasonably in treating it as a sufficient reason for dismissing the employee, and

(b) shall be determined in accordance with equity and the substantial merits of the case."

The tribunal must, then, be satisfied that the decision of the employer to dismiss was reasonable, rather than unreasonable. Whereas the burden of proof in respect of the reason for dismissal is upon the employer, when it comes to the question of reasonableness, the burden is neutral. In other words, it is for the tribunal to determine, taking into account the evidence and arguments of the parties.

In considering reasonableness, some general factors need to be looked at first, and this is done in the next section. Then an attempt is made to examine what is reasonable in respect of each of the potentially fair reasons for dismissal.

The band of reasonableness

9.57   Central to the enquiry into reasonableness is the principle that the tribunal must not substitute its own judgment for that of the employer. Its judicial task is not to decide whether the members of the tribunal would have dismissed, but rather whether the decision of the employer to dismiss was reasonable or unreasonable. That formula reflects the wording of the statute, which was fleshed out in the case of *Iceland Frozen Foods Ltd v Jones* [1982] I.R.L.R. 439, EAT. The principles stated in that case are worth setting out, because they address the most common misconception about unfair dismissal cases—particularly those concerned with misconduct. That misconception is that the case is really about whether the employee is "guilty" of the misconduct alleged. That is not an issue in the case. The crucial point is whether the employer acted reasonably or not. The difference is highlighted by the following summary of the principles in *Iceland Frozen Foods*:

(1) The starting point should always be the words of what is now s.98(4) of the ERA 1996 (see para.9.56).

(2) The tribunal must consider the reasonableness of the employer's conduct, rather than whether the members of the tribunal consider the dismissal to be fair.

(3) In judging the reasonableness of the employer's conduct, the tribunal must not substitute its own decision as to what was the right course for that of the employer.

(4) In many (though not all) cases there is a band of reasonable responses to the employee's conduct within which one employer might reasonably take one view, another quite reasonably take another.

(5) The function of the tribunal, as an industrial jury, is to determine whether in the particular circumstances of each case the decision

to dismiss the employee fell within the band of reasonable responses which a reasonable employer might have adopted. If the dismissal falls within the band, the dismissal is fair. If it falls outside the band, it is unfair.

After a brief period in the late 1990s when *Iceland Frozen Foods* was doubted, it was firmly stated to be the law in *Post Office v Foley, HSBC Bank Ltd v Madden* [2000] I.R.L.R. 827. Further, it sets out the right approach not only when considering whether dismissal is an appropriate response to the misconduct (or lack of capability, etc.) in question, but also when looking at the procedure which the employer adopted. As it was put in *Sainsbury's Supermarkets Ltd v Hitt* [2003] I.R.L.R. 23, CA:

"the objective standards of the reasonable employer must be applied to all aspects of the question whether an employee was fairly and reasonably dismissed."

The wording of s.98(4) states that the tribunal must take into account the "size and administrative resources" of the employer in deciding whether it acted reasonably. This is not meant to provide small employers with a defence if they act unfairly. It is rather a recognition that they will not always be able to implement such a detailed disciplinary procedure as a large employer. For example, they may not be able to ensure such elaborate appeals machinery as an employer with a number of senior managers. In addition, the opportunities for alternative employment in a small employer are likely to be more restricted where, for example, an employee's position is found redundant.

Human Rights Act

Since the enactment of the Human Rights Act 1998, tribunals must, as **9.58** far as possible, interpret domestic legislation (for example, the ERA 1996) in such a way as to be compatible with the rights set out in the European Convention on Human Rights ("ECHR"). Guidance as to the situation with regard to private employers was set out in *X v Y* [2004] I.R.L.R. 625 CA, where Mummery L.J. suggested that a tribunal should, whenever a Human Rights Act point was raised in an unfair dismissal case, deal with it in the following way:

(1) Do the circumstances of the dismissal fall within the ambit of one or more articles of the ECHR? If not, Convention rights are not engaged, and need not be considered further.

(2) If they do, does the state have a positive obligation to secure enjoyment of the right in question between private persons? If it does not, the Convention right is unlikely to affect the outcome of an unfair dismissal claim against a private employer.

(3) If it does have such a positive obligation, is the interference with the employee's right under the ECHR by his dismissal justified? If it is, then proceed to (5).

(4) If it is not justified, was there a permissible reason for the dismissal under the ERA 1996, which does not involved unjustified interference with a right under the ECHR? If there was no permissible reason, the dismissal will be unfair for the absence of a permissible reason to justify it.

(5) If there was a permissible reason which does not involve unjustified interference with an ECHR right, is the dismissal fair? This question must be tested by the provisions of s.98 of the ERA, reading and giving effect to them under s.3 of the HRA so as to be compatible with the ECHR.

In *McGowan v Scottish Water* [2005] I.R.L.R. 167, EAT, an employer suspected that an employee was acting dishonestly by falsifying his time-sheets. The employer considered whether it was possible to investigate the matter internally, but found that it was not practicable to do so. As a result, they employed private investigators who secreted themselves opposite the front door of his house and filmed his comings and goings over the course of a week. It was argued on the employee's behalf that this was a breach of his right to respect for private life (Art.8 of the ECHR). The tribunal found that the dismissal was not unfair. The EAT, in dealing with the appeal, held that Art.8 was engaged, but that whether a surveillance operation breached the right to respect for private life was a question of proportionality. In this case, the employer's surveillance of the employee's home was not disproportionate. They were bound to carry out an investigation in order to protect the assets of the company. They considered alternatives, but formed the view that they were impracticable and ineffective. It had to be borne in mind that their suspicions were found to be established, and the subsequent disciplinary process was not challenged as unfair.

The ACAS Code of Practice

9.59   The Arbitration, Conciliation and Advisory Service ("ACAS") has issued a Code of Practice on Disciplinary and Grievance Procedures, having been given the power to do so by the Trades Union and Labour Relations (Consolidation) Act 1992. Although a failure to comply with the Code is not in itself unlawful, tribunals will take its provisions into account in deciding what is reasonable. It provides commonsense guidance for employers in dealing with disciplinary matters, and a set of standards by which employees can measure the way in which they are treated. The latest edition of the Code (4th edn, 2004) deals with the implementation of the statutory DDP and GP, as well as the employer's internal procedures. The contents are not summarised here, as the Code is reproduced in full as Appendix 3. However, it is worth emphasising that tribunals do have regard to the Code when determining what is reasonable. That does not mean that any failure to comply with a particular recommendation (e.g. that written records should be kept of the disciplinary process) will mean that a subsequent dismissal is unfair. But any defects in the procedure by comparison with the ACAS guidance will be taken into account, and will go into the scales in deciding whether the process as a whole was reasonable or unreasonable.

One point of contention in the past was whether the scope of the ACAS Code of Practice was restricted to misconduct cases. Does it have application beyond the sphere of misconduct, for example? The 2004 edition of the Code throws some light on this question in para.2:

> "Disciplinary rules tell employees what behaviour employers expect from them. If an employee breaks specific rules about behaviour, this is often called misconduct. . . . Disciplinary procedures may also be used where employees don't meet their employer's expectations in the way that they do their job. These cases, often known as unsatisfactory performance (or capability), may require different treatment from misconduct, and disciplinary procedures should allow for this."

In para.19, the Code sets out the suggested "First formal action" in relation to "unsatisfactory performance", and there are references to this and other capability questions at various points in the Code.

It would seem, then, that the Code has some application to capability cases as well as those concerned with conduct. It does not seem to be of the same degree of relevance to hearings in cases of redundancy, for example. It is worth emphasising that the statutory DDP, by contrast, applies to all forms of dismissal (other than retirement, which is governed by the "duty to consider" procedure—see paras 9.73 to 9.80).

Natural justice and fair hearings

The employer does not have to follow all the rules of natural justice **9.60** which the common law has evolved. However, there are certain basic requirements which any internal disciplinary procedure should comply with:

(1) the employee must know the nature of the case against him;

(2) he should be given an opportunity to state his case; and

(3) the body deciding whether to dismiss him should act in good faith.

(*Khanum v Mid-Glamorgan Area Health Authority* [1978] I.R.L.R. 215, EAT.)

As to (1), it is the nature of the case which must be made clear to the employee. There is no requirement that in all cases an employee must be shown copies of witness statements, for example: *Hussain v Elonex plc* [1999] I.R.L.R. 420, CA.

The question sometimes arises whether the person or body deciding whether to dismiss is sufficiently impartial to hear the case, e.g. because of their previous involvement with the employee in danger of dismissal. It is possible for a person who carried out a preliminary investigation to conduct the disciplinary hearing itself with fairness although no doubt it is better for someone fresh to the matter to adjudicate upon it. Again, if a person has been a witness he should preferably not be given the task of carrying out the hearing, but it may be difficult to avoid that duplication of roles e.g. in the case of a small employer (*Slater v Leicestershire Health Authority* [1989] I.R.L.R. 16, CA).

Appeals

9.61   The statutory DDP lays down an appeal stage, as step 3 of the dismissal and disciplinary process. More generally, the ACAS Code of Practice states that employees should be allowed to appeal. Both state that, in so far as it is reasonably practicable, the appeal should be heard by a more senior manager, the implication being that a more junior manager would not have the "clout" to overturn the original decision. A person may not be suitable to hear an appeal because of his involvement in the events that led to the dismissal, the investigation, or the decision to dismiss. Of course, events may mean that it is impossible for the employer to conduct the manner in such a way that a completely new person deals with the appeal, especially in a small company. In the last resort, the issue is one of reasonableness.

The "no difference" rule

9.62   Assume that there is an element of procedural unfairness about the employer's decision to dismiss—for example, the employee is not given a fair hearing before the dismissal. Assume also that, even if a fair procedure had been adopted, the employee would have been dismissed in any event— that the unfairness made "no difference" to the result. Is the dismissal unfair or not?

The position at common law, as a result of the decision of the House of Lords in *Polkey v A E Dayton Services Ltd* [1987] I.R.L.R. 503, HL, was that, where the employer fails to take the proper procedural steps, a tribunal must not ask whether it would have made any difference if the right procedure had been followed. The question to ask was: did the employer act reasonably or unreasonably? If there was a fundamental flaw in the procedure, then the dismissal would not be regarded as fair merely because the procedural unfairness did not affect the end result. The question: what would the result have been under a fair procedure did not affect the issue of reasonableness (although it did affect the issue of compensation—see para.10.17). However, the position has been changed by the Employment Act 2002, which inserted a new s.98A in the ERA 1996, reading in part as follows:

> "98A(1) An employee who is dismissed shall be regarded for the purposes of this part as unfairly dismissed if—
>
>   (a) one of the procedures set out in Part 1 of Schedule 2 to the Employment Act 2002 (dismissal and disciplinary procedures) applies in relation to the dismissal,
>   (b) the procedure has not been completed, and
>   (c) the non-completion of the procedure is wholly or mainly attributable to failure by the employer to comply with its requirements.
>
> (2) Subject to subsection (1), failure by an employer to follow a procedure in relation to the dismissal of an employee shall not be regarded for the purposes

of s.98(4)(a) as by itself making the employer's action unreasonable if he shows that he would have decided to dismiss the employee if he had followed the procedure".

The result is that:

(1) for dismissals where the statutory DDP has not been completed due to a failure of the employer to comply with its requirements, the dismissal is automatically unfair (see the section on the statutory DDP above). For that sort of procedural defect, the hypothetical outcome under a fair procedure is irrelevant.

(2) For all other dismissals, the failure by an employer to follow "a procedure" in relation to the dismissal of an employee shall not be regarded as making the employer's action unreasonable if he shows that he would have decided to dismiss the employee if he had followed "the procedure."

The precise meaning of the new rule in (2) was dealt with in a series of **9.63** conflicting decisions in the EAT during 2006. In summary, there are two ways in which the phrase "a procedure" in s.98A(2) has been interpreted:

(a) the wide interpretation—it applies to any procedure with which the tribunal considers that the employer should have complied. This is an interpretation which favours the employer, as it means that a dismissal will be regarded as fair if *any* procedural failure made no difference to the result, no matter how important a safeguard the procedure in question provided.

(b) The narrow interpretation—it applies only to "a procedure which indicates some formality", e.g. to those incorporated in contracts. But it does not cover a lapse from the standard of reasonableness, or from the ACAS Code, which provides guidance as to the principles which ought to underlie a procedure, rather than the procedure itself. This approach favours employees, since it denies the employer the defence where the procedural failure is one which can be described as more than a mere formality.

In *Alexander v Bridgen Enterprises Ltd* [2006] I.R.L.R. 422, EAT, the wide interpretation was favoured. Elias P. stated *obiter* that s.98A(2) covered any procedure (other than the statutory DDP) that the tribunal considers that the employer ought in fairness to have complied with. It applied to all procedures, in the sense of the steps which ought to be taken by an employer before determining that he will dismiss a particular employee. There was no magic in the word "procedure". Nor was there any justification for seeking to redefine some steps which would naturally be described as "procedural" such as the duty to consult in a redundancy case, as "substantive" merely on the basis that they were said to provide important safeguards for employees.

In *Mason v Governing Body of Ward End Primary School* [2006] I.R.L.R. 432, EAT, the narrow interpretation was adopted, again obiter, by a division of the EAT presided over by H.H. Judge McMullen. He stated that s.98A(2) did not apply to any failure to comply with the standards of a reasonable employer, whether as exemplified by the ACAS Code of Practice or not. The Code was not "a procedure". Further, he focused attention on the wording of s.98A(2) and in particular the phrase "by itself". This meant that the subsection did not apply where there was a breach of a specific procedure accompanied by a more general criticism deriving from the standards of a reasonable employer or from the Code. Similar remarks were made by H.H. Judge McMullen, again obiter in *Pudney v Network Rail* EAT 070/05. However, in *Kelly-Madden v Manor Surgery* [2007] I.R.L.R. 17, the EAT presided over by Elias P held that "procedure" for the purposes of s.98A(2) meant any procedure rather than a specific procedure, and includes 'informal' unwritten practices even if they are drawn from the standards of a reasonable employer.

9.64   At the time of writing, the conflicting decisions of the EAT had not been resolved, although it must be a matter of time before the issue is referred to the Court of Appeal. It is respectfully submitted that the statutory provision ought to be narrowly construed, in accordance with interpretation (b) set out in para.9.61. The wording of the subsection does tend to favour such a construction. The phrase "by itself" would seem to exclude cases where the defect is really about a failure to meet the standards of the reasonable employer, or the principles of good industrial practice and reasonable behaviour set out in the ACAS Code of Practice. The "no difference" principle, and the *Polkey* reduction which is associated with it are further examined in dealing with remedies for unfair dismissal in para.10.17.

Reasonableness and dismissals for capability

9.65   A lack of capability should at the outset be distinguished from misconduct. "Capability" should be treated as applying to cases where the shortfall from the requisite standard is due to inherent incapacity. A failure to measure up to what is required through negligence or idleness, on the other hand, is properly described as misconduct: *Sutton & Gates (Luton) Ltd v Boxall* [1978] I.R.L.R. 486, EAT There are various categories of incapability, the main ones being:

(a) incompetence; and

(b) ill health.

9.66   Incompetence. In *James v Waltham Holy Cross UDC* [1973] I.C.R. 398, NIRC, it was suggested that reasonableness in the context of a dismissal for incompetence relied essentially upon three factors:

(1) Was there proper investigation and appraisal of the employee's performance and identification of the problem?

(2) Was he warned about the consequences of failure to improve?

(3) Was he given a reasonable chance to improve?

Fleshing this framework out, in examining whether the employer has acted reasonably, a tribunal is likely to be concerned with such issues as:

- Was there a proper assessment system in place e.g a form of appraisal or performance management?

- Is there other evidence of incompetence, e.g. the results of an investigation?

- Was the employee warned of the problem and the need to improve?

- Was he given an opportunity to improve?

- Was training appropriate and, if so, was it available?

- If an alternative post is available for which the employee was suitable, was it offered to him?

Ill-health. As far as ill-health is concerned, the approach of the reason-   **9.67** able employer is likely to differ according to whether the problem is one of long-term absence, or persistent short-term absences.

As far as long-term sickness is concerned, the procedure adopted by the employer must be a fair one. The statutory DDP (see paras 9.30 to 9.39) must in any event be followed, but that is of course only a bare minimum. What is further required in order for the employer's actions to be considered reasonable is:

(1) proper consultation with the employee. This ought to include discussions periodically throughout the duration of the illness. The employee ought, in particular to be told if the stage when dismissal may be considered is approaching. The employee's views on his condition ought to be considered.

(2) Medical investigation. Employers should inform themselves as to the true medical position in order to make an informed decision to dismiss.

(3) Consideration of any appropriate alternative employment.

(See *East Lindsey District Council v Daubney* [1977] I.R.L.R. 181, EAT).

As far as persistent short-term absence is concerned, the fundamentals of reasonableness were said in *International Sports Co Ltd v Thomson* [1980] I.R.L.R. 340, EAT to be:

(a) a fair review by the employer of the absence record and the reasons for it;

(b) the opportunity for the employee to make representations

(c) appropriate warnings thereafter.

However, it was said to be placing too heavy a burden on an employer to make the sort of medical investigation which was set out in *Daubney*. Such a procedure was applicable rather to long-term absences.

9.68   In relation to absences for ill health generally, the procedure is obviously relevant, and the factors set out above for long-term and persistent short-term absence will be important. As to the matters which an employer ought to take into account before deciding to dismiss, the following are among the factors to be considered:

(a) the nature and length of the illness;

(b) the likely future position as far as the illness is concerned;

(c) the effect upon other employees;

(d) the effect upon the business.

Some employers have a strict attendance policy due to the demands of their business. This is the case for postal workers, for example, where a certain number of absences, or days absent, will trigger off automatic warnings culminating in dismissal if there is no improvement. Dismissal in such a case has been held to be for "some other substantial reason" rather than incapability, even though the absences in question have been caused by ill health.

It is worth noting that the employer must be alert to the possibility that the employee is disabled within the meaning of the Disability Discrimination Act ("DDA") 1995. Any action in such a case must be taken in such a way that it is not unlawful under the DDA (see paras 6.38 to 6.53).

Reasonableness and dismissals for misconduct

9.69   Many of the unfair dismissal cases which find their way to the tribunal are cases where the employer has dismissed for misconduct. As with other types of dismissal, the employer must comply with the statutory DDP. Over and above that, the employer must act reasonably in accordance with s.98(4) of the ERA 1996. The principles in relation to a reasonable procedure in misconduct cases are well-established, and are set out in *British Home Stores Ltd v Burchell* [1978] I.R.L.R. 379 EAT. Where the employer suspects an act of misconduct and dismisses as a result, there are three issues for the tribunal in relation to the procedure:

(1) Did the employer genuinely believe that the employee was guilty of that misconduct?

(2) Did the employer have within his mind reasonable grounds upon which to sustain that belief?

(3) At the time at which he formed that belief on those grounds, had the employer carried out as much investigation into the matter as was reasonable?

There is then the further question of whether dismissal was an appropriate sanction in the circumstances.

In considering each of these matters, the tribunal should apply the "band of reasonable responses" test, rather than judging the employer's actions by what it (the tribunal) would have done in the circumstances. The band of reasonable responses test applies not only to whether dismissal was an appropriate penalty, but also to the procedures which are adopted to investigate: *Sainsbury's Supermarket v Hitt* [2003] I.R.L.R. 23, CA.

In dealing with dismissal where the reason is related to conduct, it is sometimes important to distinguish gross misconduct from other sorts of misconduct. Gross misconduct can be defined as misconduct which is sufficiently serious to allow the employer to dismiss summarily, i.e. without notice. Exactly what sort of conduct is entailed will vary according to the nature of the working situation. A list of examples of gross misconduct is set out in the ACAS Code of Practice, para.57 (see Appendix 3). Conduct dismissals are not confined to gross misconduct. However, where the misconduct in question cannot be classified as gross, there will be two important consequences:

(a) the employer cannot usually dismiss without notice; and

(b) it is difficult to justify dismissal without a warning (see the ACAS Code of Practice: para.60: "Good disciplinary procedures should. . .provide that no employee is dismissed for a first breach of discipline, except in cases of gross misconduct").

One issue which sometimes arises in dismissals for misconduct is the **9.70** question of consistency of treatment as between employees. Assume that an employee has been found fighting, and has been dismissed after a fair procedure was followed. Dismissal for fighting in the workplace would normally be regarded as a reasonable response. But what if another employee had been given a warning for fighting, rather than being dismissed? The problem would then be one of unequal treatment between two employees.

In *The Post Office v Fennell* [1981] I.R.L.R. 221, the Court of Appeal said that the word "equity" in the phrase "having regard to equity and the substantial merits of the case" in s.98(4) meant that employees who behave in much the same way should have meted out to them much the same punishment. In *Paul v East Surrey District Health Authority* [1995] I.R.L.R. 305, however, the Court of Appeal emphasised that an employer was entitled to take into account not only the nature of the conduct and the surrounding facts but also any mitigating personal circumstances in relation to the employees concerned. Clearly, the tribunal must be careful to determine that like is being compared with like. In the example given in the previous paragraph, the label "fighting" will cover a multitude of sins. To take but one aspect, what area did the fight take place in? An employer might be able to explain satisfactorily a lenient view taken of a fight outside the gaze of the public, and with no dangerous machinery in the vicinity.

Such an approach might not be inconsistent with a decision to dismiss where members of the public were present or the fight took place in a foundry.

Reasonableness and dismissals for redundancy

9.71   In the case of multiple redundancy dismissals, there are specific duties on the employer to consult employee representatives, and to notify the Department of Trade and Industry (see paras 11.16 to 11.18). These duties are additional to the prospect of any claim for unfair dismissal. As to the applicability of the statutory DDP, it is excluded where there is a collective redundancy of 20 or more employees, and there is a duty to consult and inform representatives.

If the employer states that the reason for dismissal was redundancy, it needs to establish that there was a redundancy situation, the tribunal will be reluctant to question a commercial decision to reduce the number of employees required, unless the good faith of the employer is questioned, i.e. is it a genuine redundancy, or has something else been dressed up as redundancy? Once the existence of a redundancy situation is established, the employer must go on to show that redundancy was in fact the reason for the dismissal, in the same way as any other potentially fair reason must be established.

With regard to reasonableness, the main focus is usually upon the selection process. Further, there are some types of redundancy dismissal which are automatically unfair. There are also potential issues related to individual consultation, and alternative employment. These matters are considered further in paras 11.24 to 11.26.

Reasonableness and dismissals for statutory illegality

9.72   The statutory DDP does not apply to a dismissal where it is no longer legal for an employee to do his job as a result of a statutory prohibition or restriction (reg.4 of the Dispute Resolution Regulations).

However, the employer must still act reasonably in deciding to dismiss. This is likely to involve considering:

(a) the extent of the ban. Does it affect all the employee's work, or only part of it?

(b) How long will the ban last?

(c) Are there alternative posts available?

Reasonableness and dismissals for retirement

9.73   The Employment Equality (Age) Regulations 2006 ("the Age Regulations") brought about a major revision to the law on unfair dismissal. Central to the change is the introduction of a new, potentially fair reason for dismissal: retirement of the employee (see paras 9.53 and 9.54). Alongside that change is the "duty to consider" procedure, which plays the key role in determining whether the retirement is procedurally fair. It should be stressed that the statutory DDP does not apply to dismissals for retirement. It is replaced by the "duty to consider" procedure. The matters to be considered when determining whether a dismissal for retirement is fair are set out in flow chart form in para.6.68. The deadlines for the "duty to consider" procedure are tabulated in para.6.65.

The "duty to consider" procedure is set out in Sch.6 to the Age Regulations. It operates in the following way.

The duty to notify. The employer must notify the employee of the date upon which he intends the employee to retire, and of the employee's right to request not to be retired on that date. The notification must be in writing, and it must be given not more than a year and not less than six months before the intended date of retirement. The duty applies regardless of any term in the employee's contract indicating when retirement is to take place, and irrespective of any other notification about his date of retirement or right to make a request, given at any time. As a result, it is not possible for the employer to avoid compliance with the duty within the six month–twelve month window by giving notice within the contract or at any other time. **9.74**

Where the employer has failed to serve notice within the period of six to twelve months, he will incur a limited penalty. In addition, he must notify the employee by the 14th day before the intended date of retirement. So the position is that:

(a) the employer should comply with the duty to notify between six and twelve months before the intended date of retirement;

(b) if he fails to do so, he should nevertheless notify no later than the 14th day before dismissal.

The consequence of failing to comply with (a) is an award to the employee of up to eight weeks pay. The consequence of failing to comply with (b) may be much more serious for the employer—the dismissal will be automatically unfair.

The right to request. The employee is given a statutory right to request not to retire, which corresponds to the employer's duty to notify. Just as the notification is about the date of intended retirement, so the right is to request not to retire on the intended date of retirement. The request must be in writing and state that it is made under the statutory procedure. **9.75**

The request must propose that the employee should continue in employment:

(a) indefinitely;

(b) for a stated period; or

(c) until a stated date.

It can be made even if the employer has failed to notify. If so, it must identify the date upon which the employee believes that the employer intends to retire him.

If the employer has, in fact, notified between six and twelve months prior to the intended date of retirement, then the employee is bound by time limits: his request must be made at least three months but not more than six months before the intended date of retirement. If, on the other hand, the employer has failed to give between six and twelve months notice, the employee's request can be made at any time within the six month period before the intended date of retirement.

9.76   The employee is entitled to make only one statutory request in relation to any one intended date of retirement.

9.77   Considering the request.   Once the employer has received a request under the procedure, he is under a duty to consider it. He must hold a meeting to discuss it with the employee within a reasonable period after receiving it. There is an exception where they reach an agreement that the employee's employment will continue—either indefinitely or to an agreed date. If no such agreement is reached, employer and employee must take all reasonable steps to attend a meeting. In the event that it is impracticable to hold a meeting within a reasonable period, the employer must consider any representations made by the employee.

After the meeting has been held (or the request considered in the event that a meeting is impracticable), the employer must notify the employee of his decision. He does not have to give reasons. All he has to do is:

(a) where the decision is that the employment will continue indefinitely, state that fact;

(b) where the decision is that the employment will continue for a further period, state the length of that period or the date on which it will end; or

(c) where the decision is to refuse the request, confirm that he wishes to retire the employee, and the date on which dismissal is to take effect.

(d) In addition, where he has refused the request, or granted an extension for a period shorter than the employee requested, he must inform the employee of his right to appeal. All notices in connection with the meeting (e.g. accepting or refusing the request to continue in employment, notifying the right to appeal etc.) must be in writing and dated.

If the employer has

(a) received a valid request from the employee not to retire;

(b) has not yet given notice of his decision about that request; and

(c) dismisses him,

then Sch.6, para.10 of the Age Regulations applies. This provides that, where the employer dismisses the employee in these circumstances:

"the contract of employment shall continue in force for all purposes, including the purpose of determining for any purpose the period for which the employee has been continuously employed."

In other words, the dismissal is ineffective. The employee will continue in **9.78** employment (with the right to be paid etc) until the day following the day on which notice of the decision is given.

The employee has a right to appeal from the employer's decision, where it is to refuse his request or to allow a shorter period of continued employment than was requested. A similar procedure is laid down for the appeal procedure as pertains to the original meeting to consider the request. The employee is supposed to "set out grounds of appeal". This is something of a tall order, given that there is no requirement on the employer to set out reasons for the decision which is being appealed against. Again, all notices under in connection with the appeal must be written and dated.

Right to be accompanied. The employee has a right to be accompanied to **9.79** a meeting to consider his request to continue after the intended retirement date, or a meeting to appeal against a refusal to comply with his request. The right is triggered off where the employee:

"reasonably requests to be accompanied at the meeting' by a companion who is 'a worker employed by the same employer as the employee."

Where the employer fails, or threatens to fail, to comply with a request to be accompanied, the employee may make a claim to an Employment Tribunal. In the event that the claim succeeds, the tribunal can award an amount of up to two weeks pay.

Protection for those who exercise their right to be accompanied is provided. An employee is entitled not to be subjected to a detriment for doing so, as is the companion whom he chooses. Further, an employee is entitled to be regarded as unfairly dismissed if the reason (or principal reason) for his dismissal is that he used (or tried to use) the right to be accompanied. The companion is provided with similar protection.

Section 98(4) of the ERA 1996 has no part to play In determining **9.80** whether a dismissal for retirement is fair or not. Nor does the statutory DDP which applies to most reasons for dismissal. Instead, the duty to consider procedure takes centre stage.

As far as retirement dismissals are concerned, a new s.98ZG of the ERA (inserted by the Age Regulations) determines whether the dismissal is fair or not. Of course, it applies only where the employer has established (with or without the help of the presumptions set out in paras 9.53 to 9.54) that the dismissal was by reason of retirement. Section 98ZG lays down that the issue for the tribunal to determine is whether the employer complied with

the core obligations contained within the "duty to consider" procedure.
Those core obligations are:

- to serve notice of the date of intended retirement and of the right
  to make a request, at least by the fourteenth day before the date in
  question;

- consideration of any request to continue in employment after the
  intended date of retirement (usually by holding a meeting, but
  considering the request in any event where a meeting is not
  practicable);

- considering any appeal against a decision to refuse a request.

The requirements are purely formal. Concepts such as "reasonableness",
"equity" and "merits" do not enter into the equation. If the core
obligations are complied with, the retirement dismissal is deemed to be fair.
If they are not, it is automatically unfair.

Reasonableness and dismissals for some other substantial reason

9.81   The statutory DDP applies where reason for the dismissal is "some other
substantial reason". Provided that the statutory procedure has been followed (or any failure to do so cannot be laid at the door of the employer)
then the dismissal will not be automatically unfair. The tribunal will still
need to consider whether the employer acted reasonably or unreasonably in
deciding to dismiss for the substantial reason in question. The fact that the
category is a catch-all one means that it is difficult to generalise about what
constitutes reasonableness in relation to it. To take a couple of the more
common situations which have cropped up under this heading:

- where the substantial reason is that the employee was on a fixed-
  term contract, the employer should be given the opportunity of
  being considered if a full-time position becomes available: *Beard v
  St Joseph's School* [1978] I.C.R. 1234;

- where the substantial reason is a business reorganisation, the
  tribunal must examine the employer's motives for the changes,
  and satisfy itself that they are not being imposed for arbitrary
  reasons: *Catamaran Cruisers Ltd v Williams* [1994] I.R.L.R. 386,
  EAT;

- where the substantial reason is outside pressure from a customer,
  the employer should act reasonably before deciding to dismiss, e.g.
  by considering and taking into account any injustice to the
  employee: *Dobie v Burns International Security Services (UK) Ltd*
  [1984] I.R.L.R. 329, CA.

CHAPTER TEN

REMEDIES FOR UNFAIR DISMISSAL

If a tribunal decides that the claimant has been unfairly dismissed, it can **10.01** order:

(a) Reinstatement—the claimant returns to his old job, with arrears of pay; etc. from a date specified by the Tribunal;

(b) Re-engagement—the claimant must be engaged in employment comparable to that from which he was dismissed, or other suitable employment; or

(c) Financial compensation.

Section 112 of the ERA 1996 lays down that the tribunal must consider the remedies available in the above order. In *Pirelli General Cable Works Ltd v Murray* [1979] I.R.L.R. 190, the EAT stated that in every case where a dismissal is found to be unfair the employment tribunal must explain reinstatement and re-engagement and ask the claimant if he wants such an order made. If he does, it must go on to consider each of those possibilities, giving both parties the opportunity to be heard. The EAT stated that this procedure must be followed even where the claimant is professionally represented. It would seem that this guidance must be adhered to even where the claimant has indicated on the claim form that he wishes to seek compensation, rather than reinstatement or re-engagement. However, as a procedural matter, the claimant ought to have given notice to the respondent of his changed intentions, so as to avoid the necessity for an adjournment and the possibility of a costs order.

In practice, despite the prominence given by the statute to re-employment, it is only ordered in a tiny proportion of those cases where the claimant has been successful—less than one per cent in any given year.

Before making an order for reinstatement or re-engagement, the Tribunal must consider:

(a) the claimant's wishes;

(b) whether the order is practicable; and

(c) whether it would be just if the claimant caused or contributed to the dismissal.

As to (a), if the claimant does not want such an order, the tribunal will move directly to consider compensation. Most frequently, the dispute between the parties is about (b)—whether the order is practicable. In *Meridian Ltd v Gomersall* [1977] I.R.L.R. 425, the EAT stated that, in deciding on this question, a tribunal should look at the circumstances of the case taking a broad commonsense view, rather than trying to analyse in detail the word "practicable".

10.02   Generally, it will not be practicable to order an employer to re-employ a dismissed employee if that would entail significant overstaffing, or redundancies among the other workers. However, employing a permanent replacement for a dismissed employee will not make re-employment impracticable of itself. The tribunal is instructed by s.116(5) and (6) of the ERA 1996 to ignore the fact that a replacement has been engaged unless:

    (a) it was not practicable for the employer to arrange for the employee's work to be done without such a replacement; and

    (b) the replacement was only engaged after a reasonable period had elapsed without an indication from the dismissed employee that he wished to be reinstated, and the only reasonable way to arrange for the work to be done was to engage a permanent replacement.

Another factor to be taken into account in determining practicability is the relationship between the dismissed employee and his colleagues. Where relationships are acrimonious, then a tribunal is unlikely to order re-employment. A related factor is whether there has been a breakdown of trust and confidence between employer and employee. In *Wood Group Heavy Industrial Turbines Ltd v Crossan* [1998] I.R.L.R. 680, EAT, for example, it was stated that it would only be in the rarest of cases that re-employment would be ordered where there was a breakdown of trust and confidence. In that case, the employer continued to believe that the employee had been dealing in drugs at work, and his re-engagement was held to be impracticable.

In addition to practicability, the tribunal must also take into account the justice of making an order for re-employment where the employee caused or contributed to the dismissal. A finding that the employee has contributed to his dismissal is not fatal to the prospect of an order for re-employment, but it must be taken into account, and will make it less likely.

10.03   Coupled with any order for reinstatement or re-engagement, there needs to be an order for compensation for the period since the claimant was unfairly dismissed. This is assessed on principles broadly similar to those set out under the heading "Financial Compensation" below. However, there is no "cap" on the amount of back pay and benefits which can be awarded, by contrast to the position with regard to the compensatory award.

If reinstatement or re-engagement is ordered, and the employer fails to comply, the matter will return to the tribunal for a second remedies hearing. It is possible at this second hearing for the employer to argue that complying with the order was impracticable, but the onus would be on him to show that it was.

10.04   **Additional award.** In the event that the tribunal finds that the order was practicable, and that the employer failed to comply with it, it will assess the compensation due to the employee in the light of the fact that he is not to be re-employed. In addition, compensation will be increased by an "additional award" of between 26 and 52 weeks—a special form of punitive damages (s.117(3)(b) Employment Rights Act 1996).

The tribunal will have to decide where to fix its award along the spectrum of 26 to 52 weeks. In *Mabirizi v National Hospital for Nervous Diseases* [1990] I.R.L.R. 133, EAT, the following factors were held to have been properly taken into account by the tribunal in carrying out this process:

(a) the degree of culpability on the part of the employer in failing to reinstate despite an order;

(b) compensation to the employee for her arrears of wages; and

(c) the employee's failure to mitigate her loss by getting another job.

Financial compensation

This is the remedy for unfair dismissal in the great majority of cases. It consists of a basic and a compensatory award.   **10.05**

Basic award.   This represents a number of weeks' gross pay, calculated in accordance with s.119 of the ERA 1996, which lays down that the unfairly dismissed employee should receive: **10.06**

(a) one and a half weeks' pay for each year of employment in which he was not below the age of 41;

(b) one week's pay for each year of employment not within (a) above, in which he was not below the age of 22; and

(c) half a week's pay for each year of employment not within (a) or (b) above.

There are various points to note about the formula. In particular:

• The weekly pay in question is gross wages, i.e. before deduction of tax, etc., and includes allowances and commission if contractual.

• It is subject to a limit which is raised annually (£310 with effect from February 1, 2007).

• Only complete years are counted.

Deductions may be made from the basic award where it would be "just and equitable to reduce the basic award" (s.122(3) of the ERA). But no deduction should be made because of a failure by the employee to mitigate, nor should it be reduced because the employee has suffered no financial loss. The principle is that the employee should receive the basic award, even if he steps straight into another job immediately after being unfairly dismissed, and even if the new job is more highly paid than the one which he has lost.

For example:

- a dismissal takes place which is automatically unfair because the employer has failed to comply with the "duty to consider" procedure. The employee is aged 60, had twelve years continuous employment with the employer, and was paid £390 gross per week at the time of the dismissal. He finds alternative employment, which is better paid, immediately. Leaving to one side any compensatory award, he should receive £310 (the statutory maximum) x 12 x 1.5 by way of basic award—£5,580.

In certain cases, the basic award is subject to a minimum. In the following cases, there is a minimum basic award of £4,000:

(a) where the dismissal (or selection for redundancy) was automatically unfair because it was for a trade union reason;

(b) where the dismissal was automatically unfair by reason of s.100 of the ERA 1996, because the employee was carrying out certain health and safety activities or duties;

(c) where the dismissal was automatically unfair by reason of s.101A of the ERA 1996 (Working Time Regulations cases);

(d) where the dismissal was automatically unfair by reason of s.102(1) of the ERA 1996 (occupational pension trustees);

(e) where the dismissal was automatically unfair under s.103 of the ERA (consultation about a transfer under the TUPE Regulations or about collective redundancies).

There is a minimum basic award of four weeks' pay subject to the statutory maximum (currently £310 per week) in the following circumstances:

(a) where the employee is found to be automatically unfairly dismissed as a result of the employer's failure to comply with the statutory DDP;

(b) where the employee is found to be automatically unfairly dismissed as a result of the employer's failure to follow the "duty to consider" procedure in a retirement case.

The tribunal may, in certain circumstances set out in s.122 of the ERA 1996, reduce the amount of the basic award. In summary, these are:

(a) where the claimant has unreasonably refused an offer of reinstatement;

(b) where the claimant's conduct before dismissal (or, in a case where dismissal was with notice, before notice was given) makes it just and equitable to reduce the basic award;

(c) where the claimant has been awarded any amount under a designated dismissal procedure;

(d) where the claimant has received a redundancy payment.

It is only in these limited circumstances that a basic award can be reduced. Unlike the compensatory award, it is not subject to reduction for failure to mitigate; nor is it liable to a *Polkey* reduction (see the section on *Polkey* reductions later in this chapter).

The most important of these reductions is that set out in (b)—where a **10.07** reduction is just and equitable because of the claimant's conduct before dismissal (or before being given notice). It is not necessary that his conduct should have contributed to the dismissal.

Compensatory award. The basic principle is that this element of the **10.08** award should compensate the employee for financial loss suffered as a result of the dismissal. A statutory cap is placed on most forms of unfair dismissal by s.124 ERA (see the section "Maximum compensatory award" below).

The compensatory award includes:

(a) Immediate loss of wages and benefits. This deals with the period from the effective date of termination (EDT) to the remedy part of the hearing. The loss is the net amount which the employee would have earned, less the amount earned in fresh employment (if any)

(b) Future loss of wages and benefits. This covers loss after the remedy hearing. The tribunal will look at whether the employee will suffer continuing loss, after reasonable efforts at mitigation are taken into consideration

(c) Loss of statutory protection. A figure (e.g. £250) to compensate for the loss of the right not to be unfairly dismissed from a future job

(d) Expenses incurred as a result of dismissal.

The loss under (a) immediate loss and (b) future loss above will include, where appropriate, loss of fringe benefits and pension rights. As far as fringe benefits are concerned, the following are examples of what might be claimed:

(i) Commission.

(ii) Contractual bonuses (but not Christmas gifts).

(iii) The benefit under a low interest loan. This would normally be valued at the difference between the interest payable on the company's low interest loan and the market rate.

(iv) Subsidised accommodation. The value would be the difference between the cost actually paid by the employee and the cost of obtaining equivalent accommodation elsewhere.

   (v) Special travel allowances.

  (vi) Tips.

 (vii) Luncheon vouchers.

(viii) Medical insurance.

  (ix) Benefits received under a share participation scheme.

   (x) The difference in value between shares sold back to the employer company at the time of dismissal, and the value of the shares at the date of the remedies hearing.

These are merely examples, and instructions need to be taken as to exactly what was received in the way of benefits. Care must be taken not to take into account allowances paid free of tax (for example for travel) since their function is to reimburse the employee for expense incurred, rather than to provide a benefit. A related point is that any allowance claimed which was not taxed may create the risk that the contract is tainted with illegality (see para.9.16 for details about illegal contracts).

10.09   Immediate or future loss may also include loss of the benefit which would have been received as a result of pension rights which have been reduced as a result of the unfair dismissal. In some cases, the sum concerned can be a very large one, and this is an area where, if the position is at all complicated, expert advice is required. Some guidance is to be found in the pamphlet *Employment Tribunals: Compensation for Loss of Pension Rights*, drawn up in 2003 by a group of employment tribunal chairmen with the assistance of the Government Actuary Department. In *Port of Tilbury (London) Ltd v Birch* [2005] I.R.L.R. 92, EAT, it was held that the duty of the tribunal was to consider the evidence and submissions of the parties, and to see whether a fair assessment of the loss of pension rights could be made on that basis. If that was not possible, then the guidelines might help the tribunal to come to a conclusion. In practice, where there is a complicated issue in relation to pensions, the tribunal will very often make an assessment of the other elements of compensation and put the matter back to a later date for a sum for loss of pension to be agreed, or further evidence and submissions to be made to the tribunal so that it can give proper consideration to what is often a relatively weighty question.

The main categories of pension loss in an unfair dismissal case are likely to be:

  (1) loss of the pension rights which have accrued between the date of dismissal and the hearing. The usual sum awarded for this head of loss is an amount equivalent to what the employer would have contributed to the employee's pension scheme during the period in question. The contributions which the employee would have made are ignored for this purpose.

  (2) Loss of future pension rights which would accrue between the hearing and retirement. Again, the usual way of dealing with this

area is to make an award equivalent to the amount which the employer would have made to the fund in the future for that employee. The period in question has to be fixed by the tribunal coming to a speculative conclusion. In doing so, it has to answer questions such as: how long would the employee have been employed by that employer? How long would it be before the employee acquired other pensionable employment? The questions are similar to those in respect of other forms of future loss (see below).

(3) Loss of the enhancement of rights which had already accrued at the time of dismissal. This is the part of the exercise which is complicated. It is dealt with in the pamphlet referred to above, with actuarial tables. Fortunately for the employment law practitioner, in most cases no account needs to be taken of the enhancement of accrued pension rights, and the pamphlet provides further guidance. As a result, most cases of loss of pension rights can be resolved by the relatively simple process involved in (1) and (2) above.

The fundamental principle, in calculating the compensatory award, is that it is confined to compensating for financial loss. It should not be used to express disapproval of the employer, or to mark the tribunal's sympathy for the claimant: *Lifeguard Assurance Ltd v Zadrozny* [1977] I.R.L.R. 56, EAT. Further, it is financial loss which falls to be compensated. There can be no loss for injury to feelings, humiliation or distress: *Dunnachie v Kingston upon Hull City Council* [2004] I.R.L.R. 727, HL.

Immediate loss

With regard to immediate loss, difficulties in calculation sometimes occur **10.10** when the employee obtains new employment in the period between the dismissal and the date of the tribunal hearing to determine remedies. The general principle is that earnings actually obtained in any new employment should be set off against those which could have been expected if the employee had continued in the old job. In that way, the loss suffered by the employee will be apparent. The general principle was subject to elaboration by the EAT in *Whelan v Richardson* [1998] I.R.L.R. 114 as follows:

(a) the loss must be assessed on the basis of the facts established at the date of the remedies hearing;

(b) if the claimant was unemployed for a period, he should recover what he would have earned during that period if he had not been dismissed (subject to the duty to mitigate—see below);

(c) if the claimant finds another job which pays less than the job from which he was unfairly dismissed, he should recover what he would have earned in the job he lost, less a deduction for the income received in the new job;

(d) if, at the time of the remedies hearing, the claimant has found new permanent employment which pays as much as, or more than, the job which he lost, then the tribunal should only assess the employee's loss from the date of dismissal to the date on which the new permanent employment began. In other words, the employer who dismissed him unfairly cannot rely on his increased earnings to reduce the loss suffered before taking on the new, more lucrative, employment.

In *Dench v Flynn & Partners* [1998] I.R.L.R. 653, the Court of Appeal warned that the employer's liability to compensate does not necessarily cease when the claimant obtains employment of a permanent nature at the same or a higher salary than the job he lost. The new employment might, for example, appear to be permanent when it starts, but might prove to be of short duration, due to no fault of the claimant. If so, loss consequent upon the unfair dismissal might continue.

Another issue which sometimes arises in relation to immediate loss is the position as far as earnings during the notice period is concerned. Should the claimant be paid for the notice period where he obtains other employment? In *Norton Tool Co Ltd v Tewson* [1972] I.R.L.R. 86, NIRC, it was stated that it was good industrial relations practice for an employer who dismisses without notice to make a payment in lieu of notice. As a result, no credit need be given by the employee for money earned from other employees during the notice period. The compensatory award should include full pay for the notice period, without any reduction for wages earned by way of mitigation. During the course of 2004–2006, there were several conflicting EAT decisions as to whether this remained good law. The Court of Appeal dealt with the matter in *Burlo v Langley* [2007] I.R.L.R. 145, endorsing the principle in *Norton Too*, and holding that an employee who is unfairly dismissed does not have to give credit for sums earned from other employers during the notice period.

Future loss

10.11　　As far as future loss is concerned, the tribunal is essentially involved in a speculative exercise about the future employment prospects of the claimant. How long is he likely to be unemployed? Is his employment likely to be at a lower rate than the job which he lost? The calculation is based upon the net earnings which the claimant would have received if he had not been unfairly dismissed, less the net earnings which he should receive in whatever job he takes up. As it was put in *Tradewinds Airways Ltd v Fletcher* [1981] I.R.L.R. 272, EAT, the tribunal must compare the salary prospects for the future in each job and see how long it will take the employee to reach in his new job the salary which he would have reached in the old job. His future loss is then the amount of the shortfall, measured by reference to the difference in net take home pay.

The following situations should be considered:

(1) The claimant has acquired stable permanent employment by the time of the remedies hearing, at the same or a higher wage than in the job which he lost. There should be no award for future loss.

(2) The claimant has found employment but it is at a lower wage than the old job. The tribunal must determine the extent of the shortfall, and its likely duration. For example, if the wage is £100 a week less, and the tribunal takes the view that he ought to reach his old wage rate in six months time, it will award £2,600 for future loss.

(3) The claimant is still unemployed, despite his efforts to find another job. The tribunal must decide when he is likely to obtain employment, and what the wage is likely to be. It will take into account the local job market and the claimant's characteristics, e.g. his age and skills. Based upon these and any other relevant factors, it will take a broad brush decision as to the length of the period of future unemployment and the financial loss entailed.

In situations (2) and (3), the tribunal will have regard to the claimant's duty to mitigate his loss by making reasonable efforts to obtain employment.

As far as loss of statutory protection is concerned, this is an amount to compensate the employee for the fact that he will have to work for a year for any new employer before he acquires the right not to be unfairly dismissed, and for two years before he is entitled to a redundancy payment. The tribunals make a small award to reflect this "loss of statutory industrial rights" as it is sometimes termed. The amount varies according to circumstances, but £250 is common.

The tribunal may, if it has been given evidence on the matter, also award   **10.12**
the claimant his expenses in looking for work. This would include the cost of publications which carry job advertisements, postage for job applications, travel to interviews and the like. Where the claimant has been involved in setting up in business on his own, and has incurred reasonable expenses in doing so, the compensatory award can reflect this: *Gardiner-Hill v Roland Berger Technics Ltd* [1982] I.R.L.R. 498, EAT.

Deductions from the compensatory award

There are various deductions and adjustments which fall to be made when the compensatory award is calculated.

Contributory fault

Under s.123(6) of the ERA 1996, the tribunal has the power to make a   **10.13**
reduction from the compensatory award for unfair dismissal where it decides that the employee is, in part, at fault:

"Where the tribunal finds that the dismissal was to any extent caused or contributed to by any action of the complainant, it shall reduce the amount of the compensatory award by such proportion as it considers just and equitable having regard to that finding."

The process may be compared to that where there is a finding of contributory negligence in tort. The tribunal will decide, first, whether the claimant is (at least in part) "the author of his own misfortune". Has he contributed to the dismissal? Second, was he in some way blameworthy? Finally, if his fault did in some way contribute to the dismissal, the tribunal will fix a percentage for the reduction.

General guidance on this area was given in *Morrison v Amalgamated Transport & General Workers' Union* [1989] I.R.L.R. 361, NICA as follows:

(a) the tribunal must take a broad, commonsense view of the situation;

(b) its view should not be confined to the moment when employment is terminated;

(c) what is relevant is conduct on the part of the employee which is culpable or blameworthy or unreasonable; and

(d) the employee's culpability or unreasonable conduct must have contributed to or played a part in the dismissal.

In practice, tribunals do make deductions for contributory fault in a significant minority of unfair dismissal cases. Typically, such a contribution will be 25, 50 or 75 per cent, depending on the degree of contribution, and the extent to which the employee appears to be culpable. In an appropriate case, a tribunal is not debarred from making a deduction of 100 per cent, with the result that there is no compensatory award: *W Devis & Sons v Atkins* [1977] A.C. 931. There is some case law as to the situations in which a deduction for contributory conduct may be appropriate. For example:

(a) Failure to exercise a right of appeal under the employer's internal procedure does not constitute contributory fault: *Hoover Ltd v Forde* [1980] I.C.R. 239. It may now be penalised in accordance with s.31(2) of the Employment Act 2002 (see below).

(b) Failure to use a grievance procedure in a constructive dismissal situation may constitute contributory conduct (and again, may make the employee subject to a reduction under s.31 of the Employment Act 2002).

(c) The great majority of reductions for contributory conduct occur in misconduct cases e.g. threats of violence when wrongdoing was alleged: *Munif v Cole & Kirby Ltd* [1973] I.C.R. 486. Perhaps the most bizarre basis for a reduction was for placing the wrong body in a coffin: *Coalter v Walter Craven* [1980 I.R.L.R. 262.

(d) Although usually of relevance in misconduct cases, it is possible for a reduction for contributory fault to be made where the tribunal has found the claimant was unfairly dismissed on grounds of ill health. Such a reduction will be rare, however, one possible example being where the employee persistently refused to obtain appropriate medical reports, or attend for medical examination: *Slaughter v C Brewer & Sons Ltd* [1990] I.R.L.R. 426, CA.

(e) A reduction can be made in a case where the unfair dismissal was for redundancy e.g. a refusal to take alternative work offered by the employer: *Nelson v BBC (No.2)* [1979 I.R.L.R. 346. Such a case might also fall within the category of failure to mitigate loss (by earning the amount which the employer would have paid in the alternative employment—see "Failure to mitigate loss" below).

Post-conduct dismissal

In deciding what is just and equitable, the tribunal may have regard to **10.14** misconduct on the part of the employee which has been discovered subsequent to dismissal: *W Devis & Sons Ltd v Atkins* [1977] I.R.L.R. 314, HL. However, the conduct in question must have been committed prior to dismissal (even if discovered after dismissal). Post-dismissal conduct cannot be taken into account in determining what is "just and equitable in all the circumstances": *Soros and Soros v Davison and Davison* [1994] I.R.L.R. 264, EAT.

Failure to mitigate loss

As stated earlier, in determining the claimant's loss, the overall equation **10.15** is to take the amount which he would have earned, and to deduct from that the amount which he actually did earn. This line of reasoning needs to be somewhat modified in the light of the claimant's obligation to mitigate his loss. It would clearly not be just if he could sit back (once he had been unfairly dismissed) and make no effort to find work. So he is fixed by law with the obligation to make reasonable efforts to mitigate his loss. Usually this will involve seeking out job vacancies, making applications for those which are suitable, attending for interview if asked and accepting any reasonable offer. At the tribunal hearing on remedies, if the employer contends that the claimant has not made reasonable efforts to mitigate, evidence will be heard on the issue. As a matter of practice, therefore, it is prudent for the claimant to keep copies of job applications made, advertisements replied to, etc. If the tribunal decides that the claimant has not made reasonable efforts to mitigate his loss, it must decide what the position would have been if he had made reasonable efforts of the sort required. Would he have acquired a job, and if so, when and at what salary? The tribunal must then take the answers to these questions into account in determining what the claimant's loss would have been, if he had made reasonable efforts to mitigate.

In *Wilding v British Telecommunications plc* [2002] I.R.L.R. 524, CA, the Court of Appeal stated that it was the duty of an employee to act as a reasonable person, unaffected by the prospect of compensation from his former employee. Where the employer alleges that the employee has failed to mitigate his loss, the burden of proof is on the party making the allegation: *Bessenden Properties Ltd v Corness* [1974] I.R.L.R. 338, CA. In discharging that burden of proof, it is not enough for the employer to show that it would have been reasonable for the claimant to take the steps which he suggests. He must show that it was unreasonable of the claimant not to take them. As Sedley L.J. put it in *Wilding*, this reflects the important legal principle that, if there is more than one reasonable response open to the wronged party, the wrongdoer has no right to determine his choice. It is only where the wrongdoer can show affirmatively that the other party acted unreasonably in relation to his duty to mitigate that the defence will succeed.

It is usual for a tribunal to accept that an employee need not take the first job which appears on the horizon. The question is: what is reasonable? The wages and other terms would enter into the consideration of the reasonable person in deciding what job to pursue or accept, as would the distance which he would have to travel. As time goes by, however, the scope of what is reasonable is likely to expand, so that after a lengthy period of unemployment, the claimant might be expected to be prepared to take a substantial cut in wages in order to get back in the job market, and mitigate his loss.

10.16 In certain circumstances, it may be reasonable for a claimant to seek to set up in business on his own account, rather than seek employment. In such a case, it may also be legitimate for the claimant to seek the expenses of setting up in business, again provided that it is reasonable to do so: *Gardiner-Hill v Roland Berger Technics Ltd* [1982] I.R.L.R. 498.

The *Polkey* reduction

10.17 The concept involved in this possible reduction was crystallised in *Polkey v AE Dayton Services* [1988] A.C. 344. In that case, the House of Lords considered the position in an unfair dismissal case where the employer's failure to follow a fair procedure did not affect the outcome, i.e. the employee would have been dismissed anyway. There were two aspects to their important decision:

(1) First, they held that the fact that it would not have made any difference if the employer had followed a fair procedure generally did not affect the question whether the dismissal was unfair. It remained unfair, even if the unfairness did not affect whether the employee would have been dismissed.

(2) Second, if the unfairness did not affect the result, and the employee would have been dismissed even with a fair procedure, that would have impact upon the amount of the compensatory award. Lord Bridge (at 365) stated that, if the Tribunal was in doubt about whether the employee would have been dismissed, that doubt

"can be reflected by reducing the normal amount of compensation by a percentage representing the chance that the employee would still have lost his employment."

As far as (1) is concerned, the effect of the decision in *Polkey* was radically altered by the insertion of s.98A into the ERA 1996. As this is a matter which affects the substantive law of unfair dismissal, it is dealt with in Chapter 9 (see paras 9.62 to 9.64).

With respect to (2), it is open to the employer to show that dismissal would have been likely even if a proper procedure had been followed. In some cases, the tribunal will find it difficult to envisage what would have happened in the hypothetical situation of the unfairness not having occurred. This is particularly likely to be the case where the unfairness "goes to the heart of the matter". In such a case, the tribunal may refuse to "embark upon a sea of speculation" (*King v Eaton Ltd (No.2)* [1998] I.R.L.R. 686, CS). However, in *Scope v Thornett* [2007] I.R.L.R. 155, the CA said that the task of an employment tribunal

> "when deciding what compensation is just and equitable for future loss of earnings, will almost inevitably involve a consideration of uncertainties. There may be cases in which evidence to the contrary is so sparse that a tribunal should approach the question on the basis that loss of earnings in the employment would have continued indefinitely, but, where there is evidence that it may not have been so, that evidence must be taken into account."

Where a tribunal does find a case suitable for a Polkey reduction, then it must decide:

(a) when the employer might have dismissed if it had acted according to a fair procedure; and

(b) what were the chances that it would have dismissed at that point, expressed as a percentage.

As a result of this reasoning process, the tribunal might decide, for example, that it would have taken the employer a further three weeks to hold the hearings which were required in order to act reasonably and fairly. It might also decide that, at that point, there was a 50/50 chance that the claimant would have been dismissed. The calculation of the compensatory award would then give the claimant three weeks at full pay, followed by a period on half of full pay, until such time as he acquired (or ought to have acquired) alternative employment.

Dispute resolution procedures (Employment Act 2002, s.31)

If the relevant statutory dismissal and disciplinary procedure (DDP) or **10.18** statutory grievance procedure (GP) was not completed before proceedings were commenced, the Tribunal is obliged to adjust the level of the compensatory (but not the basic) award (s.31 of the EA 2002). If the reason for non-completion was wholly or mainly due to a failure by the employee to comply with requirements or to exercise a right of appeal under the relevant procedure, the award must be reduced. If it was due to a failure by the employer, the award must be increased. The standard level of adjustment is 10 per cent. If "just and equitable in all the circumstances", that adjustment may be up to 50 per cent. On the other hand, if there are "exceptional circumstances" where a 10 per cent adjustment would be unjust or inequitable, the Tribunal may make a lesser adjustment, or none at all. At the time of writing, there had been no appellate cases in which the discretion of the tribunal in making these adjustments had been challenged. It would seem, however, that the usual position is that the reduction or increase should be 10 per cent. Where there are factors such as a deliberate attempt to avoid resolution of the dispute, or to give a fair hearing, then the increase or reduction might well be substantially more. Similarly, an employer who fails to have any sort of procedure in place might expect to be treated more harshly than one who has a procedure, but implements it in a sloppy fashion. To look at the other side of the equation, an employee who fails to exercise a right to appeal in circumstances where he genuinely believes it would be hopeless might be more leniently dealt with by the tribunal than one who "jumped the gun" and went to tribunal without appealing against the decision to dismiss because of a desire to hold the employer to account publicly.

Redundancy payment

10.19   A redundancy payment made by the employer will be deducted when determining the basic award. If there is any excess over the basic award (e.g. because it has been made on a more generous contractual basis than the statutory minimum), then it goes to reduce the compensatory award (s.123(7) of the ERA 1996, and *Rushton v Harcros Timber and Building Suppliers Ltd* [1993] I.R.L.R. 254).

Ex gratia payment

10.20   Where the employer has made an *ex gratia* payment to the employee, it will be deducted from the basic award provided it is referable to the dismissal. Any excess over the basic award will be deducted from the compensatory award, subject to the same condition. In order to ensure that credit will be given for the payment, the employer needs to make it clear that it relates to the dismissal: *Chelsea Football Club and Athletic Co Ltd v Heath* [1981] I.R.L.R. 73, EAT.

Payment in lieu of notice

10.21   If the employer makes a payment to the employee in lieu of notice, it should be deducted from the compensatory award: *Babcock FATA Ltd v Addison* [1987] I.R.L.R. 173, CA.

Maximum for compensatory award

10.22   This limits the compensatory award to £60.600 for cases where the effective date of termination ("EDT") is on or after February 1, 2007. This limit is revised annually. By contrast with the basic award, however, there is no statutory cap upon the weekly earnings of the claimant upon which the award is based.

This limit applies to the compensatory award taken by itself, and excludes the separate figure for the basic award.

There are certain unfair dismissal cases where the statutory cap on the compensatory award does not apply. In summary, these are:

(a) cases where the claimant was dismissed contrary to s.103A of the ERA 1996 for making a protected disclosure ("whistle-blowing");

(b) cases where the dismissal is automatically unfair by virtue of s.100 of the ERA 1996 (certain health and safety reasons); and

(c) selection for redundancy on the grounds of either (a) or (b) above.

Written particulars

Section 38 of the Employment Act 2002 provides that tribunals must **10.23** award compensation to an employee where, upon a claim being successful under any of a number of jurisdictions (including unfair dismissal), it becomes evident that an employer was in breach of his statutory duty to provide full and accurate particulars of employment.

The award does not have to be part of the claim made by the employee. The statute envisages that the tribunal will act of its own motion to add the amount in question if the evidence shows that the employer has failed to comply with its duty. The award for this breach of duty is a minimum of two weeks and a maximum of four weeks wages, the amount of a week's wages being subject to the same limit as that for the basic award (£310 per week where the EDT is on or after February 1, 2007).

Benefits other than job seekers' allowance and income support

If the claimant receives state benefits during the period for which he is **10.24** being compensated, that will raise the prospect of double compensation. As far as job seekers' allowance and income support are concerned, they are dealt with by means of the process of recoupment, which is discussed below. As to other benefits, in *Morgans v Alpha Plus Security Ltd* [2005] I.R.L.R. 234, the EAT held that the full amount of the incapacity benefit which the claimant had received during the period of the award should be deducted. In coming to this conclusion, the EAT reasoned that there was no power for the tribunal to disregard receipts so that a claimant might recover a sum in excess of actual loss.

The order of reductions

Those reductions which are applicable should be made in the following **10.25** order (*Digital Equipment Ltd v Clements (No.2)* 1998] I.R.L.R. 134, CA, as read with s.24A of the ERA 1996):

(1) calculate the claimant's financial loss sustained in consequence of the dismissal (s.123(1) of the ERA 1996)

(2) Deduct any payment already made by the employer as compensation for the dismissal (e.g. as an *ex gratia* payment), other than an enhanced redundancy payment.

(3) Deduct any amount earned by the claimant during the period of loss, or to reflect his failure to take reasonable steps in mitigation of his loss.

(4) Make any percentage reduction in accordance with *Polkey v AE Dayton Services* [1988] A.C. 344 to reflect the chance that the claimant would have been dismissed even if the employer had acted fairly.

(5) Increase or reduce where either employer or employee failed to comply with a relevant grievance or disciplinary procedure (s.31 of the Employment Act 2002).

(6) Increase for any failure by the employer to provide written particulars (s.38 of the Employment Act 2002).

(7) Make any percentage reduction for the employee's contributory fault (s.123(6) of the ERA 1996).

(8) Deduct any enhanced redundancy payment to the extent that it exceeds the basic award (s.123(7) of the ERA 1996).

(9) Apply the statutory cap unless one of the exceptions applies (s.124(1) of the ERA 1996—£60,600 if the EDT is on or after February 1, 2007).

Interest

10.26   The award of the tribunal for unfair dismissal will not include interest. The power to award interest is given to courts of record by the Law Reform (Miscellaneous Provisions) Act 1934. Since an employment tribunal is not a court of record, it does not have that power: *Nelson v British Broadcasting Corporation (No.2)* [1979] I.R.L.R. 346, CA.

After the award has been made, however, if the respondent delays in paying, an entitlement to interest arises. If an award is unpaid 42 days after the date upon which judgment was sent to the parties, interest begins to accrue at the rate specified in s.17 of the Judgments Act 1838: Employment Tribunals (Interest) Order 1990, art.4. That rate is 8 per cent per annum (and has been since April 1, 1993). The following sums are to be disregarded when interest is calculated:

(a) any sum claimed by the Secretary of State in a recoupment notice (see next section); and

(b) any sum which the respondent has to deduct and pay over to the authorities in respect of income tax or national insurance contributions.

If the tribunal has made an award of costs or expenses, that is also excluded from the interest calculation.

Recoupment

During any period of unemployment, it is likely that the claimant will **10.27** have received jobseeker's allowance and/or income support. If the compensatory award covers that period, then the government will wish to reclaim the amount paid to the claimant in benefits. As a result, it is necessary for the tribunal award to make it clear whether its award covers a period during which the claimant may have been in receipt of benefit. The machinery set up for this purpose is contained in the Employment Protection (Recoupment of Jobseeker's Allowance and Income Support) Regulations 1996 (SI 1996/2349: "the Recoupment Regulations"). That part of the compensatory award which reflects wages for the period from the date of dismissal to the date of the remedies hearing is known as the "prescribed element". The period in question is known as the "prescribed period". During the course of the remedies hearing, the tribunal will have ascertained whether the employee claimed jobseeker's allowance or income support during the prescribed period. In giving its decision, the tribunal is under a duty to identify the prescribed period and the prescribed element. The Benefits Agency then works out the amount received by the claimant in jobseeker's allowance or income support over the period, and serves a notice on the parties, specifying the amount which it reclaims. That notice has to be served within 21 days after the hearing or nine days after the judgment has been sent to the parties, whichever is the sooner. The respondent must then pay this amount to the Agency, and the remainder to the claimant.

This procedure applies only to jobseeker's allowance and income support. For the position with regard to other benefits, see para.?.??.

The Recoupment Regulations do not apply to the basic award. Nor do they apply to future loss. However, the claimant's entitlement to future benefits is likely to be affected by an award as to future loss. The regulations which determine entitlement to benefit lay down that a claimant is not to be treated as unemployed following a tribunal award for compensation for unfair dismissal where the payment represents remuneration which the employment tribunal considers that the employee might have earned on a particular day: Social Security (Unemployment, Sickness and Invalidity Benefit) Regulations 1983 (SI 1983/1598), reg.7.

Example. C receives £900 in income support while awaiting the hearing. At **10.28** *the remedies hearing, C is awarded £4,500, made up as follows:*

Basic Award	*£800*
Earnings between the date of	
dismissal and the date of	
the hearing (the prescribed element)	*£1,700*
Statutory industrial rights	*£250*
Future loss representing unemployment for	
eight weeks after the date of the remedies hearing	*£1,750*

The prescribed element is £1,700. The employer should pay C £2,800 immediately and tell the Benefits Agency that he has retained £1,700. The Benefits Agency should tell the employer to pay it £900. The employer should then pay £900 to the Benefits Agency, and £800 (the remainder of the prescribed element) to C.

The phenomenon of recoupment provides an incentive to the parties to settle. If there is a settlement, the Recoupment Regulations do not apply, since the settlement (even if it is endorsed by the tribunal) will not identify any prescribed amount or prescribed period. There is therefore no clawback of part of the award, and the claimant keeps the whole award as well as the benefits which he has received. Negotiators for both sides will keep this in mind, with the result that the claimant may settle for slightly less than the likely tribunal award, in the knowledge that this will be slightly more than he would receive once recoupment has taken place.

10.29 *Example.   C expects to obtain an award of £5,000 from R if the tribunal gives judgment, but is aware that £2,000 of that will be clawed back by the Benefits Agency. A settlement over £3,000 will benefit C, whilst a settlement under £5,000 will benefit R. There is therefore a substantial band of common interest which acts as an incentive to settle the case before judgment.*

Taxation

10.30   Where the award is less than £30,000, no tax is payable. This flows from the fact that tribunals assess the compensatory award on the basis of net pay. Where an award is made for termination of employment which exceeds £30,000, it is subject to tax to the extent that it exceeds £30,000. All amounts received for termination of employment go towards meeting the £30,000 threshold.

In due course, therefore, if the award exceeds the £30,000 threshold, the employee will receive a tax demand for tax on the amount over that threshold. However, the employee should receive the amount which he has lost as a result of his dismissal. In order to ensure that result, the tribunal will have to "gross up" the amount of the award. This means that it decides the amount which the employee should receive, and then adds to it an amount representing the tax which he will eventually have to pay.

10.31 *Example.   The employee's loss is £45,000. On receiving evidence about his tax position for the year in which the award is to be paid, the tribunal concludes that he will be a higher tax rate payer, and decides that the tax on the amount over the threshold will be as follows:*

£45,000–£30,000 = £15,000 x 40 per cent = £6,000

In order to put him in the position of receiving £45,000 after tax, the tribunal must award £55,000. He will then be taxed at 40 per cent on £25,000 (the excess over £30,000). As a result, he will receive after tax:

£30,000 tax free
(£25,000 less tax at 40 per cent) *£15,000*
Total *£45,000*

Overlapping claims

Frequently an employee claims for two or more of the following: **10.32**

(a) unfair dismissal

(b) wrongful dismissal;

(c) redundancy

(d) discrimination (where the alleged act of discrimination is dismissal).

It is of course perfectly possible that the claimant might succeed on one of the claims only (e.g. the tribunal finds that he was unfairly dismissed on a ground other than redundancy, that he was not wrongfully dismissed and there was no discrimination involved). Wherever overlapping claims like this succeed, however, the general principle is that there should be no double recovery.

For example, where claims for both wrongful and unfair dismissal succeed, the employee will be entitled to payment for the notice period in respect of each claim. The usual practice is for the tribunal to make an award for wrongful dismissal which consists of payment for the notice period. The compensatory award for unfair dismissal would then exclude the notice period, so as to avoid a situation where the claimant is compensated twice over.

Similarly, where an employee is unfairly dismissed for redundancy, the   **10.33** award for redundancy will normally cover the basic award, so that the award for unfair dismissal will be confined to the compensatory award.

Somewhat more complex are the rules relating to discrimination awards where the employee was also unfairly dismissed. But the same general principle applies, and s.126 of the ERA 1996 lays down that, where compensation falls to be awarded for unfair dismissal and for discrimination, the employment tribunal must wholly offset any compensation awarded under one set of provisions against the others.

CHAPTER ELEVEN

REDUNDANCY

Redundancy is a form of dismissal. Like other dismissals, it may be **11.01** carried out wrongfully (e.g. without proper notice being given) or unfairly (contrary to the statutory provisions, particularly those contained in the ERA 1996). Even where proper notice is given, proper procedures are followed and the reason is a genuine redundancy (hence for a potentially fair reason), however, it differs from most of the other reasons for dismissal. In essence, there is no obvious reason why the fact that his job has been declared redundant can be laid at the door of the redundant employee. As a result, in addition to the possible remedies for wrongful or unfair dismissal, the law recognises that the redundant employee (provided that he has worked for the employer for a substantial period of time) should receive compensation for the very fact of having been declared redundant, in the form of a redundancy payment. The right to receive a redundancy payment was introduced in the Redundancy Payments Act 1965, so that it pre-dated the right not to be unfairly dismissed, the prohibition of unlawful discrimination and all the significant statutory rights which now attach to the employment relationship.

Because dismissal is necessary before one can say that an employee has been made redundant, this chapter deals first with the concept of dismissal as it applies in the context of redundancy. It goes on to discuss the statutory definition of redundancy and the way in which that has been interpreted in the case law. The next section deals with the question of when a dismissal for redundancy is unfair. After that, the subject of entitlement to a redundancy payment is discussed. Finally, there is an overview of the duties of the employer in relation to redundancy.

Dismissal

The question of when an employee has been dismissed has been **11.02** considered in Chapter 9. There are, however, certain issues which arise particularly in the context of redundancy.

Advance warning

There may be doubt as to whether an employee has been dismissed **11.03** where the employer gives advance warning of redundancy which is interpreted as giving notice. For example, in *International Computers Ltd v Kennedy* [1981] I.R.L.R. 28, EAT, the employers told the workforce that the factory where they worked would be closed by the end of September 1980. They were also told that they would receive their redundancy payments at that time, and the claimant left shortly after the announcement to take up another job. The EAT held that she had not been dismissed. Although the date of the closure was made clear, it was not certain when the employment of the individual would come to an end. The principle to be gleaned from this and other authorities is that for a dismissal to be effective, it must be possible to ascertain the precise date of termination. A warning of future redundancies is not a dismissal.

"Voluntary redundancy"

11.04   Where an employer has decided that some redundancies are necessary, there may be a call for "volunteers" for redundancy. The idea is that, if there are sufficient people volunteering, it may avoid the necessity for compulsory redundancies. There may well be sufficient people willing to be declared redundant because they want to retire early, or move on to some other job, with the bonus of a redundancy payment, and, possibly, enhanced severance pay or an increased pension. The question which arises in this context is: are the volunteers dismissed? There is no comprehensive answer, and each case will depend on the facts. In some cases, the termination will be characterised as a resignation, in others as by mutual agreement, whilst in yet others it may indeed constitute a dismissal.

In *Birch v University of Liverpool* [1985] I.C.R. 470, the university had introduced a premature retirement scheme in 1981, making it clear that it was not a redundancy scheme and that any retirement pursuant to it could only take place if both the university and the employee agreed. In 1982, the university stated that compulsory redundancies would be declared if insufficient volunteers came forward under the premature retirement scheme. The claimants made requests for early retirement. The university replied that "the University confirms that it is in the managerial interests for you to retire. . . and requests you to do so." The Court of Appeal held that the claimants' employment had ended, not by dismissal, but by mutual agreement.

Dismissals for purposes of redundancy payment

11.05   There are certain situations which are classified as dismissals for the purpose of qualifying for a redundancy payment. In summary the situations are:

(a) Where the employee is given a trial period in alternative employment, and rejects the job during or after the trial period.

(b) Where the employer has given the employee notice of dismissal and, during the notice period, the employee leaves early, e.g. because he has found another job which requires an immediate start.

(c) Where the employee resigns because of lay-off or short-time working.

Redundancy

If the employee was dismissed, the next stage of the enquiry is: was he   **11.06**
dismissed for redundancy? In the case of a claim for a redundancy payment
only, the presumption set out in s.163 applies. The relevant part reads:

> "For the purposes of any . . . reference [as to the right of an employee to a
> redundancy payment] an employee who has been dismissed by his employer
> shall, unless the contrary is proved, be presumed to have been so dismissed by
> reason of redundancy."

It should be emphasised that this presumption is confined to redundancy
payments, and does not apply, for example, to unfair dismissal. The
statutory definition of redundancy is set out in s.139 of the ERA 1996, and
reads in part as follows:

> "139(1) For the purposes of this Act an employee who is dismissed shall be
> taken to be dismissed by reason of redundancy if the dismissal is wholly or
> mainly attributable to—
>
> (a) the fact that his employer has ceased or intends to cease—
>
>   (i) to carry on the business for the purposes of which the employee was
>   employed by him, or
>   (ii) to carry on that business in the place where the employee was so
>   employed, or
>
> (b) the fact that the requirements of that business—
>
>   (i) for employees to carry out work of a particular kind, or
>   (ii) for employees to carry our work of a particular kind in the place
>   where the employee was employed by the employer,
>
> have ceased or diminished or are expected to cease or diminish."

To summarise the statute, there are three different types of redundancy
situation:

(1) where the business ceases completely (s.139(1)(a)(i));

(2) where the business ceases at the employee's workplace
    (s.139(1)(a)(ii); and

(3) where the demand for employees to carry out work of a particular
    kind ceases or diminishes (s.139(1)(b)).

The business ceases

The situation here is that the employer closes down the business   **11.07**
completely. This does not often give rise to a dispute, since the position is
usually clear-cut. If the business has been taken over by another enterprise,
then the Transfer of Undertakings (Protection of Employment) Regulations come into the equation—see Chapter 12 for details of TUPE
transfers.

The business ceases at the employee's workplace

11.08   If the employee works in a shop, depot, office or factory which is sited at a particular place, and it closes, then his dismissal will be on grounds of redundancy, even if the employer's business carries on elsewhere. That is the clear implication of s.139(1)(a)(ii) of the ERA 1996.

What, then, is the employee's place of work? Many employees have within their contract of employment a mobility clause, which gives the employer the right to move them (perhaps after giving notice) to another place of work. Is the employee's place of work, for the purposes of the redundancy provisions, their contractual place of work, or the place at which they have in fact been working? Is the test a contractual one, or a factual one?

In *High Table Ltd v Horst* [1997] I.R.L.R. 513, Mrs Horst was employed as a waitress by her employer, which provided catering services for firms in the City of London and elsewhere. Her letter of appointment stated that she was appointed as a waitress for Hill Samuel. She worked there for some five years. Her contract stated:

> "Your place of work is as stated in your letter of appointment, which acts as part of your terms and conditions. However, given the nature of our business, it is sometimes necessary to transfer staff on a temporary or permanent basis to another location. Whenever possible, this will be within reasonable travelling distance of your existing place of work".

In due course, the employer decided that it needed fewer waitresses working for longer hours. Mrs Horst and others were dismissed as redundant, and claimed that they had been unfairly dismissed. The employer argued that they were in fact redundant, with the result that there was a fair reason for their dismissal. The tribunal held that they were, but the EAT decided that the case should be sent back to be re-heard on the question of whether there was a redundancy, given the contractual position. The case went to the Court of Appeal on the question whether the statute imposed a contractual or a factual test for the determination of the employee's place of work. The CA came firmly down on the side of the factual test, Peter Gibson L.J. stating:

> "If an employee has worked in only one location under his contract of employment for the purposes of the employer's business, it defies common sense to widen the extent of the place where he was so employed, merely because of the existence of a mobility clause. Of course, the refusal by the employee to obey a lawful requirement under the contract of employment may constitute a valid reason for dismissal, but the issues of dismissal, redundancy and reasonableness in the actions of an employer should be kept distinct. . .it cannot be right to let the contract be the sole determinant, regardless of where the employee actually worked for the employer. . . It is plain that for all of the employees the place where they were employed by the employers was Hill Samuel and that there was a redundancy situation there which caused the employees to be dismissed."

It appears, therefore, that the geographical or factual test has the blessing of the Court of Appeal when it comes to determining the employee's place of work.

Diminution in the requirements of the business

The third situation is where there is a reduction in the requirement for **11.09** employees to perform work of a particular kind. The first point to make is that it is not necessary for the *work* to have diminished. There may be just as much work to be done, but the employer has decided that it should be done by fewer people. There are many reasons why this decision could be taken. For example, it may be due to the introduction of new technology, which means that fewer people are necessary; or it may be that there has been a falling off of demand; or the employer may have decided that fewer people can do the job if they work for longer hours. The employer's right to make decisions of this sort cannot generally be challenged under the law relating to redundancy. The fundamental question is: has the requirement for employees to do work of the particular kind which the employee was doing ceased or diminished, either generally or at his workplace? Alternatively, are those requirements expected to cease or diminish?

The question then arises: what is the work which the employee was doing? Is it the work which was specified in his contract (the contract test), or the work which he actually did (the function test)? A number of appellate cases pointed in different directions on this question, until the House of Lords came to what was hailed as the definitive decision in *Murray v Foyle Meats Ltd* [1999] I.R.L.R. 562, HL. The claimants were employed as meat plant operatives. They normally worked in the slaughter hall, but under their contracts of employment they could be required to work elsewhere in the factory, and occasionally had done so. Employees working in other parts of the factory, such as the boning hall or the loading bay were also employed as meat operatives, on similar contracts. In 1995, the company needed to close down one of the killing lines in the hall, with the result that fewer employees were required. The claimants were dismissed as redundant. The employers argued that their dismissals were wholly attributable to the fact that the requirements of the business to carry out work of a particular kind, on the slaughter line, had diminished, and that they were redundant as a result. The tribunal held that they were. On appeal to the House of Lords, it was argued on behalf of the employees that the statutory words "requirements for employees to carry out work of a particular kind" means "requirements for employees contractually engaged to carry out work of a particular kind". They further argued that, since the employers had engaged all their employees on similar terms, no distinction could be drawn between those who worked in the slaughter hall, and those who worked elsewhere in the factory. It followed, so they submitted, that it was wrong to select for redundancy solely from those who had worked in the slaughter hall. The House of Lords, in dismissing the appeal, regarded both the "contract test" and the "function test" as irrelevant. Lord Irvine L.C. emphasised the need to concentrate upon the statutory wording—the language of s.139(1)(b) in particular was "simplicity itself". He stated that there were two questions which had to be asked:

   (a) Were the requirements of the business to carry out work of a particular kind diminished?

(b) Was the dismissal wholly or mainly attributable to that state of affairs?

In the instant case, the tribunal had found that the answer to each of these questions of fact was "yes". That disposed of the matter. He went on to say that:

> "both the contract test and the function test miss the point. The key word in the statute is "attributable" and there is no reason in law why the dismissal of an employee should not be attributable to a diminution in the employer's need for employees irrespective of the terms of his contract or the function which he performed. Of course the dismissal of an employee who could perfectly well have been redeployed or who was doing work unaffected by the fall in demand may require some explanation to establish the necessary factual connection. But this is a question of fact, not law."

Redundancy and unfair dismissal

11.10   In Chapter 9 on "Unfair Dismissal", the role of redundancy as one of the potentially fair reasons for dismissal was discussed. If the employer has been able to establish that the reason (or principal reason) for the dismissal of the employee was redundancy, the fact that the reason is a potentially fair one in terms of the statute does not, of course, end the matter. There are important procedural questions which may make the dismissal unfair.

Statutory DDP

11.11   The statutory DDP applies to redundancy as much as it does to other types of dismissal, with certain exceptions which may be relevant to some redundancy situations, in particular the statutory DDP does not apply:

- Where there is a collective redundancy of 20 or more employees and a duty to consult and inform representatives arises; or

- Where the employer's business suddenly ceases to function, because of an event unforeseen by the employer, with the result that it is impracticable for him to employ any employees.

(See reg.4 of the Employment Act 2002 (Dispute Resolution) Regulations 2004.)

The statutory DDP will apply to other redundancies. In brief, the employer must set out the grounds in writing (Step 1) invite the employee to a meeting and hold such a meeting before dismissal (Step 2) and provide a right of appeal (Step 3). The provisions in question are contained within Sch.2 of the Employment Act 2002, which is set out in Appendix Two and some general commentary has been given in paras 9.30 to 9.39.

In *Alexander v Bridgen Enterprises Ltd* [2006] I.R.L.R. 422, EAT, Elias P, dealt generally with the ambit of the standard DDP. He also gave guidance as to the role of the statutory DDP in a redundancy case, stating that the first step may require no more than specifying that the grounds which lead the employer to contemplate dismissing the employee is redundancy. He went on to deal with the second step in the following terms:

> ". . . the reference in step two to "the basis for including in the statement . . . the ground or grounds given in it" requires that an explanation is given as to why the employer is contemplating dismissing that particular employee. . . In a redundancy context, that will involve providing information as to both why the employer considers that there is, to put it colloquially, a redundancy situation and also why the employee is being selected. . . We think that it is clearly necessary that the employer, in order to comply with step two, should, in advance of the meeting notify the employee of the selection criteria. Without that information, it is impossible for the employee to give an sensible response to the decision at all. . . In order to comply with the statutory provisions an employer should provide to the employee not only the basic selection criteria which have been used, but also the employee's own assessment."

Although not specifically stated in the judgment, it is clear that the reference to selection criteria means that this guidance relates to cases where there has to be some selection from a pool of employees, and criteria are required, rather than the case where all employees of a particular description are declared redundant, and the issue in dispute is whether there is a genuine redundancy, or whether the dismissals were carried out fairly. **11.12**

Reasonableness in dismissing for redundancy

Assuming that the employer has not failed to comply with an applicable statutory DDP, the fairness of the dismissal will be determined according to ss.98(4) and 98A(2) of the ERA 1996. **11.13**

As far as s.98(4) is concerned, the issue is whether "the employer acted reasonably or unreasonably in treating it [redundancy] as a sufficient reason for dismissing the employee." Certain guidelines as to what constitutes reasonableness in the context of redundancy were laid down in *Williams v Compair Maxam Ltd* [1982] I.R.L.R. 83, EAT. Browne-Wilkinson J. made it clear that it was impossible to lay down detailed procedures which all reasonable employers would follow in all circumstances. Further, the guidelines were stated to be appropriate for cases where employees were represented by an independent union recognised by the employer. In summary, the points set out were:

1. As much warning as possible of impending redundancies.

2. Consultation with the union as to how the desired management result can be achieved with as little hardship as possible to the employees, particularly with regard to the criteria to be applied in selecting for redundancy.

3. The establishment of criteria which so far as possible can be objectively checked against such things as attendance record, efficiency at the job, experience, length of service.

4. Fair selection in accordance with these criteria, and consideration of any union representations as to selection.

5. The employer will seek to see whether, instead of dismissing the employee, he could offer him alternative employment.

It was acknowledged that circumstances might mean that one or more of these factors was not present in a particular case, but the principles should only be departed from where there was good reason.

These guidelines were approved by the House of Lords in *Polkey v A E Dayton Services Ltd* [1988] A.C. 344, HL, where Lord Bridge said:

> "in the case of redundancy, the employer will normally not act reasonably unless he warns and consults any employees affected or their representatives, adopts a fair basis upon which to select for redundancy and takes such steps as may be reasonable to avoid or minimise redundancy within his own organisation."

11.14   Nevertheless, in some of the cases which have followed (see, for example A *Simpson & Son (Motors) v Reid and Findlater* [1983] I.R.L.R. 401, EAT) it has been stressed that failure to comply with one of "the five so-called principles" did not lead to automatic unfairness. That is certainly true, but tribunals frequently have recourse to the principles in question in deciding whether the employer acted reasonably or unreasonably in deciding to dismiss for redundancy. In the process, a tribunal will no doubt bear in mind that there may be circumstances which lead to the conclusion that it was reasonable for the employer in question to fail to implement one or other of the five points. This is perhaps more likely to be the case with a small employer than a large one.

Whether the list in *Williams v Compair Maxam* consists of principles, guidelines or factors, it provides a basis for consideration of the issues which will be looked at by a tribunal where the procedural fairness of a redundancy is contested. For that reason, the sections which follow make extensive reference to the various points in the guidelines, as well as certain other issues.

Redundancy situation

11.15   Generally, the employer will decide, usually in response to external events, as to whether redundancies need to be declared. Some of the commonest reasons for deciding that there are to be redundancies are those which are set out in the form used to notify the Department of Trade and Industry of forthcoming redundancies (for details of this obligation, see para.11.18). The main reasons cited for redundancies are:

(a) lower demand for products or services

(b) completion of all or part of a contract

(c) transfer of work to another site or employer

   (d) introduction of new technology/plant/machinery

   (e) changes in work methods or organisation.

To demonstrate the fact that the list is in no way exhaustive, the form adds:

   (f) another reason.

In determining whether there is a redundancy situation, it is the requirements of the employer which are crucial. That is the wording of the statute, and it reflects the situation on the ground. Tribunals will not attempt to re-hash the employer's decision as to whether there ought to be redundancies or not, provided that the decision is a genuine one. As Kilner Brown J. put it in *Moon v Homeworthy Furniture Ltd* [1977] I.C.R. 117, there should not be "any investigation into the rights and wrongs of the declared redundancy".

In order to show that the redundancies planned were genuine ones, however, the employer will often need to adduce evidence of the state of the business, so as to establish that the reason which drove the plan to lose jobs was related to, for example, a fall in demand. The issue for the tribunal when evaluating that evidence, however, is not whether the redundancies were inevitable, or even whether they were reasonable. It is rather to decide, in the light of the evidence, whether the requirements of the employer for employees had in fact ceased or diminished, i.e. was it a genuine redundancy situation?

Collective consultation

Although this aspect is strictly within the sphere of collective employ- **11.16** ment law, it is so closely bound up with individual rights relating to redundancy that it is necessary to deal with it here. In particular, the employer's actions (or lack of them) in consulting collectively are likely to have an impact upon any subsequent adjudication as to the fairness or otherwise of dismissals for redundancy.

Section 188 of the Trade Union and Labour Relations (Consolidation) Act 1992 lays down a duty upon the employer to consult collectively upon impending redundancies. The duty arises where it is proposed to dismiss 20 or more employees at one establishment within a period of 90 days or less. If that is what is planned, the employer must consult with the "appropriate representatives" of the employees who may be affected. Such consultation must begin "in good time". In any event, it must begin at least 90 days before the first of the dismissals takes effect if the employer is proposing to dismiss 100 or more employees, and 30 days before if it is proposed to dismiss less than 100. Notice of dismissal can be given to individual employees before or during the consultation period, provided that it does not take effect until after the consultation has ended.

The representatives with whom the employer consults should be representatives of a trade union recognised in respect of the employees in question if there is one (the employees do not have to be members of the trade union in question). If there is no recognised trade union, the duty of the employer is to consult with employee representatives with authority to deal with this particular issue. The consultation must include ways to:

(a) avoid the dismissals;

(b) reduce the number of dismissals;

(c) mitigate the consequences of the dismissals.

It must be "undertaken by the employer with a view to reaching agreement with the appropriate representatives". Prior to consultation, details have to be disclosed in writing to the representatives, including the reasons for the proposals, the numbers involved, the proposed method of selection for redundancy, and the method of carrying out the dismissals.

11.17 This collective consultation is additional to any individual consultation which is required in respect of those who are personally at risk of being declared redundant (see paras 11.24 and 11.25). In the event that it is alleged that collective consultation as the statute requires has not been carried out, a claim may be presented to the employment tribunal by the trade union or other employee representatives, or (in certain limited circumstances) by any of the employees made redundant. The claim is for a protective award, ordering the employer to pay the wages of the employees whom it has dismissed, or proposes to dismiss, for a protected period of up to 90 days. The employee is then entitled to gross wages for the whole of the protected period. Such a protective award is additional to any other compensation which the employee may receive, e.g. a redundancy payment, or an award for unfair dismissal. In *Susie Radin Ltd v GMB* [2004] I.R.L.R. 400, the Court of Appeal held that a protective award could be made in circumstances where consultation would have been futile. Further, the protective award was not linked to any loss suffered by the employee in question. It was based upon the seriousness of the employer's default in complying with the obligation to consult. The deliberateness or otherwise of the failure to consult would be relevant, as might be the availability to the employer of advice about his legal obligations. The proper approach for the tribunal in a case where there had been no consultation was to start with the maximum period of 90 days and reduce it only if there were mitigating circumstances.

Notifying the Secretary of State

11.18 Closely bound up with the obligation to consult is a duty to notify the Secretary of State for Trade and Industry. This is done by completing the form HR1 (referred to above). It must be done within the same time limits as consultation—30 days before the first dismissal takes effect if it is proposed to dismiss between 20 and 99 employees and 90 days before the first dismissal if 100 or more employees are to be dismissed. A copy of the form must be given to the trade union or employee representatives, as part of the information required under the duty to consult.

Defining the unit of selection

Where the employer's business ceases completely, there will obviously be **11.19** no need to select any employees for redundancy, as all will have to be dismissed. Similarly, where the factory or other place where the employee works is closed down, it will usually be clear which employees are to be dismissed. More difficulty arises, however, in the case where the requirement for employees to carry out work of a particular kind has diminished, rather than ceased.

In such a case, it is necessary for the employer to decide on the pool from which the employees are to be selected for dismissal—the unit of selection. The problem may be difficult to resolve, particularly if there is flexibility within the workforce, so that different people perform different jobs at different times. The employer faces a dilemma. If the unit is defined too narrowly, then those who are selected for redundancy may claim that they would not have been at risk if the pool had been larger. If the unit is broadened, then those who are selected may claim that they were wrongly included, and the decision ought to have been restricted to those whose work was directly and immediately affected by the causes of the redundancy.

Although the case of *Murray v Foyle Meats Ltd* [1999] I.R.L.R. 562, HL (discussed in the section on "Diminution in the requirements of the business" earlier in this chapter) was decided on the issue of whether there was a redundancy, it also contained within it a dispute about the proper pool for selection—was it the workers in the slaughter house or those in the factory as a whole? The rule is that the pool for selection must be reasonably defined. In *GEC Machines Ltd v Gilford* [1982] I.C.R. 725, selection from a section, rather than the whole department was held unfair since the work was interchangeable between employees within the department.

Example. A related question is "bumping". Assume that a company plans to **11.20** *declare redundancies in its detergent factory, due to falling demand. The company decides that it will consider those involved in the production of all its detergents. A is employed on the manufacture of non-biological washing powder, the demand for which remains buoyant. Her particular job will not disappear as a result of the redundancy. However, on the criteria for selection, she scores sufficiently low to be selected for redundancy. As a result, she is made redundant. B, who is working on the production of dishwasher tablets, scores better on the selection criteria, and is not declared redundant. However, as there is reduced demand for dishwasher tablets, B is moved to take over A's old job. Such a situation is termed a "bumped redundancy", and there has been controversy as to whether it does in fact constitute redundancy. In Murray, the House of Lords approved a test which would include the "bumped redundancy" within the statutory definition of redundancy.*

There still remains the question of how the employer should define the unit of selection. There is no strict rule to determine this. However, what is important is that an employer should consider the different possibilities and come to a reasonable conclusion in defining the unit of selection. Where there are consultations with the recognised trade union, the definition of the unit of selection is likely to be an important item on the agenda.

The selection process

11.21   Occasionally, the determination of the unit of selection will effectively answer the question: who is to be made redundant? That will be the case, for example, where the necessary number of redundancies is equal to the number of people in the unit of selection.

Much more usually, however, a selection has to be made from those within the pool. How should the employer go about the task of selection? The matter is central to the redundancy process, and should be an important part of the matters about which the union is consulted (*Williams v Compair Maxam*—see the list of principles in para.11.13).

There may be a procedure which has been agreed with the recognised trade union, or one which has been adopted in the past and which employees would expect to operate in the new situation. If so, the employer must clearly take such existing procedure into account. Failure to do so might arguably constitute unreasonable (rather than reasonable) behaviour when viewed in the light of s.98(4) of the ERA 1996. However, there is no absolute obligation on the employer to act in accordance with an agreed procedure or a customary arrangement, as was the case prior to the enactment of the Deregulation and Contracting Act 1994.

11.22   It is for the employer, then, in consultation with the union and taking the context into account, to determine a set of criteria for selection for redundancy. The commonest way in which this is done is by the construction of a matrix, which sets out a list of criteria. Against each criterion, the employee receives a score. Some criteria which are perceived as more important than others may receive a weighting, so that they count for more towards the total.

In *Williams v Compair Maxam,* it was stated that the employer:

> "should seek to establish criteria for selection which so far as possible do not depend solely upon the opinions of the person making the selection but can be objectively checked against such things as attendance record, efficiency at the job, experience, length of service".

Factors capable of objective measurement in this way play a part in many redundancy selection procedures. Usually the employer will also wish to include criteria which require some management judgment as to the strengths and weaknesses of the employee, e.g. adaptability, quality of work, skills.

11.23   One criterion which readily lends itself to objective assessment is the traditional LIFO (last in, first out) method of selection. This is a method which has traditionally been favoured by the trade unions, but frequently meets with employer resistance on the basis that it gives no weight to the needs of the enterprise to ensure that it has the requisite skills and competence to ensure efficient performance. The debate has now been overshadowed by the Employment Equality (Age) Regulations 2006, which outlaw age discrimination (see paras 6.54 to 6.69). Although LIFO would not constitute direct age discrimination, since those who joined most recently would not necessarily be the youngest, it is likely in a given situation to involve indirect age discrimination—those joining most recently are more *likely* to be young than those who have been employed for longer. As a result, any such method of selection would have to be objectively justified—fulfilling a legitimate aim by proportionate means. This new dimension is likely to consign LIFO to the outer margins of the debate, given that the employers' natural antipathy to this method of selection now has some legal backing.

In addition to avoiding age discrimination, the employer must take care that no criterion is discriminatory on any other ground, e.g. race, sex or disability. Particular care needs to be taken in relation to such matters as attendance records and rate of output where the possibility of disability discrimination may be an issue (see Chapter 6 on "Discrimination").

The actions of the employer in deciding upon criteria for selection will be judged by a tribunal in accordance with the "band of reasonable responses" test which applies to the determination of reasonableness in unfair dismissal cases. As it was put in *British Aerospace plc v Green* [1995] I.R.L.R. 433, CA, in general an employer who sets up a system of selection which can reasonably be described as fair and applies it without any overt sign of conduct which mars its fairness, will have done all that the law requires of him. It should be noted, however, that tribunals do scrutinise the process of selection with some care. This is in part because the way in which selection is carried out can mask one form of discrimination or another. It is also because some employers use the redundancy process to get rid of those whom they regard as a problem in terms of conduct or performance, and whom they have not been honest enough to warn about their shortcomings.

Individual consultation

Over and above the duty to carry out collective consultation with recognised trade unions or employee representatives, the employer must warn and consult the individual who is at risk of being made redundant. This should be done at the stage when the selection process has been carried out, but before notice of dismissal is given. It can only be avoided when the employer can show that consultation would be "an utterly futile exercise": *Mugford v Midland Bank* [1997] I.R.L.R. 209.   **11.24**

In *King v Eaton Ltd* [1996] I.R.L.R. 199, CS, the Scottish Court of Session adopted for the redundancy process the definition of consultation set out by Glidewell LJ in a different context in *R. v British Coal Corporation Ex p. Price* [1994] I.R.L.R. 72:

> "Fair consultation means (a) consultation when the proposals are still at a formative stage; (b) adequate information on which to respond; (c) adequate time in which to respond; and (d) conscientious consideration by an authority of a response to consultation."

It is worth emphasising that the process of consultation may overlap with the requirements of the statutory DDP in some respects. Failure to abide by the minimal standards laid down in the DDP will usually mean that the redundancy is automatically unfair. This will be the case unless it falls within one of the exclusions from the operation of the DDP, e.g. collective redundancy falling within the duty to consult collectively, or cases where the employer's business suddenly ceases to function because of an unseen event.

However, the statutory DDP does not require the employer to live up to the standards required for meaningful consultation set out in Glidewell L.J.'s definition. More stringent is the duty to act reasonably, rather than unreasonably, in deciding to dismiss for redundancy (s.98(4) of the ERA 1996). That does require proper consultation with the employee, rather than just going through the relatively mechanical exercise involved in the three steps of the DDP.

11.25　　As to the content and form of the consultation meeting, the following points should be covered:

- although it is not a legal right, it is best practice (and may be considered reasonable) to suggest that the employee is accompanied by a colleague or union representative;

- an explanation of why redundancies are being considered should be given, if this has not already been done;

- an explanation of why his job is at risk should be given to the employee;

- if a scorecard or matrix has been used, the employee should be shown at least his own score, if not those of other employees, and the basis for scoring should be explained;

- a chance should be given for the employee to consider the information which he has received and to formulate a response;

- a meeting should be fixed to discuss any points which the employee might have as a result of his consideration;

- the possibility of alternative work can be canvassed, but it may be premature to consider this topic in detail before the employee's representations have been made and considered;

- a further interview should be held at which the representations can be heard and alternative employment discussed. A notice of dismissal should not be served until this has been done.

Alternative work

11.26　　The employer should take reasonable steps to seek alternative employment for an employee who is to be made redundant. The general duty was set out in *Vokes Ltd v Bear* [1974] I.C.R. 1, NIRC. In that particular case, the employee was dismissed without any attempt being made to find him alternative employment in any of the 299 other companies which belonged to the employer's group of companies. The failure to make an attempt to find him alternative employment meant that the dismissal was unfair.

The duty to look for alternative employment is a component of reasonableness on the part of the employer. The employee's job may be redundant, but it may be possible that he can continue to work for the employer. The avoidance of dismissal, if reasonably possible, is in accordance with the first of the five principles in *Williams v Compair Maxam*.

The duty does not extend to finding an alternative job for the redundant employee. It is a duty to search, but the search must be a serious one. As it was put in *Avonmouth Construction Co Ltd v Shipway* [1979] I.R.L.R. 14, EAT, the employer has a responsibility not simply to look, but to give careful consideration to the possibility of offering the employee another job. In that case, it was suggested that the fact that a vacant position would involve demotion is something which is primarily for the employee to worry about.

Automatic unfairness

In certain circumstances, a dismissal for redundancy will be automatically **11.27** unfair. For example, if a selection for redundancy is made on any of the following grounds, it will lead to a finding of unfair dismissal:

(a) membership (or non-membership) of a trade union, or activities in a union;

(b) an employee was trustee of an occupational pension scheme;

(c) the employee was a part-time worker;

(d) assertion of a relevant statutory right;

(e) pregnancy.

(See s.105 of the ERA 1996 for a full list of the prohibited grounds.)

Redundancy payments

Dismissal for redundancy triggers off the right to a statutory redundancy **11.28** payment, where the employee has two years or more employment with that employer. It may also, where the employee has a contractual entitlement, mean that the employer is obliged to pay severance pay at a higher level than the statutory minimum. The next three sections deal with the statutory redundancy payment, and the fourth section covers the contractual position as far as severance pay is concerned.

Calculation of statutory redundancy payment

The formula for calculation is set out in s.162 of the ERA 1996. It is **11.29** virtually identical to the calculation of the basic award for unfair dismissal (see para.10.06). In summary, the employee is entitled to the following for each complete year's employment:

(a) one and a half week's pay for each year when he was not below the age of 41;

(b) one week's pay for each year In which he was not below the age of 22; and

(c) half a week's pay for each week in which he was employed which does not fall within (a) or (b) above.

The week's pay is gross (before tax), and is subject to a limit of £310 (where the date of dismissal is on or after February 1, 2007, the limit being revised annually). Only 20 years' service can be counted, with the result that the maximum statutory payment for redundancy is £9300 (20 x 1.5 x £310).

Suitable alternative employment

11.30   Generally, entitlement to a statutory redundancy payment flows from dismissal for redundancy, subject to the employee having the necessary qualifying service. However, the right to payment is extinguished if the employee's contract is renewed, or he is re-engaged in a suitable alternative position (s.138(1) of the ERA 1996) by:

(1) the same employer; or

(2) an associated employer; or

(3) in the case of a local government employee, any other local government employee.

The definition of "associated employers" is to be found in s.231 of the ERA 1996. Any two employers are to be treated as associated if—

(a) one is a company of which the other has direct or indirect control; or

(b) both are companies of which a third person has indirect control.

As a result, it covers a company controlled by, or controlling the company for which the employee has been working, or a company controlled by a company which also controls the company for which he has been working. If the new job is with a separate employer, however, then the employee retains his right to a redundancy payment.

If the employee accepts the job offer, there is no redundancy. If he refuses the job offer, then the provisions in s.141 of the ERA 1996 apply. His entitlement to a redundancy payment will depend on:

(a) where the new terms are the same as the old ones, whether his refusal was reasonable;

(b) where the new terms are different, whether the offer is of suitable alternative employment, and whether he was unreasonable to refuse it.

In each case, the burden of proof is on the employer to show suitability and unreasonableness.

As far as suitability is concerned, a tribunal would look at matters such as **11.31** the nature and status of the work, pay and hours, as well as the employee's experience, skill and aptitude. In assessing reasonableness, the employee's personal position comes into the equation, for example: Will he have travel difficulties? Does his family situation make it difficult to travel? What about the availability of accommodation in the area?

If the new job which is offered differs as to the place or the capacity in which the employee is to work, then he is entitled to a trial period of four weeks to test the new terms (s.138 of the ERA 1996). During that time, he can decide whether he wants to take up the position permanently. If he decides not to continue with the new job then he can resign and claim a redundancy payment (or unfair dismissal if he considers that he was unfairly dismissed). In the event that he claims a redundancy payment, his entitlement will depend on whether the new employment was suitable, and whether he acted reasonably, as discussed above. However, if he leaves after the four week period, then he is treated as having resigned, and will not be able to claim either a redundancy payment or unfair dismissal.

There are certain circumstances in which the employee is disqualified from receipt of a redundancy payment, e.g. where he leaves before his notice expires despite his employer's objections.

Claiming a redundancy payment

In most cases, the employer calculates and pays the amount due. If he **11.32** fails to do so, the employee should claim his entitlement in writing. If the employer still fails to make the payment due, then a claim should be made to the employment tribunal within six months of dismissal. The period for making a claim is longer than that for unfair dismissal (three months), and the tribunal can extend the period for a further six months if it considers it "just and equitable".

Contractual severance pay

Many employers have redundancy or severance schemes which are more **11.33** generous than the statutory provisions. There is sometimes an issue as to whether such a scheme is contractual or not. The mere fact that it has been used in respect of redundancies declared in the past will not make it a contractual entitlement.

On occasion, an employer will attempt to alter an enhanced contractual redundancy scheme because of the impact which it will have upon the business. For example, if employees are to be declared redundant prior to the sale of the business as a going concern, generous severance payments will greatly reduce the value of the business, making its sale less likely or less profitable. In such a case, the employer may try to replace the scheme with a less generous one, or restrict employees to their statutory entitlement. Such a change will constitute a variation of contract, and will have to be considered on general contractual principles (see Chapter 3). The variation may be agreed, but if it is not, the employer may dismiss the employees, and offer them re-employment on terms which exclude the severance scheme in question. This will constitute dismissal, and may lead to claims for unfair dismissal, which again must be considered in the light of the law relating to unfair dismissal (see Chapter 9).

Where an employee is made redundant and seeks to enforce a contractual redundancy payment, the case can be brought as a claim for breach of contract in the employment tribunal, subject to a limit of £25,000. Claims for breach of contract in excess of that amount must be brought in the county court or High Court.

Chapter Twelve

CHANGES OF OWNERSHIP, TRANSFERS OF UNDERTAKINGS AND INSOLVENCY

This chapter examines the consequences for employees when the owner- **12.01** ship of a business changes. Where the ownership of a business passes from Company A to Company B, the employees of A would lose their rights upon transfer of the business because the rules relating to privity of contract determine that their rights can only be enforced against A. As a result, if a business is sold, its employees would no longer be employed by A, with the result that their employment would be terminated. The reason for their dismissal would fit within the statutory definition of redundancy (see Chapter 11). If B bought the business as a going concern, and needed some or all of A's employees in order to continue, it would have to recruit them anew, and their employment would start from scratch. Clearly such a situation would undermine the purpose of the employment protection legislation, and potentially lend itself to evasion by employers. Various statutory rules therefore modify the common law contractual position. In the remainder of this chapter, the following situations are considered:

(a) a transfer between associated companies;

(b) the sale of shares in a company;

(c) the Transfer of Undertakings (Protection of Employment) Regulations 2006 (the "TUPE Regulations"—this is the most complex and important of the situations which we need to consider); and

(d) insolvency.

Associated companies

One common change of employer is where an employee is transferred **12.02** from one associated company to another. For example, such a change may take place as a result of a reorganisation within a group of companies, e.g. the employee is shifted from the holding company to a subsidiary, or vice versa, or from one subsidiary to another. Whatever the reason for the transfer, continuity of employment will be preserved as a result of s.218(6). This states that, wherever an employee moves from one associated employer to another, his period of employment with the first employer counts as a period of employment with the second employer, and the change does not break the continuity of employment.

The phrase "associated employer" is defined in s.231. Two employers are to be treated as associated if:

(a) one is a company of which the other (directly or indirectly) has control; or

(b) both are companies of which a third person (directly or indirectly) has control.

Transfers between associated employers are often carried out with a minimum of formality. However, there are statutory obligations to notify the employee of the change of employer (even though there may be no apparent change in his working situation)—see s.4 of the ERA 1996. In addition, it would seem that many such transfers will be covered by the TUPE Regulations, with the result that there are duties to consult trade unions or employee representatives (see below).

Transfer of shares

12.03   The fundamental principle of company law is that the company is invested with legal personality. As a result, it is the employer, rather than the shareholders. It follows that the rights and duties attendant upon the status of employer attach to the company itself.

Assume that there is a transfer of shares within company X from shareholders A and B to shareholders C and D. As a result of this, there is a change in the ownership of company X. But the employees will still be employed by Company X, and its duties and rights in respect of them will remain unchanged. The terms and conditions of the employees will not be altered by the change in ownership of the company. Any desire on the part of the new brooms who have taken over the majority of the shares to sweep old practices out will be subject to the usual restrictions on unilateral variations in contract. Equally, it is worth emphasising that the transfer of shares will not be subject to the TUPE Regulations, because there is no transfer of an undertaking to trigger those regulations off—the undertaking remains firmly in the hands of the same company where it has been all along.

The TUPE Regulations

12.04   The domestic law relating to transfers of undertakings derives from a series of Directives originating from the European Union (77/187, 98/50 and 2001/23). Over the years, there have been a large number of cases from the ECJ which have dealt with the interpretation of these Directives, and some of this case law has been reflected in the latest version of the TUPE Regulations—those which came into effect in April 2006.

The effect of the TUPE Regulations may be summarised as follows. They spell out the consequences when there is a relevant transfer. The employee's employment will usually be automatically transferred from the transferor (the former owner of the business) to the transferee (the new owner). The terms and conditions of employment will remain the same (with the exception of any occupational pension). Any employee who is dismissed as a result of the transfer is deemed to have been unfairly dismissed (other than in certain restricted circumstances). There are duties on the part of both the transferor and the transferee to consult trade unions or other employee representatives. A more detailed explanation of this briefest of summaries is provided in the sections which follow. To illustrate the practical situation to which the rules apply, it may help to envisage an example.

Example.   Conference Call Ltd (CCL) is engaged in the business of providing **12.05** *conference facilities. One part of its operation is devoted to the provision and servicing of audio-visual equipment, which is used for the conferences which it arranges. However, CCL finds that it is unable to make sufficient use of the audio-visual equipment and staff for it to be profitable. It therefore enters into an agreement with an entirely separate company, Audio Visual Ltd—(AVL), which specialises in the provision and servicing of such equipment. AVL has formed the view that it can run CCL's audio-visual business more profitably, by integrating it within its existing operations.*

Relevant transfer

The Regulations only apply where there is a "relevant transfer". This is **12.06** defined in reg.3 to include two routes, as follows:

(a) a transfer of an undertaking to another person where there is a transfer of an economic entity which retains its identity; or

(b) a service provision change.

Route (a) is the one which emerged from the 1986 version of the TUPE Regulations and has been mapped out by the various cases interpreting that set of regulations. The English authority which codifies the European case law, and provides guidance upon their interpretation is *Cheesman v R Brewer Contracts Ltd* [2001] I.R.L.R. 144, EAT. In that case, it was emphasised that there were two separate questions which the tribunal must consider in deciding whether there had been a relevant transfer. They were:

(1) is there an undertaking, and

(2) has it been transferred?

As far as question (1) is concerned, there are various factors which the tribunal needs to take into account, based upon the case law of the ECJ:

(i) There must be a stable economic entity—an organised grouping of persons and of assets which allows the exercise of an economic activity which pursues a specific objective.

(ii) It must be structured and autonomous, but need not have significant assets.

    (iii) In certain sectors (e.g. cleaning and surveillance) the assets may essentially be based upon manpower.

    (iv) An organised grouping of wage-earners may amount to an economic entity if they are permanently assigned to a common task.

    (v) The identity of an entity emerges from factors such as the workforce, management staff, operating methods and operational resources. An entity is not the same as an activity.

In answering the second question ("has there been a transfer?"), the following points were prominent in the guidance offered in *Cheesman v Brewer*:

    (i) The decisive criterion is whether the entity in question has retained its identity. Has its operation actually continued or resumed?

    (ii) All the factors characterising the transaction in question must be considered. None should be considered in isolation.

    (iii) Among the factors to be considered are:

- The type of undertaking;
- The value of its intangible assets at the time of transfer;
- Whether or not the majority of its employees are taken over by the new company;
- Whether or not its customers are transferred;
- The degree of similarity between the activities carried on before and after the transfer;
- Any period during which those activities are suspended.

12.07   The above points constitute only part of the guidance in *Cheesman v Brewer*, which is an invaluable source when a practitioner is advising upon whether there has been the transfer of an undertaking.

The TUPE Regulations 2006 also provide an additional route by which a "relevant transfer" can be established. This is the "service provision change". In recent years, there has been a growing trend for businesses to hive off some of their service functions, e.g. cleaning, security, catering, information technology. Such services are then provided externally, leaving the organisation free to concentrate upon its "core business". Such a process frequently involves "contracting out"—the organisation decides to award the ancillary business which it no longer wishes to conduct to a service provider.

There have been conflicting decisions as to whether the process of contracting out gives rise to a relevant transfer, and the matter was not particularly clear when the TUPE Regulations 1981 were applied, particularly given the confused state of European jurisprudence on the issue. The position is clarified in the 2006 Regulations, which provide that a "service provision change" will constitute a relevant transfer if:

(i) activities cease to be carried out by a client on his own behalf and are carried out instead by a "contractor" on the client's behalf;

(ii) activities cease to be carried out by a particular contractor on a client's behalf and are carried out instead ay another contractor on the client's behalf;

(iii) activities cease to be carried out by a contractor, and are carried out instead by the client on his own behalf,

and all the following conditions are satisfied:

(i) immediately before the service provision change, there is an organised grouping of employees which has as its principal purpose the conduct of the activities in question; and

(ii) the client intends that the transferee will carry out the activities, other than in connection with a single specific event or task of short-term duration, and

(iii) the activities do not consist wholly or mainly of the supply of goods for the client's use.

Some examples of the various relationships encompassed in the definition of a "service provision change" are to be found in the diagrams below.

Service provision changes

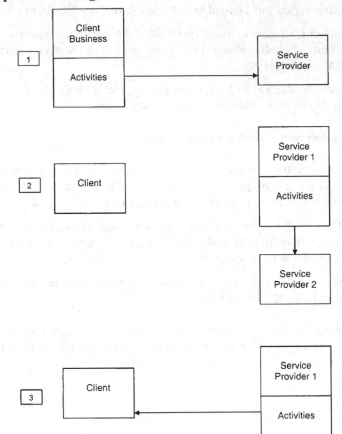

Consequences for individual employees

12.08   The TUPE Regulations 2006, reg.4 provide that

- a relevant transfer does not terminate the contract of any person employed by the transferor immediately before the transfer and assigned to the group of employees subject to the transfer (with the exception of pension rights—see para.12.10);

- any such contract of employment has effect after the transfer as if made between the employee and the transferee;

- all the transferor's rights and duties under the contract of employment are transferred to the transferee.

However, if the employee objects to the transfer of his contract and the rights and duties under it, and informs the transferor or the transferee of his objection, his contract and the rights and duties under it will not be transferred: reg.4(7). In such a case his contract is terminated, but he is not dismissed (and consequently cannot claim unfair dismissal). An objection will only be effective if it is an actual refusal to work. A mere expression of concern or unwillingness is not sufficient to prevent the transfer: *Hay v George Hanson (Building Contractors Ltd* [1996] I.C.R. 427.

As to the question of which employees are transferred across, it is those who are "assigned" to the transferred undertaking. The test is a factual, rather than a contractual one, i.e. it does not matter so much what the terms of the employee's contract state—it is rather about his function. It follows that a mobility clause which is not in fact used will be irrelevant: *Securicor Guarding Ltd v Fraser Security Services Ltd* [1996] I.R.L.R. 552.

The employees affected are those who were employed "immediately **12.09** before" the transfer. Regulation 4(3) makes it clear that this includes those who would have been so employed if they had not been dismissed unfairly. This puts in statutory form the principle which emerged from *Litster v Forth Dry Dock* [1989] I.R.L.R. 161. In that case, the House of Lords had to interpret the words "employed immediately before the transfer" in the TUPE Regulations 1981. It gave the words a purposive interpretation, so as to implement the purpose of the Acquired Rights Directive, by the imaginary insertion of additional words so as to include those who would have been so employed if they had not been unfairly dismissed for a reason connected with the transfer (see the section on Unfair Dismissal below). With the 2006 version of the TUPE Regulations, there is no need for this imaginative exercise, as it is made clear that employees who are dismissed in these circumstances are to be included in those within the scope of reg.4. As a result, they continue to be employed (unless they object) and the rights and duties under their contracts of employment transfer to the transferee.

Pensions

Unlike other rights and duties, those contained within an occupational **12.10** pension scheme are not transferred under the TUPE Regulations. However, it is only rights under an occupational pension scheme as defined in the Pension Schemes Act 1993 which are excluded in this way. A contractual provision (e.g. that the transferor will pay five per cent of salary into a personal pension scheme) would constitute a contractual term which must be honoured by the transferee. In addition, where a transferring employee was a member of an occupational pension scheme with the transferor, the transferee is obliged to make provision which meets certain standards, as laid down in s.12A of the Pension Schemes Act 1993.

Changes in terms and conditions

The employees who are transferred take with them their existing terms **12.11** and conditions of employment (with the exception of occupational pension rights—see the preceding paragraph). New recruits will not necessarily be employed upon those terms, and have no entitlement to claim them.

The fact that the existing terms are preserved for transferred employees, however, may be a source of concern to the transferee employer. Take the case of the company providing and servicing audio-visual equipment for conference, dealt within para.12.05. It formed the opinion that it could make the transferred business more profitable by integrating it within its own operations. It will already have employees who are on one set of terms and conditions. It has now acquired employees who are on an entirely different set of terms and conditions, laid down by a process in which it played no part. If there is any significant difference between the two sets, it will inevitably trigger off feelings of resentment at the group of workers who perceive themselves as worse off. At the same time, part of its strategy for making the new integrated business profitable may well be to bring the terms of the transferred employees into line with what it perceives as being commercially realistic.

Such a situation will create a desire for change on the part of the transferee business. It will clearly be faced with the usual obstacles if it attempts to bring about a unilateral variation in contract (see Chapter 3). But will it be able to remedy the situation if it achieves agreement with the transferred employees, either individually or collectively? The position is that any variation will be invalid if it is due to the transfer.

12.12   In *Wilson v St Helens BC* [1998] I.R.L.R. 706, the House of Lords made it clear that the automatic preservation of rights and duties was not restricted to the time of transfer. A purported variation at a later stage would be invalid if it was due to the transfer. However, the passage of time will make it increasingly less likely that the variation is connected with the transfer: *Daddy's Dance Hall* [1988] I.R.L.R. 315, ECJ.

The position is now dealt with in reg.4(4) and (5) of the TUPE Regulations 2006, which embody the principle in *Wilson*, but modify it to some extent. The regulations in question deal with four different kinds of case:

(a) a case which the sole or principal reason for the variation in contract is the transfer itself;

(b) a case in which the sole or principal reason for the variation is connected with the transfer, and it is not an economic, technical or organisational reason entailing changes in the workforce;

(c) a case in which the sole or principal reason for the variation is a reason unconnected with the transfer; and

(d) a case in which the sole or principal reason for the variation is connected with the transfer, but is an economic, technical or organisational reason entailing changes in the workforce.

In cases (a) and (b) the purported variation of contract will generally be void. In (c) and (d) a valid variation can be agreed.

In *Power v Regent Security Services Ltd* [2007] I.R.L.R. 226, the EAT dealt with the question whether an attempted variation will be void even if it is favourable to the employee, and he wishes to take advantage of it. Elias P held that the principle can be used by the employee as a shield to object to the changes, but does not prevent the employee from taking advantage of favourable terms which have been agreed with the transferee.

The flowchart below illustrates the way in which reg.4(4) and (5) operates.

TUPE and contractual variation

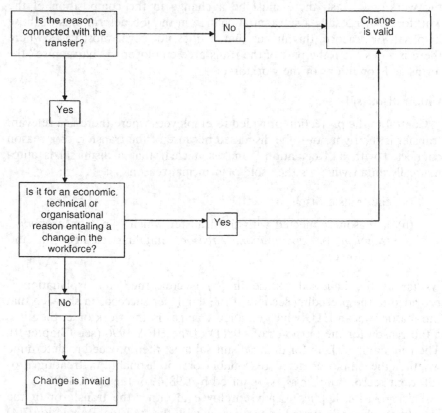

* Subject to the decision in *Power v Regent Security Services Ltd* (see above).

Two of the concepts involved require further interpretation. First, the **12.13** phrase "economic, technical or organisational reason" (usually abbreviated to ETO) is taken directly from the language of the Acquired Rights Directive. Guidance issued by the government in respect of the phrase in the context of the 1981 TUPE Regulations suggested that:

- an economic reason might apply where demand for the employer's product has fallen to such an extent that the enterprise is not profitable;

- a technical reason might arise where the transferee wishes to use new technology, and the staff transferred do not have the requisite skills.

- an organisational reason might apply where the transferee operates at a different locality from the transferor.

Where the ETO appears in the types of case set out as (d) above, it has to "entail changes in the workforce" to have any effect. In *Berriman v Delabole Slate Ltd* [1985] I.R.L.R. 305, the CA stated that, to satisfy the "change in the workforce" test, there must be a change in the composition of the workforce, or possibly a substantial change in the job descriptions of those involved. In practice, this means that it does not cover most cases where there is a desire on the part of the transferee employer to "harmonise" the terms and conditions of the workforce.

Unfair dismissal

12.14   Central to the protection provided to employees where there is a relevant transfer is the right not to be dismissed because of the transfer, or a reason connected with it. Regulation 7 makes it clear that a dismissal is automatically unfair where is the "sole or principal reason" is:

(a) the transfer itself, or

(b) a reason connected with the transfer which is not an *economic, technical or organisational reason* entailing changes in the workforce.

As far as the italicised phrase in (b) is concerned, an explanation is provided in the preceding section. If the employer succeeds in showing that the reason was an ETO which entailed changes in the workforce, then it is a fair reason for the purposes of s.98(1) of the ERA 1996 (see Chapter 9). The tribunal in a claim for unfair dismissal must then proceed to determine whether the employer acted reasonably or unreasonably in treating it as sufficient reason to dismiss, as required by s.98(4) of the ERA 1996.

This provision applies to any employee of either the transferor or the transferee who is dismissed in connection with the transfer. Regulation 7(4) makes it clear that it applies whether or not the employee in question was assigned to the transferred undertaking. Further, the dismissal could be before, at the time of, or after the transfer—the crucial point is whether it is "connected with" the transfer. It can even apply to a transfer which is still to be arranged: *Morris v John Grose Group Ltd* [1998] I.R.L.R. 499, EAT. As a result, it is likely to cover a situation where transferor and transferee come to an arrangement whereby an employee is dismissed as a necessary step towards reaching an agreement. Such collusion between transferor and transferee will mean that the dismissal is for a reason connected with the transfer. In *Wheeler v Patel* [1987] I.R.L.R. 211, the vendor of a shop employed Mrs Wheeler. He dismissed her before transferring the shop to a prospective purchaser, in order to ensure that the transfer went ahead. It was held that the dismissal was connected with the transfer. Further, an argument that this was an "economic" reason such as to ground an ETO defence failed. An economic reason was one which related to the future conduct of the business. It did not include acquiring a higher price for the business, or effecting a sale agreement.

As in most other claims for unfair dismissal, however, the employee must have accrued a year's continuous employment to bring a claim for unfair dismissal on the basis that the transfer or a reason connected with it was the sole or principal reason for his dismissal. It is different where a claimant is dismissed for asserting one of the rights conferred by the TUPE Regulations. In such a case, the dismissal is automatically unfair, and there is no requirement for a year's continuous employment: reg.19, amending s.104 of the ERA 1996.

The process of determining whether a dismissal is unfair in the context of a TUPE transfer is illustrated in the flowchart below. **12.15**

TUPE and unfair dismissal

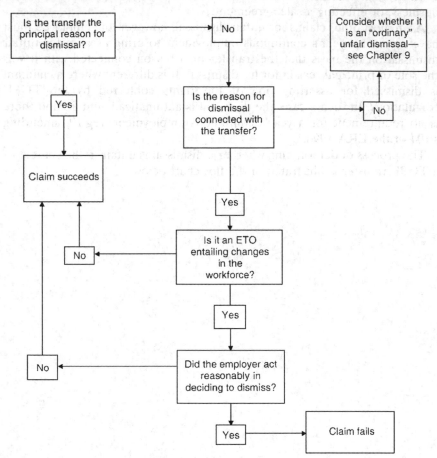

ETO = economic, technical or organisational reason

The flowchart concentrates upon the aspect of the dismissal governed by the TUPE Regulations. It assumes that the claimant has the right not to be unfairly dismissed, e.g. is an employee with at least one year's continuous employment.

It is still necessary for the employer to comply with the statutory DDP if it is applicable. In addition, s.98A(2) of the ERA 1996 will apply if the dismissal is unfair for failure to follow "a procedure" (see Chapter 9).

The TUPE Regulations 2006 introduced new provisions relating to constructive dismissal. Under the 1981 TUPE Regulations, as interpreted by the CA in *Rossiter v Pendragon* [2002] I.R.L.R. 482, the test for constructive dismissal was held to be the same as it was in other cases of unfair dismissal: did the employer resign as a result of a fundamental breach of contract by the employer? (see paras 9.21 to 9.28).

Under the TUPE Regulations 2006, this method of establishing constructive dismissal remains, but is supplemented by an alternative route, contained in reg.4(9). A transferred employee will be treated as dismissed if he resigns in response to "a substantial change in working conditions" which is to his "material detriment". This will be an easier test to satisfy in some circumstances than "a fundamental breach of contract".

Collective agreements and trade union recognition

Upon the completion of a relevant transfer, the status quo is preserved **12.16** with regard to collective agreements, including those which relate to trade union recognition. These matters are dealt with in regs 5 and 6.

Consultation with employee representatives

Both the transferor and the transferee are obliged to consult employee **12.17** representatives about the forthcoming transfer. The duty has been likened to that in relation to collective redundancies (see para.11.16) but there is no minimum number of employees which has to be involved, and no minimum period of time laid down.

The duty is to consult in relation to affected employees. It is not confined to those who are assigned to the transferred undertaking. Where there is a recognised union, the duty is to consult with that union. Otherwise, consultation must be with employee representatives appointed by the affected employees for other purposes, provided they have authority to be consulted about the transfer. If neither of these routes is available, then elections must be arranged by the employer within a statutory framework (regs 13(3) and 14).

The employer is obliged to inform the representatives of certain specified facts in relation to the transfer, including:

- the proposed date of the transfer and the reasons for it;
- the legal, economic and social implications of the transfer for any affected employees;
- any measures which he expects to take in relation to affected employees.

This information must be provided long enough before the transfer to enable consultation to take place. When it does take place, consultation must be with a view to seeking agreement, and must allow the representatives to make representations and for the employer to reply, giving reasons for the rejection of any representations.

12.18   Where consultation is defective, a claim may be made by or on behalf of the affected employees (reg.15). The employer may escape liability if he can show that there were special circumstances which rendered it not reasonably practicable for him to comply with the duty. In practice, some employers may have been reluctant to release information about a pending transfer, for reasons of commercial confidentiality, and may then seek to avail themselves of this defence.

If the complaint is well-founded, the tribunal may make an order for appropriate compensation, which is set down as

> "such sum not exceeding 13 weeks' pay . . . as the tribunal considers just and equitable having regard to the failure of the employer to comply with his duty".

The level of award is primarily punitive, so as to reflect the employer's default. The degree of loss suffered may, however, be taken on board in considering what is just and equitable: *Sweetin v Coral Racing* [2006] I.R.L.R. 252, EAT (the position is similar to that in respect of the protective award for a failure to consult over multiple redundancies—see para.11.17).

The award will usually be against whichever party failed in its own obligation to consult—either the transferor or the transferee. However, if the transferor can establish that its failure was caused by the transferee's failure to provide information, the primary award will be against the transferee (reg.15(8)). In addition, the transferee is jointly and severally liable in respect of any other primary award made against the transferee (reg.15(9)).

Transferor's duty to pass information to the transferee

12.19   Until recently, there was no statutory duty for a transferor to inform the transferee about the employees whom it was transferring, or the obligations attaching to them. Of course, as part of any agreement to transfer, it made sense for the transferee to insist upon such information, but it was not covered by the TUPE Regulations.

Regulation 11(2) of the TUPE Regulations 2006 now sets out the information which the transferor must provide in relation to each employee who will transfer (including those who would transfer if not dismissed prior to the transfer in contravention of the unfair dismissal provisions of reg.7). This information must be given in writing or "in a readily accessible form" no later than 14 days before the transfer, unless special circumstances make it not reasonably practicable to do so. It must not be more than 14 days old when given, and it should be updated if it changes. The required details are:

- the identity and age of the employee;
- the particulars of employment pursuant to s.1 of the ERA 1996 (see para.3.13);
- information about any disciplinary procedure taken against, or grievance procedure taken by, an employee within the previous

two years, in circumstances where the Employment Act 2002 (Dispute Resolution) Regulations 2004 apply;

- information about any court or tribunal claim brought by an employee against the transferor within the previous two years;

- information about any such claim which the transferor has reasonable grounds to believe that an employee might bring against the transferee, arising out of his employment with the transferor;

- information about any collective agreement which will have effect after the transfer.

The right to receive the information is that of the transferee, and not of the employees. As a result, it is the transferee who is entitled to bring a claim if the transferor fails to comply with these provisions. The claim must be presented within three months (subject to a "not reasonably practicable" extension—see Chapter 14 on Time Limits). In the event that the tribunal finds the claim to be well-founded, it may award such compensation as is "just and equitable". The award should have regard to any loss sustained by the transferee, and the terms of any contract, but shall be not less than £500 per employee to whom the failure relates, unless it would be just and equitable to award a lesser sum. According to government guidance, the £500 minimum reflects the fact that it will often be difficult for the transferee to prove loss related to the lack of information, but there should nevertheless be a substantial penalty for default, to ensure compliance.

TUPE and insolvency

Frequently, a TUPE transfer is related to the insolvency of the trans- **12.20** feror. Generally, the fact that it is insolvency which has caused the transfer does not affect the position, but there are two major exceptions.

First, reg.4 of the TUPE Regulations 2006 (dealing with the transfer of contracts of employment and related rights and duties) and reg.7 (unfair dismissal) do not apply:

> "if there are bankruptcy proceedings or any analogous insolvency proceedings which have been instituted with a view to the liquidation of the assets of the transferor and are under the supervision of an insolvency practitioner"

(reg.8(7)).

Second, there are different provisions if the transferor is, at the time of the transfer, the subject of "relevant insolvency proceedings". These are defined as proceedings which are under the supervision of an insolvency practitioner and which are "not with a view to the liquidation of the assets of the transferor" (reg.8(2) to (6)). In these circumstances, certain sums which the transferor is liable to pay to employees do not become a claim against the transferee. Instead, they are recoverable from the National Insurance Fund. The sums in question are:

(a) redundancy payments; and

(b) the items covered by Pt XII of the ERA 1996 (which are listed in the section on Insolvency which follows).

12.21   In addition, employee representatives are given the power to agree to certain variations in the contracts of the employees whom they represent. As has been discussed in paras 12.11 and 12.12 above, employees and their representatives may not be able to agree to variations which are connected with the transfer, unless they are for an ETO reason (regs 4(4) and (5)). However, where the transferor is the subject of "relevant insolvency proceedings" at the time of the transfer, then certain variations are permitted. They are variations which are "designed to safeguard employment opportunities by ensuring the survival of the undertaking, business or part [of it] that is the subject of the relevant transfer (reg.9(7)(b)).

Insolvency

12.22   The consequences of insolvency in a general way are beyond the scope of a book on employment law, and reference should be made to works on company law. However, where an employer becomes insolvent, the ownership of the business will clearly be affected, and with it the contracts of employment of its employees.

Where an administrator, receiver or liquidator ("insolvency practitioner") is appointed by the court, the contracts of employment of all employees are automatically terminated, by virtue of redundancy. However, where the insolvency practitioner is appointed as an agent of the company, this will have no effect on the employees' contracts of employment. The insolvency practitioner may dismiss some of the employees in order to reduce expenditure, and this will usually constitute a redundancy. Where the aim is to ensure that the company can in due course be sold as a going concern, then it is likely that the TUPE Regulations will apply, with the prospect that the dismissal of the employees in question will be automatically unfair (see para.12.14 above).

Insolvency may mean that employees of the company are left with rights against the company, and have difficulty in enforcing them. There are two sets of rights:

(a) those against the assets of the insolvent employer; and

(b) those against the National Insurance Fund.

Payments from the insolvent employer

12.23   In the event of insolvency, there is a statutory order of priority which the insolvency practitioner must follow in attempting to meet the claims of outstanding creditors. It is:

(a) the costs of realising the assets;

(b) the costs and remuneration to the practitioner himself;

(c) claims from holders of fixed charges;

(d) preferential claims;

(e) claims from holders of floating charges; and

(f) unsecured claims.

Each of the categories must be met in full before the practitioner moves on to consider the claims within the next category. If there is insufficient to meet the claims in a particular category then they will be satisfied pro rata (e.g. 50 pence in the pound) and any remaining categories will not receive any payment.

An employee has preferential creditor status (thus ranking in category (d) in the order of priority) against the assets of an employer who becomes insolvent in respect of certain debts. These are set out in Sch.6 of the Insolvency Act 1986, as follows:

(a) four months' wages, to a maximum set by the Secretary of State (currently £800);

(b) any guarantee payment for lay-off because of a temporary short-age of work;

(c) payment for time off for trade union duties or for ante-natal care; and

(d) a protective award for failure to consult over redundancies.

Any other debts owed to the employee would rank in category (f) as an unsecured claim. As a result, typically the employee might just receive some payment in respect of those debts for which he was a preferential creditor, but would only very rarely receive anything in respect of unsecured claims.

Payments from the National Insurance Fund

Because of the difficulties which employees encounter in obtaining **12.24** payment of the debts which they are owed by insolvent employers, European Directive 80/987 requires member states to provide some protection for such employees. In the United Kingdom, this is effected through the ERA 1996, Pt XII. Section 184 sets out the debts which will be paid to employees from the National Insurance Fund where the employer is insolvent (within the definition contained in s.183), as follows:

(a) arrears of pay up to eight weeks;

(b) statutory notice pay;

(c) holiday pay up to six weeks; provided it accrued within the year preceding the insolvency;

(d) the basic award for unfair dismissal

(e) guarantee payments in respect of lay-off;

(f) payment for time off for trade union duties;

(g) remuneration for suspension on medical grounds or maternity grounds;

(h) any protective award in respect of failure to consult over redundancy in accordance with s.189 of the Trade Union and Labour Relations (Consolidation) Act 1992.

The calculation is subject to the statutory maximum of £310 in respect of a week's pay (where the material date is on or after February 1, 2007—the limit is annually updated).

In addition to these rights, the government will pay pension contributions which the insolvent employer has failed to pay, in respect of arrears accrued within the 12 months prior to insolvency, subject to a maximum of ten per cent of the pay of the employees covered by the scheme.

As far as redundancy payments are concerned, s.166 of the ERA 1996 entitles an employee to claim a redundancy payment direct from the National Insurance Fund provided that he is entitled to such a payment, and

(a) the employer is insolvent; or

(b) the employee has taken all reasonable steps, other than legal proceedings, to recover the payment and the employer has failed to make the payment (or part of it).

Where the Fund makes a payment, it takes over the rights of the employee against the employer, and will recover payment in appropriate circumstances. Finally, an employee may make a claim from the Maternity Fund for maternity pay under the Statutory Maternity Pay (General) Regulations 1986, reg.7. Although such payment will be particularly applicable where the employer is insolvent, it is not confined to that situation.

Chapter Thirteen

TRIBUNAL PROCEDURE

The great majority of employment cases are dealt with in the employ-   **13.01**
ment tribunals. There are important exceptions, for example, where an
injunction is sought, then it will be on the courts that the parties must rely.
Where damages for breach of contract are claimed, the jurisdiction of the
employment tribunal is limited to £25,000, so the claimant will have to take
this into account in deciding the appropriate forum to pursue his claim.
Where it is the employer (rather than the employee) who makes the claim
then, with the exception of the potential for a counterclaim to a claim for
breach of contract, the tribunals have no jurisdiction, and it is the ordinary
courts which provide a potential remedy.

Where an employment case is heard in the ordinary courts, then the
usual rules of civil procedure apply, and reference will have to be made to
the Civil Procedure Rules and the various commentaries upon those rules.
In the more usual employment cases, litigated in the tribunal, however, the
rules are laid down in the Employment Tribunal (Constitution and Rules of
Procedure) Regulations 2004 (SI 2004/1861). The statutory instrument
consists of a set of Regulations, to which are appended six schedules. Each
of the schedules deals with the procedure of the employment tribunals in a
particular context e.g. in relation to training levy appeal, equal value cases,
etc. By far the most important schedule, both for our purposes and
generally, is Sch.1, which is entitled "The Employment Tribunals Rules of
Procedure". This will be referred to as "the Rules of Procedure", and
references to particular rules in the remainder of this chapter relate to the
Rules of Procedure as laid down in Sch.1. It is occasionally necessary to
refer to the Regulations themselves, which lay down general principles, and
in so far as this is necessary, they will be referred to as "the Regulations".
Both the Regulations and the Rules of Procedure are reproduced in
Appendix Three.

Perhaps the most important of the Regulations is reg.3, which contains
the overriding objective. All the rules need to be subject to this objective,
which reads as follows:

> "3(1) The overriding objective of these Regulations and the rules in Schedules
> 1, 2, 3, 4, 5 and 6 is to enable tribunals and chairmen to deal with cases justly.
> (2) Dealing with a case justly includes, so far as practicable-
>
> (a) ensuring that the parties are on an equal footing;
> (b) dealing with the case in ways which are proportionate to the complexity or
> importance of the issues;

(c) ensuring that it is dealt with expeditiously and fairly; and
(d) saving expense.

(3) A tribunal or chairman shall seek to give effect to the overriding objective when it or he:

(a) exercises any power given to it or him by these Regulations or the rules in Schedules 1, 2, 3, 4, 5 and 6; or
(b) interprets these Regulations or any rule in Schedules 1, 2, 3, 4, 5 and 6.

(4) The parties shall assist the tribunal or the chairman to further the overriding objective."

History

13.02   The present system of employment tribunals was created by the Industrial Training Act 1964. Its sole purpose at that time was to hear appeals against the industrial training levies—where a particular employer objected to the levy imposed under legislation in order to provide the revenue for training in a particular industry. In 1965, the power was given to the tribunals (which at that time were called industrial tribunals) to deal with issues under the Contracts of Employment Act 1963 and the Redundancy Payments Act 1965. All three of these early jurisdictions remain to-day, but the scope of the tribunals' work has been expanded beyond recognition. In 1971, the Industrial Relations Act created the legal right not to be unfairly dismissed, and jurisdiction in respect of the new right was given exclusively to the industrial tribunals. Adjudication in unfair dismissal cases rapidly became their core function. During the 1970s, they acquired important new jurisdictions in relation to discrimination cases, which have expanded greatly as the breadth of anti-discrimination legislations has grown. In 1998 they were renamed employment tribunals.

Composition

13.03   A full employment tribunal consists of three members—a chairman and two wing members. Each of the three members is drawn from a different panel, as follows:

(a) the chairman is drawn from a panel of legally qualified chairmen appointed by the Lord Chancellor. Each of them must have been qualified as a barrister or a solicitor for at least seven years on appointment to the panel. Some are full-time, some are salaried part-time and some are fee-paid part-time. Typically, the fee-paid chairmen will be in practice as a barrister or solicitor, but some are retired full-time chairmen and a few are lecturers in law;

(b) one of the wing-members is drawn from a panel consisting of those with experience of employment relations from the perspective of the employer. In part, this panel is made up of those who have been nominated by organisations such as the CBI; and in part (since 1999) it consists of those appointed after public application.

(c) The other wing-member is drawn from a panel consisting of those with experience of employment relations from the perspective of the employee. Again, this panel consists partly of those nominated by the trade unions, and partly of those appointed after public application.

A number of matters are heard by a chairman sitting alone. This will be the case in interlocutory matters, including pre-hearing reviews (see para.13.27) except where one of the parties has requested a hearing by a full tribunal. It will also be the case in an uncontested matter. Further, s.4(3) of the Employment Tribunals Act 1996 sets out a number of jurisdictions where it will be usual for a chairman sitting alone to hear the proceedings, including deductions from wages and breach of contract claims. In such cases, the assumption is that the chairman will hear such cases alone, unless there are particular circumstances which make a full tribunal desirable, e.g. the likelihood of a significant dispute on the facts or the representations of the parties in favour of a full tribunal.

Where a full tribunal hears the case, the legally qualified chairman will conduct proceedings, but all three members play a full part by asking questions and participating in the decisions made by the tribunal. The eventual judgment of the tribunal on the case may be unanimous or by a majority. In practice, it is almost invariably unanimous, which is an interesting reflection of the way in which the wing-members, in particular, give priority to their judicial role, rather than their partisan origins.

Occasionally, one of the wing members may be absent, leaving the tribunal "one down", i.e. consisting of two members only. In such a case it is possible for the tribunal to proceed, provided that the parties consent. If the two remaining members disagree, then the chairman has a casting vote. The agreement of the parties to proceed with a two-person tribunal must be based upon informed consent. In order for such consent to be informed, the parties should be told whether the absent member was from panel (b) or (c) above, and should also be informed that the chairman will have a casting vote in the event of disagreement.   **13.04**

The claim

The claim must be presented in time. The law which governs this important area is dealt with in Chapter 14.   **13.05**

In addition, the claim must be presented in proper form. There is a standard form (the ET1) which must be used to present any claim to the tribunal. It is nine pages long, and is reproduced as Appendix One. It can also be found, together with useful guidance, at the website of the employment tribunals: *www.employmenttribunals.gov.uk*.

The claim must be presented on this form (r.1(3)) but either the online or the hard copy version can be used. As will be seen from examination of the form, it requires information to be given about a number of different matters. Some of these are required by r.1, as follows:

(a) the name(s) of the claimant(s);

(b) the address(es) of the claimant(s);

(c) the name(s) of the respondent(s);

(d) the address(es) of the respondent(s);

(e) the details of the claim;

(f) whether or not the claimant is or was an employee of the respondent;

(g) whether or not the claim includes a complaint as to dismissal;

(h) whether or not the claimant has raised the subject matter of the claim with the respondent in writing at least 28 days prior to the presentation of the claim; and

(i) if the claimant has not done as described in (h), why he has not done so.

13.06   Various points arise from this list.

- The claim can be presented on behalf of a number of claimants, provided that names and addresses are supplied for each of them (r 1(7)).

- The respondent will usually be the employer, and this is certainly the case in claims for unfair dismissal, deduction from wages, breach of contract and the like. However, in discrimination cases, the claimant may well decide to name individuals who are alleged to have discriminated against him, as well as the employer.

- If the claimant is not or was not an employee of the respondent, the information in points (g) to (i) is not required (r.1(5)(a)).

- Where the claimant was an employee and the claim consists only of a complaint that he was dismissed, the information in points (h) and (i) is not required (r.1(5)(b)). Dismissal in this context does not, however, include constructive dismissal (r.1(6)).

- The information about whether the subject matter of the claim has been raised at least 28 days before it is presented to the tribunal is in order to ascertain whether the statutory grievance procedure ("GP") has been complied with (see para.3.32).

The procedure on presentation of the claim is that it must be considered by the Regional Secretary (in practice, one of the tribunal staff). The member of staff must reject the claim if it is not on the prescribed form, and return it to the claimant with an explanation and a copy of the correct form. The Secretary must not accept the form if:

- it does not include the required information as set out in the list (a) to (i) above;

- the tribunal has no power to consider the claim; or

- the claim has been presented in breach of the statutory GP (see para.3.32 above).

In such a case, however, the Secretary has no power to reject the claim but must refer it to a chairman to decide whether it should be accepted.

Prior to the introduction of the 2004 version of the rules, the only statutory requirement was that a claim should be in writing. It was therefore feared that the list, set out as items (a) to (i) above, could result in claims being refused by the tribunal staff even though they represent sound legal claims, because of a failure to abide by the required formality. The reported cases on these particular provisions appear to display a desire on the part of the EAT to ensure that potentially sound cases are not thrown out for lack of compliance with formality. In *Richardson v U Mole Ltd* [2005] I.R.L.R. 668, the EAT held that the tribunal had erred in refusing to accept the claimant's claim because it did not expressly state that he was an employee of the respondent as required by r.1(4)(f). The form asserted he was an employee by implication, e.g. by answering questions such as "Please give the dates of your employment" and should have been allowed.

In *Grimmer v KLM Cityhopper UK* [2006] I.R.L.R. 596, the EAT held **13.07** that the claimant had provided sufficient details of her claim relating to the employers' refusal to accede to her request for flexible working, and it should have been accepted. In giving judgment, H.H. Judge Prophet stated:

> "The Rules cannot be seen in isolation. The chairman, unlike the secretary whose functions are administrative has, as an independent judicial person, to do more than merely run down a checklist. He or she must have in mind the overall interests of justice. It is a very serious step to deny a claimant or for that matter a respondent the opportunity of having an employment rights matter resolved by an independent judicial body i.e. an employment tribunal. Most chairmen would not wish to feel forced to do so without there being a very good reason. . . The test for "details of the claim" emerges as being whether it can be discerned from the claim as presented that the claimant is complaining of an alleged breach of an employment right which falls within the jurisdiction of the employment tribunal. It follows that if that test is met, there is no scope for either the Secretary or a chairman interpreting 'details of the claim' as being 'sufficient particulars of the claim'."

What should the ET1 contain?

Leaving aside the question of the degree of detail required by the rules **13.08** for the claim to be accepted, there is also the question of what the claimant should include in the ET1 for the effective pursuit of the case. The central purpose is to explain what the claimant is complaining about, and why he says that it is unlawful. This has to be done in fairness to the respondent, so that it can see what case it has to meet, both legally and factually. It is also of potential value as far as the tribunal is concerned as a piece of written advocacy on behalf of the claimant—if it is persuasive, it will create a favourable impression when the ET1 is viewed later on, as it must be in the course of the hearing. It is also important that what is said in the ET1 is consistent with the case which is to be run at the hearing. Any anomalies are likely to provide ammunition for the respondent when the case has to be presented and argued.

Bearing all this in mind, there is no need to set out all the evidence at this very early stage of the case. At the same time, it is important (as a matter of written advocacy) for the claimant to set out in broad terms all the factual complaints, and make clear in the briefest fashion why the respondent acted unlawfully. As to the degree of detail, it would clearly be inadequate for the claimant to say "My dismissal was discriminatory" without further explanation. She would need to explain what sort of discrimination (sex, race, etc.) was alleged and the essential facts which go to show that her dismissal constituted discrimination. If she fails to do so, she may have to try to amend the claim later and run the risk that leave to amend will be refused. But she should not go into anything like the degree of detail which she needs to display in her witness statement. The crucial distinction is between the important facts (which ought to be set out in the claim) and equally important evidence of those facts (which ought to be left to the hearing).

The response

13.09   On receipt of the claim form, the tribunal staff give it a date stamp and a case number. They then send it to the respondent named on the form, together with a blank response form (ET3) and an explanatory booklet.

The ET3 is reproduced as part of Appendix One. The respondent is obliged to use that form if it wishes to respond, and it must be presented to the tribunal office within 28 days of the date on which it was sent. Again, it must include all the required information, but this is less extensive than that which is needed for the claimant to complete the ET1. The required information is (r.4(3)):

    (a) the respondent's full name;

    (b) its address;

    (c) whether it wishes to resist the claim in whole or in part; and, if so

    (d) on what grounds.

If a response is sent in time and it is accepted, it will be copied to the claimant and the case will proceed in the usual way. If no response is entered within the time limit, or the response is not on the prescribed form ET3, or it is inadequate in the sense that it does not supply the required information, then the regional secretary cannot accept it. It must be referred to a chairman who has to decide whether to accept it in accordance with the rules. A respondent who has not presented a response which has been accepted is barred from taking any further part in proceedings (r.9) other than to:

    (a) make an application for review;

(b) be called as a witness; or

(c) be sent copies of certain documents e.g. judgments.

The main difficulty in this area has been in connection with the time limit of 28 days. The respondent is entitled to apply for an extension of time (r.4(4)) but the application must be made before the time limit expires. If the application is made after the expiry of the deadline, then the respondent will be in danger of being unable to take any further part in proceedings. *Moroak t/a Blake Envelopes v Cromie* [2005] I.R.L.R. 535 deals with the situation where an employer lodges its response late, and the tribunal refuses to accept it. It has power to review its decision under r.34, e.g. on the grounds that the interests of justice require such a review. Burton P. said that the tribunal should decide whether to review, and whether to extend time, on the basis of what is just and equitable. In doing so, it should take into account all relevant factors, including the explanation for the delay and the merits of the employer's defence.

Rule 8 gives a tribunal chairman the power to issue a default judgment in certain circumstances: **13.10**

(a) where there has been no response presented to the tribunal within the time limit;

(b) where the response has not been accepted, and there has been no application for a review;

(c) where a response has been accepted, but the respondent says in it that he does not intend to resist the claim.

A default judgment can be as to liability only, or it may also determine remedy.

What should the ET3 contain?

Clearly, the ET3 must cover the information which is required under the rules. Like the ET1, however, it needs to go somewhat further in order to be an effective tool in pursuit of the case. Where the factual allegations made by the claimant are relevant, then they should be refuted or explained. Where those allegations do not amount to a case in law, that should be stated. Again, the astute representative will bear in mind that the tribunal will focus upon the ET3 during the full merits hearing, and that it therefore needs to set out the respondent's case clearly and persuasively. It is neither necessary nor advisable to set out the evidence which the respondent intends to adduce to support its case. But it is necessary to outline the essential facts which that evidence will establish. **13.11**

Employer's counterclaim

Generally, it is the employee who makes a claim in the employment tribunal, and the employer who responds to it. By s.3 of the Employment Tribunals Act 1996, however, the employer is given the right to make a **13.12** claim of breach of contract in the tribunal. This is an alternative to a claim for breach of contract by the employer in the ordinary courts.

The employer is only able to claim by way of a counterclaim to a claim for breach of contract by the employee (Employment Tribunals Extension of Jurisdiction Order (England and Wales Order 1994, art.5). Consequently, if the employee's claim is limited to race discrimination and unfair dismissal, the employer will not be able to pursue any claim which it might have that the employee breached his contract of employment in the tribunal. It will have to pursue such a claim in the courts, where it will generally prove less convenient and more expensive, and take longer. If the same employee alleges at the same time that he was wrongfully dismissed, however, that will be a claim for breach of contract. It will trigger off the right of the employer to make a counterclaim for breach of contract. This raises an important strategic point for claimants and those who advise them. If a substantial employer's claim for breach of contract is anticipated, it may be better for the claimant to avoid opening the door to such a counterclaim. That may mean not claiming for breach of contract, or alternatively framing the claim as one for deduction of wages, for example.

The procedure in relation to a counterclaim is set out in r.7 of the Rules. It is required to be in writing, and must include details broadly equivalent to those required for the response (see para.13.09 above). It may not include any claim for breach of contract relating to intellectual property, a duty of confidentiality, a covenant in restraint of trade, or the provision of living accommodation. It must be presented within six weeks starting with the day on which the employer received the employee's claim for breach of contract, unless it was not reasonably practicable for the employer to present his counterclaim within that period, and he does so within a reasonable period thereafter (compare the relevant case law on "reasonably practicable" in relation to claims in general in paras 14.10 to 14.13).

Preparing for the hearing

13.13   As is usual in litigation, an important dimension of the preparation for a tribunal case is to be found in the relations between the parties. Although the rules concentrate upon the role of the parties in relation to the tribunal, much of the work in getting the case into shape, ready to be heard, ought to be carried out in co-operation between the parties. The tribunal will expect the parties to liaise in order to ensure that the process runs smoothly, particularly if they are legally represented.

For example, where one of the parties requires the disclosure of particular documents (see para.13.18 below), a request should be sent to the other party asking for production of the documents, setting out a realistic deadline. Only if the deadline is not met should an application be made to the tribunal for an order that the documents should be disclosed. That application should enclose a copy of the request, as the tribunal chairman will want to know that a request has been made. If the application is granted, the resultant order is likely to cross-refer to the original request.

The tribunal's interlocutory powers

Proceedings which take place before the main hearing of a case are **13.14** sometimes referred to as interlocutory matters. The tribunal has a number of powers in relation to interlocutory matters, most of which are set out in r.10 of the Rules. It is worth quoting the rule in full, partly in order to show its breadth and partly because it provides an introduction to a summary of the more important and frequently used powers:

"**10.**—(1) Subject to the following rules, the chairman may at any time either on the application of a party or on his own initiative make an order in relation to any matter which appears to him to be appropriate. Such orders may be any of those listed in paragraph (2) or such other orders as he thinks fit. Subject to the following rules, orders may be issued as a result of a chairman considering the papers before him in the absence of the parties, or at a hearing (see regulation 2 for the definition of "hearing").

(2) Examples of orders which may be made under paragraph (1) are orders—

(a) as to the manner in which the proceedings are to be conducted, including any time limit to be observed;

(b) that a party provide additional information;

(c) requiring the attendance of any person in Great Britain either to give evidence or to produce documents or information;

(d) requiring any person in Great Britain to disclose documents or information to a party to allow a party to inspect such material as might be ordered by a County Court (or in Scotland, by a sheriff);

(e) extending any time limit, whether or not expired (subject to rules 4(4), 11(2), 25(5), 30(5), 33(1), 35(1), 38(7) and 42(5) of this Schedule, and to rule 3(4) of Schedule 2);

(f) requiring the provision of written answers to questions put by the tribunal or chairman;

(g) that, subject to rule 22(8), a short conciliation period be extended into a standard conciliation period;

(h) staying (in Scotland, sisting) the whole or part of any proceedings;

(i) that part of the proceedings be dealt with separately;

(j) that different claims be considered together;

(k) that any person who the chairman or tribunal considers may be liable for the remedy claimed should be made a respondent in the proceedings;

(l) dismissing the claim against a respondent who is no longer directly interested in the claim;

(m) postponing or adjourning any hearing;

(n) varying or revoking other orders;

(o) giving notice to the parties of a pre-hearing review or the Hearing;

(p) giving notice under rule 19;

(q) giving leave to amend a claim or response;

(r) that any person who the chairman or tribunal considers has an interest in the outcome of the proceedings may be joined as a party to the proceedings;

(s) that a witness statement be prepared or exchanged; or

(t) as to the use of experts or interpreters in the proceedings.

(3) An order may specify the time at or within which and the place at which any act is required to be done. An order may also impose conditions and it shall inform the parties of the potential consequences of non-compliance set out in rule 13.

(4) When a requirement has been imposed under paragraph (1) the person subject to the requirement may make an application under rule 11 (applications in proceedings) for the order to be varied or revoked."

As can be seen, the powers of the tribunal are wide-ranging, and it is worth bearing in mind that the list above is not exhaustive. When considering what requests to make of the other party or parties, and (if the requests are not met) what applications to make, a representative will wish to bear the powers of the tribunal in mind.

Applications

13.15   An application for an order (or for an order to be varied or revoked) is governed by r.11 of the Rules. Such an application should be made at least 10 days before the hearing at which it is to be considered, although many applications are applied for and granted or refused in correspondence, so that there is no hearing which considers them.

The application must be in writing, include the case number, and set out the reasons why an order should be granted, and how it will assist the tribunal or chairman in dealing with the case efficiently and fairly. Where a party is legally represented, all other parties must be provided, at the time of the application, with details of the application and the reasons why it is sought. They must also be notified that any objection to the application must be sent to the tribunal office within seven days of receipt of the application (or before the hearing if that is earlier), and that any objection to the application must be copied to the tribunal and the other parties to the case. The party or his representative must confirm that these obligations have been complied with. The requirements of r.11 are worth remembering as failure to comply with them is a frequent cause for delay while the tribunal reminds the party making the application of its terms and the need to comply with them.

Additional information

13.16   In r.10(2)(b), the tribunal is given the power to order that a party provide additional information. This was referred to in the old version of the Rules as "further and better particulars". That meant, in effect, further and better particulars of the case which the party in question intended to run at the hearing. Additional information is a broader concept, and might, for example, include information which will assist the tribunal to understand the case, or even information which will assist an opponent.

Nevertheless, the primary purpose of this power is to fill in the gaps where an opponent will not be able to see with clarity, from reading the claim or the response, what case it will have to meet at trial. In that context, the tribunal will have in mind the following principles in deciding whether to grant an order for additional information:

(a) is the information necessary in the interests of justice, or to prevent an adjournment?

(b) Will refusal mean that the party denied the information will be taken by surprise?

(c) Will the order if granted be oppressive?

(d) Will the information help to identify the issues in the case (a proper purpose), or are they a disguised means of eliciting evidence prematurely?

(See *Byrne v Financial Times* [1991] I.R.L.R. 417.)

Written answers

A tribunal has power to order a party to provide written answers to **13.17** questions which it puts, by virtue of r.10(2)(f). In deciding whether to do so, it will consider whether such an order is necessary to dispose fairly of the case, or to save costs. The questions must of course be relevant to the issues which the Tribunal has to determine. They should be based upon the contentions being put forward by the parties, and they should not be a concealed means of seeking a preview of evidence.

One frequent order made by the tribunal is for the claimant to provide a "Schedule of Loss". This will set out the compensation which is sought, and is likely to be of assistance to all concerned at an early stage of proceedings. It will focus the mind of the claimant upon the need to prove his loss. It will give the respondent a picture of the size of the claim which it has to meet, and enable it to perform the exercise of balancing the costs of fighting the claim as against settling it. From the tribunal's point of view, it will assist case management in showing the issues which have to be determined as part of a remedies hearing, and enable a decision to be made as to whether it is better to hear liability and remedies separately or together.

Disclosure of documents

The power to order disclosure of documents is contained in r.10(2)(d)). **13.18** A party is entitled to know what documents the other party has in its possession which are relevant to the case and, subject to appropriate safeguards, to inspect them. It is usual for the tribunal to make an order for general disclosure—that is for each party to reveal to the other(s) such documents as it has which are relevant to the case, and to allow inspection. In practice, inspection is carried out by the supply of photocopies. Sometimes an order for disclosure and inspection is controversial, e.g. where an employer regards certain documents relating to other employees as confidential. From the point of view of the employee, however, sight of such documents may be important where, for example, it is contended that the claimant's selection for redundancy was unfair and it is desired to look at how the other candidates for redundancy scored on the criteria which the employer chose to make its decision. In such a case, it will be for the tribunal to decide.

The test is that which is contained within the Civil Procedure Rules: an order should be made if it is necessary for the fair disposal of the case, or in order to save costs. Crucially, the document(s) must be relevant to an issue which has been raised: *British Aerospace v Green* [1995] I.R.L.R. 433, CA. Where the party from whom disclosure is sought raises confidentiality as an issue, that is a matter which the tribunal ought to take into account.

However, it does not automatically mean that disclosure must be withheld. In appropriate circumstances, documents may be redacted—e.g. details covered up, names substituted by letters of the alphabet, etc. (see *Science Research Council v Nasse* [1979] I.C.R. 921, HL).

Sometimes there is no order from the tribunal in relation to disclosure. In such a case, a party choosing to make voluntary disclosure of documents in its possession must not be unfairly selective in that process: *Birds Eye Walls Ltd v Harrison* [1985] I.C.R. 278, EAT.

13.19   The rules relating to privilege, e.g. of "without prejudice" communications, and legal professional privilege, apply to the Tribunals just as they do to the courts, notwithstanding the relative informality of proceedings. It follows that documents subject to such forms of privilege are not susceptible to disclosure, just as they may not be introduced in evidence at the hearing itself (see para.15.07).

Witness statements

13.20   The tribunal is given power to order parties to prepare or exchange witness statements by r.10(2)(s). Frequently, the tribunal will order that the parties should exchange witness statements simultaneously in advance of the hearing. If such an order is made, then expressly or by implication, no other witness may be called without the leave of the tribunal. Similarly, the evidence in chief of the witness is confined to the matters dealt with in the witness statement, unless leave is granted to add or amend. Occasionally, the tribunal may order *sequential* exchange of witness statements, if such a course of action helps to clarify the issues.

As a matter of practice, witness statements should:

(a) deal with the factual evidence known to the witness, rather than presenting argument;

(b) be couched in the witness' own terms;

(c) deal with matters chronologically;

(d) incorporate references to documents, preferably by reference to the trial bundle;

(e) be in short numbered paragraphs;

(f) be collated separately from the trial bundle.

The manner in which witness statements are dealt with by the tribunal at the hearing varies considerably. They can be (for example):

(a) read silently by the tribunal after the witness has sworn or affirmed;

(b) read in advance of the hearing, or during an adjournment, in the absence of the witness and the parties.

The normal practice, however, is for the witness (after the oath or affirmation) to read the statement out loud to the tribunal, unless there is a good reason to adopt an alternative method of proceeding, e.g. because of the constraints of time, or because a witness has difficulty in reading.

Similarly, tribunals vary in the extent to which they allow the witness statement to be augmented by supplementary questions in chief. To allow a representative to ask as many questions as they like would defeat the purpose of requiring the exchange of written witness statements in advance. At the same time, to refuse to allow any supplementary questions would mean that matters which have arisen, or become important, since the statement was written, cannot be put before the tribunal. A frequent course adopted by the tribunal is to require the representative to explain why the matter in question was not dealt with in the original statement, and decide whether it is right that it should be admitted in the light of that explanation. **13.21**

Witness orders

The power to make an order for a witness to attend and give evidence is contained in r.10(2)(c). Before it makes an order for a witness to attend, the tribunal will need to be satisfied as to the following matters: **13.22**

(a) Is the witness likely to give evidence relevant to an issue in dispute in the case? (A summary should be provided.)

(b) Is the witness unlikely to attend if no order is made?

(c) What is the witness' correct name and address?

The party applying for the witness order is not obliged to tell the other parties to the case of the application (it is an exception to the general rule contained within r.11—see para.13.15 above).

An application for a witness order may be useful where a witness is reluctant to give evidence. The reluctance may, for example, be displayed by a fellow employee who does not wish to be seen by the employer to help the claimant voluntarily, but will accept the inevitable if the tribunal orders him to give evidence.

A common misconception is that a party will benefit from obtaining a witness order against someone who is hostile to their case and who is not being called by the other side. In such circumstances, there is the usual bar upon cross-examining (or even leading) your own witness. Generally, tribunals are reluctant to import the rules which apply in the ordinary courts and which permit the cross-examination of a witness who has been declared "hostile". In any event, it is often difficult, even where those rules are applied, to establish that the witness is "hostile" in the sense of "not being desirous of telling the truth at the instance of the party calling him". One possible alternative is to ask the tribunal to order the witness as its own witness, so that he can be cross-examined by the parties.

Trial bundles

Although the power is not specifically mentioned in r.10, the tribunal will frequently order the parties to agree a joint bundle containing the documents which each party intends to rely upon at the hearing. **13.23**

Inclusion in the agreed bundle does not imply that all the parties agree that the document in question is authentic, let alone that it is important. It should only be included, however, if it is relevant, in the sense that at least one of the parties wishes to make reference to it. It is desirable to ensure that the bundle is no more bulky than is necessary, and where appropriate, an extract may be sufficient, e.g. rather than including the whole of the staff handbook in the bundle, relevant parts such as the disciplinary rules may be included.

Ideally, the bundle should be agreed by the parties sufficiently in advance of the hearing to enable the witness statements to refer to page numbers. This will speed up the process of dealing with the documents by witnesses at the hearing itself. The witness statements should not be included in the bundle, but should be separate, for ease of use during the hearing.

13.24   The bundle should be consecutively paginated, and should be numbered according to pages, rather than according to documents. This will enable those at the hearing (and particularly the chairman) to take a note which refers to the precise page when evidence is given.

In addition to the copies required by the parties, a set should be prepared for the witness table, and three sets for the members of the Tribunal (one if the case is to be heard by the chairman alone).

Leave to amend a claim or response

13.25   The tribunal has power (r.10(2)(q)) to give leave for a claim or response to be amended. A party may wish to amend its claim or response if the original document fails to set out its case properly. The tribunal will have to consider whether to allow it to do so, exercising a judicial discretion.

Where leave is sought to amend the ET1 (the claim), the tribunal will be particularly careful not to allow the claimant to evade the time limit by, in effect, introducing a new claim. The leading case is *Selkent Bus Co Ltd v Moore* [1996] I.R.L.R. 661, EAT. The position was that the claim alleged unfair dismissal. It gave brief details, but made no mention of any relationship between the dismissal and membership of, or activities in connection with, a trade union. The response stated that the reason for dismissal was the claimant's conduct. The claimant's representative then sought to amend the claim to one of dismissal for trade union membership or activities. The amendment was granted by the chairman, and the respondent appealed. The EAT set aside the the chairman's decision, and refused the amendment. It set out three matters for the chairman or tribunal to consider in exercising a discretion whether or not to allow an amendment, as follows:

(a) The nature of the amendment. Is it a simple error, or does it expand existing grounds? If so, it is likely to be accepted. On the other hand, if it is a substantial alteration, changing the basis of the claim, it is more likely to be refused.

(b) If it is a new claim, is it out of time? If so, then an extension of time will have to be considered in accordance with the usual principles (see Chapter 14 on "Time Limits").

(c) The timing and manner of the application, i.e. why was it not made earlier?

As far as an amendment to the response is concerned, the position is somewhat different. There is no problem of a lack of jurisdiction where a response is out of time, as there is with a claim. However, the tribunal will be careful to ensure that the claimant is not prejudiced by any late change of tack on the part of the respondent. In the case of a substantial amendment, the closer to the hearing, the greater the likelihood of prejudice to the claimant. Again, the reason for the amendment will be important.

Even if an amendment (to the claim or the response) is granted, it may **13.26** be necessary for the tribunal to grant an adjournment to enable the other party to meet the new case, and this will have cost implications (see paras 13.33 to 13.36).

Types of Hearing

Rule 14 deals generally with hearings, and states in part: **13.27**

"**14.**—(1)A chairman or a tribunal (depending on the relevant rule) may hold the following types of hearing—

(a) a case management discussion under rule 17;
(b) a pre-hearing review under rule 18;
(c) a Hearing under rule 26; or
(d) a review hearing under rule 33 or 36."

A *case management discussion* (r.17) is an interim hearing, held by the chairman sitting alone. It deals with matters of procedure and management of the proceedings. It may be held in private. It may deal, for example, with any of the matters listed in r.10(2) above. It may not deal with "any determination of a person's civil rights and obligations" (the phrase echoes the European Convention on Human Rights, Art.6).

A *pre-hearing* review (r.18) is also an interim hearing. It is usually conducted by a chairman alone. There are, however, provisions for it to be heard by a full tribunal if so requested in writing by one of the parties, at least ten days before it is due to take place, and agreed by a chairman because one or more substantive issues of fact are likely to be determined at it. Subject to very limited exceptions, it will take place in public. The chairman (or tribunal) has the power at a pre-hearing review to determine any interim or preliminary matter. Preliminary hearings are used, for example, to determine whether a claim was made in time, or whether the claimant was an employee.

In addition, the chairman or tribunal conducting the pre-hearing review **13.28** has power to strike out or dismiss proceedings, so that no further hearing is necessary, on any of the bases set out in rr.18(7)(b) to (f), which reads as follows:

"(b) striking out or amending all or part of any claim or response on the grounds that it is scandalous, or vexatious or has no reasonable prospect of success;

(c) striking out any claim or response (or part of one) on the grounds that the manner in which the proceedings have been conducted by or on behalf of the claimant or the respondent (as the case may be) has been scandalous, unreasonable or vexatious;

(d) striking out a claim which has not been actively pursued;

(e) striking out a claim or response (or part of one) for non-compliance with an order or practice direction;

(f) striking out a claim where the chairman or tribunal considers that it is no longer possible to have a fair Hearing in those proceedings."

In *Blockbuster Entertainment Ltd v James* [2006] I.R.L.R. 630, the claimant had failed to comply with various procedural orders for disclosure and exchange of witness statements. The tribunal struck out the claim on the grounds that the case had been conducted unreasonably. The CA held that the "draconic power" to strike out should only be exercised if the unreasonable conduct has:

(1) taken the form of deliberate and persistent disregard of required procedural steps; or

(2) made a fair trial impossible.

In any event, the CA said, a claim should only be struck out if it is proportionate to do so.

At a pre-hearing review, the chairman or tribunal may also do anything which could be done at a case management discussion, and has certain other powers, notably to order the payment of a deposit under r.20. Such a deposit (maximum £500) may be ordered as a condition of being permitted to continue to take part in proceedings relating to contentions which appear to have "little reasonable prospect of success".

13.29   Rules 33 and 36 deal with *review hearings* (see paras 13.39 to 13.42).

The most important category of hearing is that which is governed by r.26, and this is dealt with in the next section.

The full merits hearing

13.30   The only species of hearing which is designated by a capital H in the Rules is that which is described in r.26, which reads in part:

"(1) A Hearing is held for the purpose of determining outstanding procedural or substantive issues or disposing of the proceedings. In any proceedings there may be more than one Hearing and there may be different categories of Hearing, such as a Hearing on liability, remedies, costs (in Scotland, expenses) or preparation time."

It follows that a hearing may deal, for example, with remedies alone, or be confined to the question of costs. However, the most important hearing is that which deals with liability, and is sometimes referred to as the "full merits hearing". This is the hearing which will determine liability (and

THE FULL MERITS HEARING

possibly remedies and costs as well). The following points can be made about the way in which it is usually conducted:

(a) the hearing is in public, unless the very limited circumstances set out in r.16 apply. Rule 16 sets out the following exceptions to the general rule that a hearing must be conducted in public:

- evidence which a witness could not disclose without contravening a statutory prohibition;
- evidence which has been communicated to, or obtained by, the witness in confidence;
- evidence which would cause substantial injury to any undertaking of his or in which he works (other than evidence which might have such an effect by reason of its effect upon collective bargaining as statutorily defined).

(b) The procedure adopted at the hearing is similar to that adopted in the courts, although somewhat less formal e.g. advocates remain seated while addressing the Tribunal or questioning witnesses. The Tribunal is addressed through the chairman ("Sir" or "Madam").

(c) Where a party is represented by a professional advocate, the normal rules as to questioning witnesses apply, e.g.

- no leading of disputed matters in evidence-in-chief;
- put your case in cross-examination;
- deal only with matters raised in questioning by the other party or the Tribunal when re-examining;
- save argument for closing speeches, rather than rehearsing it with the witnesses;

(d) The party bearing the initial onus normally goes first (subject to the Tribunal's discretion). Although the rule is simple, its application is sometimes tricky.

(e) The Tribunal will sometimes decide to deal with both liability and remedies in a single hearing. Sometimes it will split these two aspects of the case, so that remedies is dealt with only if the claimant is successful. If it is unclear, the advocates should check—and where the hearing is split, they should determine which side of the line issues such as contributory conduct and a *Polkey* reduction fall.

(f) Opening speeches are discouraged. Closing submissions, by contrast, are crucial to the Tribunal's consideration although occasionally (usually due to pressure of time) they are not delivered orally but written submissions are made, according to a timetable laid down by the tribunal. Even where closing submissions are delivered orally, a written summary is increasingly put in front of the tribunal by the professional advocate.

(g) The use made of witness statements varies—see para.13.20.

(h) Where a witness is absent but has provided a statement, the tribunal frequently takes the course (subject to the representations of the parties) of admitting the statement subject to reduced weight (because the witness has not been sworn or affirmed, and cannot be cross-examined). A similar approach is adopted generally with respect to hearsay evidence.

The order of proceedings in a typical hearing is set out in the chart below.

The hearing—order of proceedings

13.31

A's Case	
A's first witness	1. Examination-in chief
	2. Cross-examination
	3. Questions from Tribunal
	4. Re-examination
A's second and subsequent witnesses	Repeat the steps 1–4 above
A closes case	
B's Case	
B's first witness	Steps 1–4 above
B's second and subsequent witnesses	Steps 1–4 above
B closes case	
B's closing submissions	
A's closing submissions	
Tribunal retires to decide on judgment (or reserves judgment)	
Tribunal delivers judgment (or sends it to the parties)	

In the above table, A is the party bearing the initial onus, and B is the opposing party.

Judgments

13.32   A judgment is a final determination of the whole or part of a claim (r.28(1)), and may include an award of compensation, a declaration or a recommendation. An order is an interim decision in relation to an interlocutory matter.

The usual position is that the tribunal will consider its judgment at the end of the hearing, after an adjournment to consider, and announce it to the parties. Sometimes, where the matter is more complicated or time does not allow for an early decision, the tribunal will reserve its judgment and issue it in writing later. In any event, the judgment must be recorded in writing, signed by the chairman, and given to the parties.

Where the judgment has been reserved, it will be accompanied by written reasons when sent to the parties. Where it has been announced to the parties at the conclusion of the hearing, written reasons will only be given if requested orally by one of the parties at the hearing, or within 14 days of the day upon which judgment was sent to the parties (r.30(5)). The written reasons must include the following information (r.30(6)):

(a) the issues which the tribunal or chairman has identified as being relevant to the claim;

(b) if some identified issues were not determined, what those issues were and why they were not determined;

(c) findings of fact relevant to the issues which have been determined;

(d) a concise statement of the applicable law;

(e) how the relevant findings of fact and applicable law have been applied in order to determine the issues; and

(f) where the judgment includes an award of compensation or a determination that one party make a payment to the other, a table showing how the amount or sum has been calculated or a description of the manner in which it has been calculated.

Costs

A party is entitled to make an application for its costs. This is for the cost **13.33** of legal representation, which is defined so as to be restricted to solicitors and barristers. Historically, tribunals have been slow to award legal costs. The position is greatly different from that in the ordinary courts where the usual rule is that "costs follow the event", i.e. the winner is entitled to his costs. In the tribunal there is no such presumption and costs are awarded in a minority of cases.

The main power to make a costs order is contained within r.40, which lays down that:

(a) a costs order may be made when there is the postponement or adjournment of a hearing. The award may be in favour of, or against, the party applying for the postponement or adjournment. The tribunal will not necessarily make an award of costs in such a case but, where it does, it will usually decide, in effect, who is to blame for the postponement or adjournment, and award the costs which the other party has had to incur against the party causing the delay.

(b) A costs order may be made where a party has in bringing or conducting the proceedings, acted vexatiously, abusively, disruptively or otherwise unreasonably. This provision also applies where the conduct in question is that of the party's representative.

(c) It may also be made where the bringing or conducting of the proceedings has been misconceived.

(d) A costs order may be made against a party who has not complied with an order or direction of the tribunal.

As to "misconceived", an interpretation is provided in reg.2 of the Regulations to which the Rules are attached: "misconceived includes having no reasonable prospect of success". The mere fact that a party has lost is not sufficient to show that they had no reasonable prospect of success. The question is rather: was it clear that the claim or defence was going to fail? One factor which the tribunal will regard as important in relevant cases is whether the case was set down for a pre-hearing review with a view to a deposit being ordered, and (if so) what conclusion the chairman came to.

As far as unreasonable conduct is concerned, typical grounds for a costs application might include:

- Failure to follow the orders of the tribunal, e.g. as to disclosure or the exchange of witness statements.
- Late amendment of a claim or response.
- Threats or intimidation (including unwarranted threats that the other party will have to pay costs).
- Refusal to agree to a settlement offer which is clearly reasonable.
- Unfounded allegations against the other party or his witnesses or those representing him.

13.34   In making a decision as to whether to award costs under any of these heads, the tribunal has to decide whether its power to do so has been triggered off e.g. because it was misconceived to bring proceedings. Once it has done so, it then has a discretion as to whether costs should be awarded. Hence, the word "may" is used in each of the provisions summarised above.

Once the tribunal has decided whether to make an award of costs, it then has to decide how much that award should be. This is governed by r.41 which lays down that:

- the tribunal may specify the sum, up to a limit of £10,000;
- the parties may agree a sum;
- the tribunal may order that costs should be determined by way of a detailed assessment in the county court (in Scotland, the sheriff court);
- the tribunal may have regard to the ability of the paying party to pay when considering whether to make a costs order, and what its amount should be.

In deciding how to exercise its discretion as to whether to award costs, and in deciding the amount of costs, the tribunal is likely to have the following factors in mind, among others:

(a) the seriousness of any unreasonable conduct relied upon;

(b) how clear it was that the claim or the defence was misconceived;

(c) any warnings given by the other party about the possibility of a costs application (although threats—as opposed to warnings—might themselves constitute unreasonable conduct);

(d) the means of the paying party;

(e) the means of the party seeking costs;

(f) the conduct of the party seeking costs.

Preparation time orders

13.35 Since 2004, the tribunals have a new power to order a payment in respect of preparation time. Where a party is not legally represented, they can apply for a preparation time order (r.42) to cover the preparation which they have done in person, or which has been done on their behalf by someone who is not a lawyer. The tribunal may make a preparation time order in circumstances similar to those where it may order costs (except that the party in whose favour the order is made is not legally represented). No such order can, however, be made in addition to a costs order in favour of the same party in the same case. The tribunal is asked to make an order for the costs of preparation time at a fixed amount per hour—£26 per hour with effect from April 6, 2006, and rising by £1 a year thereafter. The order does not, however, cover the time spent at the hearing itself.

Again, the tribunal has a discretion to whether to make an order for preparation time, and as to the number of hours in respect of which it is made. Similar considerations are likely to apply to those mentioned for costs orders.

Wasted costs orders

13.36 The Employment Tribunal Rules 2004 introduced a new power for the tribunal to make an order for wasted costs against a *representative* (r.48). The tribunal may order a representative to meet all or part of the wasted costs of any party (including the party whom he is representing!). "Wasted costs" are defined to include those incurred as a result of any improper, unreasonable or negligent act or omission on the part of the representative in question. "Representative" is defined to exclude the employee of a party (e.g. the firm's HR manager) or a representative not acting for profit in the proceedings (e.g. an unpaid CAB adviser or the claimant's father).

Seeking to alter the judgment

13.37 There are three ways in which a party who is dissatisfied with a judgment can seek to change it:

(a) by seeking a certificate of correction;

(b) by applying for a review;

(c) by appealing.

The next three sections deal with each of these possibilities in turn.

Certificate of correction

13.38 The chairman has a power to "correct clerical mistakes in an order, judgment, decision or reasons, or errors arising in those documents from an accidental slip or omission" (r.37). The power is confined to clerical errors, such as a mistake in the arithmetic. It does not extend to the substance of the decision.

Review

13.39 An application can be made for the tribunal to review a judgment, or the decision not to accept a claim, a response, or a counterclaim. The aim is to get the same tribunal to look at the decision again.

As far as an application to *review a judgment* is concerned, the application must be presented to the tribunal within 14 days of the date on which the decision was sent to the parties. The application must be on one or more of the following grounds:

(a) the decision was wrongly made as a result of an administrative error;

(b) a party did not receive notice of the proceedings leading to the decision;

(c) the decision was made in the absence of a party;

(d) new evidence has become available since the conclusion of the hearing to which the decision relates, provided that its existence could not have been reasonably known of or foreseen at that time; or

(e) the interests of justice require such a review.

The application will normally be considered, without a hearing, by the chairman of the tribunal which heard the case. He acts as a filter mechanism, and must decide whether there are grounds for review and whether the application has a reasonable prospect of success. If it does not, then he must refuse the application, and the staff must inform the party applying of the reasons for the refusal. If it does have a reasonable prospect of success, then he must set it down for review by the chairman or tribunal who made the original decision. A hearing will take place at which evidence/argument may be put forward. The original decision may then be revoked, varied or confirmed. If the decision is revoked, then it must be taken again, with a hearing being held if one was held prior to the original decision.

An application for review of a judgment is likely to be made, for **13.40** example, where a party did not receive notice of the hearing, with the result that they failed to attend. Similarly, where there was an emergency which prevented a party from attending, or notifying the tribunal of their likely absence, e.g. a serious accident en route for the tribunal.

Where new evidence is relied upon as the basis for a review, it must be evidence which was not available at the time of the hearing, and whose existence could not reasonably have been foreseen. An example might be where a claimant is compensated for a period of unemployment at the original hearing, and the employer subsequently receives information from a third party that he employed the claimant during the period in question. The tribunal would of course examine whether the evidence in question could have been discovered by the respondent, given reasonable diligence.

A review of the decision not to accept a claim, response or counterclaim is dealt with in a similar fashion to that outlined above. However, the grounds for review are confined to:

- the decision was wrongly made as a result of administrative error; or

- the interests of justice require such a review.

The review of a default judgment is dealt with in r.33. It applies where no **13.41** response in proper form was made to the claim within the time limit of 28 days for the submission of a response, and default judgment was issued by a chairman as a result. There is a 14 day time limit within which a review must be applied for, subject to extension where it is just and equitable. The application must state the grounds for varying or revoking the default judgment. It must include:

(a) the respondent's proposed response to the claim;

(b) an application for extending the time limit; and

(c) an explanation for the failure to comply with the requirements to submit a response in time and in proper form.

The review is conducted by the chairman in public. In considering the application for a review of a default judgment, the chairman must have regard to whether there was a good reason for failing to present the response in time, e.g. the claimant put the wrong address on the claim form, so that there was a delay before the tribunal's notification of the claim arrived.

The chairman may:

(a) refuse the application for review;

(b) vary the default judgment;

    (c) revoke the default judgment in whole or in part;

    (d) confirm the default judgment.

13.42   If the claim was satisfied or settled before the judgment, then the chairman must revoke the default judgment. If he concludes that the respondent has a reasonable prospect of defending the claim successfully, then he may revoke or vary the judgment.

    If it results in the revocation of the default judgment, then the respondent can respond to the claim, which proceeds in the usual way.

Appeals

13.43   An appeal on a point of law is available to the Employment Appeal Tribunal. Points of law arise where the tribunal wrongly construed or applied a statutory provision, or reached a decision which no reasonable tribunal could have reached on the facts of the case (i.e. the decision was perverse). It is not enough to ground a successful appeal that the appellate court would not have come to that decision on the facts, or that it would not have exercised a discretion in that way.

    Consequently, an allegation that the tribunal erred in its decision as to which witnesses to believe, or deciding whether a party acted reasonably, will not generally constitute a ground for appeal. Unless the decision is clearly perverse, the EAT will not be prepared to overturn the decision of the tribunal, which heard the witnesses in question and observed the way in which they gave evidence and has a "feel" for the case in a way that the EAT cannot.

    The appeal is started by serving a prescribed notice on the EAT. This must be done within 42 days of the date when written reasons for the Tribunal's decision were sent to the appellant. Time runs even when questions of remedy were adjourned, or if a review has been applied for.

13.44   The EAT's composition reflects that of an employment tribunal. A judge presides over proceedings, flanked by two wing members, one with a trade union background and one with managerial experience. It does not usually hear evidence, and will base its decision upon the papers, illuminated by arguments from the parties or their representatives. In particular, it will examine with some care the judgment and reasons of the tribunal, in order to determine whether it displays an error of law.

    The EAT has power to:

    (a) dismiss the appeal;

    (b) allow the appeal and substitute its own decision for that of the ET;

    (c) allow the appeal and remit the case to the same or a different ET, either for a complete rehearing or for further consideration of a particular point.

    The EAT sometimes adopts a practice of adjourning appeals and inviting an employment tribunal to amplify its reasons for its decision. The practice was explained in *Burns v Consignia (No.2)* [2004] I.R.I..R. 425, EAT, as applying where a tribunal was alleged to have failed to deal with an issue at all, or to have given no or inadequate reasons for a decision. In such circumstances, the EAT may request the tribunal to clarify, supplement or give its written reasons at the start of the process before the EAT finally hears the appeal. In *Barke v Seetec Business Technology Centre Limited* [2005] I.R.L.R. 633 the CA approved this procedure, rejecting the argument that it should only be applied with considerable caution and in tightly defined circumstances. The CA made it clear that the alternative might be remitting the whole case back to the same or a different tribunal for reconsideration, with all the cost and delay which might result.

If a party is dissatisfied with a decision of the EAT, further appeals, again **13.45** on points of law only, lie to the Court of Appeal and thence to the House of Lords.

CHAPTER FOURTEEN

TIME LIMITS

For a claim to be heard by the employment tribunal, it must be presented **14.01**
in time. This is not a mere procedural rule. If the claim is not presented in
time, the tribunal will have no jurisdiction to hear it: *Rogers v Bodfari
(Transport) Ltd* [1973] I.R.L.R. 172, NIRC. That means that the parties
cannot waive the time limit by agreeing that the case should be decided
even if it is out of time. The tribunal will have no power to act in that way.
Nor can the tribunal decide that a respondent should not be allowed to
avail itself of the time limit defence because of its own behaviour, or
because the lateness of the claim is the employer's fault. The rule is
jurisdictional, and must be applied strictly be the tribunal, subject to the
limited discretion outlined below.

There are different time limits, depending upon the nature of the claim,
and a series of rules of more general application. This chapter begins by
dealing with what is involved in presentation of the claim, and the cases
which have been decided on this point. It then goes on to describe the
different time limits in respect of the main jurisdictions dealt with by the
tribunals. The next section deals with the concept of a "continuing act",
which is of importance in discrimination cases. Thereafter, the extensions to
time limits available as a result of the operation of the statutory grievance
and dismissal and disciplinary procedures are considered. That is followed by
a discussion of the tribunal's discretion to extend time limits. Finally, there is
consideration of the practicalities of ensuring that time limits are met.

Presenting the claim

The date upon which the claim is "presented" to the tribunal is crucial to **14.02**
determining whether it is in time. A claim is presented when it is received
by the tribunal office—not when it is sent. The receipt can be by hand, post,
fax or email, and rules have evolved to deal with these different media.

Presentation of a claim by post was dealt with by the CA in *Consignia plc
v Sealy* [2002] I.R.L.R. 624. It laid down the following rules which appear to
be applicable to tribunal claims generally:

(a) A claim is "presented" when it arrives at the Central Office of
Employment Tribunals or at an office of the tribunals.

(b) If a claimant chooses to present a complaint by post, presentation
will be assumed to be effected, unless the contrary is proved, at

the time when the letter would be delivered in the ordinary course of post.

(c) If the letter is sent by first class post, it can be assumed that in the ordinary course of post it would be delivered on the second day after it was posted (excluding Sundays, Bank holidays, Christmas Day and Good Friday).

(d) If a form is date-stamped on Monday by a tribunal office when the period for presentation ends on a Saturday or Sunday, and it was posted by first-class post on the preceding Thursday, the tribunal may find that it arrived on the Saturday.

(e) If the letter arrives earlier than the second day after it was posted, then it is presented on the day on which it arrives.

Consignia plc v Sealy sets out further rules which have particular relevance to the "reasonably practicable" concept when a tribunal considers whether to exercise its discretion in relation to a time limit, and these are dealt with later. It is now possible to present a claim to the tribunal by email, and this development has meant that the rules relating to postal delivery have had to undergo adaptation. In *Tyne and Wear Autistic Society v Smith* [2005] I.R.L.R. 336, EAT, the issue was: when did a claimant present his claim online? Was it when it was submitted to the Employment Tribunals Service website? Or was it the later date when the website host forwarded it to the tribunal office computer. It was held that the relevant point was when it was successfully submitted online to the Employment Tribunals Service website, rather than the date at which it was forwarded from the website to the office.

14.03   In *Initial Electronic Security Systems Ltd v Avdic* [2005] I.R.L.R. 671, the EAT considered how the expectation of delivery of first class post within two days ought to be translated when considering the submission of a claim by email. It was held that the reasonable expectation of the sender of an email was that it would be delivered and would arrive normally within 30 to 60 minutes of transmission.

The various time limits

14.04   Each of the jurisdictions of the employment tribunals has its own time limits. These are set out in the table in para.14.06. A couple of points should be made by way of explanation:

- The tribunal has a discretion, in the case of most types of claim, to accept a claim which is out of time. This is either where it was "not reasonably practicable" to present the claim in time, or where it is "just and equitable" to accept it notwithstanding that it is late. Both of these formulae are discussed later in this chapter.

- For some types of claim (such as unfair dismissal), time begins to run from the "effective date of termination". This concept is discussed in chapter on "Unfair Dismissal".

- The various discrimination claims are subject to rules relating to time limits which are in practice identical.

Calculating the time limit

The time limits set out in the table (three months, six months) are calculated in the following way. If an employee was dismissed on April 27, the period of three months for the presentation of a claim of unfair dismissal will begin on that date. It will therefore expire at the end of July 26. To be within the three-month period, the claim must be presented on or before July 26 and not July 27. Further, it is calendar months which count, even though there different numbers of days in each month. Hence where the act of discrimination complained of is alleged to have taken place on November 30, 2006, the last date for presentation of a claim under the Sex Discrimination Act will be February 28, 2007.   **14.05**

Summary of the time limits for main jurisdictions

14.06

Jurisdiction	Statutory Source	Time Limit	Tribunal Discretion to extend
Unfair dismissal	ERA 1996, s.94	Three months from effective date of termination	"not reasonably practicable"
Unlawful deductions from wages	ERA 1996, s.23	Three months from date on which wages should have been paid	"not reasonably practicable"
Breach of Contract	Employment Tribunals (Extension of Jurisdiction) Order 1994	Three months from effective date of termination	"not reasonably practicable"
Holiday pay	Working Time Regulations 1998, reg.30	Three months from infringement	"not reasonably practicable"
Redundancy payment	ERA 1996, s.135	Six months from the "relevant date"	"just and equitable"
Discrimination	Various statutes	Three months from the act complained of	"just and equitable"

Jurisdiction	Statutory Source	Time Limit	Tribunal Discretion to extend
Equal pay	Equal Pay Act 1970	Six months from date of termination	None

Continuing acts in discrimination cases

14.07   The statutes and statutory instruments dealing with discrimination adopt a common approach in relation to time limits. The claim must be presented within three months of the act complained of. In some cases, the question "what is the act?" is a complicated one. Take for example a case of sexual harassment where the claimant says that she was subjected to a series of offensive remarks over a period of several months. Assume that she does not complain until just before the expiry of three months after the last such offensive remark. Are the earlier acts of alleged harassment out of time, such that she can make no claim in respect of them? The situation is covered by s.76(6)(b) of the SDA 1975 which states that "any act extending over a period shall be treated as done at the end of that period". As a result, what are sometimes called "continuing acts" are covered to the extent that the earlier manifestation of the continuing act will be in time, provided that the last manifestation of it is in time. To take an example, in *Barclays Bank v Kapur* [1991] I.R.L.R. 136, HL, the refusal of an employer to allow an employee's previous service to count towards a pension was held to be an "act extending over a period" within the meaning of s.68(7)(b) of the RRA 1976. In *Sougrin v Haringey Health Authority* [1992] I.R.L.R. 416, CA, by contrast, a decision to place the claimant upon a particular grade was held to be a one off act, rather than a continuing act of discrimination. It was stated that a one-off act could have continuing consequences, and yet not fall within the "extending over a period" formula. In *Robertson v Bexley Community Centre* [2003] I.R.L.R. 434, CA, it was stated that, to establish a continuing act, it must be shown that the employer had a practice, policy, rule or regime governing the act said to constitute it.

In *Hendricks v Commisioner of Police for the Metropolis* [2003] I.R.L.R. 96, the CA gave guidance for determining whether there was an "act extending over a period" as distinct from a succession of unconnected or isolated specific acts, for which time would begin to run from the date when each specific act was committed. The CA held that the focus in determining whether there was an act extending over a period should be on the substance of the complaints that the employer was responsible for an ongoing situation or a continuing state of affairs. The concepts of policy, rule, practice, scheme or regime in the previous authorities were given as examples of when an act extends over a period. They should not be treated as a complete and constricting statement of the limits of "an act extending over a period".

Extensions related to the statutory grievance procedure

The obligation for a claimant to present a grievance before bringing **14.08** certain types of claim has particular consequences in relation to time limits for presenting a claim. The general principle is that, where the statutory grievance procedure ("SGP") applies, the employee is expected to raise his dissatisfaction with the employer's conduct by presenting the employer with a written grievance,. As to the circumstances in which the SGP applies, see para.3.32 but it is worth pointing out for present purposes that:

- it does not apply generally to claims for unfair dismissal; but
- it does apply to claims for constructive dismissal;
- it does not apply to claims for breach of contract (e.g. notice pay);
- it only applies to employees.

The time limit for presenting a claim to employment tribunal can be extended in the following circumstances by reg.15(3) of the Employment Act 2002 (Dispute Resolution) Regulations 2004:

(a) the claim is one to which the SGP applies, and the employee takes Step 1 of the SGP within three months of the matter complained of; or

(b) a claim was presented to the tribunal within three months of the matter complained of, without taking Step 1 of the SGP; or

(c) Step 1 of the SGP was taken, and a claim was presented to the tribunal within three months of the matter complained of, but without waiting 28 days.

In each of the above situations, the time limit will be extended to six months (rather than the usual three). As far as (b) and (c) are concerned, the practical situation is that the claim has been presented to tribunal, but the tribunal is unable to accept the claim because it fails to comply with s.32 of the Employment Act 2002. The tribunal therefore rejects the claim and sends it back to the claimant, with a covering letter. The claimant can then comply with Step 1 of the SGP, and has an extension of time in order to do so.

Extension related to the statutory dismissal and disciplinary procedure

As pointed out in the preceding section, the extensions related to the **14.09** SGP do not apply to most claims for unfair dismissal, because the SGP does not apply to unfair dismissal.

However, there is an extension which is contained in the Employment Act 2002 (Dispute Resolution) Regulations 2004, and applies to some unfair dismissal claims. If, when the normal time limit expired, the claimant had reasonable grounds for believing that there was an ongoing disciplinary or dismissal procedure, then the time limit is extended by three months: reg.15(2) of the Regulations. The ongoing dismissal or disciplinary procedure need not be the statutory DDP, but it must be "followed in respect of matters that consisted of or included the substance of the tribunal complaint".

"Not reasonably practicable"

14.10   In a number of the jurisdictions exercised by the tribunal, it has the discretion to extend the deadline in circumstances where it was "not reasonably practicable" for the claimant to present the claim in time (see table in para.14.06). In such cases, the claim must in addition be presented "within such further period as the tribunal considers reasonable".

The meaning of "not reasonably practicable" was considered in *Walls Meat Co Ltd v Khan* [1978] I.R.L.R. 499, CA. In that case, the claimant believed that his claim for unfair dismissal was being handled by the tribunal which was dealing with his claim for unemployment benefit. The mistake was held to be reasonable, and Brandon L.J. stated:

> "The performance of an act is not reasonably practicable if there is some impediment which reasonably prevents or interferes with, or inhibits, such performance. The impediment may be physical, for instance the illness of the complainant or a postal strike; or the impediment may be mental, namely, the state of mind of the complainant in the form of ignorance of, or mistaken belief with regard to, essential matters. Such states of mind can, however, only be regarded as impediments making it not reasonably practicable to present a complaint within the period of three months, if the ignorance on the one hand or the mistaken belief on the other, is itself reasonable. Either state of mind will, further, not be reasonable if it arises from the fault of the complainant in not making such enquiries as he should reasonably in all the circumstances have made, or from the fault of his solicitors or other professional advisers."

Although the claimant's ignorance was held to be reasonable in *Wall's Meat*, it is worth bearing in mind that the case was heard nearly 30 years ago, and the right not to be unfairly dismissed, together with the existence of employment tribunals, has become much more widely known since then. Further, once a claimant ought reasonably to know of the right in question, he will be presumed to be put on notice to enquire about any time limit.. As was stated in *Trevelyans (Birmingham) v Norton* [1991] I.C.R. 488, as time passes, it becomes more and more difficult to persuade tribunals that a claimant does not know of the right to be unfairly dismissed, or of the time limit.

14.11   In the *Trevelyans* case, and a number of others, including *Dedman v British Building and Engineering Appliances Ltd* [1973] I.R.L.R. 379, CA, it has been made clear that any fault by a claimant's legal adviser was to be attributed to the claimant. In other words, a claimant cannot say:

> "It was not reasonably practicable for me to put my claim in on time, because my legal adviser did not tell me of the time limit (or told me the wrong time limit)".

The claimant will be fixed with the fault of the adviser. In *Marks & Spencer plc v Williams-Ryan* [2005] I.R.L.R. 562, CA, however, it was stated that this principle did not necessarily extend to a situation where advice is given by a Citizens Advice Bureau. The mere fact of seeking advice from a CAB did not, as a matter of law, rule out the possibility of demonstrating that it was not reasonably practicable to present a claim to the tribunal in time. The CA emphasised that the answer was likely to depend on who gave the advice, and in what circumstances.

These cases deal with reasonableness in the context of ignorance of rights. Another aspect of reasonableness is related to ignorance of a material fact. In *Machine Tool Industry Research Association v Simpson* [1988] I.R.L.R. 212, the CA held that it cannot be reasonably practicable to expect a claimant to bring a case based upon facts of which he is ignorant. In that case, an employee accepted her dismissal for redundancy. After the deadline for claiming unfair dismissal had expired, however, she discovered further facts which led her to believe that she had not been dismissed for redundancy. The CA held that the claim should be allowed to proceed.

A mistake as to the law will not assist a claimant who argues that it was **14.12** not reasonably practicable to present his claim: *Biggs v Somerset CC* [1996] I.R.L.R. 203, CA. In that case, an employee dismissed in August 1976 argued that her complaint of unfair dismissal was in time. She was a part-time teacher working 14 hours a week and she argued that her right to claim only ran from June 1, 1994, when the House of Lords decided *R. v Secretary of State for Employment Ex p. EOC* [1994] I.C.R. 364. In that case, it was held that part-time employees had the right to present a claim for unfair dismissal, notwithstanding restrictions in our domestic legislation, because of the provisions of the Treat of Rome. The Court of Appeal held that time began to run for Ms Biggs in 1976, and that the "not reasonably practicable" discretion could not salvage her claim.

One common basis upon which the tribunal is asked to extend the time limit is the illness—either mental or physical—of the claimant during the period for bringing the claim. Where the claimant is legally represented, then the illness is unlikely to provide a basis for extension of the time limit. The claimant will have passed the handling of the claim on to the adviser.

What about the situation where the claimant is ill for part of the three-month period? In *Schulz v Esso Petroleum Ltd* [1999] I.R.L.R. 488, CA, the claimant was dismissed for long-term absence which was caused by depression. During the first seven weeks of the three month period, he was able to give instructions to his solicitors, but then he became too ill to do so. The tribunal held that it had been reasonably practicable for him to present the claim in time (relying on the initial seven weeks), so that he was out of time, and the EAT agreed. However, the CA held that it was not right to approach the matter in this way. In cases where illness is relied upon, a period of disabling illness should not be given similar weight regardless of when in the time limit period it falls. The approach should vary according to whether the illness falls in the earlier weeks or in the far more critical weeks leading up to the expiry of the period.

Sometimes an employee believes that he should wait until any internal **14.13** appeal is exhausted before pursuing a claim in the employment tribunals. If that process is at all protracted, the result may be that the claim, when eventually presented, is out of time. As stated above, in certain circumstances, there is an extension of time in accordance with the Employment Act 2002 (Dispute Resolution) Regulations 2004, reg.15(2). However, the general rule is that time begins to run when a decision is taken to dismiss the employee. If there is a successful appeal, the dismissed employee will be reinstated, but if he is not then he may lose the chance to claim unfair dismissal in the tribunal. In *Palmer v Southend BC* [1984] I.R.L.R. 119, two local government workers were convicted of theft. The council dismissed them, but the council's appeals committee indicated that, should their conviction be overturned, they might be reinstated. The criminal convictions were then overturned by the Court of Appeal, but the council would not reinstate them. The tribunal held that it had been reasonably practicable to present their claims in time, and that it had therefore had no jurisdiction to hear them. That decision was upheld on appeal.

It follows that, in the event of an internal appeal procedure against dismissal, a claim for unfair dismissal should still be presented. The tribunal will be prepared to postpone the hearing until such time as the appeal has been heard, provided that it is going to be held in the near future.

One set of circumstances where delay because of an internal appeal may be acceptable as a reason for the tribunal to exercise the discretion to extend the time limit is when the employer encourages the claimant not to claim in time. An example is *Owen v Crown House Engineering Ltd* [1973] I.R.L.R. 233, NIRC, where the employers suggested that the trade union official dealing with the claims "hold his hand" so that negotiations could proceed.

"Within such further period as is reasonable"

14.14   In those cases where the tribunal's discretion is based upon the "not reasonably practicable" formula (e.g. unfair dismissal, unauthorised deduction from wages), there are two limbs to the test:

   (a) first, the tribunal must decide that it was not reasonably practicable to present the claim within the three month time limit;

   (b) then it must go on to decide whether it was presented "within such further period as the tribunal considers reasonable".

Point (a) is dealt with in the preceding section. As far as (b) is concerned, there are no particular time limits as to what can be regarded as a further reasonable period for presenting the claim: *Marley (UK) Ltd v Anderson* [1994] I.R.L.R. 152, EAT. In deciding what is a further reasonable period, the tribunal ought to take into account all relevant circumstances in order to achieve a fair balance. It is not concerned only with the problems faced by the claimant. Any additional difficulties which the employer would face in answering the claim as a result of an extended further period must also be taken into account: *Biggs v Somerset CC* [1996] I.R.L.R. 203, CA.

"Just and equitable"

The test in relation to the tribunal's discretion for discrimination claims **14.15** is whether it would be "just and equitable" to extend the time limit of three months. The "just and equitable" formula is also applicable to the six month time limit for claims for a redundancy payment.

As a result, the discretion permitted to the tribunal is broader than that where the "not reasonably practicable" test applies. The burden is still on the claimant to persuade the tribunal to exercise its discretion, but that discretion is "very wide" and the tribunal is entitled to consider anything that it considers relevant (*Robertson v Bexley Community Centre* [2003] I.R.L.R. 434, CA). On occasion, this can mean that there is a very considerable extension of the time limit. For example, in *Southwark LBC v Afolabi* [2003] I.R.L.R. 220, CA, the claim was presented some nine years out of time. Because the claimant had only realised that he had a potential claim when he had sight of his personnel file some nine years after he failed to gain promotion, it was held to be just and equitable to extend the time limit.

Since the test is a different one from the "not reasonably practicable" one, it is possible for seemingly conflicting decisions to be made concerning late claims from the same claimant. Take, for example, a case where the claimant alleges that he was unfairly dismissed, and that his dismissal was racially discriminatory. Assume that both claims are outside the three month time limit. It is perfectly possible that the tribunal will decide, on the facts, that it is unable to hear the unfair dismissal claim, but that it accepts jurisdiction in the discrimination claim.

In *Mills v Marshall* [1988] I.R.L.R. 494, the EAT stated that the tribunal **14.16** had to balance all relevant factors in deciding whether it was just and equitable to hear the case. This would include whether it was possible to have a fair trial of the issues raised by the claim. It follows that questions such as whether the length of the delay and the surrounding events make it more difficult for the employer to mount a defence to the case must be considered. Have relevant witnesses departed from the scene? Are necessary documents still in existence? In addition, the tribunal will take into account any contribution to the delay by the employer.

Because the test is a more relaxed one, the extent to which the claimant is fixed with the faults of his legal advisers differs from that which applies to the "not reasonably practicable" formula. In *Chohan v Derby Law Centre* [2004] I.R.L.R. 685, EAT, it was held that delay in bringing a claim in time due to incorrect legal advice ought not to prevent a claim from being heard. Again, unlike the position for the "not reasonably practicable" test, a mistake of law by a claimant is not fatal. In *British Coal Corporation v Keeble* [1997] I.R.L.R. 336, EAT, it was stated that, if the only reason for a long delay is a wholly understandable misapprehension of the law, that was a matter which the tribunal could take into account in considering whether it was just and equitable to extend time.

Ensuring that deadlines are met

14.17   Failure to meet the deadline for a tribunal claim is likely to constitute professional negligence, and the cautious adviser will set up systems to minimise the risk of this happening. For example:

- entry of the key dates, including expiry of the deadline, in a diary;
- ensuring that the diary is consulted on a daily basis so that action can be taken in advance of the deadline;
- presenting the claim well in advance of the deadline;
- where it is impossible to do so, faxing the claim and retaining a transmission confirmation on the file;
- telephoning the tribunal to confirm that the claim has in fact been received.

CHAPTER FIFTEEN

SETTLEMENT AND WITHDRAWAL

The majority of claims presented to the employment tribunals never **15.01** reach a hearing. In a typical year, of those claims presented, some 40 per cent are settled under the auspices of ACAS, 30 per cent are withdrawn and 30 per cent are heard by tribunal. Many of the cases which are withdrawn result from a unilateral decision by the claimant, but a substantial proportion are withdrawn as a result of the employer paying a sum of money e.g. the wages, notice pay or holiday pay which is claimed—in such cases, it is realistic to say that there has been some sort of informal settlement.

The focus of this chapter is upon the process of settlement. The section which follows looks at the reasons why the parties may wish to seek a settlement, and the different factors which might influence employers and employees respectively. The section thereafter deals with the important role played by ACAS in achieving settlements. A discussion then follows on the "without prejudice" nature of communications relating to negotiations seeking a settlement. The short section which follows looks at one particular matter which sometimes forms the subject of negotiation for a settlement—the provision by the employer of a favourable reference. The law relating to ensuring that a settlement is binding is dealt with in the next section, followed by an examination of the implications of withdrawing a claim.

Why settle?

The procedural regime within which the employment tribunal operates is **15.02** geared to ensuring that cases are heard as soon as possible, subject to the need to ensure that the case is tried properly. That objective creates a momentum which gathers pace as the case proceeds to trial. However, a trial may not be in the best interests of the parties, and from time to time during the build-up to the hearing, both sides should examine whether this outcome is what they really do desire. The fundamental question which each of the parties needs to ask itself is: will I achieve more by going to trial or by settling?

In answering that question, it makes sense to look first at the goals which each party might wish to achieve as a result of the case—whether by settlement or adjudication by the tribunal. The lists which follow are not, of course, exhaustive, and much will depend on the facts of the case and the personalities of those involved. The employee may want to seek:

- reinstatement to his old job;

- re-engagement to suitable alternative employment;

- a sum of money;

- an admission of liability;

- a favourable reference;

- an apology;

- a promise to adopt an equal opportunities policy or training programme;

- a commitment to transfer him to another site, or another department;

- a promise to promote him when a suitable vacancy arises;

- a commitment to take disciplinary action against someone who has been harassing or discriminating against him.

It is worth noting that only the first four of the list can usually be met by a judgment of the tribunal. Most of the rest of the list is beyond its jurisdiction (although one or two may form the subject of a recommendation in a discrimination case).

On being confronted with a claim, the objectives of the employer may well include one or more of the following:

- ensuring that the minimum of management time is spent preparing for and attending the tribunal;

- avoiding any disruption at the workplace, e.g. such as would result from witnesses having to attend tribunal;

- keeping legal costs as low as possible;

- ensuring that there is no adverse publicity for the company;

- settlement of any other claims which the claimant may have against the company;

- keeping the payment of any sum of money to the claimant as low as possible;

- avoiding any admission of liability.

Whilst the position is not so clear cut with regard to the powers of the tribunal, it can be seen that the first five objectives on the list are more likely in most cases to be met by a settlement than by a tribunal hearing.

15.03   There are some factors, however, which may weigh heavily in favour of a hearing. The most obvious is a calculation on the part of one party or the other that they will achieve more in monetary terms by fighting than by settling. In order to calculate whether this is so in any particular case, it is necessary to determine:

(a) How much will the claim be worth if fought and won? This depends upon an estimate of the likely remedies (see Chapter 10 on "Remedies for Unfair Dismissal" and Chapter 7 on "Remedies for Discrimination").

(b) What are the chances that the claim will be won?

Given the answer to these questions, a realistic figure can be put on the value to the claimant of going to hearing. If a successful claim is likely to be worth £6,000 and the chances of winning are 50 per cent, then a crude calculation suggests that the case is worth £3,000. A complication is added by the Recoupment Regulations, whose effect is, in broad terms, that a claimant will have deducted from an award from the tribunal a sum equal to the job seekers' allowance and income support which he has received over the relevant period. No such deduction will be made from any settlement.

For the employer, there may be considerations of policy which argue against a settlement. It may be seen as a precedent which will encourage other employees to "try it on" in the hope of achieving a windfall. Employees who have loyally "done the right thing" may feel that an idle or dishonest colleague is "getting away with it". The manager who made the decision to dismiss may feel that his authority is being undermined.

There are equivalent considerations pushing towards a trial from the point of view of the employee. The most important among these is the desire of some claimants to "have my day in court". Closely related to this is the belief that the claimant will achieve a sense of closure once the case has been brought to a conclusion—whether successful or not.

Some of these factors, taken together with others which are peculiar to **15.04** the case in question, combine to make a heady mix. The parties and their legal advisers have to take a cold, hard look at the advantages and disadvantages of settling, and get down to the business of preparing for trial, or negotiating, or quite frequently doing both simultaneously!

The role of ACAS

The Advisory, Conciliation and Arbitration Service ("ACAS") has a wide **15.05** role in the promotion of industrial relations. It is involved in conciliating in industrial disputes, and that part of its work falls outside the ambit of this book. It also has an important role to play in the settlement of individual claims presented to employment tribunals, and it that aspect of its work that is dealt with here.

Once the claim is presented, a copy of it is sent to the relevant regional office of ACAS, which will also receive any important communications sent by the parties to the tribunal thereafter. A conciliation officer is appointed, and he will usually contact the parties. He is under a duty to endeavour to promote a settlement between the parties before the claim is determined by the tribunal. The period of time for which this duty lasts depends upon the type of claim, the periods in question being laid down in the Employment Tribunal Rules, r.24. There are three different periods, each of which has relevance to particular categories of claim:

(a) Short conciliation period of seven weeks. This applies to a number of claims which, as a general rule, can be regarded as relatively simple (there are always horrendous exceptions!). This includes claims for breach of contract, failure to pay wages, failure to pay a redundancy payment, and a number of trade union related claims.

(b) No fixed conciliation period. This applies to proceedings which include a discrimination claim under the SDA 1975, the RRA 1976, the DDA 1995, the Equal Pay Act 1970, the various regulations dealing with discrimination on grounds of sexual orientation, religion or belief, and age. It also includes claims of having been dismissed, subjected to a detriment or selected for redundancy for making a protected disclosure.

(c) Standard conciliation period of 13 weeks. This applies to all claims which do not fall within either (a) or (b) above. The main category is unfair dismissal.

The conciliation period begins on the date that the tribunal sends a copy of the claim to the respondent. During the conciliation period, there can be no full merits hearing of the claim, but a pre-hearing review or a case management discussion can take place. The tribunal can, during the conciliation period, fix a date for the full merits hearing to take place, provided that the date in question is outside the conciliation period. There are limited provisions for extensions to be made to the period by ACAS or by a chairman of employment tribunals. There are also circumstances in which the conciliation period ends, e.g. where default judgment is issued, or the claim is withdrawn or settled, or the parties indicate that they do not wish to conciliate.

15.06   Once the conciliation period is over, the ACAS officer is no longer under a duty to conciliate, but he retains the power to do so. ACAS has set down its own criteria as to when an officer should exercise that power.

Where parties make use of the services of ACAS, they need to bear in mind that any information which they give to the conciliation officer will be passed on to the other side. In addition, the officer is not there to judge whether the case is likely to succeed, or to advise either party about whether a settlement should be accepted. In *Clarke v Redcar & Cleveland BC* [2006] I.R.L.R. 324 the EAT examined whether there is any duty upon an ACAS officer to see that the terms of a settlement are fair to a party, and advise on the merits of the case. It concluded that there is no such duty.

"Without prejudice"

15.07   In the course of trying to settle a case, it is often necessary for parties to make concessions. After all, the very fact that an indication is given that a party is willing to settle is in itself capable of being construed as a sign of weakness. If parties who were negotiating feared that their communications might become public in the course of a hearing, it would greatly reduce the chances of a settlement. There is a general rule of evidence that such communications (generally referred to as "without prejudice" communications) should not be disclosed to a court or tribunal.

As a result, a letter which deals with an attempt to settle the case will often be headed "without prejudice". Similarly, before beginning negotiations, a lawyer may say that what is said is "without prejudice". There is no particular magic in the words, however. If it is a genuine part of negotiations then it will be ruled inadmissible if any party attempts to introduce it in tribunal, irrespective of whether it is headed "without prejudice". Similarly, the mere fact that a letter or conversation is stated to be "without prejudice" will not protect it from being admitted before the tribunal if it is not a genuine part of negotiations. In *BNP Paribas v Mezzoterro* [2004] I.R.L.R. 508, EAT, it was stated that there must be an extant dispute between the parties, and the statement in question must be made in a genuine attempt to compromise that dispute.

On occasion, a letter may be headed "without prejudice as to costs". The aim of the party writing the letter is to ensure that the letter is inadmissible during the proceedings to determine liability and remedies. However, the writer is reserving his position with regard to any application as to costs— he is giving notice that he may wish to put the letter before the tribunal after it has pronounced upon the merits, so as to show that he was anxious to settle the case and was, by inference, reasonable in his conduct of it.

References

One of the issues in negotiating a settlement may be the provision of a **15.08** favourable reference for the employee by his former employer. This is not something which it is within the power of the tribunal to order, so that it can really only be achieved as part of a settlement. Nevertheless, it may be of great value to the employee as a crucial step to obtaining further employment. It is worth bearing the following points in mind:

- An employer must exercise the appropriate degree of care in providing a reference. If a reference is negligent and results in loss, it may give rise to a cause of action by the new employer as a negligent misstatement in accordance with the general principle in *Hedley Byrne & Co Ltd v Heller & Partners Ltd* [1964] A.C. 465.

- The employee may be sceptical about any reference which is provided on request. It is very difficult to lay down the terms in which such a reference should be couched, and any agreement to confine it to the stated terms may be regarded as impossible to enforce.

- An employee may be content with a guarantee, as part of the settlement, that any request for a reference will be dealt with by a named manager whom he regards as sympathetic.

- Many employers will ask job applicants to bring references with them to an interview. They often do not go on to take up references from previous employers, particularly where the job in question is a low-paid one. As a result, an "open reference" may meet the employee's needs. If it does, this method of proceeding will avoid the suspicion that any agreement as to a reference may not be honoured, since the employee will be in possession of the reference himself.

Binding settlements

15.09   Most employment rights are subject to a general principle that the parties cannot contract out of them. For example, s.203 of the ERA 1996 states:

"**203.**(1) Any provision in an agreement (whether a contract of employment or not) is void in so far as it purports—

(a) to exclude or limit the operation of any provision of this Act, or
(b) to preclude a person from bringing any proceedings under this Act before an employment tribunal."

The result is that the right to unfair dismissal, for example, cannot be signed away by the employee as part of his contract of employment. This provision is more far-reaching, however, and in practice it means that a settlement between the parties which involves withdrawal of the right to claim unfair dismissal (or any of the other rights in the ERA 1996) will be void unless it comes within one of the exceptions which are set out in s.203. The most important exceptions are:

(a) agreements reached with the involvement of ACAS; and

(b) agreements drawn up in accordance with s.203(3) of the ERA 1996.

Such agreements must meet the following strict conditions:

(i) the agreement must be in writing;

(ii) it must relate to the particular proceedings;

(iii) the employee must have received advise from a relevant independent adviser. This term is defined to include qualified lawyers, trade union officials and advice workers authorised and certified for the purpose. There are certain people who are excluded from acting as independent advisers, most importantly anyone acting in the matter for the employer or an associated employer;

(iv) the adviser must be insured against the risk of loss arising from the advice;

(v) the agreement must identify the adviser; and

(vi) it must state that the conditions regulating compromise agreements are satisfied.

Where the agreement is reached with the involvement of ACAS, it will **15.10**
be contained in a COT 3 agreement form, an example of which can be seen
on page ??. This is sent to the parties for signature and a copy then goes to
the tribunal. The settlement is binding, however, from the moment that
both parties have agreed to the terms which appear on the form. Usually
this is done over the telephone. Where the settlement is within the s.203(3)
framework, by contrast, it will not be binding until the formalities listed as
(i) to (vi) above are completed.

One area of controversy is the scope of a settlement which has been
reached in accordance with either of the routes which may result in a
binding settlement. As far as a settlement reached with ACAS involvement
is concerned, in *National Orthopaedic Trust v Howard* [2002] I.R.L.R. 849,
EAT, Mrs Howard presented a complaint alleging sex discrimination,
discrimination on grounds of marital status, and constructive dismissal. The
claim was settled with the involvement of ACAS for £12,000, the COT 3
form stating that it was:

> "in full and final settlement of these proceedings and of all claims which the
> applicant has or may have against the respondent (save for claims for personal
> injury and in respect of occupational pension rights) . . ."

Some time later Mrs Howard alleged that the hospital had victimised her
by refusing to allow her to work in a private capacity because of her
previous sex discrimination complaint. The hospital contended that the
terms of the compromise agreement precluded her further claim for
victimisation; the EAT held that it did not. Whilst there was no reason why
a party should contract out of some future claim, the question in each case
was whether that was the intention of the parties. If the parties sought to
exclude claims of which they could have no knowledge they must do so in
language which is absolutely clear and leaves no room for doubt as to what
they are contracting for. In this case, the expression "has or may have" was
apt to cover claims already in existence, whether known to the potential
claimant or not. It did not preclude future claims.

Bank of Credit and Commerce International SA v Ali (No.1) [2001] 2 **15.11**
W.L.R. 735, HL provides a further illustration. Under a COT 3 agreement,
an employee dismissed for redundancy accepted an additional payment

> "in full and final settlement of all or any claims whether under statute, common
> law or in equity of whatsoever nature that exists or may exist".

This was held not to preclude a claim for "stigma" damages in line with
Malik v Bank of Credit and Commerce International [1997] I.R.L.R. 462,
HL. The parties could not have contemplated the likelihood of a claim for
stigma damages at the time that they signed the agreement, as the House of
Lords only gave their judgment in *Malik* some years later.

With regard to those settlements reached in accordance with s.203(3)
with the involvement of a relevant independent adviser, there is a further
limitation upon the scope of the settlement. As will be seen from

requirement (ii) in para.15.09, it must "relate to the particular proceedings". In other words, it should not rule out all possible future claims. In *Hinton v University of East London* [2005] I.R.L.R 552, CA, the agreement was intended to satisfy s.203(3). It was stated:

> "in full and final settlement of all claims in all jurisdictions (whether arising under statute, common law or otherwise) which the employee has or may have against the university . . . including in particular. . ."

A list of 11 types of claim then followed. This was held not to preclude the claimant from pursuing a complaint that he had been subjected to a detriment contrary to s.47B of the ERA 1996 (a "whistle-blowing" claim). The CA held that, in order to constitute a valid compromise, an agreement must "relate to the particular proceedings". This meant that the particular proceedings to which the compromise agreement related must be clearly identified. It was not sufficient to use a rolled-up expression such as "all statutory rights". Smith L.J. stated that it would not be:

> "good practice for lawyers to draft a standard form of compromise agreement which lists every form of employment right known to the law. . .compromise agreements should be tailored to the individual circumstances of the individual case".

In the discussion above, the primary reference has been to the ERA 1996. In fact, the other main statutes and statutory instruments containing employment rights, including those which outlaw discrimination, have similar provisions (see, for example, the SDA 1975, s.77(4)(AA); the RRA 1976, s.72(4)(aa); and the DDA 1995, s.9(2)(b)). It is worth pointing out, however, that the same restrictions upon signing away rights do not apply generally to contractual rights. The distinction is illustrated by *Sutherland v Network Appliance Ltd* [2001] I.R.L.R. 12. In that case, the employee accepted a payment "in full and final settlement" of any claims against the company arising out of his employment or its termination. The agreement was not in the form required by s.203 of the ERA 1996. He later claimed damages for breach of contract, relating to failure to pay notice pay, loss from inability to exercise share options, and unpaid expenses. The tribunal ruled that these claims were not covered by s.203 of the ERA 1996, with the result that the compromise agreement was valid, and it had no jurisdiction to hear the breach of contract claim. The EAT agreed.

15.12   In a case where there has been a payment made in accordance with a settlement, but the settlement turns out not to be binding, the sum paid will be taken into account by the tribunal in the award which it makes.

Settlement at the tribunal

15.13   Frequently a settlement takes place at the door of the tribunal, when the minds of parties are concentrated upon the strengths and weaknesses of their case, and the cost in human and financial terms of going through the case. It is clearly not an ideal situation, for a large proportion of the costs will already have been incurred by the time that the parties arrive at the tribunal. Further, it can be a frustrating experience for those involved in running the tribunal, disrupting schedules and wasting time which could have been devoted to hearing another case. Despite these problems, however, the parties do often leave it to the last minute, and the tribunal will usually welcome a settlement, however late it is achieved.

Once the parties are at the tribunal, the protective requirements detailed in the previous section no longer apply, since the tribunal is entitled to refuse to give the order which the settlement entails, and is assumed to provide the necessary protection. In practice, if a settlement is achieved, the claimant withdraws the claim, whereupon the respondent applies for it to be dismissed, and the tribunal dismisses it. Taken by itself, this procedure would mean that the claimant could not continue proceedings—that is the usual result of withdrawal. As a result, the usual course is for the proceedings to be stayed until a specified date, when it will be dismissed as withdrawn by the claimant. In the meantime, until the specified date is reached, both parties have liberty to apply for the matter to be reinstated. The agreement reached by the parties is attached to the judgment as a schedule. This means that, if the claimant does not receive the agreed sum, for example, he can apply for proceedings to be reinstated, and ought to have lost nothing as a result.

15.14 An alternative is for the parties to come to a written agreement, and ask the tribunal to give judgment in accordance with the terms of that agreement (r.28(2) of the Employment Tribunal Rules 2004). This judgment will be enforceable in the county court. If this procedure is used, however, the judgment must obviously be limited to those matters which are within the jurisdiction of the tribunal, so that it may not include the provision of a favourable reference, for example. It is also possible that the recoupment provisions may apply (see Chapter 10 on "Remedies for Unfair Dismissal").

Withdrawal

15.15 At any time, the claimant can withdraw proceedings. This can be done either orally at a hearing, or in writing to the tribunal. Sometimes this is as part of a settlement (see the preceding section). Under the Employment Tribunal Rules 2004, withdrawal does not automatically entail dismissal of the claim. The respondent may apply for dismissal of proceedings against him within 28 days of the notice of withdrawal being sent to him by the tribunal, in accordance with r.25(4).

In *Khan v Heywood & Middleton Primary Care Trust* [2007] I.C.R. 24, the CA held that if a claimant sends a notice of withdrawal to the tribunal, the claim is at an end and the tribunal has no power to reinstate the claim at a later date. It further held that if the withdrawn claim is then dismissed by the tribunal, the claimant cannot bring a fresh claim based upon the same or similar facts. If the respondent's application for dismissal is refused, however, the claimant may issue a fresh claim, based upon the same or similar facts, subject to issues relating to time limits.

Where there is an employer's counterclaim for breach of contract (see para.13.12), then the counterclaim will survive the withdrawal of the original claim by the employee: *Patel v RCMS Ltd* [1999] I.R.L.R. 161, EAT. In such circumstances, the claimant would be best advised to secure a settlement which included as a term the withdrawal of the counterclaim, rather than withdrawing unilaterally.

EMPLOYMENT TRIBUNAL CLAIM FORM AND EMPLOYMENT TRIBUNAL RESPONSE FORM

A1.01

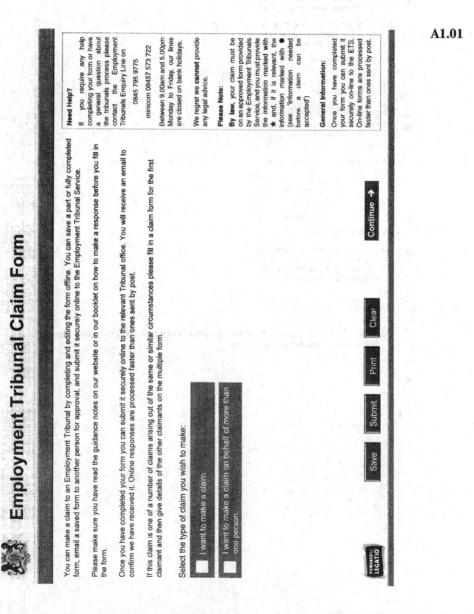

Employment Tribunal Claim Form

You can make a claim to an Employment Tribunal by completing and editing the form offline. You can save a part or fully completed form, email a saved form to another person for approval, and submit it securely online to the Employment Tribunal Service.

Please make sure you have read the guidance notes on our website or in our booklet on how to make a response before you fill in the form.

Once you have completed your form you can submit it securely online to the relevant Tribunal office. You will receive an email to confirm we have received it. Online responses are processed faster than ones sent by post.

If this claim is one of a number of claims arising out of the same or similar circumstances please fill in a claim form for the first claimant and then give details of the other claimants on the multiple form.

Select the type of claim you wish to make:

- I want to make a claim.
- I want to make a claim on behalf of more than one person.

Save   Submit   Print   Clear   Continue →

Need Help?

If you require any help completing your form or have a general question about the tribunals process please contact the Employment Tribunals Enquiry Line on

0845 795 9775

minicom 08457 573 722

Between 9.00am and 5.00pm Monday to Friday, our lines are closed on bank holidays.

We regret we **cannot** provide any legal advice.

Please Note:

By law, your claim must be on an approved form provided by the Employment Tribunals Service, and you must provide the information marked **with ★** and, if it is relevant, the information marked with ● (see "Information needed before a claim can be accepted")

General Information:

Once you have completed your form you can submit it securely on-line to the ETS. On-line forms are processed faster than ones sent by post.

1 Your details

1.1   Title: Mr   Mrs   Miss   Ms   Other

1.2* First name (or names):

1.3* Surname or family name:

1.4   Date of birth (date/month/year):   Are you: male?   female?

1.5* Address: Number or Name

                  Street

       +   Town/City

                  County

                  Postcode

1.6   Phone number (where we can contact you during normal working hours):

1.7   How would you prefer us to   E-mail   Post   Fax
      communicate with you?
      (Please tick only one box)

       E-mail address:

                          @

       Fax number:

2 Respondent's details

2.1* Give the name of your employer
      or the organisation you are claiming
      against.

2.2* Address: Number or Name

                  Street

                  Town/City

       +   County

                  Postcode

      Phone number:

2.3   If you worked at an address
      different from the one you have
      given at 2.2, please give the
      full address and postcode.

      Postcode

      Phone number:

2.4 If your complaint is against more than one respondent please give the names, addresses and
      postcodes of additional respondents.

3 Action before making a claim

■ 3.1* Are you, or were you, an employee of the respondent?   Yes   No   ■
If 'Yes', please now go straight to section 3.3.

3.2 Are you, or were you, a worker providing services to the respondent?   Yes   No
If 'Yes', please now go straight to section 4.
If 'No', please now go straight to section 6.

3.3● Is your claim, or part of it, about a dismissal by the respondent?   Yes   No
If 'No', please now go straight to section 3.5.
If your claim is about constructive dismissal, i.e. you resigned because of something
your employer did or failed to do which made you feel you could no longer continue to
work for them, tick the box here and the 'Yes' box in section 3.4.

■ 3.4● Is your claim about anything else, in addition to the dismissal?   Yes   No   ■
If 'No', please now go straight to section 4.
If 'Yes', please answer questions 3.5 to 3.7 about the
non-dismissal aspects of your claim.

3.5● Have you put your complaint(s) in writing to the respondent?

          Yes   Please give the date you put it to them in writing.

          No

If 'No', please now go straight to section 3.7.

■ 3.6● Did you allow at least 28 days between the date you put your   Yes   No   ■
complaint in writing to the respondent and the date you sent us this claim?
If 'Yes', please now go straight to section 4.

3.7● Please explain why you did not put your complaint in writing to the respondent or,
if you did, why you did not allow at least 28 days before sending us your claim.
(In most cases, it is a legal requirement to take these procedural steps. Your claim
will not be accepted unless you give a valid reason why you did not have to meet
the requirement in your case. If you are not sure, you may want to get legal advice.)

4 Employment details

4.1 Please give the following information if possible.

When did your employment start?

When did or will it end?

Is your employment continuing?   Yes   No

4.2 Please say what job you do or did.

4.3 How many hours do or did you work each week?   hours each week

4.4 How much are or were you paid?

Pay before tax   £   ,   .00   Hourly

Normal take-home pay (including   £   ,   .00   Weekly
overtime,commission, bonuses and so on)   Monthly
     Yearly

4.5 If your employment has ended, did you work
(or were you paid for) a period of notice?   Yes   No

If 'Yes', how many weeks or months did   weeks   months
you work or were you paid for?

5 Unfair dismissal or constructive dismissal

Please fill in this section only if you believe you have been unfairly or constructively dismissed.

5.1 • If you were dismissed by your employer, you should explain why you think your dismissal
was unfair. If you resigned because of something your employer did or failed to do which
made you feel you could no longer continue to work for them (constructive dismissal)
you should explain what happened.

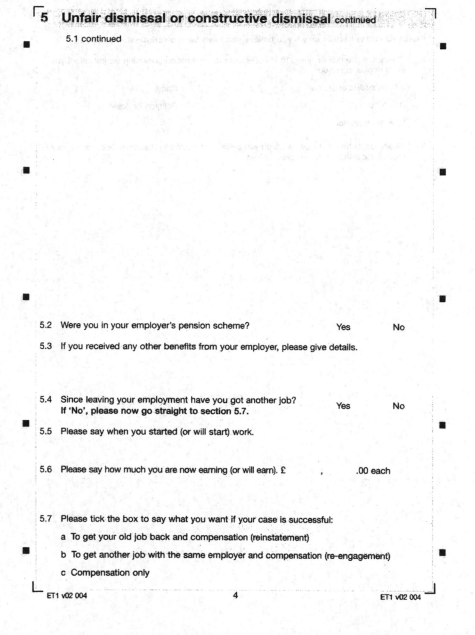

5 Unfair dismissal or constructive dismissal continued

5.1 continued

5.2 Were you in your employer's pension scheme?   Yes   No

5.3 If you received any other benefits from your employer, please give details.

5.4 Since leaving your employment have you got another job?   Yes   No
     If 'No', please now go straight to section 5.7.

5.5 Please say when you started (or will start) work.

5.6 Please say how much you are now earning (or will earn). £   ,   .00 each

5.7 Please tick the box to say what you want if your case is successful:

     a To get your old job back and compensation (reinstatement)

     b To get another job with the same employer and compensation (re-engagement)

     c Compensation only

6   Discrimination

Please fill in this section only if you believe you have been discriminated against.

6.1 • Please tick the box or boxes to indicate what discrimination (including victimisation) you are complaining about:

Sex (including equal pay)   Race

Disability   Religion or belief

Sexual orientation

6.2 • Please describe the incidents which you believe amounted to discrimination, the dates of these incidents and the people involved.

7 Redundancy payments

Please fill in this section only if you believe you are owed a redundancy payment.

7.1 Please explain why you believe you are entitled to this payment and set out the steps you have taken to get it.

8 Other payments you are owed

Please fill in this section only if you believe you are owed other payments.

8.1 Please tick the box or boxes to indicate that money is owed to you for:

unpaid wages?

holiday pay?

notice pay?

other unpaid amounts?

8.2 How much are you claiming?   £   ,   .00

Is this: before tax?   after tax?

8.3 Please explain why you believe you are entitled to this payment. If you have specified an amount, please set out how you have worked this out.

9 Other complaints

Please fill in this section only if you believe you have a complaint that is not covered elsewhere.

9.1 Please explain what you are complaining about and why.
Please include any relevant dates.

10 Other information

10.1 Please do not send a covering letter with this form.
You should add any extra information you want us to know here.

11 Disability

11.1 Please tick this box if you consider yourself to have a disability   Yes   No
If 'Yes', please say what this disability is and tell us what assistance, if any, you will
need as your claim progresses through the system.

12 Your representative

Please fill in this section only if you have appointed a representative. If you do fill this section in, we will in future only send correspondence to your representative and not to you.

12.1 Representative's name:

12.2 Name of the representative's
organisation:

12.3 Address: Number or Name

Street

+   Town/City

County

Postcode

12.4 Phone number:

12.5 Reference:

12.6 How would you prefer us to   Post   Fax   E-mail
communicate with them? (Please tick only one box)
Fax number:

E-mail address:
@

13 Multiple cases

13.1 To your knowledge, is your claim one of a number of claims   Yes   No
arising from the same or similar circumstances?

Please sign and date here

Signature: Date:

Data Protection Act 1998. We will send a copy of this form to the respondent(s) and Acas. We will put some of the
information you give us on this form onto a computer. This helps us to monitor progress and produce statistics.
Information provided on this form is passed to the Department of Trade and Industry to assist research into the use
and effectiveness of Employment Tribunals.

Additional space for notes.

Equal Opportunities Monitoring Form

You are not obliged to fill in this section but, if you do so, it will enable us to monitor our processes and ensure that we provide equality of opportunity to all. The information you give here will be treated in strict confidence and this page will not form part of your case. It will be used only for monitoring and research purposes without identifying you.

1. What is your country of birth?

England   Wales

Scotland

Northern Ireland

Republic of Ireland

Elsewhere, *please write in the present name of the country*

2. What is your ethnic group?
Choose ONE section from A to E, then ✓ the appropriate box to indicate your cultural background.

A White

British   Irish

Any other White background *please write in*

B Mixed

White and Black Caribbean

White and Black African

White and Asian

Any other Mixed background *please write in*

C Asian or Asian British

Indian   Pakistani

Bangladeshi

Any other Asian background *please write in*

D: Black or Black British

Caribbean   African

Any other Black background *please write in*

E Chinese or other ethnic group

Chinese

Any other, *please write in*

3. What is your religion?
✓ box only

None

Christian (including Church of England, Catholic, Protestant and all other Christian denominations)

Buddhist

Hindu

Jewish

Muslim

Sikh

Any other religion, *please write in*

Copy 1

Employment Tribunals - Multiple Claim Form

Please use this form if you wish to present two or more claims which arise from the same set of facts. Use additional sheets if necessary.

The following claimants are represented by   (if applicable) and the relevant required information for all the additional claimants is the same as stated in the main claim of

v

Title
First name (or names)
Surname or family name
Date of birth
Number or Name
Street
Town/City
County
Postcode

Title
First name (or names)
Surname or family name
Date of birth
Number or Name
Street
Town/City
County
Postcode

Title
First name (or names)
Surname or family name
Date of birth
Number or Name
Street
Town/City
County
Postcode

ET1a v01

ET1a v01

Copy 1

Title
First name (or names)
Surname or family name
Date of birth
Number or Name
Street
Town/City
County
Postcode

Title
First name (or names)
Surname or family name
Date of birth
Number or Name
Street
Town/City
County
Postcode

Title
First name (or names)
Surname or family name
Date of birth
Number or Name
Street
Town/City
County
Postcode

Title
First name (or names)
Surname or family name
Date of birth
Number or Name
Street
Town/City
County
Postcode

Case number:

1   Name of respondent company or organisation

1.1* Name of your organisation:

Contact name:

1.2* Address   Number or Name

+   Address Line 1

Address Line 2

Address Line 3

Postcode

1.3   Phone number:

1.4   How would you prefer us to   E-mail   Post   Fax
       communicate with you? (Please tick
       only one box)
          E-mail address:
          Fax number:

1.5   What does this organisation mainly make or do?

1.6   How many people does this organisation employ in Great Britain?

1.7   Does this organisation have more than one site in Great Britain?   Yes   No

1.8   If 'Yes', how many people are employed at the place where the
       claimant worked?

2   Action before a claim

2.1   Is, or was, the claimant an employee?   Yes   No
       If 'Yes', please now go **straight to section 2.3.**

2.2   Is, or was, the claimant a worker providing services to you?   Yes   No
       If 'Yes', please now go **straight to section 3.**
       If 'No', please now go **straight to section 5.**

2.3   If the claim, or part of it, is about a dismissal,   Yes   No
       do you agree that the claimant was dismissed?
       If 'Yes', please now go **straight to section 2.6.**

2.4   If the claim includes something **other than** dismissal,   Yes   No
       does it relate to an action you took on
       grounds of the claimant's conduct or capability?
       If 'Yes', please now go **straight to section 2.6.**

2.5   Has the substance of this claim been raised by the claimant   Yes   No
       in writing under a grievance procedure?

2.6   If 'Yes', please explain below what stage you have reached in the dismissal and disciplinary
       procedure or grievance procedure (whichever is applicable).
       If 'No' and the claimant says they have raised a grievance with you in writing, please say
       whether you received it and explain why you did not accept this as a grievance.

3 Employment details

3.1 Are the dates of employment given by the claimant correct?   Yes   No
   If 'Yes', please now go straight to section 3.3.

3.2 If 'No', please give dates and say why you disagree with the dates given by the claimant.

   When their employment started

   When their employment ended or will end

   Is their employment continuing?   Yes   No

   I disagree with the dates for the following reasons.

3.3 Is the claimant's description of their job or job title correct?   Yes   No
   If 'Yes', please now go straight to section 3.5.

3.4 If 'No', please give the details you believe to be correct below.

3.5 Is the information given by the claimant correct about being   Yes   No
   paid for, or working, a period of notice?
   If 'Yes', please now go straight to section 3.7.

3.6 If 'No', please give the details you believe to be correct below. If you gave them no notice or
   didn't pay them instead of letting them work their notice, please explain what happened and why.

3.7 Are the claimant's hours of work correct?   Yes   No
   If 'Yes', please now go straight to section 3.9.

3.8 If 'No', please enter the details you believe to be correct.   hours each week

3.9 Are the earnings details given by the claimant correct?   Yes   No
   If 'Yes', please now go straight to section 4.

3.10 If 'No', please give the details you believe to be correct below.

   Pay before tax   £   each

   Normal take-home pay (including overtime,   £   each
   commission, bonuses and so on)

4   Unfair dismissal or constructive dismissal

4.1   Are the details about pension and other benefits   Yes   No
given by the claimant correct?
If 'Yes', please now go straight to section 5.

4.2   If 'No', please give the details you believe to be correct below.

5   Response

5.1* Do you resist the claim?   Yes   No
If 'No', please now go straight to section 6.

5.2● If 'Yes', please set out in full the grounds on which you resist the claim.

3

6 Other information

6.1 Please do not send a covering letter with this form. You should add any extra information you want us to know here.

7 Your representative If you have a representative, please fill in the following.

7.1 Representative's name:

7.2 Name of the representative's
      organisation:

7.3 Address   Number or Name

                    Address Line 1

            +   Address Line 2

                    Address Line 3

                    Postcode

7.4 Phone number:

7.5 Reference:

7.6 How would you prefer us to   E-mail   Post   Fax
      communicate with them?
      (Please tick only one box)
          E-mail address:

          Fax number:

Please sign and date here

Signature: Date:

Employment Tribunal Service check list and cover sheet

You have completed stage one of your application and opted to print and post your form. We would like to remind you that applications submitted on-line are processed much faster than ones posted to us. If you wish to submit on-line please go back to the form and click the submit button, otherwise follow the **Check List** before you post the completed application form to the return address below:

Telephone:
Fax:
Email:

Please check the following:

1. Read your application to ensure the information entered is correct and truthful, and that you have not omitted any information, which you feel may be relevant to the claim.

2. You **must not attach** a covering letter to this application. If you have any further relevant information please enter it in the "Other Information" space provided in the form.

3. Please ensure that the form has been signed and dated.

4. The completed form should be returned to the address shown at the top of this page. If you are using a window envelope you may insert this page with your application. Please do not clip or staple this page to your application form.

If you have a general question about the Tribunals process please call 0845 795 9775, or minicom 0845 757 3772 between 9.00am and 5.00pm Monday to Friday.

Once your application has been received you may contact the office listed above directly.

Employment Tribunal Response Form

You can make a response to an Employment Tribunal by completing and editing the form offline. You can save a part or fully completed form, email a saved form to another person for approval, and submit it securely online to the Employment Tribunal Service.

Please make sure you have read the guidance notes on our website or in our booklet on how to make a response before you fill in the form.

Once you have completed your form you can submit it securely online to the relevant Tribunal office. You will receive an email to confirm we have received it. Online responses are processed faster than ones sent by post.

Select the type of claim you wish to make:

✓ I want to respond to a claim.

In order to proceed you must enter the case number and names of the parties printed on the form and letter we sent you:

Case Number

Names of Parties   ∨

Need Help?

If you require any help completing your form or have a general question about the tribunals process please contact the Employment Tribunals Enquiry Line on

0845 795 9775

minicom 08457 573 722.

Between 9.00am and 5.00pm Monday to Friday, our lines are closed on bank holidays.

We regret we **cannot** provide any legal advice.

Please Note:

By law, your claim must be on an approved form provided by the Employment Tribunals Service, and you must provide the information marked with ★ and, if it is relevant, the information marked with ● (see 'Information needed before a claim can be accepted')

General Information:

Once you have completed your form you can submit it securely on-line to the ETS. On-line forms are processed faster than ones sent by post.

Save   Submit   Print   Clear   Continue →

POWERED BY LEGATIO

1 Your details

1.1   Title: Mr   Mrs   Miss   Ms   Other

1.2* First name (or names):

1.3* Surname or family name:

1.4   Date of birth (date/month/year):   Are you: male?   female?

1.5* Address: Number or Name

               Street

        +   Town/City

               County

               Postcode

1.6   Phone number (where we can contact
      you during normal working hours):

1.7   How would you prefer us to   E-mail   Post   Fax
      communicate with you?
      (Please tick only one box)

      E-mail address:

                                         @

      Fax number:

2 Respondent's details

2.1* Give the name of your employer
      or the organisation you are claiming
      against.

2.2* Address: Number or Name

               Street

               Town/City

        +   County

               Postcode

      Phone number:

2.3   If you worked at an address
      different from the one you have
      given at 2.2, please give the
      full address and postcode.

      Postcode

      Phone number:

2.4● If your complaint is against more than one respondent please give the names, addresses and
      postcodes of additional respondents.

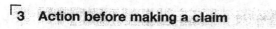

3 Action before making a claim

■ 3.1* Are you, or were you, an employee of the respondent?   Yes   No   ■
        If 'Yes', please now go straight to section 3.3.

   3.2 Are you, or were you, a worker providing services to the respondent?   Yes   No
        If 'Yes', please now go straight to section 4.
        If 'No', please now go straight to section 6.

   3.3● Is your claim, or part of it, about a dismissal by the respondent?   Yes   No
        If 'No', please now go straight to section 3.5.
        If your claim is about constructive dismissal, i.e. you resigned because of something
        your employer did or failed to do which made you feel you could no longer continue to
        work for them, tick the box here and the 'Yes' box in section 3.4.

■ 3.4● Is your claim about anything else, in addition to the dismissal?   Yes   No   ■
        If 'No', please now go straight to section 4.
        If 'Yes', please answer questions 3.5 to 3.7 about the
        non-dismissal aspects of your claim.

   3.5● Have you put your complaint(s) in writing to the respondent?

             Yes   Please give the date you put it to them in writing.

             No

        If 'No', please now go straight to section 3.7.

■ 3.6● Did you allow at least 28 days between the date you put your   Yes   No   ■
        complaint in writing to the respondent and the date you sent us this claim?
        If 'Yes', please now go straight to section 4.

   3.7● Please explain why you did not put your complaint in writing to the respondent or,
        if you did, why you did not allow at least 28 days before sending us your claim.
        (In most cases, it is a legal requirement to take these procedural steps. Your claim
        will not be accepted unless you give a valid reason why you did not have to meet
        the requirement in your case. If you are not sure, you may want to get legal advice.)

■   ■

■   ■

4   Employment details

4.1   Please give the following information if possible.

When did your employment start?

When did or will it end?

Is your employment continuing?   Yes   No

4.2   Please say what job you do or did.

4.3   How many hours do or did you work each week?   hours each week

4.4   How much are or were you paid?

Pay before tax   £   ,   .00   Hourly

Normal take-home pay (including   £   ,   .00   Weekly
overtime, commission, bonuses and so on)   Monthly
                                                 Yearly

4.5   If your employment has ended, did you work   Yes   No
(or were you paid for) a period of notice?

If 'Yes', how many weeks or months did   weeks   months
you work or were you paid for?

5   Unfair dismissal or constructive dismissal

Please fill in this section only if you believe you have been unfairly or constructively dismissed.

5.1 • If you were dismissed by your employer, you should explain why you think your dismissal
was unfair. If you resigned because of something your employer did or failed to do which
made you feel you could no longer continue to work for them (constructive dismissal)
you should explain what happened.

5 Unfair dismissal or constructive dismissal continued

5.1 continued

5.2 Were you in your employer's pension scheme?   Yes   No

5.3 If you received any other benefits from your employer, please give details.

5.4 Since leaving your employment have you got another job?
     If 'No', please now go straight to section 5.7.   Yes   No

5.5 Please say when you started (or will start) work.

5.6 Please say how much you are now earning (or will earn). £   ,   .00 each

5.7 Please tick the box to say what you want if your case is successful:

   a To get your old job back and compensation (reinstatement)

   b To get another job with the same employer and compensation (re-engagement)

   c Compensation only

6   Discrimination

Please fill in this section only if you believe you have been discriminated against.

6.1 Please tick the box or boxes to indicate what discrimination (including victimisation) you are complaining about:

Sex (including equal pay)   Race

Disability   Religion or belief

Sexual orientation

6.2 Please describe the incidents which you believe amounted to discrimination, the dates of these incidents and the people involved.

7 Redundancy payments

Please fill in this section only if you believe you are owed a redundancy payment.

7.1 ● Please explain why you believe you are entitled to this payment and set out the steps you have taken to get it.

8 Other payments you are owed

Please fill in this section only if you believe you are owed other payments.

8.1 ● Please tick the box or boxes to indicate that money is owed to you for:

unpaid wages?

holiday pay?

notice pay?

other unpaid amounts?

8.2 How much are you claiming?   £   ,   .00

Is this: before tax?   after tax?

8.3 ● Please explain why you believe you are entitled to this payment. If you have specified an amount, please set out how you have worked this out.

9 Other complaints

Please fill in this section only if you believe you have a complaint that is not covered elsewhere.

9.1 Please explain what you are complaining about and why.
Please include any relevant dates.

10 Other information

10.1 Please do not send a covering letter with this form.
You should add any extra information you want us to know here.

11 Disability

11.1 Please tick this box if you consider yourself to have a disability   Yes   No
      If 'Yes', please say what this disability is and tell us what assistance, if any, you will
      need as your claim progresses through the system.

12 Your representative

**Please fill in this section only if you have appointed a representative. If you do fill this section
in, we will in future only send correspondence to your representative and not to you.**

12.1 Representative's name:

12.2 Name of the representative's
      organisation:

12.3 Address: Number or Name

                      Street
            +
                      Town/City

                      County

                      Postcode

12.4 Phone number:

12.5 Reference:

12.6 How would you prefer us to   Post   Fax   E-mail
      communicate with them? (Please tick only one box)
         Fax number:

         E-mail address:
                                    @

13 Multiple cases

13.1 To your knowledge, is your claim one of a number of claims   Yes   No
      arising from the same or similar circumstances?

Please sign and date here

Signature: Date:

Data Protection Act 1998. We will send a copy of this form to the respondent(s) and Acas. We will put some of the
information you give us on this form onto a computer. This helps us to monitor progress and produce statistics.
Information provided on this form is passed to the Department of Trade and Industry to assist research into the use
and effectiveness of Employment Tribunals.

Additional space for notes.

Equal Opportunities Monitoring Form

■ You are not obliged to fill in this section but, if you do so, it will enable us to monitor our processes and ensure that we provide equality of opportunity to all. The information you give here will be treated in strict confidence and this page will not form part of your case. It will be used only for monitoring and research purposes without identifying you.

1. What is your country of birth?

England   Wales

Scotland

Northern Ireland

Republic of Ireland

Elsewhere, *please write in the present name of the country*

2. What is your ethnic group?
Choose ONE section from A to E, then ✓ the appropriate box to indicate your cultural background.

A White

British   Irish

Any other White background
please write in

B Mixed

White and Black Caribbean

White and Black African

White and Asian

Any other Mixed background
please write in

C Asian or Asian British

Indian   Pakistani

Bangladeshi

Any other Asian background
please write in

D: Black or Black British

Caribbean   African

Any other Black background
please write in

E Chinese or other ethnic group

Chinese

Any other, *please write in*

3. What is your religion?
✓ box only

None

Christian (including Church of England, Catholic, Protestant and all other Christian denominations)

Buddhist

Hindu

Jewish

Muslim

Sikh

Any other religion,
please write in

Copy 1

Employment Tribunals - Multiple Claim Form

Please use this form if you wish to present two or more claims which arise from the same set of facts. Use additional sheets if necessary.

The following claimants are represented by   (if applicable) and the relevant required information for all the additional claimants is the same as stated in the main claim of

V

Title
First name (or names)
Surname or family name
Date of birth
Number or Name
Street
Town/City
County
Postcode

Title
First name (or names)
Surname or family name
Date of birth
Number or Name
Street
Town/City
County
Postcode

Title
First name (or names)
Surname or family name
Date of birth
Number or Name
Street
Town/City
County
Postcode

ET1a v01   ET1a v01

Copy 1

Title
First name (or names)
Surname or family name
Date of birth
Number or Name
Street
Town/City
County
Postcode

Title
First name (or names)
Surname or family name
Date of birth
Number or Name
Street
Town/City
County
Postcode

Title
First name (or names)
Surname or family name
Date of birth
Number or Name
Street
Town/City
County
Postcode

Title
First name (or names)
Surname or family name
Date of birth
Number or Name
Street
Town/City
County
Postcode

Case number:

1   Name of respondent company or organisation

1.1* Name of your organisation:

    Contact name:

1.2* Address   Number or Name

                 Address Line 1

      +   Address Line 2

                 Address Line 3

                 Postcode

1.3   Phone number:

1.4   How would you prefer us to   E-mail   Post   Fax
       communicate with you? (Please tick
       only one box)
         E-mail address:
         Fax number:

1.5   What does this organisation mainly make or do?

1.6   How many people does this organisation employ in Great Britain?

1.7   Does this organisation have more than one site in Great Britain?   Yes   No

1.8   If 'Yes', how many people are employed at the place where the
       claimant worked?

2   Action before a claim

2.1   Is, or was, the claimant an employee?   Yes   No
       If 'Yes', please now go straight to section 2.3.

2.2   Is, or was, the claimant a worker providing services to you?   Yes   No
       If 'Yes', please now go straight to section 3.
       If 'No', please now go straight to section 5.

2.3   If the claim, or part of it, is about a dismissal,   Yes   No
       do you agree that the claimant was dismissed?
       If 'Yes', please now go straight to section 2.6.

2.4   If the claim includes something **other than** dismissal,   Yes   No
       does it relate to an action you took on
       grounds of the claimant's conduct or capability?
       If 'Yes', please now go straight to section 2.6.

2.5   Has the substance of this claim been raised by the claimant   Yes   No
       in writing under a grievance procedure?

2.6   If 'Yes', please explain below what stage you have reached in the dismissal and disciplinary
       procedure or grievance procedure (whichever is applicable).
       If 'No' and the claimant says they have raised a grievance with you in writing, please say
       whether you received it and explain why you did not accept this as a grievance.

3   Employment details

3.1   Are the dates of employment given by the claimant correct?   Yes   No
If 'Yes', please now go straight to section 3.3.

3.2   If 'No', please give dates and say why you disagree with the dates given by the claimant.

       When their employment started

       When their employment ended or will end

       Is their employment continuing?   Yes   No

I disagree with the dates for the following reasons.

3.3   Is the claimant's description of their job or job title correct?   Yes   No
If 'Yes', please now go straight to section 3.5.

3.4   If 'No', please give the details you believe to be correct below.

3.5   Is the information given by the claimant correct about being   Yes   No
paid for, or working, a period of notice?
If 'Yes', please now go straight to section 3.7.

3.6   If 'No', please give the details you believe to be correct below. If you gave them no notice or
didn't pay them instead of letting them work their notice, please explain what happened and why.

3.7   Are the claimant's hours of work correct?   Yes   No
If 'Yes', please now go straight to section 3.9.

3.8   If 'No', please enter the details you believe to be correct.   hours each week

3.9   Are the earnings details given by the claimant correct?   Yes   No
If 'Yes', please now go straight to section 4.

3.10 If 'No', please give the details you believe to be correct below.

       Pay before tax   £   each

       Normal take-home pay (including overtime,   £   each
       commission, bonuses and so on)

4   Unfair dismissal or constructive dismissal

4.1   Are the details about pension and other benefits   Yes   No
      given by the claimant correct?
      If 'Yes', please now go straight to section 5.

4.2   If 'No', please give the details you believe to be correct below.

5   Response

5.1* Do you resist the claim?   Yes   No
      If 'No', please now go straight to section 6.

5.2● If 'Yes', please set out in full the grounds on which you resist the claim.

6 Other information

6.1 Please do not send a covering letter with this form. You should add any extra information you want us to know here.

7 Your representative   If you have a representative, please fill in the following.

7.1 Representative's name:

7.2 Name of the representative's organisation:

7.3 Address   Number or Name
                   Address Line 1
            +   Address Line 2
                   Address Line 3
                   Postcode

7.4 Phone number:

7.5 Reference:

7.6 How would you prefer us to   E-mail   Post   Fax
    communicate with them?
    (Please tick only one box)
        E-mail address:

        Fax number:

Please sign and date here

Signature: Date:

Data Protection Act 1998. We will send a copy of this form to the claimant and Acas. We will put some of the information you give us on this form onto a computer. This helps us to monitor progress and produce statistics. Information provided on this form is passed to the Department of Trade and Industry to assist research into the use and effectiveness of Employment Tribunals.

Employment Tribunal Service check list and cover sheet

You have completed stage one of your application and opted to print and post your form. We would like to remind you that applications submitted on-line are processed much faster than ones posted to us. If you wish to submit on-line please go back to the form and click the submit button, otherwise follow the **Check List** before you post the completed application form to the return address below:

Telephone:
Fax:
Email:

Please check the following:

1.   Read your application to ensure the information entered is correct and truthful, and that you have not omitted any information, which you feel may be relevant to the claim.

2.   You **must not attach** a covering letter to this application. If you have any further relevant information please enter it in the "Other Information" space provided in the form.

3.   Please ensure that the form has been signed and dated.

4.   The completed form should be returned to the address shown at the top of this page. If you are using a window envelope you may insert this page with your application. Please do not clip or staple this page to your application form.

If you have a general question about the Tribunals process please call 0845 795 9775, or minicom 0845 757 3772 between 9.00am and 5.00pm Monday to Friday.

Once your application has been received you may contact the office listed above directly.

THE STATUTORY DISMISSAL AND DISCIPLINARY PROCEDURE AND THE GRIEVANCE PROCEDURE FORM—SCHEDULE 2 TO THE EMPLOYMENT ACT 2002

SCHEDULES   A2.01

SCHEDULE 2   Section 29

STATUTORY DISPUTE RESOLUTION PROCEDURES

Part 1

DISMISSAL AND DISCIPLINARY PROCEDURES

Chapter I

Standard procedure

Step 1: statement of grounds for action and invitation to meeting

1   (1) The employer must set out in writing the employee's alleged conduct or characteristics, or other circumstances, which lead him to contemplate dismissing or taking disciplinary action against the employee.

(2) The employer must send the statement or a copy of it to the employee and invite the employee to attend a meeting to discuss the matter.

Step 2: meeting

2   (1) The meeting must take place before action is taken, except in the case where the disciplinary action consists of suspension.

(2) The meeting must not take place unless —

(a) the employer has informed the employee what the basis was for including in the statement under paragraph 1(1) the ground or grounds given in it, and

(b) the employee has had a reasonable opportunity to consider his response to that information.

(3) The employee must take all reasonable steps to attend the meeting.

(4) After the meeting, the employer must inform the employee of his decision and notify him of the right to appeal against the decision if he is not satisfied with it.

Step 3: appeal

3 (1) If the employee does wish to appeal, he must inform the employer.

(2) If the employee informs the employer of his wish to appeal, the employer must invite him to attend a further meeting.

(3) The employee must take all reasonable steps to attend the meeting.

(4) The appeal meeting need not take place before the dismissal or disciplinary disciplinary action takes effect.

(5) After the appeal meeting, the employer must inform the employee of his of his

Chapter 2

Modified procedure

Step 1: statement of grounds for action

4 The employer must—

(a) Set out in writing—

(i) the employee's alleged misconduct which has led to the dismissal,
(ii) what the basis was for thinking at the time of the dismissal that the employee was guilty of the alleged misconduct, and
(iii) the employee's right to appeal against dismissal, and

(b) send the statement or a copy of it to the employee.

Step 2: appeal

5 (1) If the employee does wish to appeal, he must inform the employer.

(2) If the employee informs the employer of his wish to appeal, the employer must invite him to attend a meeting.

(3) The employee must take all reasonable steps to attend the meeting.

(4) After the appeal meeting, the employer must inform the employee of his final decision.

PART 2

GRIEVANCE PROCEDURES

Chapter 1

Standard procedure

Step 1: statement of grievance

6   The employee must set out the grievance in writing and send the statement or a copy of it to the employer.

Step 2: meeting

7   (1) The employer must invite the employee to attend a meeting to discuss the grievance.

    (2) The meeting must not take place unless —

        (a) the employee has informed the employer what the basis for the grievance was when he made the statement under paragraph 6, and
        (b) the employer has had a reasonable opportunity to consider his response to that information.

    (3) The employee must take all reasonable steps to attend the meeting.

    (4) After the meeting, the employer must inform the employee of his decision as to his response to the grievance and notify him of the right to appeal against the decision if he is not satisfied with it.

Step 3: appeal

8   (1) If the employee does wish to appeal, he must inform the employer.

    (2) If the employee informs the employer of his wish to appeal, the employer must invite him to attend a further meeting.

    (3) The employee must take all reasonable steps to attend the meeting.

    (4) After the appeal meeting, the employer must inform the employee of his final decision.

Chapter 2

Modified procedure

Step 1: statement of grievance

9   The employee must —

    (a) set out in writing —
        (i) the grievance, and
        (ii) the basis for it, and
    (b) send the statement or a copy of it to the employer.

Step 2: response

10   The employer must set out his response in writing and send the statement or a copy of it to the employee.

Part 3

General requirements

Introductory

11   The following requirements apply to each of the procedures set out above (so far as applicable).

Timetable

12   Each step and action under the procedure must be taken without unreasonable delay.

Meetings

13 (1) Timing and location of meetings must be reasonable.

    (2) Meetings must be conducted in a manner that enables both employer and employee to explain their cases.

    (3) In the case of appeal meetings which are not the first meeting, the employer should, as far as is reasonably practicable, be represented by a more senior manager than attended the first meeting (unless the most senior manager attended that meeting).

PART 4

SUPPLEMENTARY

Status of meetings

14   A meeting held for the purposes of this Schedule is a hearing for
        the purposes of section 13(4) and (5) of the Employment Rela-
        tions Act 1999 (c. 26) (definition of "disciplinary hearing" and
        "grievance hearing" in relation to the right to be accompanied
        under section 10 of that Act).

Scope of grievance procedures

15 (1) The procedures set out in Part 2 are only applicable to matters
        raised by an employee with his employer as a grievance.

    (2) Accordingly, those procedures are only applicable to the kind of
        disclosure dealt with in Part 4A of the Employment Rights Act
        1996 (c. 18) (protected disclosures of information) if information
        is disclosed by an employee to his employer in circumstances
        where—

        (a) the information relates to a matter which the employee could
            raise as a grievance with his employer, and

        (b) it is the intention of the employee that the disclosure should
            constitute the raising of the matter with his employer as a
            grievance.

EMPLOYMENT TRIBUNALS (CONSTITUTION AND RULES OF PROCEDURE) REGULATIONS 2004— REGULATIONS AND SCHEDULE 1

STATUTORY INSTRUMENTS

2004 No. 1861

EMPLOYMENT TRIBUNALS

The Employment Tribunals (Constitution and Rules of Procedure) Regulations 2004

Made - - - -	*19th July 2004*
Laid before Parliament	*20th July 2004*
Coming into force - -	*1st October 2004*

ARRANGEMENT OF REGULATIONS

SCHEDULE 2   Regulation 16(2)

THE EMPLOYMENT TRIBUNALS (NATIONAL SECURITY) RULES OF PROCEDURE

SCHEDULE 3   Regulation 16(3)(a)

THE EMPLOYMENT TRIBUNALS (LEVY APPEALS) RULES OF PROCEDURE

For use only in proceedings on levy appeals

SCHEDULE 4   Regulation 16(3)(b)

THE EMPLOYMENT TRIBUNALS (HEALTH AND SAFETY— APPEALS AGAINST IMPROVEMENT AND PROHIBITION NOTICES) RULES OF PROCEDURE

1. Application of Schedule 1
2. Definitions
3. Notice of appeal
4. Time limit for bringing appeal
5. Action on receipt of appeal
6. Application for a direction suspending the operation of a prohibition notice
7. General power to manage proceedings
8. Appointment of an assessor
9. Right to withdraw proceedings
10. Costs and expenses
11. Provisions of Schedule 1 which do not apply to appeals against improvement notices or prohibition notices
12. Modification of Schedule 1

SCHEDULE 5   Regulation 16(3)(c)

THE EMPLOYMENT TRIBUNALS (NON-DISCRIMINATION NOTICES APPEALS) RULES OF PROCEDURE

1. Application of Schedule 1
2. Definitions
3. Notice of Appeal
4. Action on receipt of appeal
5. Provisions of Schedule 1 which do not apply to appeals against non-discrimination notices
6. Modification of Schedule 1

The Secretary of State, in exercise of the powers conferred on her by section 24(2) of the Health and Safety at Work etc. Act 1974(**a**), sections 1(1), 4(6), and (6A), 7(1), (3), (3ZA), (3A), and (5), 7A(1) and (2), 9(1), (2) and (4), 10(2), (5), (6) and (7), 10A(l), 11(1), 12(2), 13, 13A(1) and (2), 19 and 41(4) of the Employment Tribunals Act 1996(**b**) and paragraph 36

(**a**) 1974 c. 37; "prescribed" is defined by section 53(1) of the Act as meaning prescribed by regulations.
(**b**) 1996 c. 17; by virtue of section 1 of the Employment Rights (Dispute Resolution) Act 1998 (c. 8) industrial tribunals were renamed employment tribunals and references to "industrial tribunal" and "industrial tribunals" in any enactment were substituted with "employment tribunal" and "employment tribunals". Section 4(6) was amended by paragraph 12(4) of Schedule 1 to the Employment Rights (Dispute Resolution) Act 1998 and section 4(6A) was inserted by section 3(6) of that Act. Section 7 was interpreted by section 239(4) of the Trade Union and Labour Relations (Consolidation) Act 1992 (c. 52), as inserted by paragraph 1 of Schedule 5 to the Employment Relations Act 1999 (c. 26). Paragraph 7(3)(f)(i) was repealed by paragraph 14(2) of Schedule 1 to the Employment

of Schedule 8 to the Government of Wales Act 1998(**c**), and paragraph 37 of Schedule 6 to the Scotland Act 1998(**d**), and after consultation with the Council of Tribunals, in accordance with section 8(1) of the Tribunals and Inquiries Act 1992(**e**), hereby makes the following Regulations:—

Citation, commencement and revocation

1.—(1) These Regulations may be cited as the Employment Tribunals (Constitution and Rules of Procedure) Regulations 2004 and the Rules of Procedure contained in Schedules 1, 2, 3, 4 and 5 to these Regulations may be referred to, respectively, as—

(a) the Employment Tribunals Rules of Procedure;

(b) the Employment Tribunals (National Security) Rules of Procedure;

(c) the Employment Tribunals (Levy Appeals) Rules of Procedure;

(d) the Employment Tribunals (Health and Safety—Appeals against Improvement and Prohibition Notices) Rules of Procedure; and

(e) the Employment Tribunals (Non-Discrimination Notices Appeals) Rules of Procedure.

(2) These Regulations shall come into force on 1 October 2004.

(3) Subject to the savings in regulation 20, the Employment Tribunals (Constitution and Rules of Procedure) Regulations 2001(**f**) and the Employment Tribunals (Constitution and Rules of Procedure) (Scotland) Regulations 2001(**g**) are revoked.

Rights (Dispute Resolution) Act 1998 and paragraph 7(3)(f)(i) was inserted by section 24(1) of the Employment Act 2002 (c.22) and section 7(3ZA) was inserted by section 25 of that Act. Sections 7(3 A) to 7(3C) were inserted by section 2 of the Employment Rights (Dispute Resolution) Act 1998 and section 7(3A) was then substituted by section 26 of the Employment Act 2002. Section 7A was inserted by section 27 of the Employment Act 2002. The sum in paragraph (a) of section 9(2) was substituted by article 2 of S.I. 2001/237 and section 9(2A) was inserted by section 28 of the Employment Act 2002. Section 9(4) was amended by paragraph 15 of Schedule 1 to the Employment Rights (Dispute Resolution) Act 1998. Section 10 was substituted, and section 10A was inserted, by paragraph 3 of Schedule 8 to the Employment Relations Act 1999. Section 13(1) was substituted by subsections (1), (1A) to (1C), by section 22(1) of the Employment Act 2002. Section 13(2) was amended by paragraph 4 of Part III of Schedule 4 to the Employment Relations Act 1999 and section 13A was inserted by section 22(2) of the Employment Act 2002. Section 19(1) was numbered as such by section 24(4) of the Employment Act 2002, and was amended by paragraph 23(1) and (3) of Schedule 7 and Schedule 8 of that Act. Section 19(2) was inserted by section 24(4) of the Employment Act 2002.

(**c**) 1998 c. 38.
(**d**) 1998 c. 46.
(**e**) 1992 c. 53.
(**f**) S.I. 2001/1171.
(**g**) S.I. 2001/1170.

Interpretation

2. In these Regulations and in Schedules 1, 2, 3, 4 and 5:—

"ACAS" means the Advisory, Conciliation and Arbitration Service referred to in section 247 of TULR(C)A;

"appointing office holder" means, in England and Wales, the Lord Chancellor, and in Scotland, the Lord President;

"chairman" means the President or a member of the panel of chairmen appointed in accordance with regulation 8(3)(a), or, for the purposes of national security proceedings, a member of the panel referred to in regulation 10 selected in accordance with regulation 1 l(a), and in relation to particular proceedings it means the chairman to whom the proceedings have been referred by the President, Vice President or a Regional Chairman;

"compromise agreement" means an agreement to refrain from continuing proceedings where the agreement meets the conditions in section 203(3) of the Employment Rights Act;

"constructive dismissal" has the meaning set out in section 95(1)(c) of the Employment Rights Act;

"Disability Discrimination Act" means the Disability Discrimination Act 1995(**a**);

"electronic communication" has the meaning given to it by section 15(1) of the Electronic Communications Act 2000(**b**);

"Employment Act" means the Employment Act 2002(**c**); "Employment Rights Act" means the Employment Rights Act 1996(**d**); "Employment Tribunals Act" means the Employment Tribunals Act 1996(**e**);

"Employment Tribunal Office" means any office which has been established for any area in either England & Wales or Scotland specified by the President and which carries out administrative functions in support of functions being carried out by a tribunal or chairman, and in relation to particular proceedings it is the office notified to the parties in accordance with rule 61(3) of Schedule 1;

"enactment" includes an enactment comprised in, or in an instrument made under, an Act of the Scottish Parliament;

"Equal Pay Act" means the Equal Pay Act 1970(**f**);

"excluded person" means, in relation to any proceedings, a person who has been excluded from all or part of the proceedings by virtue of:—

(a) a direction of a Minister of the Crown under rule 54(1)(b) or (c) of Schedule 1, or

---

(**a**) 1995 c. 50.
(**b**) 2000 c. 7.
(**c**) 2002 c. 22.
(**d**) 1996 c. 18.
(**e**) 1996 c.l 7.
(**f**) 1970 c.41; section 2A was inserted by the Equal Pay (Amendment) Regulations 1983 (S.I. 1983/1794).

(b) an order of the tribunal under rule 54(2)(a) read with 54(1)(b) or (c) of Schedule 1;

"hearing" means a case management discussion, pre-hearing review, review hearing or Hearing (as those terms are defined in Schedule 1) or a sitting of a chairman or a tribunal duly constituted for the purpose of receiving evidence, hearing addresses and witnesses or doing anything lawful to enable the chairman or tribunal to reach a decision on any question;

"legally represented" has the meaning set out in rule 38(5) of Schedule 1; "Lord President" means the Lord President of the Court of Session; "misconceived" includes having no reasonable prospect of success;

"national security proceedings" means proceedings in relation to which a direction is given under rule 54(1) of Schedule 1, or an order is made under rule 54(2) of that Schedule;

"old (England & Wales) regulations" means the Employment Tribunals (Constitution and Rules of Procedure) (Scotland) Regulations 2001;

"old (Scotland) regulations" means the Employment Tribunals (Constitution and Rules of Procedure) Regulations 2001;

"panel of chairmen" means a panel referred to in regulation 8(3)(a);

"President" means, in England and Wales, the person appointed or nominated by the Lord Chancellor to discharge for the time being the functions of the President of Employment Tribunals (England and Wales), and, in Scotland, the person appointed or nominated by the Lord President to discharge for the time being the functions of the President of Employment Tribunals (Scotland);

"Race Relations Act" means the Race Relations Act 1976(**a**);

"Regional Chairman" means a member of the panel of chairmen who has been appointed to the position of Regional Chairman in accordance with regulation 6 or who has been nominated to discharge the functions of a Regional Chairman in accordance with regulation 6;

"Register" means the Register of judgments and written reasons kept in accordance with regulation 17;

"Secretary" means a person for the time being appointed to act as the Secretary of employment tribunals either in England and Wales or in Scotland;

"Sex Discrimination Act" means the Sex Discrimination Act 1975(**b**);

"special advocate" means a person appointed in accordance with rule 8 of Schedule 2;

"tribunal" means an employment tribunal established in accordance with regulation 5, and in relation to any proceedings means the tribunal to which the proceedings have been referred by the President, Vice President or a Regional Chairman;

(**a**) 1976 c. 74.
(**b**) 1975 c. 65.

"TULR(C)A" means the Trade Union and Labour Relations (Consolidation) Act 1992(a);

"Vice President" means a person who has been appointed to the position of Vice President in accordance with regulation 7 or who has been nominated to discharge the functions of the Vice President in accordance with that regulation;

"writing" includes writing delivered by means of electronic communication.

Overriding objective

3.—(1) The overriding objective of these regulations and the rules in Schedules 1, 2, 3, 4 and 5 is to enable tribunals and chairmen to deal with cases justly.

(2) Dealing with a case justly includes, so far as practicable:—

(a) ensuring that the parties are on an equal footing;

(b) dealing with the case in ways which are proportionate to the complexity or importance of the issues;

(c) ensuring that it is dealt with expeditiously and fairly; and

(d) saving expense.

(3) A tribunal or chairman shall seek to give effect to the overriding objective when it or he:—

(a) exercises any power given to it or him by these regulations or the rules in Schedules 1, 2, 3, 4 and 5; or

(b) interprets these regulations or any rule in Schedules 1, 2, 3, 4 and 5.

(4) The parties shall assist the tribunal or the chairman to further the overriding objective.

President of Employment Tribunals

4.—(1) There shall be a President of Employment Tribunals (England and Wales), responsible for the administration of justice by tribunals and chairmen in England and Wales, who shall be appointed by the Lord Chancellor and shall be a person described in paragraph (3).

(2) There shall be a President of Employment Tribunals (Scotland), responsible for the administration of justice by tribunals and chairmen in Scotland, who shall be appointed by the Lord President and shall be a person described in paragraph (3).

(3) A President shall be a person:—

(a) 1992 c. 52.

(a) having a seven year general qualification within the meaning of section 71 of the Courts and Legal Services Act 1990(a);

(b) being an advocate or solicitor admitted in Scotland of at least seven years standing; or

(c) being a member of the Bar of Northern Ireland or solicitor of the Supreme Court of Northern Ireland of at least seven years standing.

(4) A President may resign his office by notice in writing to the appointing office holder.

(5) If the appointing office holder is satisfied that the President is incapacitated by infirmity of mind or body from discharging the duties of his office, or the President is adjudged to be bankrupt or makes a composition or arrangement with his creditors, the appointing office holder may revoke his appointment.

(6) The functions of President under these Regulations may, if he is for any reason unable to act or during any vacancy in his office, be discharged by a person nominated for that purpose by the appointing office holder.

Establishment of employment tribunals

5.—(1) Each President shall, in relation to that part of Great Britain for which he has responsibility, from time to time determine the number of tribunals to be established for the purposes of determining proceedings.

(2) The President, a Regional Chairman or the Vice President shall determine, in relation to the area specified in relation to him, at what times and in what places in that area tribunals and chairmen shall sit.

Regional Chairmen

6.—(1) The Lord Chancellor may from time to time appoint Regional Chairmen from the panel of full-time chairmen and each Regional Chairman shall be responsible to the President (England and Wales) for the administration of justice by tribunals and chairmen in the area specified by the President (England and Wales) in relation to him.

(2) The President (England and Wales) or the Regional Chairman for an area may from time to time nominate a member of the panel of full time chairmen to discharge for the time being the functions of the Regional Chairman for that area.

Vice President

7.—(1) The Lord President may from time to time appoint a Vice President from the panel of full time chairmen and the Vice President shall be responsible to the President (Scotland) for the administration of justice by tribunals and chairmen in Scotland.

(a) 1990 c. 41.

(2) The President (Scotland) or the Vice President may from time to time nominate a member of the panel of full time chairmen to discharge for the time being the functions of the Vice President.

Panels of members of tribunals—general

8.—(1) There shall be three panels of members of Employment Tribunals (England and Wales), as set out in paragraph (3).

(2) There shall be three panels of members of Employment Tribunals (Scotland), as set out in paragraph (3).

(3) The panels referred to in paragraphs (1) and (2) are:—

(a) a panel of full-time and part-time chairmen appointed by the appointing office holder consisting of persons—

(i) having a seven year general qualification within the meaning of section 71 of the Courts and Legal Services Act 1990;

(ii) being an advocate or solicitor admitted in Scotland of at least seven years standing; or

(iii) being a member of the Bar of Northern Ireland or solicitor of the Supreme Court of Northern Ireland of at least seven years standing;

(b) a panel of persons appointed by the Secretary of State after consultation with such organisations or associations of organisations representative of employees as she sees fit; and

(c) a panel of persons appointed by the Secretary of State after consultation with such organisations or associations of organisations representative of employers as she sees fit.

(4) Members of the panels constituted under these Regulations shall hold and vacate office under the terms of the instrument under which they are appointed but may resign their office by notice in writing, in the case of a member of the panel of chairmen, to the appointing office holder and, in any other case, to the Secretary of State; and any such member who ceases to hold office shall be eligible for reappointment.

(5) The President may establish further specialist panels of chairmen and persons referred to in paragraphs (3)(b) and (c) and may select persons from such specialist panels in order to deal with proceedings in which particular specialist knowledge would be beneficial.

Composition of tribunals—general

9.—(1) For each hearing, the President, Vice President or the Regional Chairman shall select a chairman, who shall, subject to regulation 11, be a member of the panel of chairmen, and the President, Vice President or the Regional Chairman may select himself.

(2) In any proceedings which are to be determined by a tribunal comprising a chairman and two other members, the President, Regional

Chairman or Vice President shall, subject to regulation 11, select one of those other members from the panel of persons appointed by the Secretary of State under regulation 8(3)(b) and the other from the panel of persons appointed under regulation 8(3)(c).

(3) In any proceedings which are to be determined by a tribunal whose composition is described in paragraph (2) or, as the case may be, regulation 1 l(b), those proceedings may, with the consent of the parties, be heard and determined in the absence of any one member other than the chairman.

(4) The President, Vice President, or a Regional Chairman may at any time select from the appropriate panel another person in substitution for the chairman or other member of the tribunal previously selected to hear any proceedings before a tribunal or chairman.

Panels of members of tribunals— national security proceedings

10. In relation to national security proceedings, the President shall:—

(a) select a panel of persons from the panel of chairmen to act as chairmen in such cases; and

(b) select:—

(i) a panel of persons from the panel referred to in regulation 8(3)(b) as persons suitable to act as members in such cases; and

(ii) a panel of persons from the panel referred to in regulation 8(3)(c) as persons suitable to act as members in such cases.

Composition of tribunals— national security proceedings

11. In relation to national security proceedings:—

(a) the President, the Regional Chairman or the Vice President shall select a chairman, who shall be a member of the panel selected in accordance with regulation 10(a), and the President, Regional Chairman or Vice President may select himself; and

(b) in any such proceedings which are to be determined by a tribunal comprising a chairman and two other members, the President, Regional Chairman or Vice President shall select one of those other members from the panel selected in accordance with regulation 10(b)(i) and the other from the panel selected in accordance with regulation 10(b)(ii).

Modification of section 4 of the Employment Tribunals Act (national security proceedings)

12.—(l)For the purposes of national security proceedings section 4 of the Employment Tribunals Act shall be modified as follows.

(2) In section 4(1)(a), for the words "in accordance with regulations made under section 1(1)" substitute the words "in accordance with

regulation 11 (a) of the Employment Tribunals (Constitution and Rules of Procedure) Regulations 2004".

(3) In section 4(1)(b), for the words "in accordance with regulations so made" substitute the words "in accordance with regulation 11 (b) of those Regulations".

(4) In section 4(5), for the words "in accordance with Regulations made under section 1(1)" substitute the words "in accordance with regulation 10(**a**) of the Employment Tribunals (Constitution and Rules of Procedure) Regulations 2004".

Practice directions

13.—(l)The President may make practice directions about the procedure of employment tribunals in the area for which he is responsible, including practice directions about the exercise by tribunals or chairmen of powers under these Regulations or the Schedules to them.

(2) The power of the President to make practice directions under paragraph (1) includes power:—

    (a) to vary or revoke practice directions;

    (b) to make different provision for different cases or different areas, including different provision for specific types of proceedings.

(3) The President shall publish a practice direction made under paragraph (1), and any revocation or variation of it, in such manner as he considers appropriate for bringing it to the attention of the persons to whom it is addressed.

Power to prescribe

14.—(1) The Secretary of State may prescribe—

    (a) one or more versions of a form, one of which shall be used by all claimants for the purpose of commencing proceedings in an employment tribunal ("claim form") except any claim or proceedings listed in paragraph (3);

    (b) one or more versions of a form, one of which shall be used by all respondents to a claim for the purpose of responding to a claim before an employment tribunal ("response form") except respondents to a claim or proceedings listed in paragraph (3); and

    (c) that the provision of certain information and answering of certain questions in a claim form or in a response form is mandatory in all proceedings save those listed in paragraph (3).

(2) The Secretary of State shall publish the forms and matters prescribed pursuant to paragraph (1) in such manner as she considers appropriate in order to bring them to the attention of potential claimants, respondents and their advisers.

(3) The proceedings referred to in paragraph (1) are:—

(a) those referred to an employment tribunal by a court;

(b) proceedings to which any of Schedules 3 to 5 apply; or

(c) proceedings brought under any of the following enactments:—

> (i) sections 19, 20 or 22 of the National Minimum Wage Act 1998(a);
> (ii) section 11 of the Employment Rights Act where the proceedings are brought by the employer.

Calculation of time limits

15.—(1) Any period of time for doing any act required or permitted to be done under any of the rules in Schedules 1, 2, 3, 4 and 5, or under any decision, order or judgment of a tribunal or a chairman, shall be calculated in accordance with paragraphs (2) to (6).

(2) Where any act must or may be done within a certain number of days of or from an event, the date of that event shall not be included in the calculation. For example, a respondent is sent a copy of a claim on 1st October. He must present a response to the Employment Tribunal Office within 28 days of the date on which he was sent the copy. The last day for presentation of the response is 29th October.

(3) Where any act must or may be done not less than a certain number of days before or after an event, the date of that event shall not be included in the calculation. For example, if a party wishes to submit representations in writing for consideration by a tribunal at a hearing, he must submit them not less than 7 days before the hearing. If the hearing is fixed for 8th October, the representations must be submitted no later than 1st October.

(4) Where the tribunal or a chairman gives any decision, order or judgment which imposes a time limit for doing any act, the last date for compliance shall, wherever practicable, be expressed as a calendar date.

(5) In rule 14(4) of Schedule 1 the requirement to send the notice of hearing to the parties not less than 14 days before the date fixed for the hearing shall not be construed as a requirement for service of the notice to have been effected not less than 14 days before the hearing date, but as a requirement for the notice to have been placed in the post not less than 14 days before that date. For example, a hearing is fixed for 15th October. The last day on which the notice may be placed in the post is 1st October.

(6) Where any act must or may have been done within a certain number of days of a document being sent to a person by the Secretary, the date when the document was sent shall, unless the contrary is proved, be regarded as the date on the letter from the Secretary which accompanied the document. For example, a respondent must present his response to a

---

(a) 1998 c.39.

claim to the Employment Tribunal Office within 28 days on the date of which he was sent a copy of the claim. If the letter from the Secretary sending him a copy of the claim is dated 1st October, the last day for presentation of the response is 29th October.

Application of Schedules 1-5 to proceedings

16.—(1) Subject to paragraphs (2) and (3), the rules in Schedule 1 shall apply in relation to all proceedings before an employment tribunal except where separate rules of procedure made under the provisions of any enactment are applicable.

(2) In proceedings to which the rules in Schedule 1 apply and in which any power conferred on the Minister, the tribunal or a chairman by rule 54 (national security proceedings) of Schedule 1 is exercised, Schedule 1 shall be modified in accordance with Schedule 2.

(3) The rules in Schedules 3, 4 and 5 shall apply to modify the rules in Schedule 1 in relation to proceedings which consist, respectively, in:—

(a) an appeal by a person assessed to levy imposed under a levy order made under section 12 of the Industrial Training Act 1982(**b**);

(b) an appeal against an improvement or prohibition notice under section 24 of the Health and Safety at Work etc Act 1974; and

(c) an appeal against a non-discrimination notice under section 68 of the Sex Discrimination Act, section 59 of the Race Relations Act or paragraph 10 of Schedule 3 to the Disability Rights Commission Act 1999(**a**).

Register

17.—(1) The Secretary shall maintain a Register which shall be open to the inspection of any person without charge at all reasonable hours.

(2) The Register shall contain a copy of all judgments and any written reasons issued by any tribunal or chairman which are required to be entered in the Register in accordance with the rules in Schedules 1 to 5.

(3) The Register, or any part of it, may be kept by means of a computer.

Proof of decisions of tribunals

18. The production in any proceedings in any court of a document purporting to be certified by the Secretary to be a true copy of an entry of a judgment in the Register shall, unless the contrary is proved, be sufficient evidence of the document and of the facts stated therein.

(**b**) 1982 c. 10.
(**a**) 1999 c. 17.

Jurisdiction of tribunals in Scotland and in England & Wales

19.—(1) An employment tribunal in England or Wales shall only have jurisdiction to deal with proceedings (referred to as "English and Welsh proceedings") where—

(a) the respondent or one of the respondents resides or carries on business in England and Wales;

(b) had the remedy been by way of action in the county court, the cause of action would have arisen wholly or partly in England and Wales;

(c) the proceedings are to determine a question which has been referred to the tribunal by a court in England and Wales; or

(d) in the case of proceedings to which Schedule 3, 4 or 5 applies, the proceedings relate to matters arising in England and Wales.

(2) An employment tribunal in Scotland shall only have jurisdiction to deal with proceedings (referred to as "Scottish proceedings") where—

(a) the respondent or one of the respondents resides or carries on business in Scotland;

(b) the proceedings relate to a contract of employment the place of execution or performance of which is in Scotland;

(c) the proceedings are to determine a question which has been referred to the tribunal by a sheriff in Scotland; or

(d) in the case of proceedings to which Schedule 3, 4 or 5 applies, the proceedings relate to matters arising in Scotland.

Transitional provisions

20.—(1) These Regulations and Schedules 1 to 5 to them shall apply in relation to all proceedings to which they relate where those proceedings were commenced on or after 1 October 2004.

(2) These Regulations and Schedules 1 and 2 to them (with the exception of rules 1 to 3 and 38 to 48 of Schedule 1) shall apply to proceedings:—

(a) which were commenced prior to 1 October 2004; and

(b) to which Schedule 1 to either the old (England & Wales) regulations or the old (Scotland) regulations applied;

provided that a copy of the originating application was not sent to the respondent prior to 1 October 2004.

(3) In relation to the proceedings described in paragraph (2), the following provisions of Schedule 1 to the old (England & Wales) regulations or the old (Scotland) regulations (as the case may be) shall continue to apply:—

(a) rule 1 (originating application);

(b) rule 2 (action upon receipt of originating application) with the exception of paragraphs (2), (4) and (5) of that rule; and

(c) rule 14 (costs).

(4) In relation to proceedings described in paragraph (2) but where a copy of the originating application was sent to the respondent prior to 1 October 2004, Schedules 1 and 2 to these Regulations shall apply with the exception of rules 1 to 9, 21 to 24, 33 and 38 to 48 of Schedule 1 and rules 2, 3 and 4 of Schedule 2.

(5) In relation to proceedings described in paragraph (4), the following provisions of the old (England & Wales) regulations or the old (Scotland) regulations (as the case may be) shall continue to apply:—

(a) in Schedule 1:—

(i) rule 1 (originating application);
(ii) rule 2 (action upon receipt of originating application) with the exception of paragraphs (2), (4) and (5) of that rule;
(iii) rule 3 (appearance by respondent);
(iv) rule 8 (national security);
(v) rule 14 (costs); and

(b) rule 1 of Schedule 2.

(6) In relation to proceedings commenced prior to 1 October 2004 and to which Schedule 4, 5 or 6 to the old (England & Wales) regulations or the old (Scotland) regulations (as the case may be) applied, the provisions of those schedules shall continue to apply to such proceedings.

Gerry Sutcliffe,
Parliamentary Under Secretary of State for Employment
Relations, Competition and Consumers,
19th July 2004   Department of Trade and Industry

SCHEDULE 1   Regulation 16

THE EMPLOYMENT TRIBUNALS RULES OF PROCEDURE

HOW TO BRING A CLAIM

Starting a claim

1.—(1) A claim shall be brought before an employment tribunal by the claimant presenting to an Employment Tribunal Office the details of the claim in writing. Those details must include all the relevant required information (subject to paragraph (5) of this rule and to rule 53 (Employment Agencies Act 1973)).

(2) The claim may only be presented to an Employment Tribunal Office in England and Wales if it relates to English and Welsh proceedings (defined in regulation 19(1)). The claim may only be presented to an Employment Tribunal Office in Scotland if it relates to Scottish proceedings (defined in regulation 19(2)).

(3) Unless it is a claim in proceedings described in regulation 14(3), a claim which is presented on or after 6 April 2005 must be presented on a claim form which has been prescribed by the Secretary of State in accordance with regulation 14.

(4) Subject to paragraph (5) and to rule 53, the required information in relation to the claim is—

    (a) each claimant's name;

    (b) each claimant's address;

    (c) the name of each person against whom the claim is made ("the respondent");

    (d) each respondent's address;

    (e) details of the claim;

    (f) whether or not the claimant is or was an employee of the respondent;

    (g) whether or not the claim includes a complaint that the respondent has dismissed the claimant or has contemplated doing so;

    (h) whether or not the claimant has raised the subject matter of the claim with the respondent in writing at least 28 days prior to presenting the claim to an Employment Tribunal Office;

    (i) if the claimant has not done as described in (h), why he has not done so.

(5) In the following circumstances the required information identified below is not required to be provided in relation to that claim—

    (a) if the claimant is not or was not an employee of the respondent, the information in paragraphs (4)(g) to (i) is not required;

(b) if the claimant was an employee of the respondent and the claim consists only of a complaint that the respondent has dismissed the claimant or has contemplated doing so, the information in paragraphs (4)(h) and (i) is not required;

(c) if the claimant was an employee of the respondent and the claim does not relate to the claimant being dismissed or a contemplated dismissal by the respondent, and the claimant has raised the subject matter of the claim with the respondent as described in paragraph (4)(h), the information in paragraph (4)(i) is not required.

(6) References in this rule to being dismissed or a dismissal by the respondent do not include references to constructive dismissal.

(7) Two or more claimants may present their claims in the same document if their claims arise out of the same set of facts.

(8) When section 32 of the Employment Act applies to the claim or part of one and a chairman considers in accordance with subsection (6) of section 32 that there has been a breach of subsections (2) to (4) of that section, neither a chairman nor a tribunal shall consider the substance of the claim (or the relevant part of it) until such time as those subsections have been complied with in relation to the claim or the relevant part of it.

ACCEPTANCE OF CLAIM PROCEDURE

What the tribunal does after receiving the claim

2.—(1) On receiving the claim the Secretary shall consider whether the claim or part of it should be accepted in accordance with rule 3. If a claim or part of one is not accepted the tribunal shall not proceed to deal with any part which has not been accepted (unless it is accepted at a later date). If no part of a claim is accepted the claim shall not be copied to the respondent.

(2) If the Secretary accepts the claim or part of it, he shall—

(a) send a copy of the claim to each respondent and record in writing the date on which it was sent;

(b) inform the parties in writing of the case number of the claim (which must from then on be referred to in all correspondence relating to the claim) and the address to which notices and other communications to the Employment Tribunal Office must be sent;

(c) inform the respondent in writing about how to present a response to the claim, the time limit for doing so, what may happen if a response is not entered within the time limit and that the respondent has a right to receive a copy of any judgment disposing of the claim;

(d) when any enactment relevant to the claim provides for conciliation, notify the parties that the services of a conciliation officer are available to them;

(e) when rule 22 (fixed period for conciliation) applies, notify the parties of the date on which the conciliation officer's duty to conciliate ends and that after that date the services of a conciliation officer shall be available to them only in limited circumstances; and

(f) if only part of the claim has been accepted, inform the claimant and any respondent which parts of the claim have not been accepted and that the tribunal shall not proceed to deal with those parts unless they are accepted at a later date.

When the claim will not be accepted by the Secretary

3.—(1) When a claim is required by rule 1(3) to be presented using a prescribed form, but the prescribed form has not been used, the Secretary shall not accept the claim and shall return it to the claimant with an explanation of why the claim has been rejected and provide a prescribed claim form.

(2) The Secretary shall not accept the claim (or a relevant part of one) if it is clear to him that one or more of the following circumstances applies—

(a) the claim does not include all the relevant required information;

(b) the tribunal does not have power to consider the claim (or that relevant part of it); or

(c) section 32 of the Employment Act (complaints about grievances) applies to the claim or part of it and the claim has been presented to the tribunal in breach of subsections (2) to (4) of section 32.

(3) If the Secretary decides not to accept a claim or part of one for any of the reasons in paragraph (2), he shall refer the claim together with a statement of his reasons for not accepting it to a chairman. The chairman shall decide in accordance with the criteria in paragraph (2) whether the claim or part of it should be accepted and allowed to proceed.

(4) If the chairman decides that the claim or part of one should be accepted he shall inform the Secretary in writing and the Secretary shall accept the relevant part of the claim and then proceed to deal with it in accordance with rule 2(2).

(5) If the chairman decides that the claim or part of it should not be accepted he shall record his decision together with the reasons for it in writing in a document signed by him. The Secretary shall as soon as is reasonably practicable inform the claimant of that decision and the reasons for it in writing together with information on how that decision may be reviewed or appealed.

(6) Where a claim or part of one has been presented to the tribunal in breach of subsections (2) to (4) of section 32 of the Employment Act, the Secretary shall notify the claimant of the time limit which applies to the claim or the part of it concerned and shall inform the claimant of the consequences of not complying with section 32 of that Act.

(7) Except for the purposes of paragraph (6) and (8) or any appeal to the Employment Appeal Tribunal, where a chairman has decided that a claim or part of one should not be accepted such a claim (or the relevant part of it) is to be treated as if it had not been received by the Secretary on that occasion.

(8) Any decision by a chairman not to accept a claim or part of one may be reviewed in accordance with rules 34 to 36. If the result of such review is that any parts of the claim should have been accepted, then paragraph (7) shall not apply to the relevant parts of that claim and the Secretary shall then accept such parts and proceed to deal with it as described in rule 2(2).

(9) A decision to accept or not to accept a claim or part of one shall not bind any future tribunal or chairman where any of the issues listed in paragraph (2) fall to be determined later in the proceedings.

(10) Except in rule 34 (review of other judgments and decisions), all references to a claim in the remainder of these rules are to be read as references to only the part of the claim which has been accepted.

RESPONSE

Responding to the claim

4.—(1) If the respondent wishes to respond to the claim made against him he must present his response to the Employment Tribunal Office within 28 days of the date on which he was sent a copy of the claim. The response must include all the relevant required information. The time limit for the respondent to present his response may be extended in accordance with paragraph (4).

(2) Unless it is a response in proceedings described in regulation 14(3), any response presented on or after 6 April 2005 must be on a response form prescribed by the Secretary of State pursuant to regulation 14.

(3) The required information in relation to the response is—

   (a) the respondent's full name;

   (b) the respondent's address;

   (c) whether or not the respondent wishes to resist the claim in whole or in part; and

   (d) if the respondent wishes to so resist, on what grounds.

(4) The respondent may apply under rule 11 for an extension of the time limit within which he is to present his response. The application must be presented to the Employment Tribunal Office within 28 days of the date on which the respondent was sent a copy of the claim (unless the application is made under rule 33(1)) and must explain why the respondent cannot comply with the time limit. Subject to rule 33, the chairman shall only extend the time within which a response may be presented if he is satisfied that it is just and equitable to do so.

(5) A single document may include the response to more than one claim if the relief claimed arises out of the same set of facts, provided that in respect of each of the claims to which the single response relates—

(a) the respondent intends to resist all the claims and the grounds for doing so are the same in relation to each claim; or

(b) the respondent does not intend to resist any of the claims.

(6) A single document may include the response of more than one respondent to a single claim provided that—

(a) each respondent intends to resist the claim and the grounds for doing so are the same for each respondent; or

(b) none of the respondents intends to resist the claim.

ACCEPTANCE OF RESPONSE PROCEDURE

What the tribunal does after receiving the response

5.—(1) On receiving the response the Secretary shall consider whether the response should be accepted in accordance with rule 6. If the response is not accepted it shall be returned to the respondent and (subject to paragraphs (5) and (6) of rule 6) the claim shall be dealt with as if no response to the claim had been presented.

(2) If the Secretary accepts the response he shall send a copy of it to all other parties and record in writing the date on which he does so.

When the response will not be accepted by the Secretary

6.—(1) Where a response is required to be presented using a prescribed form by rule 4(2), but the prescribed form has not been used, the Secretary shall not accept the response and shall return it to the respondent with an explanation of why the response has been rejected and provide a prescribed response form.

(2) The Secretary shall not accept the response if it is clear to him that any of the following circumstances apply—

(a) the response does not include all the required information (defined in rule 4(3));

(b) the response has not been presented within the relevant time limit.

(3) If the Secretary decides not to accept a response for either of the reasons in paragraph (2), he shall refer the response together with a statement of his reasons for not accepting the response to a chairman. The chairman shall decide in accordance with the criteria in paragraph (2) whether the response should be accepted.

(4) If the chairman decides that the response should be accepted he shall inform the Secretary in writing and the Secretary shall accept the response and then deal with it in accordance with rule 5(2).

(5) If the chairman decides that the response should not be accepted he shall record his decision together with the reasons for it in writing in a

document signed by him. The Secretary shall inform both the claimant and the respondent of that decision and the reasons for it. The Secretary shall also inform the respondent of the consequences for the respondent of that decision and how it may be reviewed or appealed.

(6) Any decision by a chairman not to accept a response may be reviewed in accordance with rules 34 to 36. If the result of such a review is that the response should have been accepted, then the Secretary shall accept the response and proceed to deal with the response as described in rule 5(2).

Counterclaims

7.—(1) When a respondent wishes to present a claim against the claimant ("a counterclaim") in accordance with article 4 of the Employment Tribunals Extension of Jurisdiction (England and Wales) Order 1994(**a**), or as the case may be, article 4 of the Employment Tribunals Extension of Jurisdiction (Scotland) Order 1994(**b**), he must present the details of his counterclaim to the Employment Tribunal Office in writing. Those details must include—

(a) the respondent's name;

(b) the respondent's address;

(c) the name of each claimant whom the counterclaim is made against;

(d) the claimant's address;

(e) details of the counterclaim.

(2) A chairman may in relation to particular proceedings by order made under rule 10(1) establish the procedure which shall be followed by the respondent making the counterclaim and any claimant responding to the counterclaim.

(3) The President may by a practice direction made under regulation 13 make provision for the procedure which is to apply to counterclaims generally.

CONSEQUENCES OF A RESPONSE NOT BEING PRESENTED OR ACCEPTED

Default judgments

8.—(1) In any proceedings if the relevant time limit for presenting a response has passed, a chairman may, in the circumstances listed in paragraph (2), issue a default judgment to determine the claim without a hearing if he considers it appropriate to do so.

(**a**) S.I. 1994/1623.
(**b**) S.I. 1994/1624.

(2) Those circumstances are when either—

(a) no response in those proceedings has been presented to the Employment Tribunal Office within the relevant time limit; or

(b) a response has been so presented, but a decision has been made not to accept the response either by the Secretary under rule 6(1) or by a chairman under rule 6(3), and the Employment Tribunal Office has not received an application under rule 34 to have that decision reviewed;

and the claimant has not informed the Employment Tribunal Office in writing either that he does not wish a default judgment to be issued or that the claim has been settled.

(3) A default judgment may determine liability only or it may determine liability and remedy. If a default judgment determines remedy it shall be such remedy as it appears to the chairman that the claimant is entitled to on the basis of the information before him.

(4) Any default judgment issued by a chairman under this rule shall be recorded in writing and shall be signed by him. The Secretary shall send a copy of that judgment to the parties, to ACAS, and, if the proceedings were referred to the tribunal by a court, to that court. The Secretary shall also inform the parties of their right to have the default judgment reviewed under rule 33. The Secretary shall put a copy of the default judgment on the Register (subject to rule 49 (sexual offences and the Register)).

(5) The claimant or respondent may apply to have the default judgment reviewed in accordance with rule 33.

(6) If the parties settle the proceedings (either by means of a compromise agreement (as defined in rule 23(2)) or through ACAS) before or on the date on which a default judgment in those proceedings is issued, the default judgment shall have no effect.

(7) When paragraph (6) applies, either party may apply under rule 33 to have the default judgment revoked.

Taking no further part in the proceedings

9. A respondent who has not presented a response to a claim or whose response has not been accepted shall not be entitled to take any part in the proceedings except to—

(a) make an application under rule 33 (review of default judgments);

(b) make an application under rule 35 (preliminary consideration of application for review) in respect of rule 34(3)(a) and (b);

(c) be called as a witness by another person; or

(d) be sent a copy of a document or corrected entry in accordance with rule 8(4), 29(2) or 37; and in these rules the word "party" or "respondent" includes a respondent only in relation to his entitlement to take such a part in the proceedings, and in relation to any such part which he takes.

CASE MANAGEMENT

General power to manage proceedings

10.—(1) Subject to the following rules, the chairman may at any time either on the application of a party or on his own initiative make an order in relation to any matter which appears to him to be appropriate. Such orders may be any of those listed in paragraph (2) or such other orders as he thinks fit. Subject to the following rules, orders may be issued as a result of a chairman considering the papers before him in the absence of the parties, or at a hearing (see regulation 2 for the definition of "hearing").

(2) Examples of orders which may be made under paragraph (1) are orders—

(a) as to the manner in which the proceedings are to be conducted, including any time limit to be observed;

(b) that a party provide additional information;

(c) requiring the attendance of any person in Great Britain either to give evidence or to produce documents or information;

(d) requiring any person in Great Britain to disclose documents or information to a party to allow a party to inspect such material as might be ordered by a County Court (or in Scotland, by a sheriff);

(e) extending any time limit, whether or not expired (subject to rules 4(4), 11(2), 25(5), 30(5), 33(1), 35(1), 38(7) and 42(5) of this Schedule, and to rule 3(4) of Schedule 2);

(f) requiring the provision of written answers to questions put by the tribunal or chairman;

(g) that, subject to rule 22(8), a short conciliation period be extended into a standard conciliation period;

(h) staying (in Scotland, sisting) the whole or part of any proceedings;

(i) that part of the proceedings be dealt with separately;

(j) that different claims be considered together;

(k) that any person who the chairman or tribunal considers may be liable for the remedy claimed should be made a respondent in the proceedings;

(l) dismissing the claim against a respondent who is no longer directly interested in the claim;

(m) postponing or adjourning any hearing;

(n) varying or revoking other orders;

(o) giving notice to the parties of a pre-hearing review or the Hearing;

(p) giving notice under rule 19;

(q) giving leave to amend a claim or response;

(r) that any person who the chairman or tribunal considers has an interest in the outcome of the proceedings may be joined as a party to the proceedings;

(s) that a witness statement be prepared or exchanged; or

(t) as to the use of experts or interpreters in the proceedings.

(3) An order may specify the time at or within which and the place at which any act is required to be done. An order may also impose conditions and it shall inform the parties of the potential consequences of non-compliance set out in rule 13.

(4) When a requirement has been imposed under paragraph (1) the person subject to the requirement may make an application under rule 11 (applications in proceedings) for the order to be varied or revoked.

(5) An order described in either paragraph (2)(d) which requires a person other than a party to grant disclosure or inspection of material may be made only when the disclosure sought is necessary in order to dispose fairly of the claim or to save expense.

(6) Any order containing a requirement described in either sub-paragraph (2)(c) or (d) shall state that under section 7(4) of the Employment Tribunals Act, any person who without reasonable excuse fails to comply with the requirement shall be liable on summary conviction to a fine, and the document shall also state the amount of the maximum fine.

(7) An order as described in paragraph (2)(j) may be made only if all relevant parties have been given notice that such an order may be made and they have been given the opportunity to make oral or written representations as to why such an order should or should not be made.

(8) Any order made under this rule shall be recorded in writing and signed by the chairman and the Secretary shall inform all parties to the proceedings of any order made as soon as is reasonably practicable.

Applications in proceedings

11.—(1) At any stage of the proceedings a party may apply for an order to be issued, varied or revoked or for a case management discussion or pre-hearing review to be held.

(2) An application for an order must be made not less than 10 days before the date of the hearing at which it is to be considered (if any) unless it is not reasonably practicable to do so, or the chairman or tribunal considers it in the interests of justice that shorter notice be allowed. The application must (unless a chairman orders otherwise) be in writing to the Employment Tribunal Office and include the case number for the proceedings and the reasons for the request. If the application is for a case management discussion or a pre-hearing review to be held, it must identify any orders sought.

(3) An application for an order must include an explanation of how the order would assist the tribunal or chairman in dealing with the proceedings efficiently and fairly.

(4) When a party is legally represented in relation to the application (except where the application is for a witness order described in rule 10(2)(c) only), that party or his representative must, at the same time as the application is sent to the Employment Tribunal Office, provide all other parties with the following information in writing—

(a) details of the application and the reasons why it is sought;

(b) notification that any objection to the application must be sent to the Employment Tribunal Office within 7 days of receiving the application, or before the date of the hearing (whichever date is the earlier);

(c) that any objection to the application must be copied to both the Employment Tribunal Office and all other parties;

and the party or his representative must confirm in writing to the Employment Tribunal Office that this rule has been complied with.

(5) Where a party is not legally represented in relation to the application, the Secretary shall inform all other parties of the matters listed in paragraphs (4)(a) to (c).

(6) A chairman may refuse a party's application and if he does so the Secretary shall inform the parties in writing of such refusal unless the application is refused at a hearing.

Chairman acting on his own initiative

12.—(1) Subject to paragraph (2) and to rules 10(7) and 18(7), a chairman may make an order on his own initiative with or without hearing the parties or giving them an opportunity to make written or oral representations. He may also decide to hold a case management discussion or pre-hearing review on his own initiative.

(2) Where a chairman makes an order without giving the parties the opportunity to make representations—

(a) the Secretary must send to the party affected by such order a copy of the order and a statement explaining the right to make an application under paragraph (2)(b); and

(b) a party affected by the order may apply to have it varied or revoked.

(3) An application under paragraph (2)(b) must (subject to rule 10(2)(e)) be made before the time at which, or the expiry of the period within which, the order was to be complied with. Such an application must (unless a chairman orders otherwise) be made in writing to an Employment Tribunal Office and it must include the reasons for the application. Paragraphs (4) and (5) of rule 11 apply in relation to informing the other parties of the application.

Compliance with orders and practice directions

13.—(1) If a party does not comply with an order made under these rules, under rule 8 of Schedule 3, rule 7 of Schedule 4 or a practice direction, a chairman or tribunal—

   (a) may make an order in respect of costs or preparation time under rules 38 to 46; or

   (b) may (subject to paragraph (2) and rule 19) at a pre-hearing review or a Hearing make an order to strike out the whole or part of the claim or, as the case may be, the response and, where appropriate, order that a respondent be debarred from responding to the claim altogether.

(2) An order may also provide that unless the order is complied with, the claim or, as the case may be, the response shall be struck out on the date of non-compliance without further consideration of the proceedings or the need to give notice under rule 19 or hold a pre-hearing review or Hearing.

(3) Chairmen and tribunals shall comply with any practice directions issued under regulation 13.

DIFFERENT TYPES OF HEARING

Hearings—general

14.—(1) A chairman or a tribunal (depending on the relevant rule) may hold the following types of hearing—

   (a) a case management discussion under rule 17;

   (b) a pre-hearing review under rule 18;

   (c) a Hearing under rule 26; or

   (d) a review hearing under rule 33 or 36.

(2) So far as it appears appropriate to do so, the chairman or tribunal shall seek to avoid formality in his or its proceedings and shall not be bound by any enactment or rule of law relating to the admissibility of evidence in proceedings before the courts.

(3) The chairman or tribunal (as the case may be) shall make such enquiries of persons appearing before him or it and of witnesses as he or it considers appropriate and shall otherwise conduct the hearing in such manner as he or it considers most appropriate for the clarification of the issues and generally for the just handling of the proceedings.

(4) Unless the parties agree to shorter notice, the Secretary shall send notice of any hearing (other than a case management discussion) to every party not less than 14 days before the date fixed for the hearing and shall inform them that they have the opportunity to submit written representations and to advance oral argument. The Secretary shall give the parties reasonable notice before a case management discussion is held.

(5) If a party wishes to submit written representations for consideration at a hearing (other than a case management discussion) he shall present them to the Employment Tribunal Office not less than 7 days before the hearing and shall at the same time send a copy to all other parties.

(6) The tribunal or chairman may, if it or he considers it appropriate, consider representations in writing which have been submitted otherwise than in accordance with paragraph (5).

Use of electronic communications

15.—(1) A hearing (other than those mentioned in sub-paragraphs (c) and (d) of rule 14(1)) may be conducted by use of electronic communications provided that the chairman or tribunal conducting the hearing considers it just and equitable to do so.

(2) Where a hearing is required by these rules to be held in public and it is to be conducted by use of electronic communications in accordance with this rule then, subject to rule 16, it must be held in a place to which the public has access and using equipment so that the public is able to hear all parties to the communication.

Hearings which may be held in private

16.—(1) A hearing or part of one may be conducted in private for the purpose of hearing from any person evidence or representations which in the opinion of the tribunal or chairman is likely to consist of information—

(a) which he could not disclose without contravening a prohibition imposed by or by virtue of any enactment;

(b) which has been communicated to him in confidence, or which he has otherwise obtained in consequence of the confidence placed in him by another person; or

(c) the disclosure of which would, for reasons other than its effect on negotiations with respect to any of the matters mentioned in section 178(2) of TULR(C)A, cause substantial injury to any undertaking of his or any undertaking in which he works.

(2) Where a tribunal or chairman decides to hold a hearing or part of one in private, it or he shall give reasons for doing so. A member of the Council on Tribunals (in Scotland, a member of the Council on Tribunals or its Scottish Committee) shall be entitled to attend any Hearing or pre-hearing review taking place in private in his capacity as a member.

CASE MANAGEMENT DISCUSSIONS

Conduct of case management discussions

17.—(1)Case management discussions are interim hearings and may deal with matters of procedure and management of the proceedings and they may be held in private. Case management discussions shall be conducted by a chairman.

(2) Any determination of a person's civil rights or obligations shall not be dealt with in a case management discussion. The matters listed in rule

10(2) are examples of matters which may be dealt with at case management discussions. Orders and judgments listed in rule 18(7) may not be made at a case management discussion.

PRE-HEARING REVIEWS

Conduct of pre-hearing reviews

18.—(1) Pre-hearing reviews are interim hearings and shall be conducted by a chairman unless the circumstances in paragraph (3) are applicable. Subject to rule 16, they shall take place in public.

(2) At a pre-hearing review the chairman may carry out a preliminary consideration of the proceedings and he may—

(a) determine any interim or preliminary matter relating to the proceedings;

(b) issue any order in accordance with rule 10 or do anything else which may be done at a case management discussion;

(c) order that a deposit be paid in accordance with rule 20 without hearing evidence;

(d) consider any oral or written representations or evidence;

(e) deal with an application for interim relief made under section 161 of TULR(C)A or section 128 of the Employment Rights Act.

(3) Pre-hearing reviews shall be conducted by a tribunal composed in accordance with section 4(1) and (2) of the Employment Tribunals Act if—

(a) a party has made a request in writing not less than 10 days before the date on which the pre-hearing review is due to take place that the pre-hearing review be conducted by a tribunal instead of a chairman; and

(b) a chairman considers that one or more substantive issues of fact are likely to be determined at the pre-hearing review, that it would be desirable for the pre-hearing review to be conducted by a tribunal and he has issued an order that the pre-hearing review be conducted by a tribunal.

(4) If an order is made under paragraph (3), any reference to a chairman in relation to a pre-hearing review shall be read as a reference to a tribunal.

(5) Notwithstanding the preliminary or interim nature of a pre-hearing review, at a pre-hearing review the chairman may give judgment on any preliminary issue of substance relating to the proceedings. Judgments or orders made at a pre-hearing review may result in the proceedings being struck out or dismissed or otherwise determined with the result that a Hearing is no longer necessary in those proceedings.

(6) Before a judgment or order listed in paragraph (7) is made, notice must be given in accordance with rule 19. The judgments or order listed in

paragraph (7) must be made at a pre- hearing review or a Hearing if one of the parties has so requested. If no such request has been made such judgments or order may be made in the absence of the parties.

(7) Subject to paragraph (6), a chairman or tribunal may make a judgment or order:—

(a) as to the entitlement of any party to bring or contest particular proceedings;

(b) striking out or amending all or part of any claim or response on the grounds that it is scandalous, or vexatious or has no reasonable prospect of success;

(c) striking out any claim or response (or part of one) on the grounds that the manner in which the proceedings have been conducted by or on behalf of the claimant or the respondent (as the case may be) has been scandalous, unreasonable or vexatious;

(d) striking out a claim which has not been actively pursued;

(e) striking out a claim or response (or part of one) for non-compliance with an order or practice direction;

(f) striking out a claim where the chairman or tribunal considers that it is no longer possible to have a fair Hearing in those proceedings;

(g) making a restricted reporting order (subject to rule 50).

(8) A claim or response or any part of one may be struck out under these rules only on the grounds stated in sub-paragraphs (7)(b) to (f).

(9) If at a pre-hearing review a requirement to pay a deposit under rule 20 has been considered, the chairman who conducted that pre-hearing review shall not be a member of the tribunal at the Hearing in relation to those proceedings.

Notice requirements

19.—(1) Before a chairman or a tribunal makes a judgment or order described in rule 18(7), except where the order is one described in rule 13(2) or it is a temporary restricted reporting order made in accordance with rule 50, the Secretary shall send notice to the party against whom it is proposed that the order or judgment should be made. The notice shall inform him of the order or judgment to be considered and give him the opportunity to give reasons why the order or judgment should not be made. This paragraph shall not be taken to require the Secretary to send such notice to that party if that party has been given an opportunity to give reasons orally to the chairman or the tribunal as to why the order should not be made.

(2) Where a notice required by paragraph (1) is sent in relation to an order to strike out a claim which has not been actively pursued, unless the

contrary is proved, the notice shall be treated as if it were received by the addressee if it has been sent to the address specified in the claim as the address to which notices are to be sent (or to any subsequent replacement for that address which has been notified to the Employment Tribunal Office).

PAYMENT OF A DEPOSIT

Requirement to pay a deposit in order to continue with proceedings

20.—(1) At a pre-hearing review if a chairman considers that the contentions put forward by any party in relation to a matter required to be determined by a tribunal have little reasonable prospect of success, the chairman may make an order against that party requiring the party to pay a deposit of an amount not exceeding £500 as a condition of being permitted to continue to take part in the proceedings relating to that matter.

(2) No order shall be made under this rule unless the chairman has taken reasonable steps to ascertain the ability of the party against whom it is proposed to make the order to comply with such an order, and has taken account of any information so ascertained in determining the amount of the deposit.

(3) An order made under this rule, and the chairman's grounds for making such an order, shall be recorded in a document signed by the chairman. A copy of that document shall be sent to each of the parties and shall be accompanied by a note explaining that if the party against whom the order is made persists in making those contentions relating to the matter to which the order relates, he may have an award of costs or preparation time made against him and could lose his deposit.

(4) If a party against whom an order has been made does not pay the amount specified in the order to the Secretary either:—

(a) within the period of 21 days of the day on which the document recording the making of the order is sent to him; or

(b) within such further period, not exceeding 14 days, as the chairman may allow in the light of representations made by that party within the period of 21 days;

a chairman shall strike out the claim or response of that party or, as the case may be, the part of it to which the order relates.

(5) The deposit paid by a party under an order made under this rule shall be refunded to him in full except where rule 47 applies.

CONCILIATION

Documents to be sent to conciliators

21. In proceedings brought under the provisions of any enactment providing for conciliation, the Secretary shall send copies of all documents, orders, judgments, written reasons and notices to an ACAS conciliation officer except where the Secretary and ACAS have agreed otherwise.

Fixed period for conciliation

22.—(1) This rule and rules 23 and 24 apply to all proceedings before a tribunal which are brought under any enactment which provides for conciliation except national security proceedings and proceedings which include a claim made under one or more of the following enactments—

    (a) the Equal Pay Act, section 2(1);

    (b) the Sex Discrimination Act, Part II, section 63;

    (c) the Race Relations Act, Part II, section 54;

    (d) the Disability Discrimination Act, Part II, section 17A or 25(8)(**a**);

    (e) the Employment Equality (Sexual Orientation) Regulations 2003(**b**);

    (f) the Employment Equality (Religion or Belief) Regulations 2003(**a**); and

    (g) Employment Rights Act, sections 47B, 103A and 105(6A)(**b**).

(2) In all proceedings to which this rule applies there shall be a conciliation period to give a time limited opportunity for the parties to reach an ACAS conciliated settlement (the "conciliation period") In proceedings in which there is more than one respondent there shall be a conciliation period in relation to each respondent.

(3) In any proceedings to which this rule applies a Hearing shall not take place during a conciliation period and where the time and place of a Hearing has been fixed to take place during a conciliation period, such Hearing shall be postponed until after the end of any conciliation period. The fixing of the time and place for the Hearing may take place during a conciliation period. Pre-hearing reviews and case management discussions may take place during a conciliation period.

(4) In relation to each respondent the conciliation period commences on the date on which the Secretary sends a copy of the claim to that respondent. The duration of the conciliation period shall be determined in accordance with the following paragraphs and rule 23.

(**a**) These sections were inserted into the Disability Discrimination Act 1995 (c. 50) by regulations 3(1), 9 and 19 of the Disability Discrimination Act 1995 (Amendment) Regulations 2003 S.I. 2003/1673.
(**b**) S.I. 2003/1661.
(**a**) S.I. 2003/1660.
(**b**) These sections were inserted into the Employment Rights Act respectively by sections 2, 5 and 6 of the Public Interest Disclosure Act 1998 c. 23.

(5) In any proceedings which consist of claims under any of the following enactments (but no other enactments) the conciliation period is seven weeks (the "short conciliation period")—

    (a) Employment Tribunals Act, section 3 (breach of contract);

    (b) the following provisions of the Employment Rights Act—

        (i) sections 13 to 27 (failure to pay wages or an unauthorised deduction of wages);

        (ii) section 28 (right to a guarantee payment);

        (iii) section 50 (right to time off for public duties);

        (iv) section 52 (right to time off to look for work or arrange training);

        (v) section 53 (right to remuneration for time off under section 52);

        (vi) section 55 (right to time off for ante-natal care);

        (vii) section 56 (right to remuneration for time off under section 55);

        (viii) section 64 (failure to pay remuneration whilst suspended for medical reasons);

        (ix) section 68 (right to remuneration whilst suspended on maternity grounds);

        (x) sections 163 or 164 (failure to pay a redundancy payment);

    (c) the following provisions of TULR(C)A—

        (i) section 68 (right not to suffer deduction of unauthorised subscriptions)

        (ii) section 168 (time off for carrying out trade union duties);

        (iii) section 169 (payment for time off under section 168);

        (iv) section 170 (time off for trade union activities);

        (v) section 192 (failure to pay remuneration under a protective award);

    (d) regulation 11(5) of the Transfer of Undertakings (Protection of Employment) Regulations 1981 (failure to pay compensation following failure to inform or consult).

(6) In all other proceedings to which this rule applies the conciliation period is thirteen weeks (the "standard conciliation period").

(7) In proceedings to which the standard conciliation period applies, that period shall be extended by a period of a further two weeks if ACAS notifies the Secretary in writing that all of the following circumstances apply before the expiry of the standard conciliation period—

    (a) all parties to the proceedings agree to the extension of any relevant conciliation period;

    (b) a proposal for settling the proceedings has been made by a party and is under consideration by the other parties to the proceedings; and

(c) ACAS considers it probable that the proceedings will be settled during the further extended conciliation period.

(8) A short conciliation period in any proceedings may, if that period has not already ended, be extended into a standard conciliation period if a chairman considers on the basis of the complexity of the proceedings that a standard conciliation period would be more appropriate. Where a chairman makes an order extending the conciliation period in such circumstances, the Secretary shall inform the parties to the proceedings and ACAS in writing as soon as is reasonably practicable.

Early termination of conciliation period

23.—(1) Should one of the following circumstances arise during a conciliation period (be it short or standard) which relates to a particular respondent (referred to in this rule as the relevant respondent), that conciliation period shall terminate early on the relevant date specified (and if more than one circumstance or date listed below is applicable to any conciliation period, that conciliation period shall terminate on the earliest of those dates)—

(a) where a default judgment is issued against the relevant respondent which determines both liability and remedy, the date on which the default judgment is signed;

(b) where a default judgment is issued against the relevant respondent which determines liability only, the date which is 14 days after the date on which the default judgment is signed;

(c) where either the claim or the response entered by the relevant respondent is struck out, the date on which the judgment to strike out is signed;

(d) where the claim is withdrawn, the date of receipt by the Employment Tribunal Office of the notice of withdrawal;

(e) where the claimant or the relevant respondent has informed ACAS in writing that they do not wish to proceed with attempting to conciliate in relation to those proceedings, the date on which ACAS sends notice of such circumstances to the parties and to the Employment Tribunal Office;

(f) where the claimant and the relevant respondent have reached a settlement by way of a compromise agreement (including a compromise agreement to refer proceedings to arbitration), the date on which the Employment Tribunal Office receives notice from both of those parties to that effect;

(g) where the claimant and the relevant respondent have reached a settlement through a conciliation officer (including a settlement to refer the proceedings to arbitration), the date of the settlement;

(h) where no response presented by the relevant respondent has been accepted in the proceedings and no default judgment has been issued against that respondent, the date which is 14 days after the expiry of the time limit for presenting the response to the Secretary.

(2) Where a chairman or tribunal makes an order which re-establishes the relevant respondent's right to respond to the claim (for example, revoking a default judgment) and when that order is made, the conciliation period in relation to that respondent has terminated early under paragraph (1) or has otherwise expired, the chairman or tribunal may order that a further conciliation period shall apply in relation to that respondent if they consider it appropriate to do so.

(3) When an order is made under paragraph (2), the further conciliation period commences on the date of that order and the duration of that period shall be determined in accordance with paragraphs (5) to (8) of rule 22 and paragraph (1) of this rule as if the earlier conciliation period in relation to that respondent had not taken place.

Effect of staying or sisting proceedings on the conciliation period

24. Where during a conciliation period an order is made to stay (or in Scotland, sist) the proceedings, that order has the effect of suspending any conciliation period in those proceedings. Any unexpired portion of a conciliation period takes effect from the date on which the stay comes to an end (or in Scotland, the sist is recalled) and continues for the duration of the unexpired portion of that conciliation period or two weeks (whichever is the greater).

WITHDRAWAL OF PROCEEDINGS

Right to withdraw proceedings

25.—(1) A claimant may withdraw all or part of his claim at any time— this may be done either orally at a hearing or in writing in accordance with paragraph (2).

(2) To withdraw a claim or part of one in writing the claimant must inform the Employment Tribunal Office of the claim or the parts of it which are to be withdrawn. Where there is more than one respondent the notification must specify against which respondents the claim is being withdrawn.

(3) The Secretary shall inform all other parties of the withdrawal. Withdrawal takes effect on the date on which the Employment Tribunal Office (in the case of written notifications) or the tribunal (in the case of oral notification) receives notice of it and where the whole claim is withdrawn, subject to paragraph (4), proceedings are brought to an end against the relevant respondent on that date. Withdrawal does not affect proceedings as to costs, preparation time or wasted costs.

(4) Where a claim has been withdrawn, a respondent may make an application to have the proceedings against him dismissed. Such an

application must be made by the respondent in writing to the Employment Tribunal Office within 28 days of the notice of the withdrawal being sent to the respondent. If the respondent's application is granted and the proceedings are dismissed those proceedings cannot be continued by the claimant (unless the decision to dismiss is successfully reviewed or appealed).

(5) The time limit in paragraph (4) may be extended by a chairman if he considers it just and equitable to do so.

THE HEARING

Hearings

26.—(1) A Hearing is held for the purpose of determining outstanding procedural or substantive issues or disposing of the proceedings. In any proceedings there may be more than one Hearing and there may be different categories of Hearing, such as a Hearing on liability, remedies, costs (in Scotland, expenses) or preparation time.

(2) Any Hearing of a claim shall be heard by a tribunal composed in accordance with section 4(1) and (2) of the Employment Tribunals Act.

(3) Any Hearing of a claim shall take place in public, subject to rule 16.

What happens at the Hearing

27.—(1) The President, Vice President or a Regional Chairman shall fix the date, time and place of the Hearing and the Secretary shall send to each party a notice of the Hearing together with information and guidance as to procedure at the Hearing.

(2) Subject to rule 14(3), at the Hearing a party shall be entitled to give evidence, to call witnesses, to question witnesses and to address the tribunal.

(3) The tribunal shall require parties and witnesses who attend the Hearing to give their evidence on oath or affirmation.

(4) The tribunal may exclude from the Hearing any person who is to appear as a witness in the proceedings until such time as they give evidence if it considers it in the interests of justice to do so.

(5) If a party fails to attend or to be represented (for the purpose of conducting the party's case at the Hearing) at the time and place fixed for the Hearing, the tribunal may dismiss or dispose of the proceedings in the absence of that party or may adjourn the Hearing to a later date.

(6) If the tribunal wishes to dismiss or dispose of proceedings in the circumstances described in paragraph (5), it shall first consider any information in its possession which has been made available to it by the parties.

(7) At a Hearing a tribunal may exercise any powers which may be exercised by a chairman under these rules.

ORDERS, JUDGMENTS AND REASONS

Orders and judgments

28.—(1) Chairmen or tribunals may issue the following—

(a) a "judgment", which is a final determination of the proceedings or of a particular issue in those proceedings; it may include an award of compensation, a declaration or recommendation and it may also include orders for costs, preparation time or wasted costs;

(b) an "order", which may be issued in relation to interim matters and it will require a person to do or not to do something.

(2) If the parties agree in writing upon the terms of any order or judgment a chairman or tribunal may, if he or it thinks fit, make such order or judgment.

(3) At the end of a hearing the chairman (or, as the case may be, the tribunal) shall either issue any order or judgment orally or shall reserve the judgment or order to be given in writing at a later date.

(4) Where a tribunal is composed of three persons any order or judgment may be made or issued by a majority; and if a tribunal is composed of two persons only, the chairman has a second or casting vote.

Form and content of judgments

29.—(1) When judgment is reserved a written judgment shall be sent to the parties as soon as practicable. All judgments (whether issued orally or in writing) shall be recorded in writing and signed by the chairman.

(2) The Secretary shall provide a copy of the judgment to each of the parties and, where the proceedings were referred to the tribunal by a court, to that court. The Secretary shall include guidance to the parties on how the judgment may be reviewed or appealed.

(3) Where the judgment includes an award of compensation or a determination that one party is required to pay a sum to another (excluding an order for costs, expenses, allowances, preparation time or wasted costs), the document shall also contain a statement of the amount of compensation awarded, or of the sum required to be paid.

Reasons

30.—(1) A tribunal or chairman must give reasons (either oral or written) for any—

(a) judgment; or

(b) order, if a request for reasons is made before or at the hearing at which the order is made.

(2) Reasons may be given orally at the time of issuing the judgment or order or they may be reserved to be given in writing at a later date. If reasons are reserved, they shall be signed by the chairman and sent to the parties by the Secretary.

(3) Written reasons shall only be provided:—

(a) in relation to judgments if requested by one of the parties within the time limit set out in paragraph (5); or

(b) in relation to any judgment or order if requested by the Employment Appeal Tribunal at any time.

(4) When written reasons are provided, the Secretary shall send a copy of the reasons to all parties to the proceedings and record the date on which the reasons were sent. Written reasons shall be signed by the chairman.

(5) A request for written reasons for a judgment must be made by a party either orally at the hearing (if the judgment is issued at a hearing), or in writing within 14 days of the date on which the judgment was sent to the parties. This time limit may be extended by a chairman where he considers it just and equitable to do so.

(6) Written reasons for a judgment shall include the following information—

(a) the issues which the tribunal or chairman has identified as being relevant to the claim;

(b) if some identified issues were not determined, what those issues were and why they were not determined;

(c) findings of fact relevant to the issues which have been determined;

(d) a concise statement of the applicable law;

(e) how the relevant findings of fact and applicable law have been applied in order to determine the issues; and

(f) where the judgment includes an award of compensation or a determination that one party make a payment to the other, a table showing how the amount or sum has been calculated or a description of the manner in which it has been calculated.

Absence of chairman

31. Where it is not possible for a judgment, order or reasons to be signed by the chairman due to death, incapacity or absence—

(a) if the chairman has dealt with the proceedings alone the document shall be signed by the Regional Chairman, Vice President or President when it is practicable for him to do so; and

(b) if the proceedings have been dealt with by a tribunal composed of two or three persons, the document shall be signed by the other person or persons;

and any person who signs the document shall certify that the chairman is unable to sign.

The Register

32.—(1) Subject to rule 49, the Secretary shall enter a copy of the following documents in the Register—

(a) any judgment (including any costs, expenses, preparation time or wasted costs order); and

(b) any written reasons provided in accordance with rule 30 in relation to any judgment.

(2) Written reasons for judgments shall be omitted from the Register in any case in which evidence has been heard in private and the tribunal or chairman so orders. In such a case the Secretary shall send the reasons to each of the parties and where there are proceedings before a superior court relating to the judgment in question, he shall send the reasons to that court, together with a copy of the entry in the Register of the judgment to which the reasons relate.

POWER TO REVIEW JUDGMENTS AND DECISIONS

Review of default judgments

33.—(1) A party may apply to have a default judgment against or in favour of him reviewed. An application must be made in writing and presented to the Employment Tribunal Office within 14 days of the date on which the default judgment was sent to the parties. The 14 day time limit may be extended by a chairman if he considers that it is just and equitable to do so.

(2) The application must state the reasons why the default judgment should be varied or revoked. When it is the respondent applying to have the default judgment reviewed, the application must include with it the respondent's proposed response to the claim, an application for an extension of the time limit for presenting the response and an explanation of why rules 4(1) and (4) were not complied with.

(3) A review of a default judgment shall be conducted by a chairman in public. Notice of the hearing and a copy of the application shall be sent by the Secretary to all other parties.

(4) The chairman may—

(a) refuse the application for a review;

(b) vary the default judgment;

(c) revoke all or part of the default judgment;

(d) confirm the default judgment;

and all parties to the proceedings shall be informed by the Secretary in writing of the chairman's judgment on the application.

(5) A default judgment must be revoked if the whole of the claim was satisfied before the judgment was issued or if rule 8(6) applies. A chairman may revoke or vary all or part of a default judgment if the respondent has a reasonable prospect of successfully responding to the claim or part of it.

(6) In considering the application for a review of a default judgment the chairman must have regard to whether there was good reason for the response not having been presented within the applicable time limit.

(7) If the chairman decides that the default judgment should be varied or revoked and that the respondent should be allowed to respond to the claim the Secretary shall accept the response and proceed in accordance with rule 5(2).

Review of other judgments and decisions

34.—(1) Parties may apply to have certain judgments and decisions made by a tribunal or a chairman reviewed under rules 34 to 36. Those judgments and decisions are—

(a) a decision not to accept a claim, response or counterclaim;

(b) a judgment (other than a default judgment but including an order for costs, expenses, preparation time or wasted costs); and

(c) a decision made under rule 6(3) of Schedule 4;

and references to "decision" in rules 34 to 37 are references to the above judgments and decisions only. Other decisions or orders may not be reviewed under these rules.

(2) In relation to a decision not to accept a claim or response, only the party against whom the decision is made may apply to have the decision reviewed.

(3) Subject to paragraph (4), decisions may be reviewed on the following grounds only—

(a) the decision was wrongly made as a result of an administrative error;

(b) a party did not receive notice of the proceedings leading to the decision;

(c) the decision was made in the absence of a party;

(d) new evidence has become available since the conclusion of the hearing to which the decision relates, provided that its existence could not have been reasonably known of or foreseen at that time; or

(e) the interests of justice require such a review.

(4) A decision not to accept a claim or response may only be reviewed on the grounds listed in paragraphs (3)(a) and (e).

(5) A tribunal or chairman may on its or his own initiative review a decision made by it or him on the grounds listed in paragraphs (3) or (4).

Preliminary consideration of application for review

35.—(1) An application under rule 34 to have a decision reviewed must be made to the Employment Tribunal Office within 14 days of the date on which the decision was sent to the parties. The 14 day time limit may be extended by a chairman if he considers that it is just and equitable to do so.

(2) The application must be in writing and must identify the grounds of the application in accordance with rule 34(3), but if the decision to be reviewed was made at a hearing, an application may be made orally at that hearing.

(3) The application to have a decision reviewed shall be considered (without the need to hold a hearing) by the chairman of the tribunal which made the decision or, if that is not practicable, by—

(a) a Regional Chairman or the Vice President;

(b) any chairman nominated by a Regional Chairman or the Vice President; or

(c) the President;

and that person shall refuse the application if he considers that there are no grounds for the decision to be reviewed under rule 34(3) or there is no reasonable prospect of the decision being varied or revoked.

(4) If an application for a review is refused after such preliminary consideration the Secretary shall inform the party making the application in writing of the chairman's decision and his reasons for it. If the application for a review is not refused the decision shall be reviewed under rule 36.

The review

36.—(1) When a party has applied for a review and the application has not been refused after the preliminary consideration above, the decision shall be reviewed by the chairman or tribunal who made the original decision. If that is not practicable a different chairman or tribunal (as the case may be) shall be appointed by a Regional Chairman, the Vice President or the President.

(2) Where no application has been made by a party and the decision is being reviewed on the initiative of the tribunal or chairman, the review must be carried out by the same tribunal or chairman who made the original decision and —

(a) a notice must be sent to each of the parties explaining in summary the grounds upon which it is proposed to review the decision and giving them an opportunity to give reasons why there should be no review; and

(b) such notice must be sent before the expiry of 14 days from the date on which the original decision was sent to the parties.

(3) A tribunal or chairman who reviews a decision under paragraph (1) or (2) may confirm, vary or revoke the decision. If the decision is revoked, the tribunal or chairman must order the decision to be taken again. When an order is made that the original decision be taken again, if the original decision was taken by a chairman without a hearing, the new decision may be taken without hearing the parties and if the original decision was taken at a hearing, a new hearing must be held.

Correction of judgments, decisions or reasons

37.—(1) Clerical mistakes in any order, judgment, decision or reasons, or errors arising in those documents from an accidental slip or omission, may at any time be corrected by certificate by the chairman, Regional Chairman, Vice President or President.

(2) If a document is corrected by certificate under paragraph (1), or if a decision is revoked or varied under rules 33 or 36 or altered in any way by order of a superior court, the Secretary shall alter any entry in the Register which is so affected to conform with the certificate or order and send a copy of any entry so altered to each of the parties and, if the proceedings have been referred to the tribunal by a court, to that court.

(3) Where a document omitted from the Register under rules 32 or 49 is corrected by certificate under this rule, the Secretary shall send a copy of the corrected document to the parties; and where there are proceedings before any superior court relating to the decision or reasons in question, he shall send a copy to that court together with a copy of the entry in the Register of the decision, if it has been altered under this rule.

(4) In Scotland, the references in paragraphs (2) and (3) to superior courts shall be read as referring to appellate courts.

COSTS ORDERS AND ORDERS FOR EXPENSES

General power to make costs and expenses orders

38.—(1) Subject to paragraph (2) and in the circumstances listed in rules 39, 40 and 47 a tribunal or chairman may make an order ("a costs order") that—

(a) a party ("the paying party") make a payment in respect of the costs incurred by another party ("the receiving party");

(b) the paying party pay to the Secretary of State, in whole or in part, any allowances (other than allowances paid to members of tribunals) paid by the Secretary of State under section 5(2) or (3) of the Employment Tribunals Act to any person for the purposes of, or in connection with, that person's attendance at the tribunal.

(2) A costs order may be made under rules 39, 40 and 47 only where the receiving party has been legally represented at the Hearing or, in proceedings which are determined without a Hearing, if the receiving party is legally represented when the proceedings are determined. If the receiving party has not been so legally represented a tribunal may make a preparation time order (subject to rules 42 to 45). (See rule 46 on the restriction on making a costs order and a preparation time order in the same proceedings.)

(3) For the purposes of these rules "costs" shall mean fees, charges, disbursements or expenses incurred by or on behalf of a party, in relation to the proceedings. In Scotland all references to costs (except when used in the expression "wasted costs") or costs orders shall be read as references to expenses or orders for expenses.

(4) A costs order may be made against or in favour of a respondent who has not had a response accepted in the proceedings in relation to the conduct of any part which he has taken in the proceedings.

(5) In these rules legally represented means having the assistance of a person (including where that person is the receiving party's employee) who—

(a) has a general qualification within the meaning of section 71 of the Courts and Legal Services Act 1990(**a**);

(b) is an advocate or solicitor in Scotland; or

(c) is a member of the Bar of Northern Ireland or a solicitor of the Supreme Court of Northern Ireland.

(6) Any costs order made under rules 39, 40 or 47 shall be payable by the paying party and not his representative.

(7) A party may apply for a costs order to be made at any time during the proceedings. An application may be made at the end of a hearing, or in writing to the Employment Tribunal Office. An application for costs which is received by the Employment Tribunal Office later than 28 days from the issuing of the judgment determining the claim shall not be accepted or considered by a tribunal or chairman unless it or he considers that it is in the interests of justice to do so.

(8) In paragraph (7), the date of issuing of the judgment determining the claim shall be either—

(a) the date of the Hearing if the judgment was issued orally; or

(b) if the judgment was reserved, the date on which the written judgment was sent to the parties.

(9) No costs order shall be made unless the Secretary has sent notice to the party against whom the order may be made giving him the opportunity to give reasons why the order should not be made. This paragraph shall not be taken to require the Secretary to send notice to that party if the party has been given an opportunity to give reasons orally to the chairman or tribunal as to why the order should not be made.

(10) Where a tribunal or chairman makes a costs order it or he shall provide written reasons for doing so if a request for written reasons is made within 14 days of the date of the costs order. The Secretary shall send a copy of the written reasons to all parties to the proceedings.

When a costs or expenses order must be made

39.—(1) Subject to rule 38(2), a tribunal must make a costs order against a respondent where in proceedings for unfair dismissal a Hearing has been postponed or adjourned and—

(**a**) 1990 c. 41.

    (a) the claimant has expressed a wish to be reinstated or re-engaged which has been communicated to the respondent not less than 7 days before the Hearing; and

    (b) the postponement or adjournment of that Hearing has been caused by the respondent's failure, without a special reason, to adduce reasonable evidence as to the availability of the job from which the claimant was dismissed, or of comparable or suitable employment.

(2) A costs order made under paragraph (1) shall relate to any costs incurred as a result of the postponement or adjournment of the Hearing.

When a costs or expenses order may be made

    40.—(1) A tribunal or chairman may make a costs order when on the application of a party it has postponed the day or time fixed for or adjourned a Hearing or pre-hearing review. The costs order may be against or, as the case may require, in favour of that party as respects any costs incurred or any allowances paid as a result of the postponement or adjournment.

    (2) A tribunal or chairman shall consider making a costs order against a paying party where, in the opinion of the tribunal or chairman (as the case may be), any of the circumstances in paragraph (3) apply. Having so considered, the tribunal or chairman may make a costs order against the paying party if it or he considers it appropriate to do so.

    (3) The circumstances referred to in paragraph (2) are where the paying party has in bringing the proceedings, or he or his representative has in conducting the proceedings, acted vexatiously, abusively, disruptively or otherwise unreasonably, or the bringing or conducting of the proceedings by the paying party has been misconceived.

    (4) A tribunal or chairman may make a costs order against a party who has not complied with an order or practice direction.

The amount of a costs or expenses order

    41.—(1) The amount of a costs order against the paying party shall be determined in any of the following ways—

    (a) the tribunal may specify the sum which the paying party must pay to the receiving party, provided that sum does not exceed £10,000;

    (b) the parties may agree on a sum to be paid by the paying party to the receiving party and if they do so the costs order shall be for the sum so agreed;

    (c) the tribunal may order the paying party to pay the receiving party the whole or a specified part of the costs of the receiving party with the amount to be paid being determined by way of detailed assessment in a County Court in accordance with the Civil

Procedure Rules 1998(a) or, in Scotland, as taxed according to such part of the table of fees prescribed for proceedings in the sheriff court as shall be directed by the order.

(2) The tribunal or chairman may have regard to the paying party's ability to pay when considering whether it or he shall make a costs order or how much that order should be.

(3) For the avoidance of doubt, the amount of a costs order made under paragraphs (l)(b) or (c) may exceed £10,000.

PREPARATION TIME ORDERS

General power to make preparation time orders

42.—(1) Subject to paragraph (2) and in the circumstances described in rules 43, 44 and 47 a tribunal or chairman may make an order ("a preparation time order") that a party ("the paying party") make a payment in respect of the preparation time of another party ("the receiving party").

(2) A preparation time order may be made under rules 43, 44 or 47 only where the receiving party has not been legally represented at a Hearing or, in proceedings which are determined without a Hearing, if the receiving party has not been legally represented when the proceedings are determined. (See: rules 38 to 41 on when a costs order may be made; rule 38(5) for the definition of legally represented; and rule 46 on the restriction on making a costs order and a preparation time order in the same proceedings).

(3) For the purposes of these rules preparation time shall mean time spent by—

(a) the receiving party or his employees carrying out preparatory work directly relating to the proceedings; and

(b) the receiving party's legal or other advisers relating to the conduct of the proceedings;
up to but not including time spent at any Hearing.

(4) A preparation time order may be made against a respondent who has not had a response accepted in the proceedings in relation to the conduct of any part which he has taken in the proceedings.

(5) A party may apply to the tribunal for a preparation time order to be made at any time during the proceedings. An application may be made at the end of a hearing or in writing to the Secretary. An application for preparation time which is received by the Employment Tribunal Office later than 28 days from the issuing of the judgment determining the claim shall not be accepted or considered by a tribunal or chairman unless they consider that it is in the interests of justice to do so.

(a) S.I. 1998/3132.

(6) In paragraph (5) the date of issuing of the judgment determining the claim shall be either—

(a) the date of the Hearing if the judgment was issued orally; or,

(b) if the judgment was reserved, the date on which the written judgment was sent to the parties.

(7) No preparation time order shall be made unless the Secretary has sent notice to the party against whom the order may be made giving him the opportunity to give reasons why the order should not be made. This paragraph shall not be taken to require the Secretary to send notice to that party if the party has been given an opportunity to give reasons orally to the chairman or tribunal as to why the order should not be made.

(8) Where a tribunal or chairman makes a preparation time order it or he shall provide written reasons for doing so if a request for written reasons is made within 14 days of the date of the preparation time order. The Secretary shall send a copy of the written reasons to all parties to the proceedings.

When a preparation time order must be made

43.—(1) Subject to rule 42(2), a tribunal must make a preparation time order against a respondent where in proceedings for unfair dismissal a Hearing has been postponed or adjourned and—

(a) the claimant has expressed a wish to be reinstated or re-engaged which has been communicated to the respondent not less than 7 days before the Hearing; and

(b) the postponement or adjournment of that Hearing has been caused by the respondent's failure, without a special reason, to adduce reasonable evidence as to the availability of the job from which the claimant was dismissed, or of comparable or suitable employment.

(2) A preparation time order made under paragraph (1) shall relate to any preparation time spent as a result of the postponement or adjournment of the Hearing.

When a preparation time order may be made

44.—(1) A tribunal or chairman may make a preparation time order when on the application of a party it has postponed the day or time fixed for or adjourned a Hearing or a pre-hearing review. The preparation time order may be against or, as the case may require, in favour of that party as respects any preparation time spent as a result of the postponement or adjournment.

(2) A tribunal or chairman shall consider making a preparation time order against a party (the paying party) where, in the opinion of the

tribunal or the chairman (as the case may be), any of the circumstances in paragraph (3) apply. Having so considered the tribunal or chairman may make a preparation time order against that party if it considers it appropriate to do so.

(3) The circumstances described in paragraph (2) are where the paying party has in bringing the proceedings, or he or his representative has in conducting the proceedings, acted vexatiously, abusively, disruptively or otherwise unreasonably, or the bringing or conducting of the proceedings by the paying party has been misconceived.

(4) A tribunal or chairman may make a preparation time order against a party who has not complied with an order or practice direction.

Calculation of a preparation time order

45.—(1) In order to calculate the amount of preparation time the tribunal or chairman shall make an assessment of the number of hours spent on preparation time on the basis of—

(a) information on time spent provided by the receiving party; and

(b) the tribunal or chairman's own assessment of what it or he considers to be a reasonable and proportionate amount of time to spend on such preparatory work and with reference to, for example, matters such as the complexity of the proceedings, the number of witnesses and documentation required.

(2) Once the tribunal or chairman has assessed the number of hours spent on preparation time in accordance with paragraph (1), it or he shall calculate the amount of the award to be paid to the receiving party by applying an hourly rate of £25.00 to that figure (or such other figure calculated in accordance with paragraph (4)). No preparation time order made under these rules may exceed the sum of £10,000.

(3) The tribunal or chairman may have regard to the paying party's ability to pay when considering whether it or he shall make a preparation time order or how much that order should be.

(4) For the year commencing on 6th April 2006, the hourly rate of £25 shall be increased by the sum of £1.00 and for each subsequent year commencing on 6 April, the hourly rate for the previous year shall also be increased by the sum of £1.00.

Restriction on making costs or expenses orders and preparation time orders

46.—(1) A tribunal or chairman may not make a preparation time order and a costs order in favour of the same party in the same proceedings. However where a preparation time order is made in favour of a party in proceedings, the tribunal or chairman may make a costs order in favour of another party or in favour of the Secretary of State under rule 38(l)(b) in the same proceedings.

(2) If a tribunal or a chairman wishes to make either a costs order or a preparation time order in proceedings, before the claim has been determined, it or he may make an order that either costs or preparation time be awarded to the receiving party. In such circumstances a tribunal or chairman may decide whether the award should be for costs or preparation time after the proceedings have been determined.

Costs, expenses or preparation time orders when a deposit has been taken

47.—(1) When:—

(a) a party has been ordered under rule 20 to pay a deposit as a condition of being permitted to continue to participate in proceedings relating to a matter;

(b) in respect of that matter, the tribunal or chairman has found against that party in its or his judgment; and

(c) no award of costs or preparation time has been made against that party arising out of the proceedings on the matter;

the tribunal or chairman shall consider whether to make a costs or preparation time order against that party on the ground that he conducted the proceedings relating to the matter unreasonably in persisting in having the matter determined; but the tribunal or chairman shall not make a costs or preparation time order on that ground unless it has considered the document recording the order under rule 20 and is of the opinion that the grounds which caused the tribunal or chairman to find against the party in its judgment were substantially the same as the grounds recorded in that document for considering that the contentions of the party had little reasonable prospect of success.

(2) When a costs or preparation time order is made against a party who has had an order under rule 20 made against him (whether the award arises out of the proceedings relating to the matter in respect of which the order was made or out of proceedings relating to any other matter considered with that matter), his deposit shall be paid in part or full settlement of the costs or preparation time order—

(a) when an order is made in favour of one party, to that party; and

(b) when orders are made in favour of more than one party, to all of them or any one or more of them as the tribunal or chairman thinks fit, and if to all or more than one, in such proportions as the tribunal or chairman considers appropriate;
and if the amount of the deposit exceeds the amount of the costs or preparation time order, the balance shall be refunded to the party who paid it.

WASTED COSTS ORDERS AGAINST REPRESENTATIVES

Personal liability of representatives for costs

48.—(1) A tribunal or chairman may make a wasted costs order against a party's representative.

(2) In a wasted costs order the tribunal or chairman may:—

(a) disallow, or order the representative of a party to meet the whole or part of any wasted costs of any party, including an order that the representative repay to his client any costs which have already been paid; and

(b) order the representative to pay to the Secretary of State, in whole or in part, any allowances (other than allowances paid to members of tribunals) paid by the Secretary of State under section 5(2) or (3) of the Employment Tribunals Act to any person for the purposes of, or in connection with, that person's attendance at the tribunal by reason of the representative's conduct of the proceedings.

(3) "Wasted costs" means any costs incurred by a party:—

(a) as a result of any improper, unreasonable or negligent act or omission on the part of any representative; or

(b) which, in the light of any such act or omission occurring after they were incurred, the tribunal considers it unreasonable to expect that party to pay.

(4) In this rule "representative" means a party's legal or other representative or any employee of such representative, but it does not include a representative who is not acting in pursuit of profit with regard to those proceedings. A person is considered to be acting in pursuit of profit if he is acting on a conditional fee arrangement.

(5) A wasted costs order may be made in favour of a party whether or not that party is legally represented and such an order may also be made in favour of a representative's own client. A wasted costs order may not be made against a representative where that representative is an employee of a party.

(6) Before making a wasted costs order, the tribunal or chairman shall give the representative a reasonable opportunity to make oral or written representations as to reasons why such an order should not be made. The tribunal or chairman shall also have regard to the representative's ability to pay when considering whether it shall make a wasted costs order or how much that order should be.

(7) When a tribunal or chairman makes a wasted costs order, it must specify in the order the amount to be disallowed or paid.

(8) The Secretary shall inform the representative's client in writing:—

   (a) of any proceedings under this rule; or

   (b) of any order made under this rule against the party's representative.

(9) Where a tribunal or chairman makes a wasted costs order it or he shall provide written reasons for doing so if a request is made for written reasons within 14 days of the date of the wasted costs order. This 14 day time limit may not be extended under rule 10. The Secretary shall send a copy of the written reasons to all parties to the proceedings.

POWERS IN RELATION TO SPECIFIC TYPES OF PROCEEDINGS

Sexual offences and the Register

49. In any proceedings appearing to involve allegations of the commission of a sexual offence the tribunal, the chairman or the Secretary shall omit from the Register, or delete from the Register or any judgment, document or record of the proceedings, which is available to the public, any identifying matter which is likely to lead members of the public to identify any person affected by or making such an allegation.

Restricted reporting orders

50.—(1) A restricted reporting order may be made in the following types of proceedings:—

   (a) any case which involves allegations of sexual misconduct;

   (b) a complaint under section 17A or 25(8) of the Disability Discrimination Act in which evidence of a personal nature is likely to be heard by the tribunal or a chairman.

(2) A party (or where a complaint is made under the Disability Discrimination Act, the complainant) may apply for a restricted reporting order (either temporary or full) in writing to the Employment Tribunal Office, or orally at a hearing, or the tribunal or chairman may make the order on its or his own initiative without any application having been made.

(3) A chairman or tribunal may make a temporary restricted reporting order without holding a hearing or sending a copy of the application to other parties.

(4) Where a temporary restricted reporting order has been made the Secretary shall inform all parties to the proceedings in writing as soon as possible of—

   (a) the fact that the order has been made; and

   (b) their right to apply to have the temporary restricted reporting order revoked or converted into a full restricted reporting order within 14 days of the temporary order having been made.

(5) If no application under paragraph (4)(b) is made within the 14 days, the temporary restricted reporting order shall lapse and cease to have any effect on the fifteenth day after the order was made. If such an application is made the temporary restricted reporting order shall continue to have effect until the pre-hearing review or Hearing at which the application is considered.

(6) All parties must be given an opportunity to advance oral argument at a pre-hearing review or a Hearing before a tribunal or chairman decides whether or not to make a full restricted reporting order (whether or not there was previously a temporary restricted reporting order in the proceedings).

(7) Any person may make an application to the chairman or tribunal to have a right to make representations before a full restricted reporting order is made. The chairman or tribunal shall allow such representations to be made where he or it considers that the applicant has a legitimate interest in whether or not the order is made.

(8) Where a tribunal or chairman makes a restricted reporting order—

(a) it shall specify in the order the persons who may not be identified;

(b) a full order shall remain in force until both liability and remedy have been determined in the proceedings unless it is revoked earlier; and

(c) the Secretary shall ensure that a notice of the fact that a restricted reporting order has been made in relation to those proceedings is displayed on the notice board of the employment tribunal with any list of the proceedings taking place before the employment tribunal, and on the door of the room in which the proceedings affected by the order are taking place.

(9) Where a restricted reporting order has been made under this rule and that complaint is being dealt with together with any other proceedings, the tribunal or chairman may order that the restricted reporting order applies also in relation to those other proceedings or a part of them.

(10) A tribunal or chairman may revoke a restricted reporting order at any time.

(11) For the purposes of this rule liability and remedy are determined in the proceedings on the date recorded as being the date on which the judgment disposing of the claim was sent to the parties, and references to a restricted reporting order include references to both a temporary and a full restricted reporting order.

Proceedings involving the National Insurance Fund

51. The Secretary of State shall be entitled to appear as if she were a party and be heard at any hearing in relation to proceedings which may involve a payment out of the National Insurance Fund, and in that event she shall be treated for the purposes of these rules as if she were a party.

Collective agreements

52. Where a claim includes a complaint under section 6(4A) of the Sex Discrimination Act 1986(**a**) relating to a term of a collective agreement, the following persons, whether or not identified in the claim, shall be regarded as the persons against whom a remedy is claimed and shall be treated as respondents for the purposes of these rules, that is to say—

(a) the claimant's employer (or prospective employer); and

(b) every organisation of employers and organisation of workers, and every association of or representative of such organisations, which, if the terms were to be varied voluntarily, would be likely, in the opinion of a chairman, to negotiate the variation;

provided that such an organisation or association shall not be treated as a respondent if the chairman, having made such enquiries of the claimant and such other enquiries as he thinks fit, is of the opinion that it is not reasonably practicable to identify the organisation or association.

Employment Agencies Act 1973

53. In relation to any claim in respect of an application under section 3C of the Employment Agencies Act 1973(**a**) for the variation or revocation of a prohibition order, the Secretary of State shall be treated as the respondent in such proceedings for the purposes of these rules. In relation to such an application the claim does not need to include the name and address of the persons against whom the claim is being made.

National security proceedings

54.—(1) A Minister of the Crown (whether or not he is a party to the proceedings) may, if he considers it expedient in the interests of national security, direct a tribunal or chairman by notice to the Secretary to:—

(a) conduct proceedings in private for all or part of particular Crown employment proceedings;

(b) exclude the claimant from all or part of particular Crown employment proceedings;

(c) exclude the claimant's representative from all or part of particular Crown employment proceedings;

(a) 1986 c. 59.
(a) 1973 c. 35; section 3C was inserted by paragraphs 1(1) and (3) of Schedule 10 to the Deregulation and Contracting Out Act 1994 c. 40.

(d) take steps to conceal the identity of a particular witness in particular Crown employment proceedings.

(2) A tribunal or chairman may, if it or he considers it expedient in the interests of national security, by order—

(a) do anything which can be required by direction to be done under paragraph (1);

(b) order any person to whom any document (including any judgment or record of the proceedings) has been provided for the purposes of the proceedings not to disclose any such document or the content thereof:—

    (i) to any excluded person;

   (ii) in any case in which a direction has been given under paragraph (l)(a) or an order has been made under paragraph (2)(a) read with paragraph (l)(a), to any person excluded from all or part of the proceedings by virtue of such direction or order; or

  (iii) in any case in which a Minister of the Crown has informed the Secretary in accordance with paragraph (3) that he wishes to address the tribunal or chairman with a view to an order being made under paragraph (2)(a) read with paragraph (l)(b) or (c), to any person who may be excluded from all or part of the proceedings by virtue of such an order, if an order is made, at any time before the tribunal or chairman decides whether or not to make such an order;

(c) take steps to keep secret all or part of the reasons for its judgment.

The tribunal or chairman (as the case may be) shall keep under review any order it or he has made under this paragraph.

(3) In any proceedings in which a Minister of the Crown considers that it would be appropriate for a tribunal or chairman to make an order as referred to in paragraph (2), he shall (whether or not he is a party to the proceedings) be entitled to appear before and to address the tribunal or chairman thereon. The Minister shall inform the Secretary by notice that he wishes to address the tribunal or chairman and the Secretary shall copy the notice to the parties.

(4) When exercising its or his functions, a tribunal or chairman shall ensure that information is not disclosed contrary to the interests of national security.

Dismissals in connection with industrial action

55.—(1) In relation to a complaint under section 111 of the Employment Rights Act 1996 (unfair dismissal: complaints to employment tribunal) that a dismissal is unfair by virtue of section 238A of TULR(C)A**(a)** (participation in official industrial action) a tribunal or chairman may adjourn the proceedings where civil proceedings have been brought until such time as interim proceedings arising out of the civil proceedings have been concluded.

(2) In this rule—

(a) "civil proceedings" means legal proceedings brought by any person against another person in which it is to be determined whether an act of that other person, which induced the claimant to commit an act, or each of a series of acts, is by virtue of section 219 of TULR(C)A not actionable in tort or in delict; and

(b) the interim proceedings shall not be regarded as having concluded until all rights of appeal have been exhausted or the time for presenting any appeal in the course of the interim proceedings has expired.

Devolution issues

56.—(1) In any proceedings in which a devolution issue within the definition of the term in paragraph 1 of Schedule 6 to the Scotland Act 1998 arises, the Secretary shall as soon as reasonably practicable by notice inform the Advocate General for Scotland and the Lord Advocate thereof (unless they are a party to the proceedings) and shall at the same time—

(a) send a copy of the notice to the parties to the proceedings; and

(b) send the Advocate General for Scotland and the Lord Advocate a copy of the claim and the response.

(2) In any proceedings in which a devolution issue within the definition of the term in paragraph 1 of Schedule 8 to the Government of Wales Act 1998 arises, the Secretary shall as soon as reasonably practicable by notice inform the Attorney General and the National Assembly for Wales thereof (unless they are a party to the proceedings) and shall at the same time—

(a) send a copy of the notice to the parties to the proceedings; and

(b) send the Attorney General and the National Assembly for Wales a copy of the claim and the response.

(3) A person to whom notice is given in pursuance of paragraph (1) or (2) may within 14 days of receiving it, by notice to the Secretary, take part as a party in the proceedings, so far as they relate to the devolution issue. The Secretary shall send a copy of the notice to the other parties to the proceedings.

(a) Section 238A was inserted by paragraphs 1 and 3 of Schedule 5 to the Employment Relations Act 1999 (c. 26).

Transfer of proceedings between Scotland and England & Wales

57.—(1) The President (England and Wales) or a Regional Chairman may at any time, with the consent of the President (Scotland), order any proceedings in England and Wales to be transferred to an Employment Tribunal Office in Scotland if it appears to him that the proceedings could be (in accordance with regulation 19), and would more conveniently be, determined in an employment tribunal located in Scotland.

(2) The President (Scotland) or the Vice President may at any time, with the consent of the President (England and Wales), order any proceedings in Scotland to be transferred to an Employment Tribunal Office in England and Wales if it appears to him that the proceedings could be (in accordance with regulation 19), and would more conveniently be, determined in an employment tribunal located in England or Wales.

(3) An order under paragraph (1) or (2) may be made by the President, Vice President or Regional Chairman without any application having been made by a party. A party may apply for an order under paragraph (1) or (2) in accordance with rule 11.

(4) Where proceedings have been transferred under this rule, they shall be treated as if in all respects they had been presented to the Secretary by the claimant.

References to the European Court of Justice

58. Where a tribunal or chairman makes an order referring a question to the European Court of Justice for a preliminary ruling under Article 234 of the Treaty establishing the European Community, the Secretary shall send a copy of the order to the Registrar of that Court.

Transfer of proceedings from a court

59. Where proceedings are referred to a tribunal by a court, these rules shall apply to them as if the proceedings had been sent to the Secretary by the claimant.

GENERAL PRO VISIONS

Powers

60.—(1) Subject to the provisions of these rules and any practice directions, a tribunal or chairman may regulate its or his own procedure.

(2) At a Hearing, or a pre-hearing review held in accordance with rule 18(3), a tribunal may make any order which a chairman has power to make under these rules, subject to compliance with any relevant notice or other procedural requirements.

(3) Any function of the Secretary may be performed by a person acting with the authority of the Secretary.

Notices, etc

61.—(1) Any notice given or document sent under these rules shall (unless a chairman or tribunal orders otherwise) be in writing and may be given or sent—

(a) by post;

(b) by fax or other means of electronic communication; or

(c) by personal delivery.

(2) Where a notice or document has been given or sent in accordance with paragraph (1), that notice or document shall, unless the contrary is proved, be taken to have been received by the party to whom it is addressed—

(a) in the case of a notice or document given or sent by post, on the day on which the notice or document would be delivered in the ordinary course of post;

(b) in the case of a notice or document transmitted by fax or other means of electronic communication, on the day on which the notice or document is transmitted;

(c) in the case of a notice or document delivered in person, on the day on which the notice or document is delivered.

(3) All notices and documents required by these rules to be presented to the Secretary or an Employment Tribunal Office, other than a claim, shall be presented at the Employment Tribunal Office as notified by the Secretary to the parties.

(4) All notices and documents required or authorised by these rules to be sent or given to any person listed below may be sent to or delivered at—

(a) in the case of a notice or document directed to the Secretary of State in proceedings to which she is not a party and which are brought under section 170 of the Employment Rights Act, the offices of the Redundancy Payments Directorate of the Insolvency Service at PO Box 203, 21 Bloomsbury Street, London WC1B 3QW, or such other office as may be notified by the Secretary of State;

(b) in the case of any other notice or document directed to the Secretary of State in proceedings to which she is not a party (or in respect of which she is treated as a party for the purposes of these rules by rule 51), the offices of the Department of Trade and Industry (Employment Relations Directorate) at 1 Victoria Street, London, SW1H OET, or such other office as be notified by the Secretary of State;

(c) in the case of a notice or document directed to the Attorney General under rule 56, the Attorney General's Chambers, 9 Buckingham Gate, London, SW1E 7JP;

(d) in the case of a notice or document directed to the National Assembly for Wales under rule 56, the Counsel General to the

National Assembly for Wales, Crown Buildings, Cathays Park, Cardiff, CF10 3NQ;

(e) in the case of a notice or document directed to the Advocate General for Scotland under rule 56, the Office of the Solicitor to the Advocate General for Scotland, Victoria Quay, Edinburgh, EH6 6QQ;

(f) in the case of a notice or document directed to the Lord Advocate under rule 56, the Legal Secretariat to the Lord Advocate, 25 Chambers Street, Edinburgh, EH1 1LA;

(g) in the case of a notice or document directed to a court, the office of the clerk of the court;

(h) in the case of a notice or document directed to a party:—

(i) the address specified in the claim or response to which notices and documents are to be sent, or in a notice under paragraph (5); or

(ii) if no such address has been specified, or if a notice sent to such an address has been returned, to any other known address or place of business in the United Kingdom or, if the party is a corporate body, the body's registered or principal office in the United Kingdom, or, in any case, such address or place outside the United Kingdom as the President, Vice President or a Regional Chairman may allow;

(i) in the case of a notice or document directed to any person (other than a person specified in the foregoing provisions of this paragraph), his address or place of business in the United Kingdom or, if the person is a corporate body, the body's registered or principal office in the United Kingdom;

and a notice or document sent or given to the authorised representative of a party shall be taken to have been sent or given to that party.

(5) A party may at any time by notice to the Employment Tribunal Office and to the other party or parties (and, where appropriate, to the appropriate conciliation officer) change the address to which notices and documents are to be sent or transmitted.

(6) The President, Vice President or a Regional Chairman may order that there shall be substituted service in such manner as he may deem fit in any case he considers appropriate.

(7) In proceedings which may involve a payment out of the National Insurance Fund, the Secretary shall, where appropriate, send copies of all documents and notices to the Secretary of State whether or not she is a party.

(8) Copies of every document sent to the parties under rules 29, 30 or 32 shall be sent by the Secretary:—

(a) in the case of proceedings under the Equal Pay Act, the Sex Discrimination Act or the Sex Discrimination Act 1986, to the Equal Opportunities Commission;

(b) in the case of proceedings under the Race Relations Act, to the Commission for Racial Equality; and

(c) in the case of proceedings under the Disability Discrimination Act, to the Disability Rights Commission.

ACAS CODE OF PRACTICE ON DISCIPLINARY AND GRIEVANCE PROCEDURES (2004)

A4.01

acas

Code of Practice 1

Disciplinary and grievance procedures

Click here for the disciplinary and grievance procedures folder which contains six easy to follow charts to guide you through the disciplinary and grievance process

www.acas.org.uk

Helpline 08457 47 47 47

08456 06 16 00
Helpline for textphone users.

08702 42 90 90
For ordering Acas publications

Acas main offices

Scotland
151 West George Street, Glasgow G2 7JJ

North West
Commercial Union House,
2-10 Albert Square, Manchester M60 8AD

Pavilion 1, The Matchworks, Speke Road,
Speke, Liverpool L19 2PH

North East
Cross House, Westgate Road,
Newcastle upon Tyne NE1 4XX

Yorkshire & Humber
The Cube, 123 Albion Street,
Leeds LS2 8ER

West Midlands
Warwick House & Highfield Road,
Edgbaston, Birmingham B15 3ED

East Midlands
Lancaster House, 10 Sherwood Rise,
Nottingham NG7 6JE

East of England
Ross House, Kempston Way, Suffolk
Bournside Park, Bury St Edmunds,
Suffolk IP32 7AR

Wales
3 Purbeck House, Lambourne Crescent,
Llanishen, Cardiff CF14 5GJ

London
22nd & 23rd Floors, Euston Tower,
286 Euston Road, London NW1 3JJ

South West
The Waterfront, Welsh Back,
Bristol BS1 4SB

South East
Westminster House, 125 Fleet Road,
Fleet, Hampshire GU51 3QL

Suites 3-5, Business Centre,
1-7 Commercial Road, Paddock Wood,
Kent TN12 6EN

Head Office
Brandon House,
180 Borough High Street,
London SE1 1LW

For questions on managing
equality in the workplace

INVESTOR IN PEOPLE

This Code of Practice provides practical guidance to employers, workers and their representatives on:

The statutory requirements relating to disciplinary and grievance issues;

What constitutes reasonable behaviour when dealing with disciplinary and grievance issues;

Producing and using disciplinary and grievance procedures; and

A worker's right to bring a companion to grievance and disciplinary hearings.

The statutory dismissal, disciplinary and grievance procedures, as set out in the Employment Act 2002, apply only to employees as defined in the 2002 Act and this term is used throughout sections 1 and 2 of the Code. However, it is good practice to allow all workers access to disciplinary and grievance procedures. The right to be accompanied applies to all workers (which includes employees) and this term is used in section 3 of the Code.

A failure to follow any part of this Code does not, in itself, make a person or organisation liable to proceedings. However, employment tribunals will take the Code into account when considering relevant cases. Similarly, arbitrators appointed by Acas to determine relevant cases under the Acas Arbitration Scheme will take the Code into account.

A failure to follow the statutory disciplinary and grievance procedures where they apply may have a number of legal implications which are described in the Code.

The Code (from page 2 to page 36) is issued under section 199 of the Trade Union and Labour Relations (Consolidation) Act 1992 and was laid before both Houses of Parliament on 17 June 2004. The Code comes into effect by order of the Secretary of State on 1 October 2004.

More comprehensive, practical, advice and guidance on disciplinary and grievance procedures is contained in the Acas Handbook "Discipline and grievances at work" which also includes information on the Disability Discrimination Act 1995 and the Data Protection Act 1998. The Handbook can be obtained from the Acas website at www.acas.org.uk. Further information on the detailed provisions of the statutory disciplinary and grievance procedures can be found on the Department of Trade and Industry's website at www.dti.gov.uk/er.

TSO

Published by TSO (The Stationery Office) and available from:

Online
www.tso.co.uk/bookshop

Mail, Telephone, Fax & E-mail
TSO
PO Box 29, Norwich, NR3 1GN
Telephone orders/General enquiries: 0870 6005522
Fax orders: 0870 6005533
E-mail: book.orders@tso.co.uk
Textphone 0870 240 3701

TSO Shops
123 Kingsway, London, WC2B 6PQ
020 7242 6393 Fax 020 7242 6394
68-69 Bull Street, Birmingham B4 6AD
0121 236 9696 Fax 0121 236 9699
9-21 Princess Street, Manchester M60 8AS
0161 834 7201 Fax 0161 833 0634

16 Arthur Street, Belfast BT1 4GD
028 9023 6451 Fax 028 9023 5401
18-19 High Street, Cardiff CF10 1PT
029 2039 5548 Fax 029 2038 4347
71 Lothian Road, Edinburgh EH3 9AZ
0870 606 5566 Fax 0870 606 5588

TSO Accredited Agents
(see Yellow Pages)
and through good booksellers

Published with the permission of Acas on behalf of the Controller of Her Majesty's Stationery Office.
© Crown Copyright 2003

All rights reserved.

Copyright in the typographical arrangement and design is vested in the Crown. Applications for reproduction should be made in writing to the Copyright Unit, Her Majesty's Stationery Office, St Clements House, 2-16 Colegate, Norwich NR3 1BQ

First edition Crown Copyright 1991, published by HMSO

Second edition Crown Copyright 1998

Third edition Crown Copyright 2003

First published 2003

ISBN 0 11 703154 2

Printed in the United Kingdom for The Stationery Office

Id 136457 c50 5/03 837864

Further copies may also be obtained from Acas Publications, Swallow Field Way, Hayes, Middlesex, UB3 1DQ. Tel: 0870 242 9090.

Section 1

Disciplinary rules and procedures

Contents

At a glance

Drawing up disciplinary rules and procedures

- Involve management, employees and their representatives where appropriate (Paragraph 52).
- Make rules clear and brief and explain their purpose (Paragraph 53).
- Explain rules and procedures to employees and make sure they have a copy or ready access to a copy of them (Paragraph 55).

Operating disciplinary procedures

- Establish facts before taking action (Paragraph 8).
- Deal with cases of minor misconduct or unsatisfactory performance informally (Paragraphs 11-12).
- For more serious cases, follow formal procedures, including informing the employee of the alleged misconduct or unsatisfactory performance (Paragraph 13).
- Invite the employee to a meeting and inform them of the right to be accompanied (Paragraph 14-16).
- Where performance is unsatisfactory explain to the employee the improvement required, the support that will be given and when and how performance will be reviewed (Paragraphs 19-20).
- If giving a warning, tell the employee why and how they need to change, the consequences of failing to improve and that they have a right to appeal (Paragraphs 21-22).
- If dismissing an employee, tell them why, when their contract will end and that they can appeal (Paragraph 25).
- Before dismissing or taking disciplinary action other than issuing a warning, always follow the statutory dismissal and disciplinary procedure (Paragraphs 26-32).
- When dealing with absences from work, find out the reasons for the absence before deciding on what action to take. (Paragraph 37).

Holding appeals

- If the employee wishes to appeal invite them to a meeting and inform the employee of their right to be accompanied (Paragraphs 44-48).
- Where possible, arrange for the appeal to be dealt with by a more senior manager not involved with the earlier decision (Paragraph 46).
- Inform the employee about the appeal decision and the reasons for it (Paragraph 48).

Records

- Keep written records for future reference (Paragraph 49).

Guidance

Why have disciplinary rules and procedures?

1. Disciplinary rules and procedures help to promote orderly employment relations as well as fairness and consistency in the treatment of individuals. Disciplinary procedures are also a legal requirement in certain circumstances (see paragraph 6).

2. Disciplinary rules tell employees what behaviour employers expect from them. If an employee breaks specific rules about behaviour, this is often called misconduct. Employers use disciplinary procedures and actions to deal with situations where employees allegedly break disciplinary rules. Disciplinary procedures may also be used where employees don't meet their employer's expectations in the way they do their job. These cases, often known as unsatisfactory performance (or capability), may require different treatment from misconduct, and disciplinary procedures should allow for this.

3. Guidance on how to draw up disciplinary rules and procedures is contained in paragraphs 52-62.

4. When dealing with disciplinary cases, employers need to be aware both of the law on unfair dismissal and the statutory minimum procedure contained in the Employment Act 2002 for dismissing or taking disciplinary action against an employee. Employers must also be careful not to discriminate on the grounds of gender, race (including colour, nationality and ethnic or national origins), disability, age, sexual orientation or religion.

The law on unfair dismissal

5. The law on unfair dismissal requires employers to act reasonably when dealing with disciplinary issues. What is classed as reasonable behaviour will depend on the circumstances of each case, and is ultimately a matter for employment tribunals to decide. However, the core principles employers should work to are set out in the box overleaf. Drawing up and referring to a procedure can help employers deal with disciplinary issues in a fair and consistent manner.

Core principles of reasonable behaviour

- Use procedures primarily to help and encourage employees to improve rather than just as a way of imposing a punishment.
- Inform the employee of the complaint against them, and provide them with an opportunity to state their case before decisions are reached.
- Allow employees to be accompanied at disciplinary meetings.
- Make sure that disciplinary action is not taken until the facts of the case have been established and that the action is reasonable in the circumstances.
- Never dismiss an employee for a first disciplinary offence, unless it is a case of gross misconduct.
- Give the employee a written explanation for any disciplinary action taken and make sure they know what improvement is expected.
- Give the employee an opportunity to appeal.
- Deal with issues as thoroughly and promptly as possible.
- Act consistently.

The statutory minimum procedure

6. Employers are also required to follow a specific statutory minimum procedure if they are contemplating dismissing an employee or imposing some other disciplinary penalty that is not suspension on full pay or a warning. Guidance on this statutory procedure is provided in paragraphs 26-32. If an employee is dismissed without the employer following this statutory procedure, and makes a claim to an employment tribunal, providing they have the necessary qualifying service and providing they are not prevented from claiming unfair dismissal by virtue of their age, the dismissal will automatically be ruled unfair. The statutory procedure is a minimum requirement and even where the relevant procedure is followed the dismissal may still be unfair if the employer has not acted reasonably in all the circumstances.

What about small businesses?

7. In small organisations it may not be practicable to adopt all the detailed good practice guidance set out in this Code. Employment tribunals will take account of an employer's size and administrative resources when deciding if it acted reasonably. However, all organisations regardless of size must follow the minimum statutory dismissal and disciplinary procedures.

Dealing with disciplinary issues in the workplace

8. When a potential disciplinary matter arises, the employer should make necessary investigations to establish the facts promptly before memories of events fade. It is important to keep a written record for later reference. Having established the facts, the employer should decide whether to drop the matter, deal with it informally or arrange for it to be handled formally. Where an investigatory meeting is held solely to establish the facts of a case, it should be made clear to the employee involved that it is not a disciplinary meeting.

9. In certain cases, for example in cases involving gross misconduct, where relationships have broken down or there are risks to an employer's property or responsibilities to other parties, consideration should be given to a brief period of suspension with full pay whilst unhindered investigation is conducted. Such a suspension should only be imposed after careful consideration and should be reviewed to ensure it is not unnecessarily protracted. It should be made clear that the suspension is not considered a disciplinary action.

10. When dealing with disciplinary issues in the workplace employers should bear in mind that they are required under the Disability Discrimination Act 1995 to make reasonable adjustments to cater for employees who have a disability, for example providing for wheelchair access if necessary.

informal action

11. Cases of minor misconduct or unsatisfactory performance are usually best dealt with informally. A quiet word is often all that is required to improve an employee's conduct or performance. The informal approach may be particularly helpful in small firms, where problems can be dealt with quickly and confidentially. There will, however, be situations where matters are more serious or where an informal approach has been tried but is not working.

12. If informal action does not bring about an improvement, or the misconduct or unsatisfactory performance is considered to be too serious to be classed as minor, employers should provide employees with a clear signal of their dissatisfaction by taking formal action.

Formal action

Inform the employee of the problem

13. The first step in any formal process is to let the employee know in writing what it is they are alleged to have done wrong. The letter or note should contain enough information for the individual to be able to understand both what it is they are alleged to have done wrong and the reasons why this is not acceptable. If the employee has difficulty reading, or if English is not their first language, the employer should explain the content of the letter or note to them orally. The letter or note should also invite the individual to a meeting at which the problem can be discussed, and it should inform the individual of their right to be accompanied at the meeting (see section 3). The employee should be given copies of any documents that will be produced at the meeting.

Hold a meeting to discuss the problem

14. Where possible, the timing and location of the meeting should be agreed with the employee. The length of time between the written notification and the meeting should be long enough to allow the employee to prepare but not so long that memories fade. The employer should hold the meeting in a private location and ensure there will be no interruptions.

15. At the meeting, the employer should explain the complaint against the employee and go through the evidence that has been gathered. The employee should be allowed to set out their case and answer any allegations that have been made. The employee should also be allowed to ask questions, present evidence, call witnesses and be given an opportunity to raise points about any information provided by witnesses.

16. An employee who cannot attend a meeting should inform the employer in advance whenever possible. If the employee fails to attend through circumstances outside their control and unforeseeable at the time the meeting was arranged (eg illness) the employer should arrange another meeting. A decision may be taken in the employee's absence if they fail to attend the re-arranged meeting without good reason. If an employee's companion cannot attend on a proposed date, the employee can suggest another date so long as it is reasonable and is not more than five working days after the date originally proposed by the employer. This five day time limit may be extended by mutual agreement

Decide on outcome and action

17. Following the meeting the employer must decide whether disciplinary action is justified or not. Where it is decided that no action is justified the employee should be informed. Where it is decided that disciplinary action is justified the employer will need to consider what form this should take. Before making any decision the employer should take account of the employee's disciplinary and general record, length of service, actions taken in any previous similar case, the explanations given by the employee and – most important of all – whether the intended disciplinary action is reasonable under the circumstances.

18. Examples of actions the employer might choose to take are set out in paragraphs 19-25. It is normally good practice to give employees at least one chance to improve their conduct or performance before they are issued with a final written warning. However, if an employee's misconduct or unsatisfactory performance – or its continuance – is sufficiently serious, for example because it is having, or is likely to have, a serious harmful effect on the organisation, it may be appropriate to move directly to a final written warning. In cases of gross misconduct, the employer may decide to dismiss even though the employee has not previously received a warning for misconduct. (Further guidance on dealing with gross misconduct is set out at paragraphs 35-36.)

First formal action – unsatisfactory performance

19. Following the meeting, an employee who is found to be performing unsatisfactorily should be given a written note setting out:

- the performance problem;
- the improvement that is required;
- the timescale for achieving this improvement;
- a review date; and
- any support the employer will provide to assist the employee.

20. The employee should be informed that the note represents the first stage of a formal procedure and that failure to improve could lead to a final written warning and, ultimately, dismissal. A copy of the note should be kept and used as the basis for monitoring and reviewing performance over a specified period (eg six months).

First formal action – misconduct

21. Where, following a disciplinary meeting, an employee is found guilty of misconduct, the usual first step would be to give them a written warning setting out the nature of the misconduct and the change in behaviour required.

22. The employee should be informed that the warning is part of the formal disciplinary process and what the consequences will be of a failure to change behaviour. The consequences could be a final written warning and ultimately, dismissal. The employee should also be informed that they may appeal against the decision. A record of the warning should be kept, but it should be disregarded for disciplinary purposes after a specified period (eg six months).

23. Guidance on dealing with cases of gross misconduct is provided in paragraphs 35-36.

Final written warning

24. Where there is a failure to improve or change behaviour in the timescale set at the first formal stage, or where the offence is sufficiently serious, the employee should normally be issued with a final written warning – but only after they have been given a chance to present their case at a meeting. The final written warning should give details of, and grounds for, the complaint. It should warn the employee that failure to improve or modify behaviour may lead to dismissal or to some other penalty, and refer to the right of appeal.

The final written warning should normally be disregarded for disciplinary purposes after a specified period (for example 12 months).

Dismissal or other penalty

25. If the employee's conduct or performance still fails to improve, the final stage in the disciplinary process might be dismissal or (if the employee's contract allows it or it is mutually agreed) some other penalty such as demotion, disciplinary transfer, or loss of seniority/ pay. A decision to dismiss should only be taken by a manager who has the authority to do so. The employee should be informed as soon as possible of the reasons for the dismissal, the date on which the employment contract will terminate, the appropriate period of notice and their right of appeal.

26. It is important for employers to bear in mind that before they dismiss an employee or impose a sanction such as demotion, loss of seniority or loss of pay, they must as a minimum have followed the statutory dismissal and disciplinary procedures. The standard statutory procedure to be used in almost all cases requires the employer to:

Step 1

Write to the employee notifying them of the allegations against them and the basis of the allegations and invite them to a meeting to discuss the matter.

Step 2

Hold a meeting to discuss the allegations – at which the employee has the right to be accompanied – and notify the employee of the decision.

Step 3

If the employee wishes to appeal, hold an appeal meeting at which the employee has the right to be accompanied – and inform the employee of the final decision.

inform   advise   train   work with you

27. More detail on the statutory standard procedure is set out at Annex A. There is a modified two-step procedure for use in special circumstances involving gross misconduct and details of this are set out at Annex B. Guidance on the modified procedure is contained in paragraph 36. There are a number of situations in which it is not necessary for employers to use the statutory procedures or where they will have been deemed to be completed and these are described in Annex E.

28. If the employer fails to follow this statutory procedure (where it applies), and an employee who is qualified to do so makes a claim for unfair dismissal, the employment tribunal will automatically find the dismissal unfair. The tribunal will normally increase the compensation awarded by 10 per cent, or, where it feels it is just and equitable to do so, up to 50 per cent. Equally, if the employment tribunal finds that an employee has been dismissed unfairly but has failed to follow the procedure (for instance they have failed to attend the disciplinary meeting without good cause), compensation will be reduced by, normally, 10 per cent, or, if the tribunal considers it just and equitable to do so, up to 50 per cent.

29. If the tribunal considers there are exceptional circumstances, compensation may be adjusted (up or down) by less than 10 per cent or not at all.

30. Employers and employees will normally be expected to go through the statutory dismissal and disciplinary procedure unless they have reasonable grounds to believe that by doing so they might be exposed to a significant threat, such as violent, abusive or intimidating behaviour, or they will be harassed. There will always be a certain amount of stress and anxiety for both parties when dealing with any disciplinary case, but this exemption will only apply where the employer or employee reasonably believes that they would come to some serious physical or mental harm; their property or some third party is threatened or the other party has harassed them and this may continue.

31. Equally, the statutory procedure does not need to be followed if circumstances beyond the control of either party prevent one or more steps being followed within a reasonable period. This will sometimes be the case where there is a long-term illness or a long period of absence abroad but, in the case of employers, wherever possible they should consider appointing another manager to deal with the procedure.

32. Where an employee fails to attend a meeting held as part of the statutory discipline procedure without good reason the statutory procedure comes to an end. In those circumstances the employee's compensation may be reduced if they bring a successful complaint before an employment tribunal. If the employee does have a good reason for non-attendance, the employer must re-arrange the meeting. If the employee does not attend the second meeting for good reason the employer need not arrange a third meeting but there will be no adjustment of compensation.

What if a grievance is raised during a disciplinary case?

33. In the course of a disciplinary process, an employee might raise a grievance that is related to the case. If this happens, the employer should consider suspending the disciplinary procedure for a short period while the grievance is dealt with. Depending on the nature of the grievance, the employer may need to consider bringing in another manager to deal with the disciplinary process. In small organisations this may not be possible, and the existing manager should deal with the case as impartially as possible.

34. Where the action taken or contemplated by the employer is dismissal the statutory grievance procedure does not apply. Where the action taken or contemplated is paid suspension or a warning the statutory grievance procedure and not the dismissal and disciplinary procedure applies to any grievance. However, where the employer takes, or is contemplating other action short of dismissal and asserts that the reason for the action is conduct or capability related, the statutory grievance procedure does not apply unless the grievance is that the action amounts, or would amount, to unlawful discrimination, or that the true reason for the action is not the reason given by the employer. In those cases the employee must have raised a written grievance in accordance with the statutory grievance procedure before presenting any complaint to an employment tribunal about the issue raised by the grievance. However, if the written grievance is raised before any disciplinary appeal meeting, the rest of the grievance procedure does not have to be followed, although the employer may use the appeal meeting to discuss the grievance.

Dealing with gross misconduct

35. If an employer considers an employee guilty of gross misconduct, and thus potentially liable for summary dismissal, it is still important to establish the facts before taking any action. A short period of suspension with full pay may be helpful or necessary, although it should only be imposed after careful consideration and should be kept under review. It should be made clear to the employee that the suspension is not a disciplinary action and does not involve any prejudgement.

36. It is a core principle of reasonable behaviour that employers should give employees the opportunity of putting their case at a disciplinary meeting before deciding whether or to take action. This principle applies as much to cases of gross misconduct as it does to ordinary cases of misconduct or unsatisfactory performance. There may however be some very limited cases where despite the fact that an employer has dismissed an employee immediately without a meeting an employment tribunal will, very exceptionally, find the dismissal to be fair. To allow for these cases there is a statutory modified procedure under which the employer is required to write to the employee after the dismissal setting out the reasons for the dismissal and to hold an appeal meeting, if the employee wants one. The statutory procedure that must be followed by employers in such cases is set out in Annex B. If an employer fails to follow this procedure and the case goes to tribunal, the dismissal will be found to be automatically unfair.

Dealing with absence from work

37. When dealing with absence from work, it is important to determine the reasons why the employee has not been at work. If there is no acceptable reason, the matter should be treated as a conduct issue and dealt with as a disciplinary matter.

38. If the absence is due to genuine (including medically certified) illness, the issue becomes one of capability, and the employer should take a sympathetic and considerate approach. When thinking about how to handle these cases, it is helpful to consider:

- how soon the employee's health and attendance will improve;
- whether alternative work is available;
- the effect of the absence on the organisation;

- how similar situations have been handled in the past; and
- whether the illness is a result of disability in which case the provisions of the Disability Discrimination Act 1995 will apply.

39. The impact of long-term absences will nearly always be greater on small organisations, and they may be entitled to act at an earlier stage than large organisations.

40. In cases of extended sick leave both statutory and contractual issues will need to be addressed and specialist advice may be necessary.

Dealing with special situations

If the full procedure is not immediately available

41. Special arrangements might be required for handling disciplinary matters among nightshift employees, employees in isolated locations or depots, or others who may be difficult to reach. Nevertheless the appropriate statutory procedure must be followed where it applies.

Trade union representatives

42. Disciplinary action against a trade union representative can lead to a serious dispute if it is seen as an attack on the union's functions. Normal standards apply but, if disciplinary action is considered, the case should be discussed, after obtaining the employee's agreement, with a senior trade union representative or permanent union official.

Criminal charges or convictions not related to employment

43. If an employee is charged with, or convicted of, a criminal offence not related to work, this is not in itself reason for disciplinary action. The employer should establish the facts of the case and consider whether the matter is serious enough to warrant starting the disciplinary procedure. The main consideration should be whether the offence, or alleged offence, is one that makes the employee unsuitable for their type of work. Similarly, an employee should not be dismissed solely because they are absent from work as a result of being remanded in custody.

Appeals

44. Employees who have had disciplinary action taken against them should be given the opportunity to appeal. It is useful to set a time limit for asking for an appeal – five working days is usually enough.

45. An employee may choose to appeal for example because:
- they think a finding or penalty is unfair;
- new evidence comes to light; or
- they think the disciplinary procedure was not used correctly.

It should be noted that the appeal stage is part of the statutory procedure and if the employee pursues an employment tribunal claim the tribunal may reduce any award of compensation if the employee did not exercise the right of appeal.

46. As far as is reasonably practicable a more senior manager not involved with the case should hear the appeal. In small organisations, even if a more senior manager is not available, another manager should hear the appeal, if possible. If that is not an option, the person overseeing the case should act as impartially as possible. Records and notes of the original disciplinary meeting should be made available to the person hearing the appeal.

47. The employers should contact the employee with appeal arrangements as soon as possible, and inform them of their statutory right to be accompanied at the appeal meeting.

48. The manager must inform the employee about the appeal decision, and the reasons for it, as soon as possible. They should also confirm the decision in writing. If the decision is the final stage of the organisation's appeals procedure, the manager should make this clear to the employee.

Keeping records

49. It is important, and in the interests of both employers and employees, to keep written records during the disciplinary process. Records should include:
- the complaint against the employee;
- the employee's defence;
- findings made and actions taken;
- the reason for actions taken.
- whether an appeal was lodged;

- the outcome of the appeal;
- any grievances raised during the disciplinary procedure; and
- subsequent developments.

50. Records should be treated as confidential and be kept no longer than necessary in accordance with the Data Protection Act 1998. This Act gives individuals the right to request and have access to certain personal data.

51. Copies of meeting records should be given to the employee including copies of any formal minutes that may have been taken. In certain circumstances (for example to protect a witness) the employer might withhold some information.

Drawing up disciplinary rules and procedures

52. Management is responsible for maintaining and setting standards of performance in an organisation and for ensuring that disciplinary rules and procedures are in place. Employers are legally required to have disciplinary procedures. It is good practice to involve employees (and, where appropriate, their representatives) when making or changing rules and procedures, so that everyone affected by them understands them.

Rules

53. When making rules, the aim should be to specify those that are necessary for ensuring a safe and efficient workplace and for maintaining good employment relations.

54. It is unlikely that any set of rules will cover all possible disciplinary issues, but rules normally cover:
- bad behaviour, such as fighting or drunkenness;
- unsatisfactory work performance;
- harassment or victimisation;
- misuse of company facilities (for example email and internet);
- poor timekeeping;
- unauthorised absences; and
- repeated or serious failure to follow instructions.

55. Rules should be specific, clear and recorded in writing. They also need to be readily available to employees, for instance on a noticeboard or, in larger organisations, in a staff handbook or on the intranet. Management should do all they can to ensure that every employee knows and understands the rules, including those employees whose first language is not English or who have trouble reading. This is often best done as part of an induction process.

56. Employers should inform employees of the likely consequences of breaking disciplinary rules. In particular, they should list examples of acts of gross misconduct that may warrant summary dismissal.

57. Acts which constitute gross misconduct are those resulting in a serious breach of contractual terms and are best decided by organisations in the light of their own particular circumstances. However, examples of gross misconduct might include:

- theft or fraud;
- physical violence or bullying;
- deliberate and serious damage to property;
- serious misuse of an organisation's property or name;
- deliberately accessing internet sites containing pornographic, offensive or obscene material;
- serious insubordination;
- unlawful discrimination or harassment;
- bringing the organisation into serious disrepute;
- serious incapability at work brought on by alcohol or illegal drugs;
- causing loss, damage or injury through serious negligence;
- a serious breach of health and safety rules; and
- a serious breach of confidence.

Procedures

58. Disciplinary procedures should not be seen primarily as a means of imposing sanctions but rather as a way of encouraging improvement amongst employees whose conduct or performance is unsatisfactory. Some organisations may prefer to have separate procedures for dealing with issues of conduct and capability. Large organisations may also have separate procedures to deal with other issues such as harassment and bullying.

59. When drawing up and applying procedures employers should always bear in mind the requirements of natural justice. This means that employees should be given the opportunity of a meeting with someone who has not been involved in the matter. They should be informed of the allegations against them, together with the supporting evidence, in advance of the meeting. Employees should be given the opportunity to challenge the allegations before decisions are reached and should be provided with a right of appeal.

60. Good disciplinary procedures should:

- be put in writing;
- say to whom they apply;
- be non-discriminatory;
- allow for matters to be dealt without undue delay;
- allow for information to be kept confidential;
- tell employees what disciplinary action might be taken;
- say what levels of management have the authority to take disciplinary action;
- require employees to be informed of the complaints against them and supporting evidence, before a meeting;
- give employees a chance to have their say before management reaches a decision;
- provide employees with the right to be accompanied;
- provide that no employee is dismissed for a first breach of discipline, except in cases of gross misconduct;
- require management to investigate fully before any disciplinary action is taken;
- ensure that employees are given an explanation for any sanction; and
- allow employees to appeal against a decision.

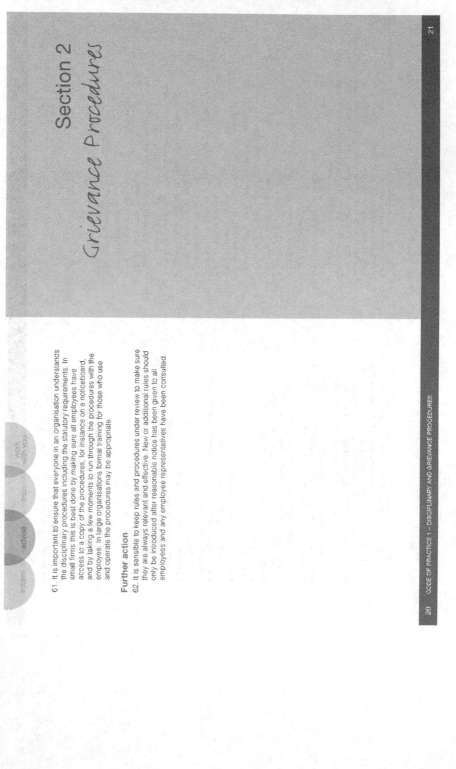

Section 2

Grievance Procedures

61 It is important to ensure that everyone in an organisation understands the disciplinary procedures including the statutory requirements. In small firms this is best done by making sure all employees have access to a copy of the procedures, for instance on a noticeboard, and by taking a few moments to run through the procedures with the employee. In large organisations formal training for those who use and operate the procedures may be appropriate.

Further action

62 It is sensible to keep rules and procedures under review to make sure they are always relevant and effective. New or additional rules should only be introduced after reasonable notice has been given to all employees and any employee representatives have been consulted.

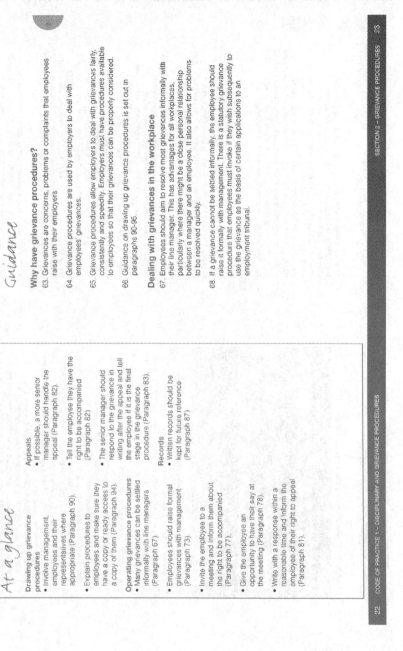

At a glance

Drawing up grievance procedures

- Involve management, employees and their representatives where appropriate (Paragraph 90).
- Explain procedures to employees and make sure they have a copy or ready access to a copy of them (Paragraph 94).

Operating grievance procedures

- Many grievances can be settled informally with line managers (Paragraph 67).
- Employees should raise formal grievances with management (Paragraph 73).
- Invite the employee to a meeting and inform them about the right to be accompanied (Paragraph 77).
- Give the employee an opportunity to have their say at the meeting (Paragraph 78).
- Write with a response within a reasonable time and inform the employee of their right to appeal (Paragraph 81).

Appeals

- If possible, a more senior manager should handle the appeal (Paragraph 82).
- Tell the employee they have the right to be accompanied (Paragraph 82).
- The senior manager should respond to the grievance in writing after the appeal and tell the employee if it is the final stage in the grievance procedure (Paragraph 83).

Records

- Written records should be kept for future reference (Paragraph 87).

Guidance

Why have grievance procedures?

63. Grievances are concerns, problems or complaints that employees raise with their employers

64. Grievance procedures are used by employers to deal with employees grievances.

65. Grievance procedures allow employers to deal with grievances fairly, consistently and speedily. Employers must have procedures available to employees so that their grievances can be properly considered.

66. Guidance on drawing up grievance procedures is set out in paragraphs 90–95.

Dealing with grievances in the workplace

67. Employees should aim to resolve most grievances informally with their line manager. This has advantages for all workplaces, particularly where there might be a close personal relationship between a manager and an employee. It also allows for problems to be resolved quickly.

68. If a grievance cannot be settled informally, the employee should raise it formally with management. There is a statutory grievance procedure that employees must invoke if they wish subsequently to use the grievance as the basis of certain applications to an employment tribunal.

69. Under the standard statutory procedure, employees must:

Step 1

Inform the employer of their grievance in writing.

Step 2

Be invited by the employer to a meeting to discuss the grievance where the right to be accompanied will apply and be notified in writing of the decision. The employee must take all reasonable steps to attend this meeting.

Step 3

Be given the right to an appeal meeting if they feel the grievance has not been satisfactorily resolved and be notified of the final decision.

More detail on the standard statutory procedure is set out in Annex C.

70. There are certain occasions when it is not necessary to follow the statutory procedure for example, if the employee is raising a concern in compliance with the Public Interest Disclosure Act or a grievance is raised on behalf of at least two employees by an appropriate representative such as an official of an independent trade union. A full list of exemptions is set out in Annex E.

71. It is important that employers and employees follow the statutory grievance procedure where it applies. The employee should (subject to the exemptions described in Annex E) at least have raised the grievance in writing and waited 28 days before presenting any tribunal claim relating to the matter. A premature claim will be automatically rejected by the tribunal although (subject to special time limit rules) it may be presented again once the written grievance has been raised. Furthermore if a grievance comes before an employment tribunal and either party has failed to follow the procedure then the tribunal will normally adjust any award by 10 per cent or, where it feels it just and equitable to do so, by up to 50 per cent, depending on which party has failed to follow the procedure. In exceptional cases compensation can be adjusted by less than 10 per cent or not at all.

72. Wherever possible a grievance should be dealt with before an employee leaves employment. A statutory grievance procedure ("the modified grievance procedure" described in Annex D), however, applies where an employee has already left employment, the standard procedure has not been commenced or completed before the employee left employment and both parties agree in writing that it should be used instead of the standard statutory procedure. Under the modified procedure the employee should write to the employer setting out the grievance as soon as possible after leaving employment and the employer must write back setting out its response.

Raising a grievance

73. Employees should normally raise a grievance with their line manager unless someone else is specified in the organisation's procedure. If the complaint is against the person with whom the grievance would normally be raised the employee can approach that person's manager or another manager in the organisation. In small businesses where this is not possible, the line manager should hear the grievance and deal with it as impartially as possible.

74. Managers should deal with all grievances raised, whether or not the grievance is presented in writing. However, employees need to be aware that if the statutory procedure applies, they will not subsequently be able to take the case to an employment tribunal unless they have first raised a grievance in writing and waited a further 28 days before presenting the tribunal claim.

75. Setting out a grievance in writing is not easy – especially for those employees whose first language is not English or who have difficulty expressing themselves on paper. In these circumstances the employee should be encouraged to seek help for example from a work colleague, a trade union or other employee representative. Under the Disability Discrimination Act 1995 employers are required to make reasonable adjustments which may include assisting employees to formulate a written grievance if they are unable to do so themselves because of a disability.

76. In circumstances where a grievance may apply to more than one person and where a trade union is recognised it may be appropriate for the problem to be resolved through collective agreements between the trade union(s) and the employer.

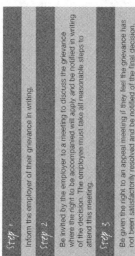

Grievance meetings

77. On receiving a formal grievance, a manager should invite the employee to a meeting as soon as possible and inform them that they have the right to be accompanied. It is good practice to agree a time and place for the meeting with the employee. Small organisations might not have private meeting rooms, but it is important that the meeting is not interrupted and that the employee feels their grievance is being treated confidentially. If an employee's companion cannot attend on a proposed date, the employee can suggest another date so long as it is reasonable and is not more than five working days after the date originally proposed by the employer. This five day time limit may be extended by mutual agreement.

78. The employee should be allowed to explain their complaint and say how they think it should be settled. If the employer reaches a point in the meeting where they are not sure how to deal with the grievance or feel that further investigation is necessary the meeting should be adjourned to get advice or make further investigation. This might be particularly useful in small organisations that lack experience of dealing with formal grievances. The employer should give the grievance careful consideration before responding.

79. Employers and employees will normally be expected to go through the statutory grievance procedures unless they have reasonable grounds to believe that by doing so they might be exposed to a significant threat, such as violent, abusive or intimidating behaviour, or they will be harassed. There will always be a certain amount of stress and anxiety for both parties when dealing with grievance cases, but this exemption will only apply where the employer or employee reasonably believes that they would come to some serious physical or mental harm, their property or some third party is threatened or the other party has harassed them and this may continue.

80. Equally, the statutory procedure does not need to be followed if circumstances beyond the control of either party prevent one or more steps being followed within a reasonable period. This will sometimes be the case where there is a long-term illness or a long period of absence abroad but wherever possible the employer should consider appointing another manager to deal with the procedure.

81. The employer should respond in writing to the employee's grievance within a reasonable time and should let the employee know that they can appeal against the employer's decision if they are not satisfied with it. What is considered reasonable will vary from organisation to organisation, but five working days is normally long enough. If it is not possible to respond within five working days the employee should be given an explanation for the delay and told when a response can be expected.

Appeals

82. If an employee informs the employer that they are unhappy with the decision after a grievance meeting, the employer should arrange an appeal. It should be noted that the appeal stage is part of the statutory procedure and if the employee pursues an employment tribunal claim the tribunal may reduce any award of compensation if the employee did not exercise the right of appeal. As far as is reasonably practicable the appeal should be with a more senior manager than the one who dealt with the original grievance. In small organisations, even if there is no more senior manager available, another manager should, if possible, hear the appeal. If that is not an option, the person overseeing the case should act as impartially as possible. At the same time as inviting the employee to attend the appeal, the employer should remind them of their right to be accompanied at the appeal meeting.

83. As with the first meeting, the employer should write to the employee with a decision on their grievance as soon as possible. They should also tell the employee if the appeal meeting is the final stage of the grievance procedure.

84. In large organisations it is good practice to allow for a further appeal to a higher level of management, such as a director. However, in smaller firms the first appeal will usually mark the end of the grievance procedure.

Special considerations

85. Complaints about discrimination, bullying and harassment in the workplace are sensitive issues, and large organisations often have separate grievance procedures for dealing with these. It is important that these procedures meet the statutory minimum requirements.

86. Organisations may also wish to consider whether they need a whistleblowing procedure in the light of the Public Interest Disclosure Act 1998. This Act provides protection to employees who raise concerns about certain kinds of wrongdoing in accordance with its procedures.

Keeping records

87. It is important, and in the interests of both employer and employee, to keep written records during the grievance process. Records should include:

• the nature of the grievance raised;
• a copy of the written grievance;
• the employer's response;
• action taken;
• reasons for action taken;
• whether there was an appeal and, if so, the outcome; and
• subsequent developments.

88. Records should be treated as confidential and kept in accordance with the Data Protection Act 1998, which gives individuals the right to request and have access to certain personal data.

89. Copies of meeting records should be given to the employee including any formal minutes that may have been taken. In certain circumstances (for example to protect a witness) the employer might withhold some information.

Drawing up grievance procedures

90. When employers draw up grievance procedures, it pays to involve everybody they will affect, including managers, employees and, where appropriate, their representatives.

91. Grievance procedures should make it easy for employees to raise issues with management and should:

• be simple and put in writing;
• enable an employee's line manager to deal informally with a grievance, if possible;
• keep proceedings confidential; and
• allow the employee to have a companion at meetings.

92. Issues that may cause grievances include
• terms and conditions of employment;
• health and safety;
• work relations;
• bullying and harassment;
• new working practices;
• working environment;
• organisational change; and
• equal opportunities.

93. Where separate procedures exist for dealing with grievances on particular issues (for example, harassment and bullying) these should be used instead of the normal grievance procedure.

Section 3

A worker's right to be accompanied

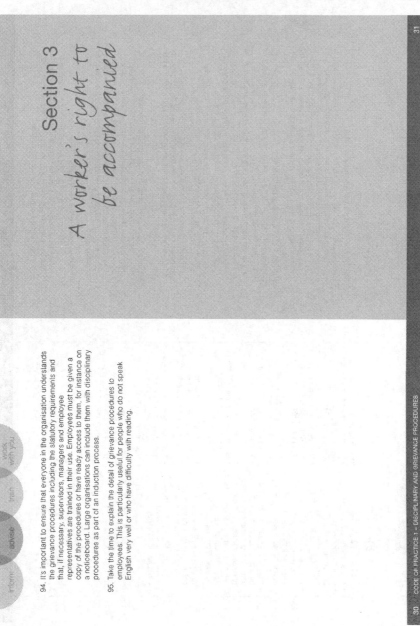

31

---

work with you

train

advise

inform

94. It's important to ensure that everyone in the organisation understands the grievance procedures including the statutory requirements and that, if necessary, supervisors, managers and employee representatives are trained in their use. Employees must be given a copy of the procedures or have ready access to them, for instance on a noticeboard. Large organisations can include them with disciplinary procedures as part of an induction process.

95. Take the time to explain the detail of grievance procedures to employees. This is particularly useful for people who do not speak English very well or who have difficulty with reading.

At a glance

The right to be accompanied

- All workers have the right to be accompanied at a disciplinary or grievance hearing (Paragraph 96).

- Workers must make a reasonable request to the employer if they want to be accompanied (Paragraph 96).

- Disciplinary hearings, for these purposes, include meetings where either disciplinary actions or some other actions might be taken against the worker. Appeal hearings are also covered (Paragraphs 97-99).

- Grievance hearings are defined as meetings where an employer deals with a worker's complaint about a duty owed to them by the employer (Paragraphs 100-102).

The companion

- The companion can be a fellow worker or a union official (Paragraph 104).

- Nobody has to accept an invitation to act as a companion (Paragraph 107).

- Fellow workers who are acting as companions can take paid time off to prepare for and go to a hearing (Paragraph 109).

Applying the right

- Agree a suitable date with the worker and the companion (Paragraph 110).

- The worker should tell the employer who the chosen companion is (Paragraph 112).

- The companion can have a say at the hearing but cannot answer questions for the worker (Paragraph 113-114).

- Do not disadvantage workers who have applied the right, or their companions (Paragraph 116).

Guidance

What is the right to be accompanied?

96. Workers have a statutory right to be accompanied by a fellow worker or trade union official where they are required or invited by their employer to attend certain disciplinary or grievance hearings. They must make a reasonable request to their employer to be accompanied. Further guidance on what is a reasonable request and who can accompany a worker appears at paragraphs 103-109.

What is a disciplinary hearing?

97. For the purposes of this right, disciplinary hearings are defined as meetings that could result in:

- a formal warning being issued to a worker (ie a warning that will be placed on the worker's record);

- the taking of some other disciplinary action (such as suspension without pay, demotion or dismissal) or other action; or

- the confirmation of a warning or some other disciplinary action (such as an appeal hearing).

98. The right to be accompanied will also apply to any disciplinary meetings held as part of the statutory dismissal and disciplinary procedures. This includes any meetings held after an employee has left employment.

99. Informal discussions or counselling sessions do not attract the right to be accompanied unless they could result in formal warnings or other actions. Meetings to investigate an issue are not disciplinary hearings. If it becomes clear during the course of such a meeting that disciplinary action is called for, the meeting should be ended and a formal hearing arranged at which the worker will have the right to be accompanied.

What is a grievance hearing?

100. For the purposes of this right, a grievance hearing is a meeting at which an employer deals with a complaint about a duty owed by them to a worker, whether the duty arises from statute or common law (for example contractual commitments).

101. For instance, an individual's request for a pay rise is unlikely to fall within the definition, unless a right to an increase is specifically provided for in the contract or the request raises an issue about equal pay. Equally, most employers will be under no legal duty to provide their workers with car parking facilities, but a grievance about such facilities would carry no right to be accompanied at a hearing by a companion. However, if a worker were disabled and needed a car to get to and from work, they probably would be entitled to a companion at a grievance hearing, as an issue might arise as to whether the employer was meeting its obligations under the Disability Discrimination Act 1995.

102. The right to be accompanied will also apply to any meetings held as part of the statutory grievance procedures. This includes any meetings after the employee has left employment.

What is a reasonable request?

103. Whether a request for a companion is reasonable will depend on the circumstances of the individual case and, ultimately, it is a matter for the courts and tribunals to decide. However, when workers are choosing a companion, they should bear in mind that it would not be reasonable to insist on being accompanied by a colleague whose presence would prejudice the hearing or who might have a conflict of interest. Nor would it be reasonable for a worker to ask to be accompanied by a colleague from a geographically remote location when someone suitably qualified was available on site. The request to be accompanied does not have to be in writing.

The companion

104. The companion may be:
- a fellow worker (ie another of the employer's workers);
- an official employed by a trade union, or a lay trade union official, as long as they have been reasonably certified in writing by their union as having experience of, or having received training in, acting as a worker's companion at disciplinary or grievance hearings. Certification may take the form of a card or letter.

105. Some workers may, however, have additional contractual rights to be accompanied by persons other than those listed above (for instance a partner, spouse or legal representative). If workers are disabled, employers should consider whether it might be reasonable to allow them to be accompanied because of their disability.

106. Workers may ask an official from any trade union to accompany them at a disciplinary or grievance hearing, regardless of whether the union is recognised or not. However, where a union is recognised in a workplace, it is good practice for workers to ask an official from that union to accompany them.

107. Fellow workers or trade union officials do not have to accept a request to accompany a worker, and they should not be pressurised to do so.

108. Trade unions should ensure that their officials are trained in the role of acting as a worker's companion. Even when a trade union official has experience of acting in the role, there may still be a need for periodic refresher training.

109. A worker who has agreed to accompany a colleague employed by the same employer is entitled to take a reasonable amount of paid time off to fulfil that responsibility. This should cover the hearing and it is also good practice to allow time for the companion to familiarise themselves with the case and confer with the worker before and after the hearing. A lay trade union official is permitted to take a reasonable amount of paid time off to accompany a worker at a hearing, as long as the worker is employed by the same employer. In cases where a lay official agrees to accompany a worker employed by another organisation, time off is a matter for agreement by the parties concerned.

Applying the right

110. Where possible, the employer should allow a companion to have a say in the date and time of a hearing. If the companion cannot attend on a proposed date, the worker can suggest an alternative time and date so long as it is reasonable and it is not more than five working days after the original date.

111. In the same way that employers should cater for a worker's disability at a disciplinary or grievance hearing, they should also cater for a companion's disability, for example providing for wheelchair access if necessary.

Section 4
Annexes

112. Before the hearing takes place, the worker should tell the employer who they have chosen as a companion. In certain circumstances (for instance when the companion is an official of a non-recognised trade union) it can be helpful for the companion and employer to make contact before the hearing.

113. The companion should be allowed to address the hearing in order to:

- put the worker's case
- sum up the worker's case
- respond on the worker's behalf to any view expressed at the hearing.

114. The companion can also confer with the worker during the hearing. It is good practice to allow the companion to participate as fully as possible in the hearing, including asking witnesses questions. The companion has no right to answer questions on the worker's behalf, or to address the hearing if the worker does not wish it, or to prevent the employer from explaining their case.

115. Workers whose employers fail to comply with a reasonable request to be accompanied may present a complaint to an employment tribunal. Workers may also complain to a tribunal if employers fail to re-arrange a hearing to a reasonable date proposed by the worker when a companion cannot attend on the date originally proposed. The tribunal may order compensation of up to two weeks' pay. This could be increased if, in addition, the tribunal finds that the worker has been unfairly dismissed.

116. Employers should be careful not to disadvantage workers for using their right to be accompanied or for being companions, as this is against the law and could lead to a claim to an employment tribunal.

inform   advise   train   work with you

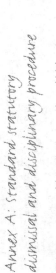

Annex A: standard statutory dismissal and disciplinary procedure

(This is a summary of the statutory procedure which is set out in full in Schedule 2 to the Employment Act 2002.)

This procedure applies to disciplinary action short of dismissal (excluding oral and written warnings and suspension on full pay) based on either conduct or capability. It also applies to dismissals (except for constructive dismissals) including dismissals on the basis of conduct, capability, expiry of a fixed-term contract, redundancy and retirement. However, it does not apply in certain kinds of excepted cases that are described in Annex E.

Step 1

Statement of grounds for action and invitation to meeting

- The employer must set out in writing the employee's alleged conduct or characteristics, or other circumstances, which lead them to contemplate dismissing or taking disciplinary action against the employee.

- The employer must send the statement or a copy of it to the employee and invite the employee to attend a meeting to discuss the matter.

Step 2

The meeting

- The meeting must take place before action is taken, except in the case where the disciplinary action consists of suspension.

- The meeting must not take place unless:

  i) the employer has informed the employee what the basis was for including in the statement under Step 1 the ground or grounds given in it; and

  ii) the employee has had a reasonable opportunity to consider their response to that information.

- The employee must take all reasonable steps to attend the meeting.

- After the meeting, the employer must inform the employee of their decision and notify them of the right to appeal against the decision if they are not satisfied with it.

- Employees have the right to be accompanied at the meeting (see section 3).

Step 3

Appeal

- If the employee wishes to appeal, they must inform the employer.

- If the employee informs the employer of their wish to appeal, the employer must invite them to attend a further meeting.

- The employee must take all reasonable steps to attend the meeting.

- The appeal meeting need not take place before the dismissal or disciplinary action takes effect.

- Where reasonably practicable, the appeal should be dealt with by a more senior manager than attended the first meeting (unless the most senior manager attended that meeting).

- After the appeal meeting, the employer must inform the employee of their final decision.

- Employees have the right to be accompanied at the appeal meeting (see section 3).

Annex B: Modified statutory dismissal and disciplinary procedure

(This is a summary of the statutory procedure which is set out in full in Schedule 2 to the Employment Act 2002.)

Step 1

Statement of grounds for action

- The employer must set out in writing:
  i) the employee's alleged misconduct which has led to the dismissal;
  ii) the reasons for thinking at the time of the dismissal that the employee was guilty of the alleged misconduct; and
  iii) the employee's right of appeal against dismissal.
- The employer must send the statement or a copy of it to the employee.

Step 2

Appeal

- If the employee does wish to appeal, they must inform the employer.
- If the employee informs the employer of their wish to appeal, the employer must invite them to attend a meeting.
- The employee must take all reasonable steps to attend the meeting.
- After the appeal meeting, the employer must inform the employee of their final decision.
- Where reasonably practicable the appeal should be dealt with by a more senior manager not involved in the earlier decision to dismiss.
- Employees have the right to be accompanied at the appeal meeting (see section 3).

Annex C: standard statutory grievance procedure

(This is a summary of the statutory procedure which is set out in full in Schedule 2 to the Employment Act 2002.)

Step 1

Statement of grievance

- The employee must set out the grievance in writing and send the statement or a copy of it to the employer.

Step 2

Meeting

- The employer must invite the employee to attend a meeting to discuss the grievance.
- The meeting must not take place unless:
  i) the employee has informed the employer what the basis for the grievance was when they made the statement under Step 1; and
  ii) the employer has had a reasonable opportunity to consider their response to that information;
- The employee must take all reasonable steps to attend the meeting.
- After the meeting, the employer must inform the employee of their decision as to their response to the grievance and notify them of the right of appeal against the decision if they are not satisfied with it.
- Employees have the right to be accompanied at the meeting (see section 3).

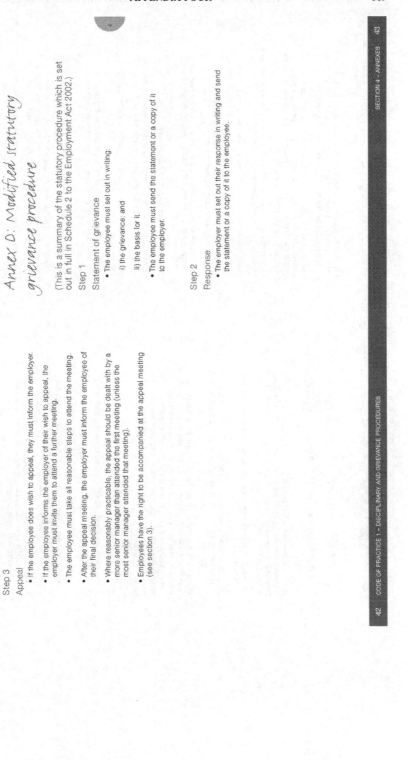

Step 3

Appeal

• If the employee does wish to appeal, they must inform the employer.

• If the employee informs the employer of their wish to appeal, the employer must invite them to attend a further meeting.

• The employee must take all reasonable steps to attend the meeting.

• After the appeal meeting, the employer must inform the employee of their final decision.

• Where reasonably practicable, the appeal should be dealt with by a more senior manager than attended the first meeting (unless the most senior manager attended that meeting).

• Employees have the right to be accompanied at the appeal meeting (see section 3).

Annex D: Modified statutory grievance procedure

(This is a summary of the statutory procedure which is set out in full in Schedule 2 to the Employment Act 2002.)

Step 1

Statement of grievance

• The employee must set out in writing:

  i) the grievance; and

  ii) the basis for it.

• The employee must send the statement or a copy of it to the employer.

Step 2

Response

• The employer must set out their response in writing and send the statement or a copy of it to the employee.

Annex E: Statutory Procedures: Exemptions and Deemed Compliance

The Employment Act 2002 (Dispute Resolution) Regulations 2004 contain detailed provisions about the application of the Statutory Dispute Resolution Procedures. This Annex summarises the particular provisions of the 2004 Regulations which describe:

(a) certain situations in which the statutory procedures will not apply at all; and

(b) other situations in which a party who has not completed the applicable procedure will nevertheless be treated as though they had done so

Where a statutory procedure applies and one of the conditions for extending time limits contained in the 2004 Regulations has been met, then the normal time limit for presenting an employment tribunal claim will be extended by three months. The guidance notes accompanying tribunal application forms describe those conditions. However, in cases where the procedures do not apply at all, there can be no such extension.

(a) Situations in which the Statutory Procedures do not apply at all

The Disciplinary and Dismissal Procedures do not apply where:

• factors beyond the control of either party make it impracticable to carry out or complete the procedure for the foreseeable future; or

• the employee is dismissed in circumstances covered by the modified dismissal procedure and presents a tribunal complaint before the employer has taken step 1; or

• all of the employees of the same description or category are dismissed and offered re-engagement either before or upon termination of their contract; or

• the dismissal is one of a group of redundancies covered by the duty of collective consultation of worker representatives under the Trade Union and Labour Relations (Consolidation) Act 1992; or

• the employee is dismissed while taking part in unofficial industrial action, or other industrial action which is not "protected action" under the 1992 Act, unless the employment tribunal has jurisdiction to hear a claim of unfair dismissal; or

• the employee is unfairly dismissed for taking part in industrial action which is "protected action" under the 1992 Act; or

• the employer's business suddenly and unexpectedly ceases to function and it becomes impractical to employ any employees; or

• the employee cannot continue in the particular position without contravening a statutory requirement; or

• the employee is one to whom a dismissal procedure agreement designated under section 110 of the Employment Relations Act 1996 applies.

The Grievance Procedures do not apply where:

• the employee is no longer employed, and it is no longer practicable for the employee to take step 1 of the procedure; or

• the employee wishes to complain about an actual or threatened dismissal; or

• the employee raises a concern as a "protected disclosure" in compliance with the public interest disclosure provisions of the 1996 Act.

• the employee wishes to complain about (actual or threatened) action short of dismissal to which the standard disciplinary procedure applies, unless the grievance is that this involves unlawful discrimination (including under the Equal Pay Act) or is not genuinely on grounds of capability or conduct.

In addition, neither party need comply with an applicable statutory procedure where to do so would be contrary to the interests of national security.

(b) Situations in which the Statutory Procedures have not been completed but are treated as having been complied with

The Disciplinary and Dismissal Procedures are treated as having been complied with where all stages of the procedure have been completed, other than the right of appeal, and:

- the employee then applies to the employment tribunal for interim relief; or

- a collective agreement provides for a right of appeal, which the employee exercises.

The Grievance Procedures are treated as having been complied with where:

- the employee is complaining that action short of dismissal to which the standard disciplinary procedure applies is not genuinely on grounds of conduct or capability, or involves unlawful discrimination, and the employee has raised that complaint as a written grievance before any appeal hearing under a statutory procedure or, if none is being followed, before presenting a tribunal complaint; or

- the employment has ended and the employee has raised a written grievance, but it has become not reasonably practical to have a meeting or an appeal. However, the employer must still give the employee a written answer to the grievance; or

- an official of a recognised independent union or other appropriate representative has raised the grievance on behalf of two or more named employees. Employees sharing the grievance may choose one of their number to act as a representative; or

- the employee pursues the grievance using a procedure available under an industry-level collective agreement.

(c) Other Special Circumstances in which the Statutory Procedures need not be begun or completed

In addition, neither the employer nor employee need begin a procedure (which will then be treated as not applying), or comply with a particular requirement of it (but will still be deemed to have complied) if the reason for not beginning or not complying is:

- the reasonable belief that doing so would result in a significant threat to themselves, any other person, or their or any other persons' property;

- because they have been subjected to harassment and reasonably believe that doing so would result in further harassment; or

- because it is not practicable to do so within a reasonable period.

WRITTEN STATEMENT OF TERMS

Section 1 of the Employment Rights Act 1996 requires an employer to **A5.01**
supply an employee employed for one month or more with a written statement
of terms and conditions (see Chapter 3 for the relevant provisions and their
interpretation).
What follows is an example of such a statement.

Sample initial employment particulars

1. Employee: Sarah Higgins   **A5.02**

2. Employer: R. R. Fisher and Company Ltd

3. Your employment began on October 1, 2003. Your period of continuous employment began on April 1, 1999 (this takes into account your
   previous employment with Fisher Enterprises Ltd).

4. Your gross pay is £295 per week, payable at weekly intervals on
   Fridays.

5. Your hours of work are from 9 a.m. until 5 p.m. from Monday until
   Friday inclusive. You are entitled to a break of one hour for lunch.

6. You are entitled to 20 days paid holiday per year, to be taken at times
   which are agreed by your line manager. This entitlement is additional
   to public holidays. The holiday year runs from January 1 to December
   31 each calendar year. On termination of employment, you will be
   entitled to accrued holiday pay on a pro rata basis for your service
   during the holiday year in which termination takes place.

7. You will be paid in accordance with paragraph 4 for any absence due to
   illness or injury, up to a maximum of six weeks in any 12 month period.
   The procedures with regard to absence set out in the Staff Handbook
   (see paragraph 10) must be followed, and credit for sickness benefits
   received from other sources must be given as set out there.

8. You are entitled to join the Staff Superannuation Scheme, details of
   which are set out in the Pensions Handbook, which can be obtained
   from the Pensions Manager in the HR Department or accessed on the
   company intranet. A contracting out certificate is in force for your
   employment.

9. The title of your job is Information Retrieval Assistant.

10. The disciplinary rules applicable to you are set out in the Staff Handbook under the heading "Disciplinary Rules". A copy of the Staff Handbook is kept in the HR Department, and it can be accessed on the company intranet.

11. If you are dissatisfied with any disciplinary decision relating to you, or any decision to dismiss you, you can apply to the HR Manager for the matter to be reconsidered. The relevant steps are set out in more detail in the Staff Handbook (see paragraph 10 for availability).

12. If you wish to seek redress of any grievance relating to your employment, you should set out the basis of the grievance and send it to the HR manager by letter or email. For details of any further steps to be taken you should refer to the Staff Handbook under the heading "Grievance Procedure" (see paragraph 10 for access to the Staff Handbook).

13. You are entitled to receive one month's notice to terminate your employment (subject to any greater statutory entitlement). You are obliged to give one month's notice of termination.

14. Your place of work is Slough.

Dated_____

Signed_____ (Employee)

Signed_____ (for R R Fisher Ltd)

INDEX

LEGAL TAXONOMY
FROM SWEET & MAXWELL

This index has been prepared using Sweet and Maxwell's Legal Taxonomy. Main index entries conform to keywords provided by the Legal Taxonomy except where references to specific documents or non-standard terms (denoted by quotation marks) have been included. These keywords provide a means of identifying similar concepts in other Sweet & Maxwell publications and online services to which keywords from the Legal Taxonomy have been applied. Readers may find some minor differences between terms used in the text and those which appear in the index. Suggestions to *sweetandmaxwell.taxonomy@thomson.com*

(All references are to paragraph number)

ABUSIVE LANGUAGE
  see UNFAIR DISMISSAL
ACAS
  Code of Practice on Disciplinary and
      Grievance Procedures
    generally, 9.59
    text, Appendix 4
  settlement, 15.05–15.06
ADDITIONAL MATERNITY LEAVE
  and see MATERNITY LEAVE
  generally, 8.06–8.07
ADOPTION LEAVE
  generally, 8.12
  unfair dismissal, 8.21–8.22
AGE DISCRIMINATION
  challenges, 6.69
  "duty to consider" procedure, 6.64–6.65
  exceptions, 6.59
  fixed-term workers, 6.72
  forms, 6.56–6.58
  generally, 6.54
  introduction, 6.09
  justification, 6.56
  part-time workers, 6.70–6.71
  recruitment, 6.60
  retirement, 6.62–6.68
  scope, 6.55
  terms of service, 6.61
  trade union membership, 6.73–6.74
  unfair dismissal, 6.63
AGENCY WORKERS
  contractual arrangement with bureau, 2.29
  contractual arrangement with hirer,
      2.27–2.28
  Dacas decision, 2.30
  generally, 2.26
AGGRAVATED DAMAGES
  discrimination, 7.12

AGREEMENTS
  termination of contract, 3.19
ANNUAL LEAVE
  working time, 5.11
ANTENATAL CARE
  see TIME OFF FOR ANTENATAL CARE
APPEALS
  generally, 13.43–13.45
ASSAULT
  unfair dismissal, 9.49
ASSOCIATED COMPANIES
  transfer of undertakings, 12.02
AUTOMATICALLY FAIR REASONS
  see UNFAIR DISMISSAL
AUTOMATICALLY UNFAIR DISMISSAL
  and see UNFAIR DISMISSAL
  generally, 9.45
  redundancy, 11.27

BASIC AWARDS
  unfair dismissal, 10.06–10.07
BELIEF DISCRIMINATION
  and see DISCRIMINATION
  generally, 6.07
BENEFITS
  compensatory award, 10.24
BENEFITS IN KIND
  discrimination, 6.28
"BLUE PENCIL TEST"
  restrictive covenants, 4.14
BREACH OF CONTRACT
  remedies
    damages for employee, 3.28–3.29
    damages for employer, 3.30
    injunctions, 3.31
    introduction, 3.27
    time limit for claims, 14.06
BURDEN OF PROOF
  discrimination, 6.82